The Economics of Pandemics

S. Niggol Seo

The Economics of Pandemics

Exploring Globally Shared Experiences

S. Niggol Seo
Muaebak Institute of Global Warming Studies
Bangkok, Thailand

ISBN 978-3-030-91020-4   ISBN 978-3-030-91021-1   (eBook)
https://doi.org/10.1007/978-3-030-91021-1

This Palgrave Macmillan imprint is published by the registered company Springer Nature Switzerland AG.
The registered company address is: Gewerbestrasse 11, 6330 Cham, Switzerland

All beings tremble at the whip.
All fear death.
All love life.
—Buddha Shakyamuni—

PREFACE

This book entitled *The Economics of Pandemics: Exploring Globally Shared Experiences: How Should Globally Shared Resources Be Managed?* is a treatise on the decisions and consequences vis-à-vis a worldwide pandemic whose experiences are deeply shared by the citizens of the planet. It provides a grand synthesis of a large array of the choices and decisions faced by numerous economic agents who seek to minimize the harm inflicted upon them by the pandemic, both economically and on their health, which strikes only very rarely, therefore, is unpredictable.

With an integrative framework, this book clarifies and analyzes a full spectrum of the decisions made during the pandemic by individual citizens, businesses, local governments, national governments, pharmaceutical companies, international organizations, judicial systems, and numerous political movements. This book is written as a textbook for a course on the economics of pandemics and epidemics or the economics of globally shared goods which may be taught at colleges and universities.

The present author had two goals in setting out to write this book. The first is to reflect vividly on a full range of experiences shared by the global community in 2020 and 2021 since the outbreak of the COVID-19 pandemic. The second is to develop the economics of pandemics that elucidates and then integrates a full scope of the economic choices and decisions faced by various economic actors at different time frames.

The idea of writing a book on planetwide pandemics was conceived at around the peak of the first wave of the COVID-19 pandemic during April 2020. While closely observing national and international policy reactions around the world, which appeared haphazardly, the present author was struck by the realization that there is no widely read economics publication on this grave planetary challenge and by how little economists have paid attention to pandemic events as deadly as the COVID-19.

Soon it dawned on the present author, however, that that is also quite understandable. The last pandemic event at a scale of the COVID-19 happened in 1919, that is, the H1N1 influenza pandemic more commonly referred to as Spanish Flu, exactly and by great chance, a hundred years ago. A worldwide pandemic is a very rare event, that is, a 1-in-100-years event. That being the case, when a pandemic comes and is over, it will soon go out of people's memories overwhelmed by other important daily matters of life. And then it may not occur again in their lifetime.

The present author came to realize that the aforementioned Spanish Flu pandemic broke out long before the publications of Irving Fisher's *The Theory of Interest* in 1930, J.M. Keynes' *The General Theory* in 1934, and Paul Samuelson's *Foundations of Economic Analysis* in 1947, all of which, along with other cherished publications in economics, opened a golden age of economic analysis of the twentieth century (Fisher 1930, Keynes 1936, Samuelson 1947). Because of this historical timeline of major events, an inquiry into pandemic problems in economics has, by and large, escaped economists' careful attention.

A big merit of this book is that it was being written right at the depths of the COVID-19 pandemic, to be specific, from April 2020 to October 2021. The book was written while the memories of the present author and the global community were still very fresh on a myriad of day-to-day happenings across the globe during the COVID-19. Owing to the commitment to write this book, it was natural, although highly unusual, for the present author to keep close eyes on such a big matrix of actions and experiences during the pandemic.

Economists have come to contact with pandemic events intellectually via the study of globally shared goods, commonly referred to as global commons or global public goods. The economics of globally shared goods has reached today's prominence in academia and has established a solid intellectual tradition during the past three decades, both of which are largely attributable to its contributions to the planet's climate change debates and negotiations (Nordhaus 1994). The economics of pandemics as a globally shared good, which is one of the two afore-declared goals of this book, is a special area of the economics of globally shared goods and has not yet come about in the literature.

If you have lived through the COVID-19 pandemic in 2020 and 2021, I believe most of the readers of this book have, then you would certainly have witnessed that fear, control, and big governmental hands overwhelmed reason and rationality in nearly all major decisions in those two years. This book hopes to offer to the readers a lucid exposition of a complex pandemic universe with a calm rational economic mind. For those of you who have passed through the pandemic as a teenager or a pre-teenager, this book hopes to offer you a full account of a myriad of tiny and big decisions faced and made by humanity, which is hoped to serve as a reminder of what really happened in those two years.

Lastly, I would like to express my gratitude to the anonymous reviewers who offered invaluable comments on the proposal at an early stage of this book. I owe thanks to Wyndham H. Pain, Ruby Panigrahi, Srishti Gupta, and other editorial team members at Palgrave Macmillan for their support and outstanding editorial works in producing this book.

Bangkok, Thailand   S. Niggol Seo

REFERENCES

Fisher, Irving. 1930. *The Theory of Interest*. New York, NY: Macmillan.
Keynes, John. M. 1936. *The General Theory on Employment, Interest and Money*. London: Palgrave Macmillan.
Samuelson, Paul A. 1947. *Foundations of Economic Analysis*. Cambridge, MA: Harvard University Press.
Nordhaus, William D. 1994. *Managing the Global Commons*. Cambridge, MA: The MIT Press.

CONTENTS

ABOUT THE AUTHOR

Professor S. Niggol Seo is a natural resource economist who specializes in the study of global warming and globally shared goods. He holds a PhD in Environmental and Natural Resource Economics from Yale University (May 2006) with a dissertation on microbehavioral models of global warming. Since 2003, he has worked on various World Bank projects on climate change in Africa, Latin America, and Asia. He held Professor positions in the UK, Spain, and Australia from 2006 to 2015. Seo has published over a hundred (peer-reviewed) articles on global warming economics, which includes eight books. He received an Outstanding Applied Economic Perspectives and Policy Article Award from the Agricultural and Applied Economics Association (AAEA) in Pittsburgh in June 2011. He is the editor-in-chief of the *Handbook of Behavioural Economics and Climate Change* to be published in 2022.

LIST OF FIGURES

LIST OF TABLES

CHAPTER 1

The COVID-19 Pandemic as a Globally Shared Experience: An Introduction

1 THE COVID-19 PANDEMIC OVERWHELMS THE PLANET

At the time when the present author started to write this book in mid-April 2020, the world was already in the depths of the global pandemic caused by the novel coronavirus. The disease was named the COVID-19, short for Corona Virus Disease of 2019, and declared a pandemic by the World Health Organization (WHO) in the preceding month (WHO 2020a). First reported from Wuhan, China, on the last day of 2019, the novel coronavirus had quickly spread to Asian neighbors, Europe, and the US. As of April 2020, over 2.5 million people worldwide were tested positive and about 180,000 people lost their lives. Many state governments in the US declared a statewide lockdown since late March and nearly all businesses in the US were advised or forced to close during April. By the middle of August 2020, the number of people infected passed 22.3 million and the total number of fatalities was near 800,000 worldwide. Entering November of that year, the third wave of the COVID-19 hit the world spurred by the winter cold temperature. By the end of January 2021, the number of infections passed 100 million (Fig. 1.1) and the number of the dead topped 2.2 million (Fig. 1.2) worldwide (JHU 2021). By early July 2021, the number of the dead was near 4 million worldwide as the Delta (Indian) variant started to become a dominant strain.

S. N. Seo, *The Economics of Pandemics*,
https://doi.org/10.1007/978-3-030-91021-1_1

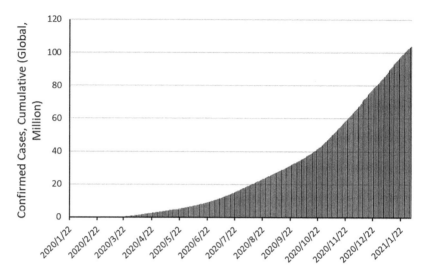

Fig. 1.1   COVID-19 confirmed cases (world, cumulative, as of end January 2021)

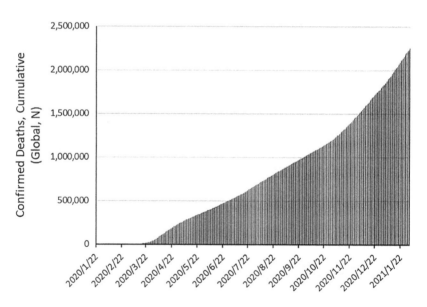

Fig. 1.2   COVID-19 confirmed deaths (world, cumulative, as of end January 2021)

Before we proceed further, let me clarify one thing. To deliver vivid lively descriptions of the happenings during the pandemic, this book has been written with anchors at several critical points in time during 2020 and 2021. The most important reference date is mid-December 2020 when the first vaccine shot was administered. Readers may refer to Fig. 7.6 in Chap. 7 for the fourth wave trend and to Fig. 7.7 in Chap. 7 for the fifth wave trend of the case and fatality data in 2021.

The year 2020 was overwhelmed by the rapid contagion of the novel coronavirus, named the SARS-CoV-2, among the planet's population ever since it was first reported and confirmed. As Figs. 1.1 and 1.2 reveal, the daily increase in the number of infections of the pandemic virus has not been slowed down by the beginning of February 2021, neither has the daily increase in the number of deaths globally.

As deadly as the novel coronavirus has been in terms of the numbers of infections and fatalities, the suffering that people on the planet have endured in the first two years of the pandemic was far beyond what these statistics can inform. Through government orders, people were forced to remain in a sustained lockdown multiple times; infected individuals were isolated; the people who were in close proximity to an infected individual were forced to enter into a quarantine period (White House 2020; NYT 2020). Businesses and shops were ordered to close, making many small businesses unable to pay the building rent or let go of their employees. Ordered school closures forced children to remain at their homes for many months resorting to distance online learning (UNESCO 2020). International travel to and from most countries was suspended during 2020. Senior citizens at nursing homes were defenseless against the lethal virus, often getting infected *en masse* and often fatally (NYT 2021a). When a person died from the virus attack, family members and relatives were not allowed to observe the funeral of the dead because of the extremely high contagiousness of the SARS-CoV-2 virus. In developing countries, dead bodies were often piled up in a town commons remotely located, burned collectively, or buried all together without any notice to their families. With the lack of hospital beds or the lack of family resources, infected family members were sometimes abandoned on the remote town corners.

The economic shock caused by the pandemic was very severe, if not unparalleled. As all businesses, except a small number of government-defined "essential businesses" such as postal service, delivery service, and public transportations, were ordered to close, the US unemployment rate in the second quarter (Q2) of 2020 shot up alarmingly. A historically low unemployment rate, which stood at 3.5% in the US before the pandemic, increased sharply to 14.5% in April 2020 (USBLS 2020). The Gross Domestic Product (GDP) growth, which stood at 2.4% in the fourth quarter (Q4) of 2019, fell precipitously to -31.4% in the second quarter (Q2) of 2020 (USBEA 2020). When the COVID-19 pandemic appeared to be over by the end of May 2020, most businesses returned but were ordered to operate at a limited capacity. While some businesses, for example, Big Tech companies such as Google, Apple, Amazon, and Facebook flourished during the pandemic, small businesses, restaurant services, hotel services, and travel businesses were among the hardest hit by the pandemic.

A shock on individuals' lives and civil liberty may have been even more acute across the planet. It started with a universal mask mandate on all citizens at all places to which many people resisted. A national lockdown prevented people from talking to their next-door neighbors (NYT 2020). The governments then started to keep track of every citizen as part of a contact tracing program. All restaurants and cafes were ordered to keep a register of visitors with their contact mobile numbers recorded. Then, all benches and pavilions in streets and parks were ordered off-limits and sealed off. A group of people gathering for a protest against a government policy was soon banned and prosecuted. In-person church and religious services in many parts of the world were prohibited by law because these events were considered super-spreader events (WSJ 2020). Despite the empirical data that showed school children were mostly unaffected by the virus, primary and secondary schools were not able to open because of the opposition by the teachers' unions (Marianno 2021).

At another realm of the planet, an extreme social unrest was unfolding simultaneously, specifically in the US, ignited by the racial tension between the police force and Black people. At the peak in May and June of 2020 during which the novel coronavirus was spreading at an alarming rate across the planet but silently, there were over 300 protests per day staged simultaneously across the US, of which nearly 100 protests per day were categorized as a violent riot (US Crisis Monitor 2020).

It is considered a miracle by many that two highly effective mRNA vaccines were successfully developed and approved for emergency use in just about nine months and before the close of 2020. A Pfizer-BioNTech vaccine was authorized for emergency use on December 7 by the US Food and Drug Administration (FDA) and a Moderna vaccine was authorized a week later (USFDA 2020a, 2020b). By February 1, 2021, nearly all developed countries were administering vaccine shots to their citizens. More than 108 million shots were administered by then globally, of which 35 million shots were given in the US (OWID 2021). An early result from the examination of Israel's vaccination efforts was much positive, from which the world community first saw a glimmer of hope for an end of the pandemic (Jerusalem Post 2021). By early May 2021, over 220 million vaccine doses were administered in the US alone and roughly 65% of the UK population over the age of 18 were vaccinated, which caused dramatic reductions in daily COVID-19 cases in the two countries (refer to Fig. 7.6 in Chap. 7; OWID 2021). By mid-June 2021, however, the Delta variant of the SARS-CoV-2, also known as the Indian variant and three times as contagious as to break an individual's vaccine defense, was surging across the globe to become a dominant strain, starting from India, the UK, and Russia (CNBC 2021). By mid-September 2021, the world was at the peak of the fifth wave with nearly 750,000 new cases per day while the percentage of people vaccinated appears to approach a plateau in Germany, the US, and others (refer to Fig. 7.8 in Chap. 7).

2   THE NOVEL CORONAVIRUS: SARS-CoV-2

The novel coronavirus which caused the worldwide pandemic in 2020 was formally named the SARS-CoV-2 by the WHO. It is one of the three coronaviruses, all betacoronaviruses, that attacked humankind seriously since the opening of the twenty-first century (Weiss 2020). The coronavirus that caused the Severe Acute Respiratory Syndrome (SARS) in 2002–2004 was the first coronavirus, named the SARS-CoV. The coronavirus that caused the Middle Eastern Respiratory Syndrome (MERS) in 2012–2015 was the second one, named the MERS-CoV (Coleman and Frieman 2014). The infectious disease that was caused by the SARS-CoV-2 was named the COVID-19 by the WHO (WHO 2020a).

The coronaviruses are named as such because they are notable for their crown-like spikes. A corona is a Latin word which means a crown in English. A two-dimensional shape of the novel coronavirus is depicted in Fig. 1.3 (NIAID 2020). Inside the ball enclosed by an outer lipid envelope, there is a Ribonucleic Acid (RNA) strand. The outer lipid envelope is protruded by many protein spikes (USFDA 2020c). Unlike the previous coronaviruses, the gene sequence of the SARS-CoV-2, which was released within weeks of the pandemic outbreak, showed "a furin cleavage site in the S1/S2 junction" (Weiss 2020).

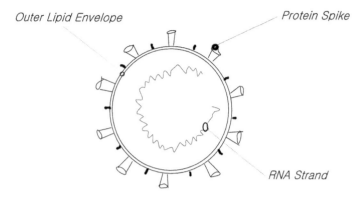

Fig. 1.3   The SARS-CoV-2

When the SARS-CoV-2 virus enters the human lungs, it attaches to the receptor of a healthy lung cell via the protein spikes. Through the protein spike, the RNA strand enters the healthy cell and kills it. When the novel coronavirus kills the healthy cell, it replicates itself and continues to attack the other healthy cells in the body (refer to Fig. 7.1 in Chap. 7 for the depiction of this process).

Coronavirus research began as early as in the 1930s, while the first international coronavirus symposium was held in Wurzburg, Germany, in 1980. During the twentieth century, the research community was largely focused on animal coronaviruses, for example, in a mouse. The first two decades of the twenty-first century witnessed the three human coronaviruses: SARS-CoV, MERS-CoV, and SARS-CoV-2 (Weiss 2020).

The novel coronavirus or the SARS-CoV-2 virus is believed by some to have "emerged in China from bats into a presumed intermediate species and then into humans," the most notable of whom are the widely publicized Lancet letter authors in March 2020 (Weiss 2020; Calisher et al. 2020). The previous two coronaviruses originated naturally from bats. For the SARS-CoV, the intermediary species was civets, while it was camels for the MERS-CoV. The SARS-CoV-2 then spread to other countries and by the end of the first six months of 2020, nearly all countries on the planet had a confirmed case of the COVID-19 (refer to Fig. 8.1 in Chap. 8). The WHO declared it as a pandemic on March 11, 2020 (WHO 2020a). However, despite the extensive search by the research community, an intermediate species has not been found for the COVID-19 virus, as of mid-September 2021 (Mallapaty 2021).

The WHO still promotes four hypotheses on the origin of the virus, as of September 2021, but has supported the above-described animal origin hypotheses (WHO 2021). The most notable of the four hypotheses which have been increasingly supported by the scientific community is that the SARS-CoV-2 was leaked accidentally during the coronavirus experiments at the Wuhan Institute of Virology in China (Reuters 2021). The scientific basis for the laboratory leak hypothesis is twofold, as far as the present author can tell from the experts' statements: first, the virus' unprecedented efficiency in transmission among humans, according to former CDC Director Robert Redfield (Reuters 2021); second, the furin cleavage site in the protein spikes (Wade 2021).

The laboratory leak hypothesis has been gaining increasing support from the scientific community as well as from the general public since the joint WHO-China mission to China in January and February of 2021, owing partly to the report of three sick researchers at the Wuhan Institute that received hospital care and the report of thousands of blood samples collected at an early stage of the pandemic destroyed before the Joint mission's investigation (WHO 2021; WSJ 2021b). A detailed explanation of the origin of the SARS-CoV-2 is provided in Chap. 9 of this book as one of the mysteries of the COVID-19.

3   The Pandemics in the History of Mankind

A worldwide contagion of an infectious agent befell humanity not a few times throughout its history. The COVID-19 pandemic is the most recent and current one. During the first two decades of the twenty-first century alone, human society suffered from three pandemics: the COVID-19, the 2009 H1N1 influenza pandemic, the 2002–2004 SARS pandemic. The frequency of pandemic outbreaks in the twenty-first century is exceptional, compared with any historical time period of the same length. As Table 1.1 summarizes the influenza pandemics since the early sixteenth century, a pandemic came to pass very rarely, that is, roughly once or twice in a century (Potter 2001).

Table 1.1   Influenza pandemics in human history

Pandemics	Year	Virus	Origin	# of cases	# of fatalities
2009 H1N1 Pandemic (swine flu)	Spring 2009	H1N1pdm09 virus	Mexico	60.8 million (US)	12,469 (US); 151,700–575,400 (world)
Pandemic of 1957–1958	1957	H2N2 virus	Yunan Province, China		Mortality rate ~ 1 in 4000; fatality~ 80,000 (US)
Pandemic of 1918–1920: 1918 influenza pandemic	1918: "The greatest medical holocaust"	H1N1 virus	Not known: China, US	~50% of world's population	40–50 million
Pandemic of 1898–1900	1898–1900				
Pandemic of 1830–1833	1830–1833		China	~20 ± 25% of the population in China	The mortality rate was not exceptionally high
Pandemic of 1781–1782	1781–1782			At the peak of the pandemic, 30,000 fell ill each day in St. Petersburg; two-thirds of the population of Rome became ill; and the outbreak is reported to have raged through Britain during the summer of 1782	
Pandemic of 1729			Russia		
Pandemic of 1580	1580: the first influenza pandemic		Asia	8000 deaths were reported from Rome, and some Spanish cities were decimated	
Pandemic of 1510	1510: probable				

Source: Potter (2001)

The first influenza pandemic in the record occurred in the sixteenth century, the 1580 pandemic. The eighteenth-century pandemics struck in 1729 and 1781, respectively. During the latter, it is estimated that two-thirds of the Rome population fell sick and, at the peak of it, 30,000 people got sick in St. Petersburg every day. The nineteenth-century pandemics broke out in 1830 and 1898, respectively. For the former, 20–45% of the Chinese population got infected (Potter 2001).

The twentieth century saw the deadliest pandemic in mankind's history, the 1918 H1N1 influenza pandemic commonly referred to as Spanish Flu. It is estimated to have infected roughly 50% of the world's population. It is estimated to have killed 40–50 million people worldwide. The second pandemic of the twentieth century occurred in 1957 caused by the H2N2 virus (Henderson et al. 2009). The mortality rate was not high, estimated to be 1 in 4000.

The twenty-first century saw the first influenza pandemic via the 2009 H1N1 pandemic. The century first encountered the human coronavirus pandemic in the SARS in 2002. The coronaviruses have emerged as one of the greatest challenges via the emergence of the subsequent MERS-CoV in 2012 and the SARS-CoV-2 in 2020. The COVID-19 virus, still highly contagious at the time of this writing, has resulted in roughly 4.5 million deaths worldwide. The MERS disease, although not classified as a pandemic by the WHO, had an exceptionally high mortality rate: three to four out of ten people infected with the MERS-CoV died.

In addition to the influenza pandemics, one of the most feared infectious diseases in human history was smallpox which was declared by the WHO in 1980 to be eradicated from the planet. The smallpox virus, referred to as *variola* (*major, minor*) virus, was highly contagious and at the same time extremely deadly, with a mortality rate of 30% in general population (CDC 2020). The establishment of the science of a vaccine and the development of a smallpox vaccine, named the *Dryvax*, was crucial in the eradication of the smallpox disease (Schwartz 2001; Plotkin 2009).

The most fatal pandemic recorded in history is the bubonic plague pandemic during the fourteenth century, commonly referred to as the Black Death. It was caused by the contagion of *bacterium Yersinia pestis* carried by vectors. It is estimated to have killed over 25–75 million in Europe and over 37 million in Asia, roughly a quarter of the world's population at that time (Gould and Pyle 1896).

4   HUMAN AND ECONOMIC TOLLS OF THE COVID-19

The tragedy of the COVID-19 pandemic has many dimensions of which the human and economic tolls are of the most often highlighted. The human dimension of the tragedy can be best explained by the number of deaths from the pandemic, especially the daily number of fatalities (Fig. 1.4). Right after the pandemic declaration by the WHO in early

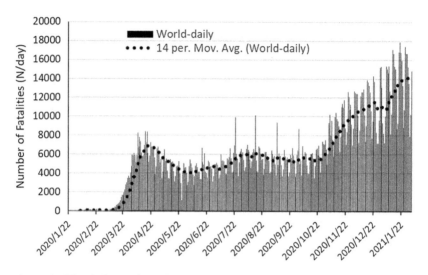

Fig. 1.4   The daily number of COVID-19 fatalities (world)

March 2020, the number of deaths per day surpassed 1000 worldwide. At the peak of the first wave of the pandemic which occurred around mid-April 2020, the number of fatalities per day was over 8000 globally (JHU 2020).

As spring passed by and then summer rolled on in that year, it seemed as if, to most people, the pandemic may give way to a hot summer. The number of fatalities dropped through May and June, *albeit* only slightly, appeared to be plateaued through the second wave in the summer and fall. Then, there approached the winter. Betraying the hope of the global community, the world was soon gripped by the third wave of the COVID-19 pandemic, which was even more contagious and deadlier. After the vaccine rollout in mid-December of 2020 followed by swift vaccination campaigns in rich countries, the fourth wave struck low-vaccination countries hard, for example, India and Brazil, from April 2021 onward (refer to Fig. 7.6 in Chap. 7 for the fourth wave and Fig. 7.7 in Chap. 7 for the fifth wave in 2021).

As Fig. 1.4 illustrates, the number of fatalities started to rise again with the start of November 2020, which started the third wave. At the peak, the number of deaths worldwide reached nearly 18,000 per day. The 14-day moving average of the daily deaths, which is depicted as the dotted

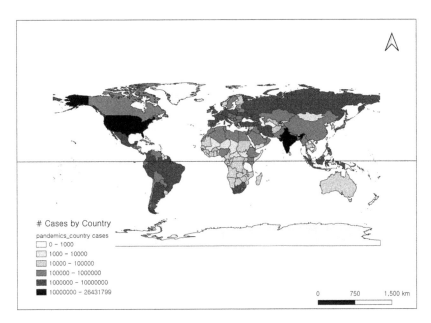

Fig. 1.5 The number of total cases by country across the planet (as of early February 2021)

line in the figure, tells us that the daily number of deaths may still rise further in the months ahead.

Across the planet, the COVID-19 has quickly spread from one country to another, as the geographical analysis of new infections in Fig. 1.5 shows. As of early February 2021, the number of COVID-19 cases surpassed 10 million people in the US and India, respectively. This is followed by the European countries, South and Central American countries (Brazil, Argentina, Mexico, etc.), Russia, and South Africa, in all of which the number of the total infections surpassed 1 million per country (JHU 2020).

Relatively fewer infections occurred in some regions. As of the afore-mentioned date, Sub-Saharan countries, with the exception of South Africa, Kenya, Nigeria, had fewer than 100,000 total infections in each country. Southeast Asian countries, as well as Oceanian countries, had also a smaller number of COVID-19 infections.

Figure 1.6 shows the geographical distribution across the planet of the number of fatalities from the COVID-19 pandemic, as of February 2,

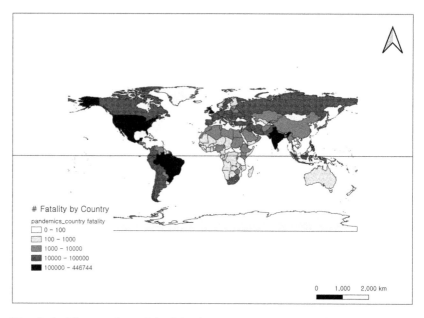

Fatality by Country
pandemics_country fatality
☐ 0 – 100
☐ 100 – 1000
■ 1000 – 10000
■ 10000 – 100000
■ 100000 – 446744

0   1,000   2,000 km

Fig. 1.6 The number of fatalities by country across the planet (as of early February 2021)

2021. The largest number of deaths occurred in the US, Brazil, Mexico, India, and the UK where it surpassed 100,000 in respective countries. By the aforementioned date, the total number of fatalities was 446,774 for the US, roughly 223,000 for Brazil, roughly 160,000 for Mexico, roughly 150,000 for India, and roughly 110,000 for the UK (JHU 2020).

A large number of countries across the planet had over 10,000 human deaths from the COVID-19 pandemic by early February 2021. An overwhelming majority of the countries in Europe, the Middle East, and South America belong to this group. A relatively smaller number of human deaths resulted from the COVID-19 in most countries of Sub-Saharan Africa, Southeast Asia, and Australasia.

The tragedy of the COVID-19 pandemic was far beyond the human health dimension, specifically hospitalizations and deaths, which was rather limited to the individuals and families directly struck by such events. The economic toll of the COVID-19, on the other hand, was more pervasive across the society, affecting nearly a full spectrum of the society (Polyakova

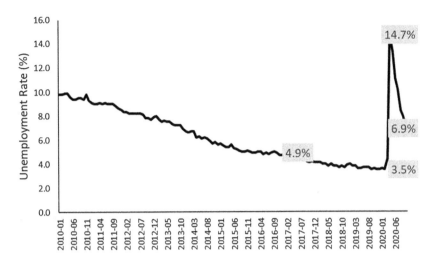

Fig. 1.7 The unemployment rate spike in the US

et al. 2020, 2021). Owing to the statewide lockdowns and business closures starting at the end of March 2020 in the US, the number of the unemployed spiked sharply and the economic production plummeted in the second quarter of 2020.

The unemployment rate in the US, shown in Fig. 1.7, shot up from as historically low as 3.5% before the pandemic to 14.5% in April 2020 (USBLS 2020). The sudden spike in the unemployment rate was attributable largely to the forced closures of small businesses as well as retail businesses, including cafes, restaurants, various shops, travels, and hotels. The unemployment rate, however, quickly bounced back in the following months as the state COVID-19 restrictions were eased in response to the declining number of new infections past the peak of the first wave (refer to Fig. 1.4).

As a vast majority of businesses were forced to remain closed in many states of the US, the US economic production similarly fell precipitously during the Q2 of 2020. From Q1 to Q2, the GDP fell by 31.4%. The GDP recovered quickly in the Q3 of 2020 as the state restrictions such as a statewide lockdown and a forced business closure were gradually lifted past the first wave (USBEA 2020).

However, as the fourth wave and the fifth wave continued to overwhelm the planet, despite high vaccination rates in developed nations, through the second year of the pandemic, a prolonged COVID-19 pandemic might be just starting to unleash its wrath on the economy, in particular, of small businesses, retailers, and low-income families in the society. They survived the pandemic's first year relying on the government's short-term emergency loans but may not be able to pay back and go bankrupt.

A center of big human and economic losses, as illustrated in Figs. 1.4, 1.5, 1.6, and 1.7, has gradually shifted from one world region to another over the course of the COVID-19 pandemic. During the first wave in 2020, big losses were concentrated in China, the US, and Europe. By the time the summer rolled on and the second wave was hitting the world, other regions began to experience similarly big losses, for example, India, Iran, Australia, Brazil, South Africa, and Japan. On September 15, 2020, for example, India reported 1290 deaths and nearly 100,000 new infections for a single day. During the third wave that began in the final quarter of 2020, South Africa reported nearly 22,000 new cases and 840 daily deaths on January 8, 2021. On January 9, 2021, Japan reported nearly 8000 daily new cases and 118 daily deaths a month later. On February 4, 2021, Brazil reported 56,873 new infections and 1232 deaths for a single day. When the fourth wave struck around March 2021, the number of infections in India surpassed 400,000 per day while the number of fatalities in the country surpassed 4000 in early May 2021 (JHU 2020).

5   Humanitarian Costs of the COVID-19

Besides the human fatalities and economic losses which are easily observable as well as quantified dimensions, the pandemic's impact on people's lives and well-being, which are not easily observable, was as severe. We may call this collectively the humanitarian cost of the COVID-19. The humanitarian cost includes, among other things, psychological effects of repeated lockdowns, the effects of school closures on children, the effects of prohibition of in-person church services, suicides and domestic violence, and various mandates forced upon the people (Hoover Institution 2020).

5.1   Lockdowns

Table 1.2 summarizes the status of COVID-19 restrictions in the US as of November 25, 2020, right after the announcements by the Pfizer-BioNTech and Moderna pharmaceuticals on their successful Phase III vaccine trials. A stay-at-home order, which is a lockdown, was issued in California, Ohio, New Mexico, and Puerto Rico. In the seven states, businesses were mostly closed: Washington, Oregon, New Mexico, Minnesota, Michigan, Illinois, and Kentucky. The mask wearing was mandatory by that time in 26 states (NYT 2020).

The lockdowns, stay-at-home orders, and other COVID-19 restrictions enforced by state governments were met with people's resistance and the concerns expressed by many groups of people in the US. The Great Barrington Declaration (GBD), which received the most attention, was the declaration by three infectious disease experts working at the world's premier universities that such lockdown policies are ineffective as well as harmful as a policy for addressing the pandemic. As an alternative, the drafters of the GBD proposed a "focused protection (FP)" approach. The FP approach places its priority on protecting the most vulnerable groups of the society, for example, the elderly, people in nursing homes, and people with co-morbidities. The declaration argued that children, young people, and healthy people face only a low risk of getting infected with the novel coronavirus and dying from it (Kulldorff et al. 2020; refer to Figs. 9.4 and 9.5 in Chap. 9).

The declaration warned of the devastating and irreparable effects of the lockdown policies on short- and long-term public health, including "lower childhood vaccination rates, worsening cardiovascular disease outcomes, fewer cancer screenings, and deteriorating mental health." It argued that

Table 1.2   COVID-19 restrictions in the US (as of November 25, 2020)

	States and territories
Businesses: mostly closed	WA, OR, NM, MN, MI, IL, KY
Masks: mandatory	WA, OR, CA, NV, UT, CO, NM, TX, LA, AL, MO, ND, MN, IO, WI, IL, MI, ID, OH, KY, WV, VA, PA, MD, NC, DL, NJ, NY, CT, MA, NH, VT, RI, MA, HW, PR
Stay-at-home orders: order of curfew	CA, OH, NM, PR

people of the working class, younger generations, and the underprivileged in the society will be disproportionately harmed by such policies (Kulldorff et al. 2020).

5.2   School Closures

Table 1.3 puts together the national-level school policies adopted across the globe with regard to school openings/closures in primary and secondary schools during the COVID-19 pandemic, which are drawn from the United Nations Educational, Scientific, and Cultural Organization's (UNESCO's) compilation of the national policies (UNESCO 2020). For each world region, country policies are classified into four categories: partially open, closed due to COVID-19, fully open, academic break. The data are compiled for April 30, 2020, when the school closures were at the peak.

The table shows that the countries that permitted primary and secondary schools to be fully open were very rare. Excluding the island nations and territories, there were only three countries that had open schools according to the UNESCO data: Belarus, Tajikistan, and Turkmenistan. In the Middle East, primary and secondary schools were fully closed in all countries. In Latin America and the Caribbean (LAC), Uruguay was the only country that was not fully closed for schools.

Many developed nations opted to partially open schools: the US, Denmark, Norway, Sweden, Russia, China, Japan, Australia, and New Zealand (AAP 2020). Many Pacific islands as well as the islands off Africa chose to fully open their schools: Madagascar, Seychelles, Kiribati, Marshall Islands, Niue, Nauru, and Vanuatu.

With the US zoomed in for a closer examination, Ohio Governor issued the first pandemic school closure order on March 12, 2020, which was soon followed by 48 other state governors. Most public schools remained closed in the fall of 2020 and even in the spring of 2021. A big obstacle in reopening schools was the opposition from teachers' unions across 13,000 school districts in the country (Grossmann et al. 2021; Marianno 2021).

The school closure orders and teachers' unions' oppositions were not in sync with the coronavirus data. The data showed that over 90% of all COVID-19 mortalities in the US occurred among people older than 55 while roughly 99% of all COVID-19 mortalities occurred among people older than 35 (CDC 2021). At odds with the prolonged school closures

Table 1.3 School closures, world (as of April 30, 2020)

Regions	Partially open	Closed due to COVID-19	Fully open	Academic break
North and Central America	Nicaragua, US	Belize, Canada, Guatemala, Honduras, Mexico, Panama, El Salvador	Greenland	
Latin America and the Caribbean (LAC)	Uruguay	Aruba, Argentina, Antigua and Barbuda, Bahamas, Bermuda, Bolivia, Brazil, Barbados, Chile, Colombia, Costa Rica, Cuba, Curacao, Dominica Dominican Republic, Ecuador, Grenada, Guyana Haiti, Jamaica, Saint Kitts and Nevis, Saint Lucia, Montserrat, Peru, Paraguay, Suriname, Turks and Caicos Island, Trinidad and Tobago, St. Vincent/ Grenadines, Venezuela, British Virgin Islands		Anguilla, Sint Maarten
Africa	Burundi, Tonga	Angola, Andorra, Benin, Burkina Faso, Cote d'Ivoire, Cameroon, Dem Republic Congo, Comoros, Cabo Verde, Djibouti, Algeria, Eritrea, Ethiopia, Gabon, Guinea, Gambia, Guinea-Bissau, Equatorial Guinea, Liberia, Libya, Lesotho, Morocco, Monaco, Mali, Montenegro, Mozambique, Mauritania, Mauritius, Malawi, Niger, Nigeria, Rwanda, Sudan, Senegal, Sierra Leone, Somalia, Serbia, South Sudan, São Tomé and Príncipe, Togo, Tunisia, Tanzania, Uganda, Yemen, South Africa	Madagascar, Seychelles	Botswana, CA Republic, Congo, Egypt, Ghana, Kenya, Namibia, Chad, Zambia, Zimbabwe

(*continued*)

Table 1.3 (continued)

Regions	Partially open	Closed due to COVID-19	Fully open	Academic break
Europe	Denmark, Faroe Islands, Iceland, Norway, Svalbard, Sweden, Russia	Albania, Armenia, Austria, Azerbaijan, Belgium, Bulgaria, Bosnia and Herzegovina, Switzerland, Cyprus, Czechia, Germany, Spain, Estonia, Finland, France, UK, Georgia, Gibraltar, Greece, Croatia, Hungary, Ireland, Italy, Liechtenstein, Lithuania, Luxembourg, Latvia, Republic of Moldova, North Macedonia, Malta, Poland, Portugal, Romania, San Marino, Slovakia, Eswatini, Ukraine	Belarus	Netherlands, Slovenia
Asia	China, Japan, Democratic People's Republic Korea,	Afghanistan, Bangladesh, Brunei Darussalam, Bhutan, Indonesia, India, Cambodia, Republic of Korea, Lao PDR, Sri Lanka, Kazakhstan, Kyrgyzstan, Myanmar, Mongolia, Malaysia, Nepal, Pakistan, Philippines, Singapore, Thailand, Uzbekistan, Viet Nam	Tajikistan, Turkmenistan	Timor-Leste
Middle East		United Arab Emirates, Bahrain, Iran, Iraq, Israel, Jordan, Kuwait, Lebanon, Oman, Palestine, Qatar, Saudi Arabia, Syrian Arab Republic, Turkey		
Oceania and Pacific Islands	Australia, New Zealand, Tokelau, Tuvalu	Cayman Is., Micronesia, Maldives, Palau, Papua New Guinea, Solomon Is., Samoa	Kiribati, Marshall Is., Niue, Nauru, Vanuatu	Cook Is., Fiji

enforced heavy-handedly in many states, schoolchildren were by and large unaffected by the SARS-CoV-2 virus during the first year of the pandemic (refer to Fig. 9.4 and 9.5 in Chap. 9).

5.3   Church Services

As the novel coronavirus was spreading with great haste in the first three months of 2020, many countries witnessed that church services are turning out to be a super-spreader event of the SARS-CoV-2 virus owing to a gathering of a large number of people in close proximity in an enclosed area coupled with frequent singing and speaking during an indoor service. Alarmed and in a rush to contain the swift contagion of the virus among church members and then into the general public, many countries, if not most, ordered a ban on in-person church services.

In these countries, church organizations resisted the government's order at first that prohibited an in-person church service but eventually they determined to comply with it. In the US, on the other hand, the Supreme Court of the United States (SCOTUS) ruled on November 26, 2020, that such a ban on in-person church services by the State of New York is not constitutional (WSJ 2020).

The SCOTUS decision was a salient outlier event in the large array of public sector decisions, to be clarified throughout this book, made and enforced during the COVID-19 pandemic. A new pandemic normal was the exact opposite: governments across the planet rushed to ban gatherings of people, be they social gatherings, civil protests, or religious worships, with a rationale of prohibiting any super-spreader event. Because such governmental orders defined a non-compliant civilian as a super-spreader killer and were enforced with an extensive police force, life and liberty of the people on the planet were undermined to an exceptional level.

The SCOTUS made the same decision again on February 5, 2021, on a similar California regulation. In a 6–3 decision, it ruled that California's ban on indoor church services during the pandemic violates the US Constitution's protection of the free exercise of religion (LAT 2021).

5.4   Domestic Violence, Suicide, and Mental Health

The lockdowns, stay-at-home orders, business closures, and school closures all render reasons for the society to be concerned about additional stress at home. An early study showed that domestic violence (DV) increased sharply in many countries during the lockdown periods (Boserup et al. 2020). The number of domestic violence has increased by +300% in February 2020, compared with February of the previous year, in Hubei Province of China to which Wuhan city belongs. France saw a 30% increase in DV since it initiated a national lockdown in March 2020. As summarized in Table 1.4, Argentina, Cyprus, and Singapore reported a similar increase in the number of DV during the first three months of 2020.

In some countries, a sharp rise in the number of suicide deaths during the COVID-19 pandemic was reported. In Japan, a monthly suicide rate increased from the previous year by +16% during the second wave from July to October 2020. The increase was far larger for females (+37%) as well as for children and adolescents (+49%) (Tanaka and Okamoto 2021).

During the second wave, a monthly increase in the number of suicides from the previous year with no COVID-19 pandemic was in the range of +100 suicides in July to +800 suicides in October 2020. In October 2020, the total number of suicides during the month topped 2153, which was larger than the total number of COVID-19 deaths until the end of November 2020 in Japan (Japan Times 2020).

The heavy-handed governmental restrictions including lockdowns and school closures may have inflicted the most severe harm on teenagers, although the quantitative evidence presented thus far is neither strong nor plenty. A quantification of it is likely to be very challenging. A rare study by the FAIR Health on the effects of the COVID-19 pandemic on pediatric mental health in the US analyzed over 32 billion private healthcare claim records in its database. The pediatric data cover the individuals aged up to 22 years. The study reports a large increase in mental health claims in the age range from 13 to 18. For the age group, the mental health claim lines, as a percentage of all medical claim lines, increased by around 100%

Table 1.4 Domestic violence and suicide during the COVID-19

	Domestic violence (first three months of 2020)	Suicide deaths	COVID-19 deaths
Hubei Province, China	+300%		
France	+30%		
Argentina	+25%		
Cyprus	+30%		
Singapore	+33%		
Japan		17,000 (January–November 2020); 2153 (October, 2020)	Fewer than 2000 (January–November 28, 2020)

from March and April in 2019 to the same period in 2020. Further, for the age group, intentional self-harm claims in March and April of 2020, as a percentage of all claims, increased by around 90–100% from the same period in 2019 (FAIR Health 2021).

6   RACE FOR A VACCINE

As the number of new cases surpassed a 10 million milestone worldwide at the end of June 2020 and the number of the dead surpassed half a million by then, the global community was in a serious race for developing an effective vaccine. However, almost no one, infectious disease experts and observers alike, believed then that an effective vaccine can be made available to people within the two years of the outbreak, that is, by the end of 2022. Experts argued that vaccines traditionally take 10–20 years to develop (Gupta 2021). Consider this! Until an eradication of smallpox viruses was declared in 1980 with the development of an effective vaccine followed by worldwide vaccination efforts, people on the planet had fallen victims to the smallpox viruses for over 200 years (Schwartz 2001).

Without an effective vaccine on the horizon, the only hope for the human society in the fight against the COVID-19 pandemic was considered by many to be herd immunity. Herd immunity is achieved when a "sufficiently" large fraction of the global population should acquire immunity against the virus via various routes, that is, antibodies or T cell immunity against the SARS-CoV-2 virus (Pierce 2019). For the COVID-19, however, achieving herd immunity naturally, that is, through infections and recoveries, seemed nearly impossible.

Shocking the world, the Pfizer pharmaceutical company announced on November 9, 2020, that it succeeded in developing a high-efficacy vaccine after completing its three stages of clinical trials. A week later, Moderna announced the same. The two pharmaceuticals' vaccines were reported to be about 95% effective in preventing the COVID-19 infection, far surpassing the experts' expectation of an effective vaccine with 60–70% efficacy rate (Fox Business 2020a, 2020b).

It took another month for the US Food and Drug Administration to approve the two vaccines for an emergency use authorization (EUA) on December 11, 2020, for the Pfizer-BioNTech vaccine and on December 18 for the Moderna vaccine (USFDA 2020a, 2020b). During the intervening period, the Vaccines and Related Biological Products Advisory

Committee reviewed the results of the clinical trials conducted of the two vaccines and voted to recommend the EUAs to the Director of the FDA.

Immediately after the Pfizer-BioNTech vaccine EUA, the vaccine doses were distributed across the US without any delay, thanks to the Operation Warp Speed (OWS) to be explained shortly (Azar II 2020). In the US, emergency healthcare professionals were given the first vaccine shots on December 14, 2020. By the first day of February in 2021, about 108 million people were given the vaccine shots in the world of which 35 million people were administered in the US. By early May 2021, 1.3 billion shots were given across 175 countries (OWID 2021). The vaccine shots administered thus far include the vaccines developed by Russia and China (NYT 2020; see also Table 7.3 in Chap. 7). There were positive signs that the vaccines, especially those developed by Pfizer-BioNTech and Moderna, were indeed having real effects on people in fighting off the COVID-19 virus. By early May 2021, multiple high-vaccination rate countries such as Israel, the UK, and the US were experiencing a sharp decline in the daily number of new infections, respectively (Jerusalem Post 2021).

The remarkable success in developing the vaccines in an unprecedentedly short period of time can be attributed to many factors, of which two are most noteworthy. One is the store of scientific knowledge accumulated on virology and especially RNA (Ribonucleic Acid) along with their applications to pharmaceutical and medical products (Plotkin 2009; Kariko et al. 2011; Pardi et al. 2018). The SARS-CoV-2 virus is a messenger RNA (mRNA) virus. Both the Pfizer-BioNTech vaccine and the Moderna vaccine are an mRNA vaccine, which is a novel scientific achievement whose efficacy and safety are being validated for the first time via the COVID-19 pandemic (NYT 2020). An mRNA vaccine is different from the established vaccine technologies such as a viral vector vaccine and a protein-based vaccine in that it only delivers genetic instructions to a person's cells to provoke the person's immune system (Pardi et al. 2018).

The other success factor was a swift national policy response to create a private-public sector partnership through the OWS (USDHHS 2020a; Azar II 2020). Through the OWS, the Trump administration mobilized the world's leading pharmaceutical companies to jump-start their vaccine developments as early as possible. It selected the most promising vaccine candidates at the earliest possible date, to each of which a funding for development efforts was allocated as early as March 30, 2020. For example, the Moderna company received US$483 million and the Johnson & Johnson company received US$456 million to start their developments.

In addition, the OWS allocated an investment funding for manufacturing and deliveries to the selected vaccine candidates, so that successful vaccines should get manufactured as soon as respective Phase II clinical trials turn out to be successful even before an EUA approval. The US government would own the manufactured vaccines and, if an EUA would be issued at a later date, the government-owned vaccines would be distributed immediately to people. Without the manufacturing and delivery funding designed in this way, the vaccine developers would not have started manufacturing their vaccine doses until the EUA approval by the FDA. Pfizer received US$1.95 billion for manufacturing and delivery and Novavax received US$1.6 billion for manufacturing (refer to Table 7.5 in Chap. 7).

7   Global Governance: WHO

A successful analysis of the COVID-19 pandemic will not be achievable without a careful examination of its characteristics as a globally shared experience, more commonly referred to as a global public good. For this special type of goods, one of the thorniest questions to address is whether global governance is properly set up to carry out the ultimate task of providing the concerned global-scale public good to the citizens of the planet (Seo 2020).

As far as the pandemics are concerned, the international organization at the top of the global governance is the World Health Organization. Established soon after the United Nations' Charter was signed in 1945, the WHO's constitution aspires to a lofty goal, that is, "attainment by all peoples of the highest possible level of health (UN 1948)." The treaty of the International Health Regulations (IHR) signed in 1969 gives the WHO a legally binding authority over 196 member nations to act as a global governance entity on an international spread of diseases (WHO 2015).

In the initial months of the COVID-19 pandemic, the WHO made a series of key decisions to inform the global community. The WHO country office in China first reported to the global community the viral pneumonia outbreak in Wuhan, China, on the last day of 2019. The WHO quickly determined that it is a novel coronavirus and declared that the virus is a public health emergency of international concern (PHEIC) on January 30, 2020. It determined the name of the disease to be the

COVID-19, short for Corona Virus Disease, on February 11, 2020. It then declared that the COVID-19 is a pandemic on March 11, 2020 (WHO 2020a).

Several criticisms were leveled against the WHO's actions through the course of the COVID-19 pandemic. The first was that the organization did not act swiftly on the COVID-19 outbreak because of the political pressure from China. Notably, the WHO stated on January 14, 2020, that "preliminary investigations by the Chinese authorities had found no clear evidence of human-to-human transmission" (WHO 2020a).

Another critique was concerned with the WHO's investigation into the origin of the SARS-CoV-2 virus. Although the first report of the disease was made on the last day of 2019, the WHO team of experts was not allowed to enter China to investigate the origin for over a year until mid-January of 2021 (WSJ 2021a). It remains still undecided, as of mid-September of 2021, whether the virus was originated from China and, if so, whether or not it was originated from the Wuhan Institute of Virology (WIV) where coronavirus experiments had been undertaken before the pandemic.

The joint WHO-China mission put forth four origin hypotheses, following the China visit, but concluded that the WIV laboratory leak hypothesis is "extremely unlikely" (WHO 2021). However, former CDC Director publicly argued on March 27, 2021, that an accidental laboratory leak from the WIV is the most likely origin of the virus, which has subsequently garnered support not only from doctors and scientists but also from a strong majority of the US citizens (Reuters 2021)

With these critiques aside, the most striking aspect of the COVID-19 policy responses may have been that the policy responses to the pandemic were mostly, if not entirely, anchored at a national control center of each nation while the international organizations did little and meant little to each nation's fights against the novel coronavirus. It swiftly dawned on each country that it should be on its own in designing a full portfolio of response strategies in urgent needs to save lives of its citizens, including the decisions on border restrictions, social distancing, a mask mandate, a lockdown, business closures, school closures, emergency productions, effective treatments, and vaccine developments (refer to Chap. 4 of this book).

Unlike many other globally shared good problems, for example, global climate change, there was no call for an international treaty or framework based upon which individual member countries should stick to and implement agreed policy measures during the pandemic crisis. Neither has there been any actual extensive global cooperation in dealing with the COVID-19 at any point in 2020 and 2021.

That the planet's COVID-19 responses were mostly individual member countries' own endeavors and initiatives sends an important message to the economics of globally shared goods and experiences (Seo 2020). A worldwide pandemic virus is a globally shared public good in the sense that by definition it easily and quickly spreads to the globe, affecting all individual citizens of the planet. Readers may refer to Fig. 8.1 in Chap. 8 to verify how quickly the COVID-19 spread to the globe and may also compare it with a rapid mixing of carbon dioxide into global atmosphere. Elimination of the pandemic-causing virus is again a globally shared good since it would benefit all citizens of the planet (Samuelson 1954).

Why then was there no call for an extensive global cooperation on COVID-19 responses? Why did individual nations act alone instead of relying on the WHO? To meet the challenges of the pandemic, each country should and had to fight her own war, with or without other countries' similar efforts, because of the rapidity of the virus contagion among the nation's population, that is, the high efficiency of the virus in human-to-humanc transmission (again, refer to Fig. 8.1 in Chap. 8).

From another angle, an end of the pandemic can be accomplished only by, to be very realistic about it, a highly effective vaccine. There is no alternative way especially in the case of a highly contagious or a highly fatal infectious disease. A high-efficacy vaccine is a backstop technology (Nordhaus 1973). The vaccine backstop development, however, does not call for an extensive global cooperation owing to a best-shot production technology for its production (Hirshleifer 1983).

These characteristics, along with the others to be explained in Chaps. 2 and 8, make a global pandemic a unique globally shared good, that is, unlike the other globally shared goods (Seo 2020). This in turn implies that a socially optimal solution to a worldwide pandemic will be unlike the other socially optimal solutions established for the other globally shared goods. An elucidation of the unique characteristics of global pandemics and the socially optimal economic solution to address them is at the heart of this book.

8   Orders and Mandates by National Governments

To state it one more time, the planetwide responses to the COVID-19 pandemic have been firmly centered around the actions of individual national governments. Each nation acted independently of the other nations as well as of the WHO. A national government had to make a series of decisions in an urgent manner on a number of pressing policy matters. The decisions made by one nation were not always in sync with the decisions made by another nation. However, many actual policy choices have turned out to be in agreement from one nation's choices to another nation's.

The series of governmental decisions made during the COVID-19 pandemic is explained in detail in Chap. 4 of this book. They include the following: (1) Is the disease a public health emergency of international concern? (2) Should the travels from the origin of the virus or neighboring countries be suspended? (3) Should social measures such as social distancing, mask wearing, hand washing, be made mandatory? (4) Should national emergency productions be ordered? (5) Should a national lockdown or a business closure be ordered? (6) How should an economic relief be designed? (7) Should certain potential treatments be approved? (8) Should a vaccine be approved for an emergency use? (9) Should schools be opened or closed?

The US and many other countries ordered a national or statewide lockdown more than one time during 2020 and 2021. A few countries took an opposite approach. Sweden, for example, carved out a no-lockdown strategy (Deccan Herald 2020; Detroit News 2020). Under the Swedish no-lockdown model, schools, restaurants, parks, cafes, shops, cinemas, and public transportations remained open as in pre-pandemic times. The nation's health authorities in Sweden resorted to voluntary compliance of her citizens to fight the COVID-19 pandemic.

Which one of the two policy models outperformed in terms of health and economic outcomes? An examination of the case and fatality data up to the end of 2020 reveals that Sweden far outperformed the countries that adopted a lockdown strategy such as the US (refer to Fig. 4.8 in Chap. 4).

The US government invoked the Defense Production Act (DPA), originally intended for emergency productions during wartimes, in an effort to rapidly produce essential emergency medical devices to fight the pandemic (USDHHS 2020b). With the DPA invocation, major private companies were called upon to produce urgent medical devices, including General Motors, Philips, General Electric, Hamilton, and Zoll. These companies produced ventilators, respirators, COVID-19 test kits, emergency medical treatment facilities, masks, needles, and syringes. The DPA-invoked productions of medical devices turned out to be a successful private-public partnership in the fight against the coronavirus. Another was the afore-described OWS which mobilized both the most advanced pharmaceutical companies in the world and multiple US federal agencies for the vaccine development efforts (USDHHS 2020a).

The treatments that received an emergency authorization from the FDA included hydroxychloroquine (revoked later), remdesivir, COVID-19 convalescent plasma, antibody cocktail (formerly known as regeneron), Abbott RealTime SARS-CoV-2 assay, and SARS-CoV-2 Polymerase Chain Reaction (PCR) test (USFDA 2020d).

The two governmental programs, that is, the OWS and the DPA, demonstrated clearly that the pre-pandemic strength of the private sector of the nation is the key to a successful fight against the pandemic. It can be said that the private sector's strength gave people hope during the COVID-19 pandemic and may eventually lead the planet to an end of the pandemic. To go further, the COVID-19 responses across the planet were most effective and consequential when the private sector had the resources and capabilities to deal with the crisis, to name only some, hospital capacities, pharmaceutical companies, doctors and nurses, medical devices, health insurances, and related sciences.

On the other hand, many government policies and regulations turned out to be dismal as well as divisive to the citizens. It only takes a look at the discontent and anger among the public against government-imposed lockdowns, forced business closures, school closures, travel bans, mask mandates, banning social gatherings, infection-contact tracing, prohibiting in-person church services, and vaccine mandates.

One of the paramount governmental actions during the pandemic was an implementation of an economic relief program for its citizens. Individual states of the US started issuing a lockdown order by the end of March 2020: California on March 19, New York on March 22, and Georgia on April 3, 2020. With a goal of alleviating the economic stress of families and businesses during the lockdown period, the Coronavirus Aid, Relief, and Economic Security Act, the CARES Act in short, was passed and signed into law on March 27, 2020 (USDOT 2020). The CARES Act provided US$2.2 trillion to the citizens for the purpose of their economic relief and security. The CARES Act has, however, turned out to be only one of the series of relief packages to be signed by the US federal government during the pandemic.

Most, if not all, countries passed and implemented an economic relief bill or program in one form or another in 2020. The economic models upon which the relief programs were based varied from one program to another. Under the CARES Act, every American citizen was to receive a one-time cash payment of the same amount from the federal government. The relief models adopted by the governments in the world are fourfold: a universal uniform cash payment like the CARES Act, a universal proportional cash payment, a selective low-income cash payment, and a selective ad hoc cash payment. The four relief models will yield very different wealth consequences. In other words, the global pandemic will force, to a degree or another, a redistribution of the nation's wealth among its citizens via the choice of one of the four relief models.

The large basket of governmental rapid responses and strategies appeared, to the observers and researchers alike, to be destined to fail in the US. This was because of a flare-up of the protests and riots, rooted in racial tension between Black people and White people, at the height of the novel coronavirus' rapid contagion in May and June of 2020 (US Crisis Monitor 2020). To give readers a rough idea, the daily number of protests during the final week of May and the first half of June reached over 500 which were erupting in all major cities across the country. Through the end of November 2020, the number of protests per day remained around 100 across major cities (Fig. 1.8).

Some of these protests also turned violent, classified as a riot, often burning, vandalizing, and rooting shops and buildings (US Crisis Monitor 2020). On the final two days of May 2020, the number of riots in the US reached nearly 100 per day (Fig. 1.9). Through the end of November 2020, violent riots did not end. Most days saw violent riots in 2 to as many as 15 cities across the country.

The sustained protests and riots during the critical phases of the COVID-19 contagion among the US public dimmed any prospect of containing the spread of the SARS-CoV-2 virus. When the third wave of the pandemic hit the country starting from early October 2020, the number of new infections, as well as the number of fatalities, nearly tripled the respective numbers recorded during the first wave of the pandemic (JHU 2020).

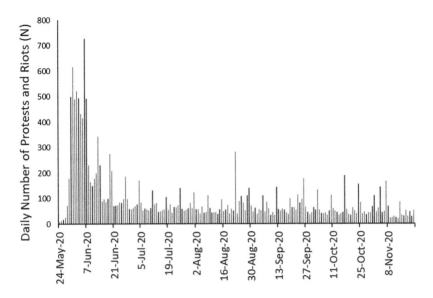

Fig. 1.8 The daily number of protests and riots in the US during 2020

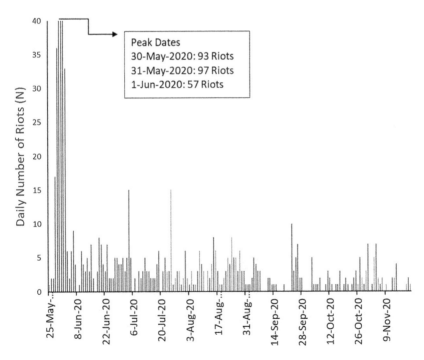

Fig. 1.9 The daily number of riots in the US during 2020

9   A GOLDEN OPPORTUNITY FOR A RADICAL SOCIAL TRANSFORMATION?

The society of humans during the COVID-19 pandemic was a drastically different one from the pre-pandemic world. It appeared as if it was transitioned into another world system or order. People were forced to be in a lockdown; private businesses were ordered to remain closed; international travels were banned; religious services were prohibited; people were ordered to wear a mask even outdoors; primary and secondary schools should remain closed; every citizen should be traceable by the government.

All of these radical as well as outlandish regulations and policies, unthinkable in the pre-pandemic worlds, meant a supreme authority of the government that was in charge at that time. The foremost of the government's authority was to feed its citizens via an economic relief aid delivered to every citizen of the country, for example, US$1200 delivered to each citizen once in a while.

This unprecedented state of the world came to being with a host of calls for a radical social transformation by way of the COVID-19 pandemic. These proposals and movements varied in the degree of radicalness as well as that of populism. In this book, the present author clarifies the spectrum of the radical transformation proposals by the following four movements: the Great Reset, a governmental capitalism, a Marxist revolution, and popular uprisings.

The Great Reset is the movement whose concept was put forward in early January 2020, not a month old since the pandemic outbreak, in the run-up to the annual meeting of the World Economic Forum in Davos, Switzerland (WEF 2020). Proponents argue that the COVID-19 pandemic presents the world a rare opportunity to reset the global economic system because, they contend, the unprecedented shock waves of the global pandemic should make people more receptive to a big vision of change (Guardian 2020a).

What is the new economic system toward which the Great Reset is driven? Although it varies from proposal to proposal, it is centered around the concepts of climate emergency, sustainable development, equity, and provisions of public goods (Schwab and Malleret 2020; Guardian 2020a). The proposed new system is owed to their identification of the COVID-19 pandemic as the result of a breakdown in the capitalist society of the relationship between mankind and nature. That is, they blame the capitalist market economy for the pandemic.

An even more radical movement than the Great Reset is a Marxist revolution. To the Marxists, the COVID-19 pandemic is "a product of capitalism" which places profit and capital over people's lives (IMT 2020). The proponents define the COVID-19 as "a trigger event," revealing and accelerating the crisis of global capitalism, for the radical transformation into a Marxist economy (SEPA 2020).

The Marxist revolution, like the Great Reset movement, pays little attention to the origin of the COVID-19 pandemic. The advocates of these movements are quick to lay blame on global capitalism but are disinclined to heed to the fact that the novel coronavirus was most likely originated from Wuhan, China, whether via a natural bat transmission or a laboratory leak (WHO 2021).

From another viewpoint, the pre-pandemic strength of the private sector in the capitalist economy, specifically the pharmaceutical enterprises and the medical sector, proved to be pivotal in the fight against the COVID-19 pandemic. The Marxist revolutionists as well as the Great Resetters do certainly overlook a critical importance of a healthy market economy, which has delivered, among other things, the advances in medical and pharmaceutical sciences that were pivotal in the COVID-19 responses including the mRNA vaccines (Pardi et al. 2018).

A popular uprising, one of the four radical social change theories examined in this book, has a weaker ideological underpinning than the others, but may turn out to present a more plausible route to social upheavals that may follow at the tail of the pandemic (Davies 1962). In one scenario, the COVID-19 pandemic may hurt different groups of citizens disproportionately and may further increase the gap between the rich and the poor, resulting in an uprising from the most hurt or the impoverished in the society (Kluth 2020).

In another scenario, personal tragedies and losses which have been kept under the roof owing to the government's tight grip on the society during the global crisis may eventually erupt. When people start to come out, they may flood the streets in protests. People may demand responsibilities for the government's actions during the pandemic or demand a restoration of civil liberty and activities in the society.

Of the four movements, however, the Great Reset may be best positioned to yield the most impact on the post-pandemic world if the US infrastructure bill and the budget bill were to pass the Congress at some point in 2021 (NYT 2021b). Both of these bills plan to heavily invest in the aforementioned programs that the Great Resetters have put forth.

10   A HARBINGER FOR A CLIMATE CHANGE DOOMSDAY?

A group of researchers and politicians, even though not organized tightly in any way, put forward a hypothesis that the COVID-19 pandemic is a result of an ongoing global climate change crisis. To them, the COVID-19 pandemic is interpreted to be only a harbinger of what will be a far worse global tragedy, that is, a climate change catastrophe (Ban and Verkooijen 2020a, 2020b; Guardian 2020b).

From the vantage point of climate change research, the proposed hypothesis is close to a climate change doomsday scenario (Lenton et al. 2008; Weitzman 2009). The advocates argue that global climate change will cause a global pandemic such as the COVID-19 more frequently and they further argue that it will cause an even deadlier pandemic more frequently. Imagine that a global pandemic that kills 10 million people worldwide would break out every 20 years!

The climate change doomsday scenario via worldwide pandemics drives those who are concerned about the relationship between climate change and wildlife. At the heart of the hypothesis is an observation that roughly 75% of all infectious diseases come from wildlife (Ban and Verkooijen 2020a). The latter is subject to alterations by changes in the climate system. They argue that the destruction of natural places and/or climate change force wildlife, especially animals, to live closer to humans, which then creates a better opportunity for pathogens to enter human hosts (Guardian 2020b).

The research on the nexus between climate change and infectious diseases is a prominent field of climate research, notwithstanding its relatively slower progress than many other fields of climate research (Patz et al. 2003). A straightforward question that could be raised by a concerned citizen is whether or not this field of climate research corroborates the above climate change doomsday scenario rooted in the pandemics (Seo 2021).

As for the climate change and infectious disease research, scientists need to look into three major actors in order to establish the links between climate change and infectious diseases: pathogens (infectious agents), vectors (carriers), and hosts (humans, animals). The three actors must be carefully studied for each of the major infectious diseases of concern. Up to the COVID-19 outbreak, scientists have paid most attention to the two infectious diseases that have long burdened humanity: malaria and influenza (Patz et al. 2003; Lopez et al. 2006). Post the COVID-19, considering the recurrence of the coronavirus diseases during the past two decades, climate researchers will no doubt add the coronaviruses to the list of infectious diseases of high concern under climate change (Weiss 2020).

Malaria is estimated to kill roughly 400,000 people annually, according to the most recent World Malaria Report (WHO 2019). The malaria deaths, however, occur in the developing countries only, especially in Sub-Saharan Africa. Influenza is estimated to kill 291,000–645,000 people worldwide annually (WHO 2019; Iuliano et al. 2018). Will malaria or influenza outbreaks turn out even deadlier as well as more frequent owing to the ongoing climate alterations?

The answers to these questions are laid out in Chap. 6. Let me give a glimpse of the chapter. Climate researchers resort to one of the three scientific methodologies to predict the impacts of climate change on humanity's burden of infectious diseases. The three methodologies, however, do not yield similar predictions, that is, they produce contrary predictions. Statistical models tend to predict little change in infectious diseases owing to climate change (Rogers and Randolph 2000). Process-based models, on the other hand, tend to forecast a severe impact of climate change on infectious diseases. To give you a rough idea, a process-based malaria model predicts an increase in the number of people at risk by 260–320 million annually by the year 2080 (Martens et al. 1999). Be reminded as well that these predictions did not take into account the malaria vaccines that are newly developed recently and tested or being developed presently (WHO 2020c).

From the review of these predictions, what can we say about the climate change doomsday scenario on the basis of repeated coronavirus pandemics in the future? There is yet no evidence that associates climate change causally to the coronaviruses, according to the World Health Organization's Q&A on the topic (WHO 2020b). In fact, there is no conclusion yet on what caused the SARS-CoV-2 pandemic, even after the WHO-China joint mission into China in January and February of 2021 (WHO 2021). As explained in Sect. 2, the four hypotheses were clarified during the press conference of the joint mission, of which the accidental laboratory escape hypothesis is gaining an increasingly large support from the public according to several polls taken in June/July 2021. As far as this discussion is concerned, it is noticeable that no attention was paid by the joint mission to the climate change origin hypothesis or the climate change doomsday scenario.

11   THE ECONOMICS OF PANDEMICS

All the considerations in the preceding sections set the stage nicely for the primary task of this book: a novel description of the economics of pandemics as a globally shared experience, which is done in Chap. 8 of this book. A pandemic, such as the COVID-19, is by definition a globally shared good. Therefore, a pandemic economics is an important sub-field of the economics literature on globally shared resources (Seo 2020).

What should constitute the economics of pandemics as a globally shared good? The essential question in the economics thereof is how the global community should manage the pandemic risk efficiently, that is, in a socially optimal manner (Nordhaus 1994; Bloom and Canning 2017). The actions that need to be taken must encompass both *ante*-pandemic outbreak decisions and *post*-pandemic outbreak decisions.

A unique economic characteristic of global pandemics at a scale of the COVID-19 is an extremely low probability of realization (Jonas 2013; Fan et al. 2018). If we relied solely on the history of pandemics, then the return time is roughly a century. The economics of pandemics, therefore, involves a dynamic model of extremely low probability events with extremely high economic consequences which deals with the question of a tail probability distribution (Schuster 1984; Weitzman 2009).

Another district characteristic of global pandemics is that the end of a pandemic may be realized only with a highly effective vaccine while the technology needed for such a vaccine development has been proven repeatedly in reality (Plotkin 2009; Pardi et al. 2018). In that sense, the high-efficacy vaccine is a backstop technology (Nordhaus 1973). The concept of a backstop becomes an integral part of the economics of pandemics. For many other globally shared goods, backstop technologies have not yet been proven, for example, nuclear fusion or solar reflector for climate change, a gravity tractor for killer asteroids (ITER 2020; Seo 2020).

The four major fault lines introduced in this book help clarify a multiplicity of actors and actions in the pandemic economics. The first is that of the private sector *versus* the public sector. The second is that of global governance *versus* national actions. The third is that of governmental orders and mandates *versus* civil liberty. The fourth is that of containment efforts *versus* vaccination efforts. The four fault lines were amply alluded in the description thus far of this chapter.

Regarding the first fault line, two programs showcased a critical role of the private sector in the management of pandemic risk. One is the vaccine development programs and the other is the invocation of the Defense Production Act (DPA) (Azar II 2020; USDHHS 2020b). Through the private-public partnerships in these programs, on the other hand, the public sector has made an important contribution.

What these two programs revealed is that the advances in biomedical sciences and virology in the private sector will show up to play a critical role in the society's efficient pandemic risk management. The strength of the private sector is also key to the availabilities and qualities of various essential resources such as test kits, hospitals, doctors, medical devices, and care staff (Romer 1990).

As for the second fault line, that the responses to the COVID-19 pandemic were anchored at a national control center and global governance did not matter much to individual nations' battles was explained above. What underlies this salient feature of humanity's responses to the pandemic is a family of unique characteristics of a global pandemic, which will be clarified in Chap. 8.

Apropos of the third fault line, that Sweden's no-lockdown strategy appears to outperform the lockdown-based strategies in most countries, particularly during the pre-vaccine period, raises the possibility that pandemic responses can be designed based on the principle of civil liberty and responsibility (Deccan Herald 2020). The hard reality in 2020 was that the world political classes were obsessed by governmental mandates and orders in a rush to contain the rapid COVID-19 contagion. However, the effects of the heavy-handed governmental mandates, including a lockdown, a universal mask mandate, a business closure, and a school closure, may have been minimal, if not even adverse causing significant side effects (Boserup et al. 2020; Bundgaard et al. 2020; Oster et al. 2021). After all, after nearly two years of implementing such hard-minded policies, the world is still struggling to contain the fifth wave of the pandemic.

As per the fourth fault line, a containment effort, that is, an endeavor to stop the virus transmission among the population, is indispensable in the fight against a pandemic, so is a vaccine development effort. A highly effective vaccine would provide a backstop solution, but it could take multiple years to get one developed and then approved for emergency use. The first one or two years from the point of a global pandemic outbreak, however, will witness millions of human deaths caused by the pandemic. After one year and nine months after the COVID-19 outbreak, the world saw nearly 5 million deaths. As such, during the pre-vaccine period, a containment effort is a central as well as an indispensable strategy.

Reflecting on the four fault lines, an economics of pandemics as a globally shared experience is elucidated in Chap. 8, highlighting and offering insights on a large set of choices available to the economic actors during the pandemic, that is, individuals, businesses, institutions, governments, and international organizations.

In designing a socially efficient pandemic strategy which is at the core of the economics of pandemics, the foremost economic question is how it anticipates and creates the right incentives to an individual actor such as an individual citizen or a business to protect oneself and the others (Coase 1960; Hart and Holmstrom 1987; Laffont and Martimort 2002; Shiller 2005). This book, especially Chap. 8, delves into this question of the incentives created by policies and strategies as well as the anticipatory and reactive behaviors of the economic actors to thus create incentives (Seo 2016, 2019).

12   The Road Ahead

This book is composed of nine chapters, including the present one which provides an introduction to the book as well as an overview of the COVID-19 pandemic. Chapter 2 provides a review of fundamental concepts, economic theories, and empirical studies currently available in the economics literature on infectious diseases and pandemics. It is a tool kit for the description of the economics of pandemics in Chap. 8.

The five chapters that follow are devoted to a critical analysis in each chapter of each of the five prominent aspects of pandemics and the pandemic risk management. Analysis I in Chap. 3 examines the role of global governance with a review of the WHO's actions during the COVID-19 pandemic. Analysis II in Chap. 4 examines the series of governmental decisions, that is, the nine decisions described previously. Analysis III in Chap. 5 examines the basket of proposals for a radical social transformation at the tail of the COVID-19 pandemic. Analysis IV in Chap. 6 examines the climate change doomsday scenario that is founded on the attribution of the COVID-19 pandemic to climate change. Analysis V in Chap. 7 examines multifarious aspects of vaccines and vaccine developments, including virology, vaccinology, history, economics, and policy thereof.

With the stage thus well set up by the five analyses, the present author integrates all the theories, concepts, observations, and empirical data discussed throughout this book to elucidate in Chap. 8 the economics of pandemics as a globally shared experience.

The book concludes with Chap. 9 where the present author provides a summary of some as of yet unresolved questions or still mysteries regarding the COVID-19 pandemic. This chapter was added because the pandemic is only a year and nine months old while many questions remain unanswered. For example, the origin of the SARS-CoV-2 is still hotly debated while the global community does not know yet why the virus was so benign to kids and school children but so fatal to seniors.

This completes Chap. 1, an introduction to the book.

REFERENCES

American Academy of Pediatrics (AAP). 2020. COVID-19 Planning Considerations: Guidance for School Re-entry. Published on June 23. Itasca, IL: AAP.

Azar II, Alex M. 2020. How Operation Warp Speed delivered a COVID Vaccine in Record Time. *Fox News*. Published on December 12. https://www.foxnews.com/opinion/hhs-azar-operation-warp-speed-covid-vaccine-record-time.

Ban, Ki-moon, and Patrick Verkooijen. 2020a. Will We Learn Lessons for Tackling Climate Change from Our Current Crisis? *CNN*. Published on April 9. https://edition.cnn.com/2020/04/09/opinions/climate-change-lessons-from-COVID-19-ban-verkooijen/index.html.

———. 2020b. Coronavirus is a Warning to Us All: We Must Heal Nature in Order to Heal Ourselves. *HuffPost*. Published on May 2. https://www.huffingtonpost.co.uk/entry/coronavirus_uk_5eac35acc5b65156135c9863.

Bloom, D.E., and D. Canning. 2017. *Epidemics and Economics*. Working Paper #9, Harvard Program on Demography of Ageing, Harvard University, Cambridge, MA.

Boserup, Brad, Mark McKenney, and Adel Elkbuli. 2020. Alarming Trends in US Domestic Violence during the COVID-19 Pandemic. *The American Journal of Emergency Medicine*. https://doi.org/10.1016/j.ajem.2020.04.077

Bundgaard, H., J.S. Bundgarrd, D.E.T. Raaschou-Pedersen, et al. 2020. Effectiveness of Adding a Mask Recommendation to Other Public Health Measures to Prevent SARS-CoV-2 Infection in Danish Mask Wearers. A Randomized Controlled Trial. *Annals of Internal Medicine*. https://doi.org/10.7326/M20-6817

Calisher, Charles, Dennis Carroll, Rita Colwell, Ronald B. Corley, Peter Daszak, Christian Drosten, Luis Enjuanes, Jeremy Farrar, Hume Field, Josie Golding, Alexander Gorbalenya, Bart Haagmans, James M. Hughes, William B. Karesh, Gerald T. Keusch, Sai Kit Lam, Juan Lubroth, John S. Mackenzie, Larry

Madoff, Jonna Mazet, Peter Palese, Stanley Perlman, Leo Poon, Bernard Roizman, Linda Saif, Kanta Subbarao, and Mike Turner. 2020. Statement in Support of the Scientists, Public Health Professionals, and Medical Professionals of China Combatting COVID-19. *Lancet* 395: E42–E43.

Centers for Disease Control and Prevention (CDC). 2020. *Smallpox.* Atlanta, G.A.: The CDC.

———. 2021. *Provisional COVID-19 Death Counts by Sex, Age, and State. Updated on April 15.* Atlanta, G.A.: The CDC. https://data.cdc.gov/NCHS/Provisional-COVID-19-Death-Counts-by-Sex-Age-and-S/9bhg-hcku.

CNBC. 2021. The UK's Covid Vaccine Program and Delta Surge Means it's Now a Test Case for the World. Published on June 25. https://www.cnbc.com/2021/06/25/uk-closely-watched-with-its-vaccine-program-and-surge-in-cases.html

Coase, R. 1960. The Problem of Social Costs. *Journal of Law and Economics* 3: 1–44.

Coleman, C.M., and M.B. Frieman. 2014. Coronaviruses: Important Emerging Human Pathogens. *Journal of Virology* 8: 5209–5212.

Davies, J.C. 1962. Toward a Theory of Revolution. *American Sociological Review* 6: 5–19.

Deccan Herald. 2020. No Lockdowns, but Sweden Seems to have Controlled the COVID-19 pandemic. Published on October 1. https://www.deccanherald.com/opinion/panorama/no-lockdowns-but-sweden-seems-to-have-controlled-the-COVID-19-pandemic-895509.html.

Detroit News. 2020. Gov. Whitmer Closing High Schools, Colleges, In-person Dining, Casinos, Movie Theaters. Published on November 15. https://www.detroitnews.com/story/news/politics/2020/11/15/gov-whitmer-expected-announce-new-COVID-19-restrictions-sunday/6304308002/.

FAIR Health. 2021. *The Impact of COVID-19 on Pediatric Mental Health: A Study of Private Healthcare Claims.* New York, N.Y.: FAIR Health.

Fan, Victoria Y., Dean T. Jamison, and Lawrence H. Summers. 2018. Pandemic Risk: How Large are the Expected Losses? *The Bulletin of the World Health Organization* 96 (2): 129–134. https://doi.org/10.2471/BLT.17.199588.

Fox Business. 2020a. Pfizer's COVID-19 Vaccine Proves 90% Effective in Latest Trials. Published on November 9. https://www.foxbusiness.com/healthcare/pfizers-COVID-19-vaccine-proves-90-effective-in-latest-trials

———. 2020b. Moderna Says its Vaccine is 94.5% Effective in Preventing COVID-19. Published on November 16. https://www.foxbusiness.com/healthcare/moderna-coronavirus-vaccine-trial-phase-3

Gould, George M., and Walter L. Pyle. 1896. Historic Epidemics. In *Anomalies and Curiosities of Medicine.* New York, NY: The Bell Publishing Company.

Grossmann, Matt, Sarah Reckhow, Katharine Strunk, and Meg Turner. 2021. *All States Close but Red Districts Reopen: The Politics of In-Person Schooling during the COVID-19 Pandemic.* EdWorkingPaper: 21-355, The Annenberg Institute, Brown University. https://doi.org/10.26300/cb1f-hq66

Guardian. 2020a. Pandemic is Chance to Reset Global Economy, says Prince Charles. Published on June 3. https://www.theguardian.com/uk-news/2020/jun/03/pandemic-is-chance-to-reset-global-economy-says-prince-charles
———. 2020b. Coronavirus: 'Nature is Sending Us a Message', says UN Environment Chief. Published on 25, March. https://www.theguardian.com/world/2020/mar/25/coronavirus-nature-is-sending-us-a-message-says-un-environment-chief
Gupta, Swati. 2021. The Application and Future Potential of mRNA Vaccine. COVID-19 & You, Yale School of Public Health, New Haven, CT. Published on May 7. https://ysph.yale.edu/news-article/the-application-and-future-potential-of-mrna-vaccines/
Hart, O., and B. Holmstrom. 1987. The Theory of Contracts. In *Advances in Economics and Econometrics*, ed. T. Bewley. Cambridge, U.K.: Cambridge University Press.
Henderson, D.A., Brooke Courtney, Thomas V. Inglesby, Eric Toner, and Jennifer B. Nuzzo. 2009. Public Health and Medical Responses to the 1957–58 Influenza Pandemic. *Biosecurity and Bioterrorism: Biodefense Strategy, Practice, and Science* 7 (3). https://doi.org/10.1089/bsp.2009.0729.
Hirshleifer, Jack. 1983. From Weakest-link to Best-shot: The Voluntary Provision of Public Goods. *Public Choice* 41: 371–386.
Hoover Institution. 2020. The Doctor Is In: *Scott Atlas and the Efficacy of Lockdowns, Social Distancing, and Closings. Uncommon Knowledge with Peter Robinson*. Palo Alto, C.A.: Hoover Institution, Stanford University. https://www.hoover.org/research/doctor-scott-atlas-and-efficacy-lockdowns-social-distancing-and-closings
International Marxist Tendency (IMT). 2020. A Socialist Program to Fight COVID-19 and the Economic Crisis. https://socialistrevolution.org/a-socialist-program-to-fight-COVID-19-and-the-economic-crisis/.
International Thermonuclear Experimental Reactor (ITER). 2020. ITER: The World's Largest Tokamak. https://www.iter.org/mach.
Iuliano, A.D., K.M. Roguski, H.H. Chang, et al. 2018. Global Seasonal Influenza-associated Mortality Collaborator Network. Estimates of Global Seasonal Influenza-associated Respiratory Mortality: A Modelling Study. *Lancet* 391 (10127): 1285–1300. https://doi.org/10.1016/S0140-6736(17)33293-2.
Japan Times. 2020. Japan Suicides Rise as Economic Impact of Coronavirus Hits Home. Published on November 11. https://www.japantimes.co.jp/news/2020/11/11/national/japan-suicide-rise-coronavirus/.
Jerusalem Post. 2021. Just 0.04% of Israelis Caught COVID-19 after Two Shots of Pfizer Vaccine. Published on January 28. https://www.jpost.com/israel-news/israel-shows-promising-results-from-pfizer-vaccination-campaign-657051
Johns Hopkins University (JHU). 2020. COVID-19 Dash Board. JHU, Baltimore, M.D.: JHU. https://data.humdata.org/dataset/novel-coronavirus-2019-ncov-cases.

————. 2021. COVID-19 Dash Board. JHU, Baltimore, M.D.: JHU.

Jonas, O.B. 2013. Pandemic Risk. Washington, DC: World Bank. https://open-knowledge.worldbank.org/bitstream/handle/10986/16343/WDR14_bp_Pandemic_Risk_Jonas.pdf?sequence=1&isAllowed=y.

Kariko, K., H. Muramatsu, J. Ludwig, and D. Weissman. 2011. Generating the Optimal mRNA for Therapy: HPLC Purification Eliminates Immune Activation and Improves Translation for Nucleoside-modified. *Protein-encoding mRNA. Nucleic Acids Research* 39: e142.

Kluth, A. 2020. This Pandemic Will Lead to Social Revolutions. *Bloomberg.* Published on April 11. https://www.bloomberg.com/opinion/articles/2020-04-11/coronavirus-this-pandemic-will-lead-to-social-revolutions.

Kulldorff, Martin, Sunetra Gupta, and Jay Bhattacharya. 2020. The Great Barrington Declaration. https://gbdeclaration.org/.

Laffont, J., and D. Martimort. 2002. *The Theory of Incentives: The Principal-Agent Model.* Princeton, N.J.: Princeton University Press.

Lenton, T.M., H. Held, E. Kriegler, J.W. Hall, W. Lucht, S. Rahmstorf, et al. 2008. Tipping elements in the earth's climate system. *Proceedings of the National Academy of Sciences in the USA* 105: 1786–1793.

Lopez, Alan D., Colin D. Mathers, Majid Ezzati, Dean T. Jamison, and Christopher J.L. Murray. 2006. *Global Burden of Disease and Risk Factors.* New York, N.Y.: World Bank and Oxford University Press.

Los Angeles Times (LAT). 2021. Supreme Court Rules California Churches May open Despite the Pandemic. Published on February 5. https://www.latimes.com/politics/story/2021-02-05/supreme-court-rules-california-churches-may-open-despite-theing-pandemic#.

Mallapaty, S. 2021. Closest Known Relatives of Virus Behind COVID-19 Found in Laos. *Nature.* https://doi.org/10.1038/d41586-021-02596-2.

Marianno, B.D. 2021. *Teachers' Unions: Scapegoats or Bad-faith Actors in COVID-19 School Reopening Decisions?* Published on March 25. Washington, D.C.: Brown Center Chalkboard, Brookings Institution.

Martens, P., R. Kovats, S. Nijhof, P. Devries, M. Livermore, D. Bradley, J. Cox, and A. McMichael. 1999. Climate Change and Future Populations at Risk of Malaria. *Global Environmental Change* 9 (October): S89–S107.

National Institute of Allergy and Infectious Diseases (NIAID). 2020. New Images of Novel Coronavirus SARS-CoV-2 Now Available. NIAID, NIH. https://www.niaid.nih.gov/news-events/novel-coronavirus-sarscov2-images.

New York Times (NYT). 2020. See Coronavirus Restrictions and Mask Mandates for All 50 States. Published on November 25. https://www.nytimes.com/interactive/2020/us/states-reopen-map-coronavirus.html.

————. 2021a. N.Y. Severely Undercounted Virus Deaths in Nursing Homes, Report Says. Published on January 29. https://www.nytimes.com/2021/01/28/nyregion/nursing-home-deaths-cuomo.html.

————. 2021b. Biden Details $2 Trillion Plan to Rebuild Infrastructure and Reshape the Economy. Published on April 15, 2021. https://www.nytimes.com/2021/03/31/business/economy/biden-infrastructure-plan.html.

Nordhaus, William D. 1973. The Allocation of Energy Resources. *Brookings Papers on Economic Activity* 1973: 529–576.

————. 1994. *Managing the Global Commons.* Boston, MA: The MIT Press.

Oster, Emily, Rebecca Jack, Clare Halloran, John Schoof, and Diana McLeod. 2021. COVID-19 Mitigation Practices and COVID-19 Rates in Schools: Report on Data from Florida, New York and Massachusetts. medRxiv 2021.05.19.21257467; https://doi.org/10.1101/2021.05.19.21257467

Our World in Data (OWID). 2021. Coronavirus (COVID-19) Vaccinations. https://github.com/owid/covid-19-data/tree/master/public/data/vaccinations.

Pardi, N., M.J. Hogan, F.W. Porter, and D. Weissman. 2018. mRNA vaccines—A New Era in Vaccinology. *Nature Reviews Drug Discovery* 17: 261–279.

Patz, J.A., A.K. Githeko, J.P. McCarty, S. Hussein, U. Confalonieri, and N. de Wet. 2003. Climate Change and Infectious Diseases. In *Climate Change and Human Health—Risks and Responses.* Geneva, CH: WHO.

Pierce, Benjamin A. 2019. *Genetics: A Conceptual Approach.* 7th ed. New York, NY: W.H. Freeman.

Plotkin, S.A. 2009. Vaccines: The Fourth Century. *Clinical and Vaccine Immunology* 16: 1709–1719.

Polyakova, Maria, Geoffrey Kocks, Victoria Udalova, and Amy Finkelstein. 2020. Initial Economic Damage from the COVID-19 Pandemic in the United States is More Widespread across Ages and Geographies than Initial Mortality Impacts. *Proceedings of the National Academy of Sciences* 117 (45): 27934–27939.

Polyakova, Maria., Victoria Udalova, Geoffrey Kocks, Katie Genadek, Keith Finlay, and Amy Finkelstein. 2021. Racial Disparities in Excess All-Cause Mortality During the Early COVID-19 Pandemic Varied Substantially Across States. *Health Affairs*, 40 (2). https://doi.org/10.1377/hlthaff.2020.02142.

Potter, C.W. 2001. A History of Influenza. *Journal of Applied Microbiology* 91 (4): 572–579.

Reuters. 2021. Former CDC Chief Redfield says he Thinks COVID-19 Originated in a Chinese Lab. Published on March 27. https://www.reuters.com/article/us-health-coronavirus-origin-redfield-idUSKBN2BI2R6.

Rogers, David J., and Sarah E. Randolph. 2000. The Global Spread of Malaria in a Future. *Warmer World. Science* 289 (5485): 1763–1766.

Romer, Paul. 1990. Endogenous Technical Change. *Journal of Political Economy* 98: S71–S102.

Samuelson, Paul. 1954. The Pure Theory of Public Expenditure. *Review of Economics and Statistics* 36: 387–389.

Schuster, E.F. 1984. Classification of Probability Laws by Tail Behavior. *Journal of the American Statistical Association* 79 (388): 936–939.

Schwab, Klaus, and Thierry Malleret. 2020. *COVID-19: The Great Reset*. Agentur Schweiz.

Schwartz, M. 2001. The Life and Works of Louis Pasteur. *Journal of Applied Microbiology*. 91 (4): 597–601.

Seo, S. Niggol. 2016. *Microbehavioral Econometric Methods: Theories, Models, and Applications for the Study of Environmental and Natural Resources*. Amsterdam, NL: Academic Press.

———. 2019. *The Economics of Global Allocations of the Green Climate Fund: An Assessment from Four Scientific Traditions of Modeling Adaptation Strategies*. Cham, CH: Springer Nature.

———. 2020. *The Economics of Globally Shared and Public Goods*. Academic Press, Amsterdam, NL: Academic Press.

———. 2021. *Climate Change and Economics: Engaging with Future Generations with Action Plans*. London, UK: Palgrave Macmillan.

Shiller, R.J. 2005. *Irrational Exuberance*. 2nd ed. Princeton, NJ: Princeton University Press.

Socialist Equality Party Australia (SEPA). 2020. The coronavirus pandemic, the crisis of capitalism and the tasks of the SEP. Published on August 26. https://www.wsws.org/en/articles/2020/08/26/res1-a26.html.

Tanaka, Takanao, and Shohei Okamoto. 2021. Increase in Suicide Following an Initial Decline during the COVID-19 Pandemic in Japan. *Nature Human Behavior*. https://doi.org/10.1038/s41562-020-01042-z.

The United Nations Educational, Scientific and Cultural Organization (UNESCO). 2020. Global Monitoring of School Closures caused by COVID-19. UNESCO Institute of Statistics Data, UNESCO. https://data.humdata.org/dataset/global-school-closures-covid19.

United Nations. 1948. *Constitution of the World Health Organization*. New York, NY: The UN.

United States Bureau of Economic Analysis (USBEA). 2020. Gross Domestic Product, Third Quarter 2020 (Advance Estimate). Suitland, MD: USBEA, US Department of Commerce. https://www.bea.gov/sites/default/files/2020-10/gdp3q20_adv.pdf.

United States Bureau of Labor Statistics (USBLS). 2020. Labor Force Statistics from the Current Population Survey. Washington, DC: USBLS, US Department of Labor. https://data.bls.gov/timeseries/LNS14000000.

United States Department of Health and Human Services (USDHHS). 2020a. Explaining Operation Warp Speed. https://www.hhs.gov/coronavirus/explaining-operation-warp-speed/index.html.

———. 2020b. Secretary Azar Statement on President Trump's Invoking the Defense Production Act. Published on March 18. https://www.hhs.gov/

about/news/2020/03/18/secretary-azar-statement-president-trumps-invoking-defense-production-act.html.
United States Department of the Treasury (USDOT). 2020. The CARES Act Works for All Americans. Washington, D.C.: USDOT. https://home.treasury.gov/policy-issues/cares.
United States Food & Drug Administration (USFDA). 2020a. Pfizer-BioNTech COVID-19 Vaccine EUA Letter of Authorization. https://www.fda.gov/media/144412/.
———. 2020b. Moderna COVID-19 Vaccine EUA Letter of Authorization. https://www.fda.gov/media/144636/download.
———. 2020c. Vaccine Development—101. https://www.fda.gov/vaccines-blood-biologics/development-approval-process-cber/vaccine-development-101.
———. 2020d. Emergency Use Authorization. Washington, DC: USFDA. https://www.fda.gov/emergency-preparedness-and-response/mcm-legal-regulatory-and-policy-framework/emergency-use-authorization.
US Crisis Monitor. 2020. Data. The Armed Conflict Location & Event Data Project (ACLED) and the Bridging Divide Initiatives (BDI) at Princeton University. https://acleddata.com/special-projects/us-crisis-monitor/.
Wade, Nicholas. 2021. The Origin of COVID: Did People or Nature Open Pandora's Box at Wuhan? Bulletin of the Atomic Scientists. Published on May 5. https://thebulletin.org/2021/05/the-origin-of-covid-did-people-or-nature-open-pandoras-box-at-wuhan/
Wall Street Journal (WSJ). 2020. Supreme Court Blocks Covid-19 Restrictions on Religious Services in New York. Published on November 26. https://www.wsj.com/articles/supreme-court-blocks-covid-19-restrictions-on-church-attendance-in-new-york-11606369004.
———. 2021a. WHO Criticizes China for Stymying Investigation Into Covid-19 Origins. Published on January 6. https://www.wsj.com/articles/world-health-organization-criticizes-china-over-delays-in-covid-19-probe-11609883140.
———. 2021b. Intelligence on Sick Staff at Wuhan Lab Fuels Debate on Covid-19 Origin. Published on May 23. https://www.wsj.com/articles/intelligence-on-sick-staff-at-wuhan-lab-fuels-debate-on-covid-19-origin-11621796228?mod=hp_lead_pos3.
Weiss, Susan R. 2020. Forty Years with Coronaviruses. *Journal of Experimental Medicine* 217 (5): e20200537. https://doi.org/10.1084/jem.20200537.
Weitzman, Martin L. 2009. On Modeling and Interpreting the Economics of Catastrophic Climate Change. *Review of Economics and Statistics* 91: 1–19.
White House. 2020. 30 Days to Slow the Spread. Published on March 16. https://www.whitehouse.gov/wp-content/uploads/2020/03/03.16.20_coronavirus-guidance_8.5x11_315PM.pdf.
World Economic Forum (WEF). 2020. The Great Reset. Davos, CH: WEF. https://www.weforum.org/great-reset/

World Health Organization (WHO). 2015. International Health Regulations (2015). Geneva, CH: WHO.

———. 2019. World Malaria Report 2019. Geneva, CH: WHO.

———. 2020a. Timeline: WHO's COVID-19 Response. Geneva, CH: WHO.

———. 2020b. Q&As on COVID-19 and Related Health Topics. Geneva, CH: WHO. https://www.who.int/emergencies/diseases/novel-coronavirus-2019/question-and-answers-hub/q-a-detail/coronavirus-disease-COVID-19.

———. 2020c. Malaria Vaccines. WHO, Geneva, CH: WHO. https://www.who.int/immunization/research/development/malaria/en/.

———. 2021. Press Conference on February 12, 2021. The Joint World Health Organization-China mission to investigate the origins of COVID-19. https://www.who.int/emergencies/diseases/novel-coronavirus-2019.

Pandemic Economics: Essential Features and Outstanding Questions

1 Introduction

Having introduced in the preceding chapter the novel coronavirus pandemic of 2020, named the COVID-19 pandemic, with a full range of issues and concerns regarding the pandemic, the present author is well-positioned to present readers with the current status of the economic literature on pandemics and infectious diseases. Integrating the review conducted in this chapter, a novel exposition of the economics of pandemics as a globally shared experience will be presented in Chap. 8.

This chapter will review the economic concepts and theories that are pertinent, either directly or indirectly, to the economic study of pandemics. In addition, it will introduce economic variables, indicators, institutions, and policies that are important in the description of pandemic economics.

A unique characteristic of a pandemic among infectious diseases is that it is a globally shared experience. An infectious disease is a disease that is easily transmitted from a person to another person, or from an animal to a person, or from an animal to another animal. When an infectious disease spreads rapidly within a given population, it is defined as an epidemic. When the epidemic spreads across the planet, it is called a pandemic (CDC 2012; Bloom and Canning 2017). As such, the economic literature on globally shared goods, also referred to as global commons or global public

© The Author(s), under exclusive license to Springer Nature Switzerland AG 2022
S. N. Seo, *The Economics of Pandemics*,
https://doi.org/10.1007/978-3-030-91021-1_2

goods, is particularly germane to an economic analysis of pandemics (Samuelson 1954; Nordhaus 1994; Seo 2020a).

Therefore, the economics of pandemics is concerned with a central question of how the global community should provide a globally shared good in a social welfare optimizing manner. The globally shared good in this context can be defined as an end of the pandemic including a prevention of the pandemic before it breaks out. To rephrase it slightly differently, the central question thereof is how the global community should manage the pandemic risk efficiently.

The answer to the question depends on the characteristic of the production function of the goods under consideration, for which three production technologies are well clarified in the literature: cumulative, best shot, and weakest link (Hirshleifer 1983). For the range of globally shared good problems, three different technologies can be easily identified and are important in the exposition of each of these problems (Seo 2020a). An eradication of an epidemic is said to have a weakest-link production function (Barrett 2003; Nordhaus 2006).

An effective vaccine is, on the other hand, an ultimate solution to the pandemic, especially, once-in-a-century pandemics. In economics language, it is a backstop (Nordhaus 1973; Hartwick and Olewiler 1997). To our dismay, such a vaccine cannot be developed preemptively, that is, before a pandemic breakout while it may take many years to find an effective vaccine (Plotkin 2009). In the first year or two since the outbreak, however, the pandemic's human tolls tend to pile up exponentially. For the COVID-19 pandemic, the number of fatalities was on route to pass 1 million by the end of 2020 and 5 million by the end of June 2021 (JHU 2020).

As for the supply of an effective vaccine in the event of a pandemic, some researchers argue that there is a market failure in its provision (Bloom and Canning 2017). However, the world's experience with the COVID-19 pandemic points otherwise. The most advanced pharmaceutical companies, which is a small group, have stepped up vigorously to develop a better vaccine before their competitors: most notably, Pfizer, Moderna, AstraZeneca, Johnson & Johnson, and Novavax (USDHHS 2020).

An aspect of the socially efficient management of the pandemic risk is prevention and preparedness (Morin et al. 2018). Instead of pouring all resources in responding to the pandemic which is already spreading among the population, the government as well as individuals can shift some of its resources to preventing a potential pandemic as well as being better prepared against such a pandemic. The question was approached by researchers through an examination of how much the national government should invest annually in the pandemic, including epidemics, preparedness, and prevention. (Fan et al. 2018; Berry et al. 2018; CEPI 2020). An answer to the question is often formulated by the economists in reliance upon the expected number of human mortalities and the expected economic cost from each event.

The hardest part in such an economic analysis is related to the rareness of a global pandemic at the scale of the COVID-19 (Jonas 2013). The COVID-19 is well-passed to be recognized as a once-in-a-century pandemic. The consequence of the pandemic of that scale tends to far exceed the "expectation" calculated from scientific models.

From another point of view, concerned scientists may ponder over whether they can predict the next pandemic or the next epidemic (Taubenberger et al. 2007). The quest will be bound to fail, considering that such a new pandemic virus will emerge from a nearly completely unknown source or process. On the other hand, the COVID-19 pandemic experience of the global community indicates that the next pandemic can be easily created by manipulations of a known virus in the laboratories.

Regarding the preparedness against a pandemic, besides the government's investments, the capacity and capabilities of the medical and pharmaceutical sectors in a nation is a key factor that determines how deadly and damaging a future pandemic may turn out to become. In enhancing the capacity and capabilities thereof, a market-oriented medical system may perform better than a government-run medical system simply because the former would create more incentives for the medical professions than the latter.

Apropos of the above objective, it is often asked whether or not a particular health insurance system is likely to outperform the other systems. The experience with the COVID-19 seems to suggest that the answer is yes, that is, disparate health outcomes across the different health systems. Health insurance in the US is largely a private system, augmented by a family of public sector programs (Finkelstein 2007; Sloan and Hsieh 2013). The National Health System (NHS) in the UK is a government-run health insurance in which the NHS covers the total cost of a patient from the general tax revenue (NHS 2020). Other countries such as Switzerland, Germany, and France chose a public health insurance system in which a respective government pays 60–70% of the health cost of a patient out of the insurance premiums paid monthly by the citizens to the government while the rest is covered directly by individuals (Ch.Ch. 2020). Across the three insurance systems, the strength of the medical sectors, including hospital capacity, medical devices, and health care resources, are varied (OECD 2019).

Once the pandemic strikes the world, an essential economic question is how to minimize the shock of the pandemic to the economy which would manifest and could be measured by such variables as, for example, small business closures, an unemployment rate spike, and a decline in total economic output. The shock to the economy was severe during the COVID-19. The US unemployment rate shot up to 15% from a historically low 3.5% pre-pandemic (USBLS 2020). The GDP in the second quarter of 2020 fell precipitously by 31% from the preceding quarter (USBEA 2020).

During the pandemic sustained for more than a year, the economic shock and losses are as dreadful as pandemic-caused human fatalities to many families as well as to the national economy. Many small businesses would have to shut down permanently with a severe financial loss. Many families would suffer from the furloughs and layoffs that result from the business closures (Polyakova et al. 2020). Confronted by all these unprecedented challenges, a crucial economic question for the government is when and how to open the economy, if it chose to close the economy in the first place, while not sacrificing the health outcomes (Romer 2020).

2   A PANDEMIC AS A GLOBALLY SHARED GOOD

The theory of a public good emerged during the first half of the twentieth century and firmly established throughout the second half of the century (Bowen 1943; Samuelson 1954; Buchanan 1965). A public good was in the beginning referred to as a jointly consumed good and later as a public consumption good by Paul Samuelson (1954, 1955). The latter was shortened to a public good. The counterpart was referred to as a private good (Seo 2020a).

The essence of the definition of a public good is that it is consumed by a large group of people once it is provided, hence a jointly consumed good. By contrast, a private good is consumed by an individual consumer exclusively. In this sense, the theory of public goods is pertinent to the economics of a pandemic which is by definition a globally experienced good shared by the citizens on the planet.

Of a basket of public goods in the economy, a worldwide pandemic is a globally shared good, so is global warming. The other types of public goods are a national public good such as national defense, a state public good such as police works, and a municipal public good such as public works (Samuelson and Nordhaus 2009).

For a global-scale public good, a globally shared good is a more apposite terminology because there is no government with a mandate, that is, the public sector, at the planet scale (Seo 2020a). This alternative terminology also avoids a wide misconception among the people that global public goods are a "universally meritorious deed." A widely used terminology that is close to a globally shared good is global commons (Nordhaus 1994).

Let me introduce the theory of a public good formulated succinctly by Paul Samuelson in his article titled "The Pure Theory of Public Expenditure" (Samuelson 1954). In Samuelson model, there are two types of goods in the economy: (1) n private consumption goods denoted by (x_1, ..., x_n); (2) m public consumption goods denoted by (x_{n+1}, ..., x_{n+m}). There are S consumers, denoted by i, in the economy: (3) i=1, 2, ..., S. His example for the former was bread, while those for the latter were outdoor circus and national defense (Samuelson 1955).

Let the market demand for a private good be denoted by x_k and the market demand for a public good by x_{n+k}. At the market clearing state for the private consumption good (Eq. 1) in the competitive market economy and at that for the public consumption good (Eq. 2), the following holds:

$$x_k = \sum_{i=1}^{s} x_k^i. \tag{1}$$

$$x_{n+k} = x_{n+k}^i, \forall i = 1,...,S. \tag{2}$$

Equation (2) captures the essence of the public good: all consumers enjoy it in common once it is supplied in the market, as such the market demand equals an individual's consumer's demand (Samuelson 1954). For private goods in Eq. (1), the market demand equals the sum of individuals' demands.

Equation (2) holds because of two unique characteristics of the public goods: non-rivalry and non-excludability. The public good is non-rivalrous in that each individual's consumption of the public good leads to no subtraction from any other individual's consumption of the good. The good is non-excludable in the sense that it is not possible to exclude an individual from the consumption of the public good (Bowen 1943).

How are the efficient levels of production/consumption of the private goods determined? And what are the efficient levels of the public goods? Put differently, what are the socially optimal or social welfare maximizing levels of the public goods? The latter has been at the heart of the economics of the public goods, especially in Samuelson's pure theory. To proceed further with this question, let's consider the simplified model, without loss of generality, in which there are only two private goods (j=1, 2) and one public good (j=3). Let subscript n denote the private goods: x_n.

Let the social welfare function be written as U = U(μ^1, ..., μ^S) with $U_j > 0$ where the subscript means a partial derivative. An individual consumer's utility function is written as $\mu^i = \mu^i\left(x_1^i, x_2^i, x_3^i\right)$ where $i = 1,2,...,S$. We can assume, without loss of generality, that the individual's utility is well defined over the goods, that is, it is summarized by a regularly smooth and convex utility index. The marginal utility from consumption of x_j for consumer i is written as μ_j^i.

For the supply side of the economy, let the Production Possibility Frontier (PPF) of the economy be $F = F(x_1, x_2, x_3)$ with $F_j > 0$. The PPF is the family of all possible combinations of the three goods that can be produced efficiently in the economy given its endowed resources and the best available technology. The slope of the PPF is the marginal rate of transformation (MRT) written as F_j/F_k. The MRT tells how much good j should be given up in production in order to supply one additional unit of good k. It measures the opportunity cost for producing the additional unit of good k.

Under these quite general conditions, Samuelson describes a "best state of the world" with the following "optimal conditions" at the equilibrium:

$$\frac{\mu_2^i}{\mu_1^i} = \frac{F_2}{F_1}, \forall i. \tag{3}$$

$$\sum_{i=1}^{s} \frac{\mu_3^i}{\mu_n^i} = \frac{F_3}{F_n}, \forall n; \tag{4}$$

$$\frac{U_i \mu_n^i}{U_q \mu_n^q} = 1, \forall i, q; \forall n. \tag{5}$$

With the budget constraint for each consumer under the competitive market prices P_j, the Eqs. (3) and (5) which are the optimality conditions for the private consumption goods can be rewritten:

$$\frac{\mu_2^i}{\mu_1^i} = \frac{P_2}{P_1} = \frac{F_2}{F_1}, \forall i. \tag{6}$$

The equilibrium conditions in Eq. ((6) restate the competitive market equilibrium of the privately consumed goods: the marginal rate of substitution (MRS) between the two private goods should equal the price ratio, which again should equal the marginal rate of transformation between the two goods (Mas-Colell et al. 1995).

According to Samuelson, Eq. (4) is the pure theory of public goods. In the model above, no decentralized pricing system can determine the optimal level of production of the public good, that is, $j = 3$. Specifically, there is no market mechanism that guarantees the equality of the two sides in Eq. (4). For the equality to hold, the MRS of an individual consumer should be summed across all the individuals in the economy, that is, $\{i|$ $i = 1, 2, ..., S\}$, which should be done for each of the private goods, that is, $\{j| j = 1, 2\}$.

It is not that there is no solution to the model, that is, that solves Eqs. (3, 4, and 5). But, the true problem is how to find it (Samuelson 1955). In the competitive market system, the marginal rate of substitution between the private good and the public good does not exist explicitly. Further, the summation of the MRS across all individuals cannot be done by market forces alone.

The preeminent economist of the twentieth century concluded his seminal article with an emphasis on the "fundamental technical difference going to the heart of the whole problem of social economy" which has two aspects, which still reverberates and even more loudly in the twenty-first century (Samuelson 1954). The "social economy" seems to refer to the social goods used by Bowen (1943) or the "public economy" by Musgrave (1939).

The following statement in the pure theory points to an impossibility of a laissez-faire solution to the public good economy because of the intrinsic "external economies" or "jointness of demand." The "external economies" here seem to refer to the externalities of the public good provision, more specifically, external benefits (Pigou 1920):

The "external economies" or "jointness of demand" intrinsic to the very concepts of collective goods and governmental activities make it impossible for the grand ensemble of optimizing equations to have that special pattern of zeros which makes laissez-faire competition even theoretically possible as an analogue computer. (Samuelson 1954)

In Samuelson's pure theory, we also come to run across the free rider problem when it was first ever mentioned in the economics literature:

By departing from his indoctrinated rules, any one person can hope to snatch some selfish benefit in a way not possible under the self-policing competitive pricing of private goods. (Samuelson 1954)

The free rider problem, the term which was coined a decade after Samuelson's pure theory, encapsulates the public good problem superbly. A free rider is one who rides, say, a public bus without paying for the ticket. Likewise, people will free ride on the public good once it is provided by the sacrifice made by other people in the society. If all individuals expect the same and act as a free rider, then the public good will not be provided at all in the free market economy.

In the theory of clubs written by Buchanan, he introduced the term "free rider" for the first time in the context of club membership and benefits (Buchanan 1965):

This is not, of course, to suggest that property rights will, in practice, always be adjusted to allow for optimal exclusion. If they are not, the "free rider" problem arises. ... If individuals think that exclusion will not be fully possible, that they can expect to secure benefits as free riders without really becoming full-fledged contributing members of the club, they may be reluctant to enter voluntarily into cost-sharing arrangements.

The club is a type of goods in between the private good and the public good. For the club members, it is a public good. For the non-club members, it is a private good. The provision of the club, therefore, depends on the excludability by the club of the club members who may not pay their fees, that is, free riders (Buchanan 1968). For the "pure" public goods, for example, national defense, such excludability does not exist.

The theory of public goods described thus far was developed within the context of a national economy, even though it was not stated that way explicitly by the afore-cited authors. By the late 1970s, a carbon dioxide problem of economic growth was apprehended by a young economist in his 30s, William Nordhaus who was a student of Paul Samuelson, who went on to define the global commons on route to laying the foundation for the theory of a global-scale public good (Nordhaus 1977, 1994). The economics of global commons or globally shared goods has advanced remarkably since then, learning from the global policy debates and tense negotiations among the nations on climate change, by integrating microbehavioral decisions, negotiation games, and a global public good fund (Seo 2016, 2019, 2020a).

The classification of a large family of public goods by their geographic scale is an apt concept for the economic study of pandemics. An infectious disease can be classified as one of the four types depending primarily on its geographic scale: outbreak, endemic, epidemic, and pandemic (CDC 2012). An endemic is defined as the presence of an infectious disease in a population within a geographic area. An epidemic is defined as a rapid spread of an infectious disease to a large number of people in a population. An outbreak refers to a rapid spread of an infectious disease but in a more limited geographic area. According to the World Health Organization (WHO), a pandemic is defined as a worldwide spread of an infectious disease (WHO 2020a).

The four types of infectious diseases can be matched, as in Table 2.1, with the four types of public goods: local, national, multi-national, and global. An epidemic can be matched, depending upon its scale, with a local public good, a national public good, or a multi-national public good. An endemic can be matched with a local public good or a national public good. An outbreak is most pertinently a local public good. A pandemic, especially a worldwide pandemic such as the COVID-19, is a global-scale public good, that is, a globally shared good as per this book's choice terminology.

Table 2.1 Public goods versus infectious diseases

		Geographic scales of public goods			
		Local	National	Multi-national	Global
Geographic scales of infectious diseases	Outbreak	V			
	Endemic	V	V		
	Epidemic	V	V	V	
	Pandemic				V

Another epidemiological indicator that is pertinent to the discussion of the scale of public goods is R_0. The R_0, referred to as the basic reproduction number, measures an infectious disease's contagiousness or "spreadability" in retrospect, that is, after the spread has occurred (Fraser et al. 2009; Morin et al. 2018). Formally, the R_0 is defined as the number of people who will contract an infectious disease, on average, from a single infected person. The larger the R_0, the more likely it is a worldwide pandemic, that is, a globally shared good. Alternatively, a global pandemic tends to have a larger R_0. For your reference, the R_0 for the 1918 H1N1 pandemic was estimated to be around 2 and that for the 2009 H1N1 pandemic was around 1.5 (Fraser et al. 2009). The R_0 of the COVID-19 was reported to be 2.5 for the original strain and as high as 6–7 for the Delta variant (CDC 2021a).

Be reminded that what the present author is seeking in this book is a systemic exposition of the economics of pandemics, in other words, a globally shared good. The title of the book "The Economics of Pandemics: Exploring Globally Shared Experiences" puts an emphasis on this primary task. A thorough exploration of the economics corpus apropos of the public goods at a planetwide scale will add much value and insights to the task.

What are such globally shared goods that the economics corpus has endeavored to explicate during the past century (Seo 2020a)? The phenomenon of global warming, or climate change if you prefer, is mentioned above more than once. Another is a possible asteroid collision with Earth. A large asteroid, for example, with its diameter greater than 1 kilometer, can seriously hurt our planet. A historical collision is associated with the extinction of dinosaurs at the end of the Cretaceous period (Chapman and Morrison 1994; NASA 2014). A nuclear war or its prevention is another example of a global-scale public good. Other globally shared goods are rooted on the fear and/or possibility of a planetwide catastrophe caused by an outlier event in advanced technologies achieved by humanity (Seo 2018). A singularity fear from computing revolutions and artificial intelligence is such a one (Kurzweil 2005; Hawking et al. 2014). Another is a strangelet fear from high-risk physics experiments such as a "God particle" experiment at the Conseil Européen pour la Recherche Nucléaire (CERN) (Ellis et al. 2008).

3 PRODUCTION TECHNOLOGIES IN PANDEMICS: WEAKEST LINK OR BEST SHOT?

The core inquiry of the economics of pandemics is how the global community should provide the globally shared good efficiently, in this case, the end of a pandemic or the prevention of it. An answer to this question depends, as will be clarified presently, on the production technologies of the goods and services that are necessary for the provision of it.

A production function specifies a technological relationship between the quantities of various inputs, that is, factors of production, and the quantity of the output. A production function can be distinguished by the type of a production technology for the production of the good of concern. Three different production technologies are identified in the economics literature: cumulative, best shot, and weakest link (Hirshleifer 1983; Nordhaus 2006).

The three production technologies are indispensable concepts for an exposition of the provisions of public goods, especially, in the context of pandemics (Table 2.2). To allude to what is to be elaborated henceforth, an eradication of an infectious agent, that is, a pathogen, takes on a specific type of production function while a development of an effective vaccine takes on another type of production function.

3.1 A Cumulative Technology

Let's start with a generic production function, with Q being the quantity of the output and x_k being the quantity of a factor of production:

$$Q = g\left(x_1, x_2, \ldots, x_K\right). \tag{7}$$

Table 2.2 Production technologies as per pandemic outcomes

		Policy outcomes		
		Flattening the curve (containing the spread through social distancing)	Eradication of a pandemic	Vaccine developments
Production technologies	Cumulative	V		
	Weakest link		V	
	Best shot			V

To explain the three types of a production technology in the context of the planet's population, let E_m be the effort by an individual community (m) to supply the public good under consideration and Q be the level of the public good actually supplied. The effort is an encompassing term of all the inputs put into the production of the good including time, material resources, and ingenuity.

First, a production function with a cumulative production technology, Q_{CU}, takes on a transformation of the weighted average of the individual communities' efforts:

$$Q_{CU} = g \left\{ \sum_{m=1}^{M} \tau_m E_m \right\}. \tag{8}$$

When the efforts by the individual communities are all of equal quality, then the weights become one: $\tau_m = 1, \forall\ m$. Simply put, the amount of the public good, Q_{CU}, is determined by the sum of the efforts by individual communities.

A salient example of a cumulative technology is found in climate policy. Consider a policy to control carbon dioxide concentration in the atmosphere. The outcome is determined by the sum of individual countries' efforts, say, abating carbon dioxide emissions from power plants, automobiles, land uses, and so on (Nordhaus and Yang 1996; Barrett 2003). A ton of carbon dioxide has the same impact on the global atmospheric concentration, regardless of from which country it is emitted (Le Treut et al. 2007). This means $\tau_m = 1, \forall\ m$.

As per the pandemic context, the cumulative production function can be applicable to a policy of "flattening the curve," that is, containing the spread of a virus in the world when there is no vaccine available. Let's consider it in a national setting. The policy goal could be achieved by the collective efforts of individuals who act to limit personal contacts. If the virus is extremely contagious, like smallpox or the COVID-19, then the collective effort may turn out to be only modestly effective. The policy outcome in such a case is determined, albeit only to some degree, by the sum of individuals' efforts.

The larger the sum, the better the policy outcome. Below a certain level of the collective effort, say, Q_{CU}^L, the policy outcome may be negligible. Beyond a certain level of the collective effort, say, Q_{CU}^U, the policy outcome may accelerate, that is, speed up at an increasing rate. A policy response and outcome to smallpox during the pre-vaccine world can be explained by this cumulative production technology.

3.2 A Weakest-Link Technology

A production function with the weakest-link technology is defined by the functional relationship in which the level of the final output is determined by the size of the least-effort factor from all factors of production. The size of the least-effort factor can be stated alternatively as the effort of the community, of all the communities, that made the least effort. As before, let E_m be the quantity of the effort by community m and τ_m be the quality of their unit effort. The weakest-link production function takes on the following functional form:

$$Q_{WL} = \min \left\{ \tau_1 E_1, \tau_2 E_2, \ldots, \tau_m E_m \right\}. \tag{9}$$

The least effort determines the quantity of the public good provided, Q_{WL}. The weakest-link production function is drawn in Fig. 2.1. Larger efforts by the other communities are of no additional benefit to the production of the good. The production function in Eq. (9) is referred to in economics as the Leontief production function or the fixed proportions production technology (Mas-Colell et al. 1995).

Imagine a seawall construction across the west coast of Sri Lanka in preparation for the sea level rise caused by climate change! As long as there

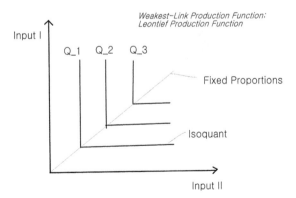

Fig. 2.1 A weakest-link production function

is one section of the coastal line with no wall or natural barrier, which is the weakest link, the seawall project will remain unfinished. That is, the seawall with the weakest link will be of no effect in stopping a flooding from the rising sea. The weakest link determines the final outcome.

The weakest-link technology is an apt concept for the description of the economic and policy decisions on infectious diseases. The goal of an infectious disease policy is an eradication of the disease or the pathogen. Let's consider an epidemic in West Africa. The goal cannot be accomplished as long as there remains the weakest link, that is to say, a community of infected people even if all the rest of West Africa is disease-free. The pathogen, which caused the epidemic, in the weakest-link community will easily spread to the other disease-free communities (Ford and Katondo 1977; Nordhaus 2006).

Malaria epidemics in Sub-Saharan countries can be explained by this production technology. The disease easily spreads from one community to another by its vector (carrier), that is, mosquitoes. So, it is of little meaning to get rid of the disease pathogen in selected communities only. Malaria remains a big threat in Sub-Sahara today, killing 400,000 people annually according to the most recent World Malaria Report (Lopez et al. 2006; WHO 2019).

In the context of the COVID-19 pandemic, the weakest-link production technology is in full display. During the pre-vaccine period in 2020, European countries, for example, struggled to contain the virus contagion with little success because the virus easily jumps from one family to another, one community to another, and from one country to another. On the other hand, small island nations and atolls of the planet were able to contain the virus contagion in the early stages more successfully, for example, Taiwan, New Zealand, and many other islands in the South Pacific (JHU 2020).

3.3   A Best-Shot Technology

The best-shot production technology is also a germane concept for an exposition of the economic properties of pandemics and infectious diseases. The best-shot production function is defined by the best effort while the inferior efforts and the second-best efforts are of little importance in the production of the concerned good.

Using the same notations, τ_m and E_m, as before, the best-shot technology production function takes on the following form:

$$Q_{BS} = \max \left\{ \tau_1 E_1, \tau_2 E_2, \ldots, \tau_m E_m \right\}. \quad (10)$$

Which public good can be described by the best-shot technology in its production function? Consider the global effort to avert an asteroid collision against Earth. Let's assume that the asteroid is fast approaching the planet and its diameter is as large as 10 kilometers. For your reference, there are about 1000 asteroids identified thus far by the National Aeronautics and Space Administration (NASA) whose diameter is larger than 1 kilometer. The asteroid could be diverted from the Earth's path by either applying a kinetic impactor or a gravity tractor well in advance (NASA 2017). The US government recently established the Planetary Defense Coordination Office in 2016 and the Space Force in 2019 to handle, among other things, the asteroid and comet problems (NASA 2017; USSF 2020).

The successful diversion of the asteroid is not determined by the sum of the efforts by, say, individual countries. Neither is it determined by the least-effort country, that is, the country with the least advanced technological capabilities. It is determined by the best effort, say, the effort by the country with the best technological capabilities.

As far as the pandemics are concerned, the best-shot technology is pertinent to the description of a provision of an effective pandemic vaccine. In a truly globalized world, there needs only one vaccine which is highly effective. Once successfully developed, it can be mass produced in individual countries and then distributed. A successful development of such a vaccine is determined by the best effort, that is, the highest quality effort by the most advanced laboratory. Taking into account many years of costly investments needed as well as large uncertainties regarding the vaccine development and the resultant profit, only a small number of firms are likely to participate in the race for vaccines.

Let's take a look at the vaccine race during the COVID-19 pandemic. According to the coronavirus vaccine tracker, the real competitors, that is, the candidate vaccine developers supported by the Operation Warp Speed (OWS) in the US were the following six: Moderna, Pfizer-BioNTech, Johnson & Johnson, AstraZeneca, Novavax, and Sanofi and GlaxoSmithKline (GSK) (USDHHS 2020). The winners of the vaccine race seem to be Pfizer-BioNTech which announced a 95% effective vaccine on November 9, 2020, and Moderna which announced on November 16,

2020, a 95% effective vaccine (Fox Business 2020a, b). The two vaccines are also only mRNA vaccines (Kariko et al. 2011; Pardi et al. 2018).

In the current state of world politics, US military competitors were actively engaged in the vaccine race. To note some, CanSino Biologics (China), Gamaleya Research Institute (Russia), Vector Institute (Russia), Sinopharm (China), Sinovac Biotech (China), and Bharat Biotech (India) (NYT 2020a).

4   Market Failures and Governmental Interventions in Pandemic Economics

The theory of public goods established by Samuelson concluded emphatically that there will be a market failure when it comes to the provision of a public good (Samuelson 1954). That being the case, governmental interventions are unavoidable to correct the market failures. The extant literature of the pandemic economics is largely framed by these two premises. In this section, the present author will examine the market failures and the governmental interventions to correct them, which have been put forth by the researchers on pandemics and epidemics.

4.1   Failures in Vaccine Developments?

Some researchers argued, just before the COVID-19 pandemic, that there is a significant market failure in vaccine developments against individual low-probability pathogens. Because of the very low probability of an individual pathogen turning into a pandemic-causing virus, the probability that a vaccine will eventually be needed is very low. On the other hand, a vaccine development requires a potential developer large research and development costs with delayed returns. Considering the risk and returns, pharmaceutical companies should be hesitant to invest in the vaccine development for a specific pathogen (Bloom and Canning 2017).

The afore-referenced authors offer three remedies and interventions to correct this failure: (1) a farsighted international collaboration, (2) motivating developing countries' participation in vaccine development, and (3) a globally centralized stockpiling of vaccines and drugs (Bloom and Canning 2017).

As for the international collaboration, they refer to the Coalition for Epidemic Preparedness Innovations (CEPI) which is a consortium of

2 PANDEMIC ECONOMICS: ESSENTIAL FEATURES AND OUTSTANDING... 61

nations: Norway, Japan, Germany, European Union, Britain. Established in 2017 with a funding from the Bill & Melinda Gates Foundation, the CEPI aims at advancing candidate vaccines, clinical testing, and scaling-up productions (CEPI 2020). The organization's vaccine developments are directed to the priority diseases declared by the WHO, which is summarized in Table 2.3 (WHO 2018). Notably, the two coronaviruses, SARS and MERS, were already a priority of the CEPI's vaccine efforts.

The market failure argument put forth by the above authors is fragile for several reasons. First, it contradicts a fundamental aspect of epidemiology and infectious diseases: a new pandemic will be caused by a "novel" virus, that is, not by a known virus today. A vaccine against one lethal pandemic virus cannot be administered to a patient with another lethal pandemic virus. Put differently, it is not realistically possible to develop a vaccine in advance against "Disease X" in Table 2.3.

A vaccine development can begin, as far as the seriousness of the effort is concerned, only after a worldwide pandemic is declared. For your reference, the vaccine development by the Pfizer corporation against the COVID-19 began on March 13, 2020, according to the company's

Table 2.3 WHO priority diseases, current (WHO 2018)

The list in 2018	Notes
1 Crimean-Congo hemorrhagic fever	
2 Ebola virus disease and Marburg virus disease	
3 Lassa fever	
4 Middle East respiratory syndrome coronavirus (MERS-CoV)	The second human coronavirus
5 Severe Acute respiratory syndrome coronavirus (SARS-CoV)	The first human coronavirus
6 Nipah and henipaviral diseases	
7 Rift Valley fever	
8 Zika	
9 Disease X	Represents the knowledge that a serious international epidemic could be caused by a pathogen currently unknown to cause human disease

updates, while the pandemic was declared by the WHO on March 11, 2020 (Pfizer 2020; WHO 2020b).

It is noticeable in Table 2.3 that there are two human coronaviruses listed as a priority disease even before the COVID-19 virus first emerged: the Middle East Respiratory Syndrome Coronavirus (MERS-CoV) and the Severe Acute Respiratory Syndrome Coronavirus (SARS-CoV). Compared even with these two coronaviruses that surfaced recently, the symptoms and characteristics of the COVID-19 virus are much different (Coleman and Frieman 2014; Weiss 2020). A SARS-CoV vaccine, if it had been developed at all before the COVID-19 outbreak, would have not been effective at all against the SARS-CoV-2.

The second recommendation by the authors, that is, motivating developing countries to participate in the vaccine developments, is not compatible with the economics of the best shot. An effective vaccine development is accomplished by the best effort, that is, the developer with the best technological capabilities. As far as the pandemic eradication is concerned, what is critical is a single vaccine which is highly effective. For those who lived through the COVID-19, it would nearly be impossible to imagine that a policy-maker might suggest a 200-nation coalition for the vaccine development during the first wave in March 2020. Global geopolitics and bureaucracies would have killed any chance at an effective vaccine development if such a proposal had been made by a powerful political leader and adopted by the nations.

The third recommendation, that is, a global stockpiling of vaccines, is unrealistic as well as contrary to what the sound economics would suggest. It is unrealistic because, *inter alia*, the storage cost is very high and the stored vaccines would not be effective against future pandemics. The Pfizer-BioNTech vaccine, for example, should be stored at roughly -70 degrees (C) for a long period of time. It is contrary to the pandemic economics because, among other things, a worldwide pandemic is an extremely rare event, say, a once-in-a-century event. It would be unwise to plan a global stockpiling of vaccines in preparation for a very low probability event which may occur only in a hundred years.

4.2   How Much Should a Nation Invest in Pandemic Preparedness and Prevention?

If the nations cannot be in possession of an effective vaccine at the time of a pandemic outbreak, then how should they be prepared for it and how well? What measures and policies can they put in place in preparation for unpredictable pandemics? What is the socially optimal level of investments by the governmental sector into pandemic prevention and preparedness?

A proposal is made to tailor the government's spending on the basis of the annual expected loss from infectious diseases including pandemics (Fan et al. 2018). Proceeding with this proposal, policy-makers must answer the thorny question of how the annual expected loss from future pandemics should be measured while taking into account the rarity of such events (Jonas 2013).

Let's start with the definition of a pandemic for which an ideal indicator is the number of human mortalities from it. Let s be the Standardized Mortality Unit (SMU). The SMU is a broadened concept of a mortality that attempts to reflect the realistic considerations, such as (1) the death by a just-born infant is different from the death by a 90-year-old man; and (2) the death by a person with a pre-existing severe illness is different from the death by a healthy person. The s can be defined in an extended analysis as the sum of the SMUs and the economics losses if both measures are expressed in value terms, that is, in dollars.

Let $\varphi(\bar{s})$ be the annual probability of a pandemic with a severity of the pandemic exceeding $\bar{s}$ SMUs. With the probability density function of s being $f(s)$,

$$\varphi(\bar{s}) = \int_{\bar{s}}^{\infty} f(s)\,ds. \tag{11}$$

Since $\varphi(s)$ measures the probability that the pandemic severity exceeds the s number of mortalities, it is a counter-cumulative distribution function (CCDF), which is also referred to in the literature as a complementary cumulative distribution function, a tail distribution, or exceedance.

The return time of the pandemic of s SMUs, which measures how often a pandemic of the severity of s SMUs would come to pass, is calculated as the inverse of the above tail distribution:

$$\tau(s) = \varphi(s)^{-1}. \tag{12}$$

The annual expected value of the SMUs is calculated by the following integral over s, that is, SMUs:

$$E[s] = \int_0^\infty \varphi(s)d(s). \tag{13}$$

To calculate the expected value of the SMUs in Eq. (13), we need to estimate the counter-cumulative distribution function $\varphi(s)$. A hyperbolic family of the CCDF can be written in a generic form as follows (Fan et al. 2018):

$$\varphi(s) = \left[1 + m(1-\chi)s\right]^{-\left[1+\frac{1}{1-\chi}\right]}. \tag{14}$$

It is a power law distribution function, referred sometimes as a fat-tail distribution. The power of the function, that is, χ, determines the fatness of the tail distribution while m is the parameter to be estimated, with $\chi < 1$ and $m > 0$ (Jamison and Jamison 2011). The closer is the χ to 1, the distribution becomes closer to a medium tail distribution. The farther apart is the χ from 1, the fatter the tail of the distribution (Pareto 1896; Zipf 1949; Schuster 1984). The authors propose $\chi = -2$, based on a batch of estimations using the historical infectious disease data.

A fat-tail distribution for the CCDF such as Eq. (14) is appropriately used when policy-makers cannot rule out an extremely large number of fatalities, however extreme that number may be (Weitzman 2009). Further, it is appropriate only when humanity has no control at all about the size of mortalities, even if it means the entire human and animal population on Earth (Seo 2020b). When the number of mortalities, SMUs (s) in the above analysis, can be reasonably bounded, that is, can be reasonably expected to be within a certain range, for example, 1% or even 10% of the world population, a medium tail distribution such as a Gaussian distribution is more appropriate (Nordhaus 2011). Such a bound is rational in the context of pandemics owing to, *inter alia*, vaccine technologies.

Applying their model of choice to estimation, the authors find, as summarized in Table 2.4, that annually 720,000 people die globally of the influenza pandemic while the annual economic loss amounts to 0.6% of the Gross National Income (GNI) at the global level. The estimation is done with the recorded historical disease data (Gould and Pyle 1896; Potter 2001). The expected health impacts are not even across the planet. The fatalities are concentrated in low-middle-income countries accounting for 54% of the world's total fatalities (390,000 deaths) and

Table 2.4 Expected mortalities and economic losses from influenza pandemic

	Income group				*World*
	Low	*Low-middle*	*Upper-middle*	*High*	*World*
Expected mortality (1000 s/yr)	120 (16.6%)	390 (54.1%)	180 (25.0%)	28 (3.8%)	720
Expected economic loss (% GNI/yr)	1.1	1.6	1.0	0.3	0.6

Source: Fan et al. (2018)

upper-middle-income countries accounting for 25% of the total (180,000 deaths). The cohort of high-income countries accounts for just 3.8% of the total world fatalities (28,000 deaths).

As per the expected economic loss, it amounts to as high as 1.6% of the GNI per year of the low-middle-income group and as low as 0.3% of the GNI per year of the high-income group. In the low-income group, it amounts to 1.1%, while in the upper-middle-income group, it amounts to 1.0%. The figures demonstrate that the pandemic-caused economic damage is very severe in low-income countries of the planet while it is by far minor in high-income countries.

The analytical framework and the estimates in Table 2.4 offer a benchmark for the national government's intervention efforts to prevent and reduce the damage from future influenza pandemic events. For example, a low-middle income country may decide to set aside 1.6% of the national income annually for a pandemic prevention and preparedness policy. For a worldwide policy, if adopted through an international treaty, about 0.6% of the world income should be allocated to a portfolio of pandemic policy programs. This is no small amount of money, roughly US$500 billion in 2020 dollars. According to this approach, the annual budget set aside for the pandemic policy by an international policy organization or as an international pandemic fund may be allocated to a host of programs implemented worldwide (Berry et al. 2018; Seo 2019).

For our useful reference, the biennial budget of the WHO is US$5.84 billion for 2020–2021, which is US$2.42 billion/year. There is no specific category in the WHO's budget allocations for the pandemic prevention and preparedness. It has the budget category of emergency operations and appeals for which US$1 billion is allocated and the category of health emergencies for which US$889 million is allocated (WHO 2020c).

4.3   Which Policy Options and Market Responses Are Possible?

Several qualifications are called for with regard to the above model and its policy recommendations. First, it should be emphasized that the estimates in Table 2.4, even if they were estimated correctly, do not prescribe a social welfare optimizing intervention by an individual government, nor by the global community, for pandemic preparedness and prevention (Morin et al. 2018). The numbers in Table 2.4 point to the potential benefits of a pandemic policy by reducing the fatalities from future pandemics (Liu et al. 2005; Burns et al. 2008). For an efficient decision, the government should weigh the costs of the range of pandemic prevention and preparedness policies to choose the optimal policy (Baumol and Oates 1975; Arrow et al. 1996).

Second, the above framework does not tell us which individual policy options are available for the government and the international organization, from which what policy options should be chosen given different circumstances and diseases (Nordhaus 2008). This is the main topic of Chap. 4 of this book.

Third, the estimates in Table 2.4 and the model itself do not separate market and individuals' responses to the pandemics from governmental responses to them (Morin et al. 2018; Seo 2020a). To mention some examples of the former, consider a private health insurance system or the biomedical sectors of the country. The strengths of these private sectors can significantly contribute to the pandemic preparedness and prevention. Of the multitude of individuals' behaviors, some are effective prevention measures, for example, taking regular health check-ups which reduce the chances of comorbidities and help enhance the immune system, avoiding places where a large crowd gathers in close physical contact.

Fourth, the above model is retrospective in that it relies on the past pandemic data. As such, the model does not tell whether or not future pandemics may occur more frequently; or whether or not they may be more catastrophic than past pandemics. Such changes may be forced by an emergence of a novel virus which has been unknown before to humanity (Weiss 2020). Such changes may also be caused by a new environmental stress, for example, climate change (Martens et al. 1999; Rogers and Randolph 2000; Patz et al. 2003). The latter is the main topic of Chap. 6 of this book.

5   NATIONAL HEALTH SYSTEMS DURING PANDEMICS

A nation's preparedness against a pandemic depends, among other things, on the strength of its health system. During the first year of the COVID-19 pandemic, that is, the pre-vaccine period, individual nations' health system capacities may have played a significant role in determining the relative successes or failures of their responses against the previously unknown pandemic virus in terms of mortality rates and infection cases (ECDPC 2020).

The health system capacity and capabilities of a nation may have determined the readiness of the nation in supplying such crucial variables during the COVID-19 pandemic as test kits, hospital beds, hospital treatment facilities, availability of doctors and nurses, personal protective equipment, and essential medical devices such as ventilators and respirators (OECD 2019).

The strength of a nation's health system can be measured in more ways than one, one of which is the performance of the nation's health insurance system. To begin with, there is no health insurance anywhere in the globe, private or public, offered against a pandemic which is unknown at the time of a contract signing but may be materialized at a future time, on which an individual buyer can rely in the event of a pandemic.

The national health insurance system, public or private, affects the nation's biomedical sectors, which in turn could influence the nation's ability to deal with an unpredictable pandemic effectively. The capacity of the national health system can be measured by the indicators such as the number of doctors and nurses, the number of hospital beds, the number of Computed Tomography (CT) scanners, the number of Magnetic Resonance Imaging (MRI) units, and the number of medical school graduates (OECD 2019).

What are the types of the national health insurance system? Broadly, there are three distinct systems that are adopted by the nations across the planet, that is, excluding the countries without any health insurance at all: a freely available national health service, a nationalized government-run health insurance system (NHI), a privately based health insurance system (PHI). The first system is adopted by the UK, Italy, Spain, and others, while the third system by the US. Many countries rely on the second system, for example, Switzerland, Germany, France, Japan, and South Korea (Sloan and Hsieh 2013).

The NHS system, adopted by the UK, Spain, and Italy, provides a variety of health services to its citizens free of charge. The resources needed for the services provided come from a general taxation of the nation (NHS 2020). That is, the citizens do not pay an earmarked tax for the national health service. Nor are they required to pay monthly insurance premiums for the health services they would receive from the NHS.

The NHI system, on the other hand, maintains a nationally managed health insurance system. The citizens are obligated by law to pay insurance premiums monthly to a national health insurance corporation (NHIC) where the size of the premium is determined by law (Ch.Ch. 2020). From the insurance premiums collected from its citizens which are invested into financial and physical assets, the NHI corporation pays on behalf of its member citizen a partial cost of the treatments s/he receives. The rest is paid by the citizen patient. The fraction of the NHIC payment is determined by law.

A breakdown of the total cost of a treatment in the NHI system is diagramed in Fig. 2.2. The total cost of a treatment that its member receives is broken down into two categories: the NHI corporation payment items and the NHI corporation non-payment items. The non-payment items may account for about 20% of the total medical cost, for example, dental treatments which are not covered by the NHIC in most countries. For the NHI corporation payment items, the total cost is shared by the corporation and the patient. The ratio of the patient payment over the total medical cost varies by disease types as well as hospital types vis-à-vis the treatment: it may vary from 20% to 60%, for example. Even for the NHIC payment items, there is a category of the "patient-pays-all" cost which occurs when, for example, a patient defaulted on monthly insurance premium payments to the NHIC.

The third type of the national health insurance system is a privately based or market-based health insurance system. This is the system adopted saliently by the US. In the country's system, the private health insurance market is augmented by a variety of public sector insurance programs such as Medicare, Medicaid, and the Affordable Care Act (Finkelstein 2007; Rice et al. 2013; Sloan and Hsieh 2013).

How did the three national health insurance systems perform during the COVID-19 pandemic? The COVID-19 mortality rates of selected nations adopting one of the three health insurance systems are summarized in Table 2.5, which are calculated from the data provided by the European Center for Disease Prevention and Control (ECDPC 2020).

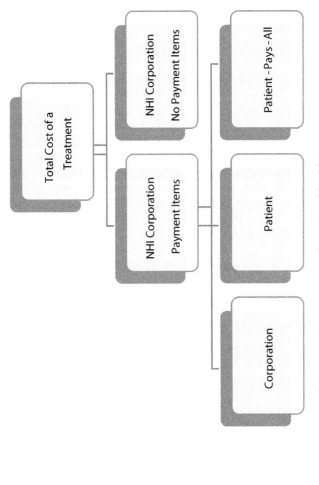

Fig. 2.2 A breakdown of the cost of a treatment in the national health insurance system

The time frame of the data is the pre-vaccine period, specifically, from the COVID-19 outbreak to the middle of November 2020, the time of the vaccine success announcements by the Pfizer and the Moderna pharmaceutical corporations.

The mortality rate, which is the case-fatality ratio calculated from the reported data, is far lower in the NHI system countries than that in the other two systems. The mortality rate of Switzerland was 1.15% and that of Germany was 1.58%. The worst performing system was the NHS system, freely available to the public. The mortality rate was close to 4% in Italy and 3.89% in the UK. The privately based health insurance system in the US reported a far lower mortality rate than that of the UK or Italy, but a higher mortality rate than the NHI system countries. The US mortality rate was 2.2%.

Has the choice of one of the national health insurance systems determined the performances of the nations in their preparedness and responsiveness against the COVID-19 pandemic? That the mortality rates are significantly different across the three systems gives us a reason to posit such a causality. A closer examination of the three health systems reveals, as also shown in Table 2.5, that the capacities of the three health systems were varied substantially right before the pandemic outbreak. The number of hospital beds per 1000 people is far larger in the NHI system countries: 8 beds for Germany, compared with 2.8 beds for the US and 2.5 beds for the UK. The number of doctors per 1000 people is also far larger in the NHI system: 4.3 doctors for Germany, compared with 2.6 doctors for the US and 2.8 doctors for the UK (OECD 2019).

On the other hand, the country with a privately based health insurance system is outperforming the countries with the other health systems in the area of advanced medical devices. The number of CT scanner available is 43 units per 1 million people for the US, compared with 35 units in Germany and 9 units for the UK. The number of MRI units available is 38 units per 1 million people for the US, compared with 35 units for Germany and 7 units for the UK (OECD 2019).

The health system statistics from the biennial health indicator report by the Organisation for Economic Co-operation and Development (OECD) indicate that there may be a correlation, if not a causality, between the choice of a national health insurance system and the pandemic preparedness of a nation, more specifically, the COVID-19 mortality rate. Having said that, a more sophisticated analysis on this topic calls for an examination of many other variables that vary across the three systems, for

Table 2.5   Performances of the national health systems under the COVID-19

	National health service (NHS)	National health insurance (NHI)	Private insurances based (PHI)
Main characteristics	A national health service freely available to its citizens	A nationally managed health insurance by a corporation	Private insurance market; augmented by Medicaid, Medicare, and Affordable Care Act
Who pays the medical cost	Government payment from general taxation: 100%	Government-run insurance: 63.8%; individual payment: 19.6%; no payment by government: 16.6%	Private insurers pay agreed medical costs while the insured pay the rest; the insured pay monthly insurance premiums
Nations	UK, Italy, Spain	Switzerland, Germany, France, South Korea	US
Mortality rate (COVID-19)	3.89% (UK), 3.98 (It)	1.58% (G), 1.15%(SW)	2.29%
CT scanners (N)/million	9 (UK), 36 (It)	35 (G), 39 (SW)	43
MRI units (N)/million	7 (UK), 29 (It)	35 (G), 23 (SW)	38
Hospital beds (N)/1000	2.5 (UK), 3.2 (It)	8 (G), 4.5 (SW)	2.8
Doctors (N)/1000	2.8 (UK), 4.0 (It)	4.3 (G), 4.3 (SW)	2.6

Note: The mortality data are from the ECPDC (2020) and the health data are from the OECD (2019)

example, health status of citizens, prevalence of certain diseases in a nation, and socio-economic variables. Some of these, analyzed in Chap. 9, may be responsible for a higher mortality rate in certain countries.

Notwithstanding, what this simple analysis of the national health insurance systems tells us, among other things, is that the governmental intervention to provide the public good, that is, pandemic preparedness and responsiveness, is not simply a question of how much money should be set aside for, say, the national disease centers and other related programs, as the analysis in the above model implied (Fan et al. 2018; Berry et al. 2018). If the national health system does not motivate individuals and organizations in the health-related sectors to innovate ceaselessly and be competitive, then any amount of dollars set aside by the government for the health services to its citizens will surely fail to achieve a strong and responsive pandemic-prepared system. The question of incentives will be a key element in the economics of pandemics to be elucidated in Chap. 8.

6   THE IMPACTS OF THE PANDEMIC ON ECONOMY

The impacts of the COVID-19 pandemic on the general economy, small businesses, and households were severe. These may be best illustrated by the dramatic changes in the US unemployment rate during 2020, the time series of which was shown in Fig. 1.7 of Chap. 1. The figure shows the monthly unemployment rate covered the 11-year period from January 2010 to October 2020 reported by the US Bureau of Labor Statistics (USBLS 2020).

The US reported a historically low unemployment rate just before the pandemic, which was as low as 3.5% in December 2019. The COVID-19 shock on the economy resulted in a sharp increase of the unemployment rate to 14.7% at the peak of the first wave in April 2020. By October 2020, it fell down to 6.5%.

The sudden spike in the unemployment rate was well expected because many states had issued a statewide lockdown order starting from California on March 19, immediately followed by New York, Georgia, Illinois, Michigan, Indiana, and others. As late as November 2020, businesses were mostly closed in many states, including Washington, Oregon, New Mexico, Minnesota, Illinois, and Kentucky (NYT 2020b).

The economy's productivity, another indicator of the economy's performance, suffered severely from the COVID-19 shock. The growth rate of the Gross Domestic Product (GDP) stood at 2.4% in the fourth quarter (Q4) of 2019, which fell to -5% in the first quarter (Q1) of 2020, followed by a sharp drop to -31.4% in the second quarter (Q2) of 2020 (Fig. 2.3). However, the GDP growth rate rebounded strongly, in pace with the rebounding unemployment rate, with a +33.1% growth rate in the third quarter (Q3) of 2020 (USBEA 2020).

The economic impact of the COVID-19 pandemic may have been more dispersed geographically than the mortality impact of the COVID-19 which was concentrated in major cities, especially during the first and second waves of the pandemic in 2020 (Polyakova et al. 2020). The pandemic may also have hurt the poor more heavily in economic terms across the globe (Mahler et al. 2020). The economic impact may have varied across people's races. In the US, the adjusted excess all-cause mortality calculated from January 2011 to April 2020 data was 6.8 for Black people, 4.3 for Hispanic people, 2.7 for Asian people, and 1.5 for White people, all per 10,000 people (Polyakova et al. 2021).

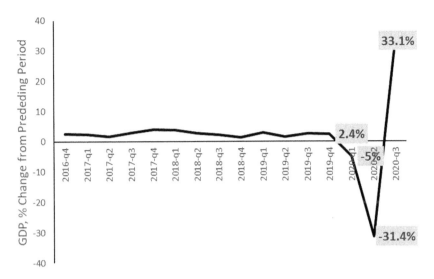

Fig. 2.3 The impact of COVID-19 on GDP growth rate in the US

As shocking as the impacts of the COVID-19 on the economy were, they appeared quite different from those observed in the Great Depression of the 1930s. As shown in Fig. 2.3 of this chapter and Fig. 1.7 in Chap. 1, the unemployment rate as well as the new economic production rebounded quickly during the pandemic. During the Great Depression, by contrast, the unemployment rate stayed above 12% for the entire decade, according to Robert Shiller who has long studied historical economic crashes (Shiller 2005; Reuters 2020). The economics of pandemics is fundamentally different from the economics of the great financial market crashes driven primarily by a creation of a bubble by market participants.

The economic impacts of the pandemic were also felt strongly at the sectoral level. Especially, the shutdowns ordered by the major global economies resulted in marked changes in the global energy sector as well as in key policy indicators of climate change. For example, global fossil-fuel CO_2 emissions dropped by 17% in April 2020 (WMO 2020; Le Quere et al. 2020). A decrease in energy demands was most severe in the countries that implemented a full national lockdown strategy: as large as 30% in India and 17% in Europe (IEA 2020).

A fuller analysis of the impacts on the global energy sector will be provided in Chap. 6 where the present author will explain changes in energy production and consumption, changes in the greenhouse gas emissions and carbon dioxide emissions, and changes in the demands for fossil fuels such as coal, oil, and natural gas.

7   Pandemic Policy Choices and Economic Outcomes

In responding to the COVID-19 pandemic, an essential policy question apropos of the economy is how the society can minimize the economic losses while at the same time minimizing the human and humanitarian costs of the pandemic. Is shutting down the entire country and economy the best option for achieving this goal? Regrettably, economists have not raised this question, as far as the present author is aware of. However, a similar question was framed by virologists and infectious disease experts during the first wave of the COVID-19 (Kulldorff et al. 2020)

The medical experts raised whether lockdowns and stay-at-home orders are a better way for the society to deal with the pandemic than a focused protection (FP) approach. While the former policy closes the society in a blanket fashion, the latter directs the society's resources to the protection of the most vulnerable populations in the society. In the COVID-19, the most vulnerable were seniors and people with comorbidities (CDC 2021b; refer to Fig. 9.4 in Chap. 9 of this book).

The FP approach was proposed as the Great Barrington Declaration (GBD) by the virology experts at the world's premier universities and signed subsequently by hundreds of medical experts (Kulldorff et al. 2020). The core argument of the GBD is that a nationwide or statewide lockdown is not as effective a policy option to slow the spread of the pandemic while it leads to other major long-term health problems such as addictions, mental stress, suicide, domestic conflicts, and non-COVID health problems (Hoover Institution 2020).

After the initial lockdowns in the US during the first and second waves in 2020, a case for safely reopening the economy gained a broader support (Romer 2020). Some states decided to reopen their economies with additional safety measures required of the reopened businesses while other states decided to remain under the lockdowns. This second phase of the pandemic economic policy-making during 2020 is marked by the choice between a continue-to-lockdown option versus a safely reopen option.

The policy options regarding the economy's running during the pandemic in 2020 are summarized in Fig. 2.4. Combining Phase I and II

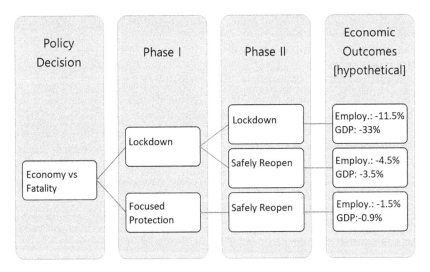

Fig. 2.4 Policy dilemma and economic outcomes: lockdown or not lockdown?

decisions, there are three options. Option I is a lockdown-lockdown policy. Option II is a lockdown-safely reopen policy. Option III is a focused protection-safely reopen policy.

Does the choice of one of these policy options by a nation affect the performance of the national economy during the pandemic? This question is a rephrase of the essential economic question raised at the top of this section. With a number of simplifying assumptions, the present author hopes to offer some rough estimates of the economic outcomes under the three policy options. Disparate economic outcomes from the three policy options can be interpreted as an economics answer to the Great Barrington Declaration debate.

The lockdown-safely reopen policy, Option II, is the one that approximates what most US state governments have followed. For the year-to-year changes in the economic indicators, the present author calculates the average unemployment rate in 2020 and the average GDP growth rate in the same year. Compared with the pre-pandemic 2019 economic performances, the unemployment rate in the US rose by 4.5%. The GDP growth, measured as the average quarterly growth rate, fell by 3.5% from 2019 to 2020.

The lockdown-lockdown policy, Option I, can be thought of as a continuation of the US second quarter policy. Extending the second quarter outcomes, the unemployment rate would stand at 15% under this policy at the end of 2020. For the GDP growth rate, the present author also extends the second quarter outcome, therefore, -30% of the GDP growth. As for the year-to-year changes from 2019 to 2020, the unemployment is up by 11.5% and the GDP growth is down by 33% from the pre-pandemic 2019.

For the focused protection-safely reopen policy option, Option III, we do not have the empirical economic data to rely upon from the US experiences. However, there is a nation that experimented with this option very closely, that is, Sweden's no-lockdown approach during the pandemic which sparked big debates and controversies (Financial Times 2020).

The Sweden's no-lockdown strategy relies on voluntary compliance measures based on the rationale of individual responsibility. The following is indicative of the Swedish model:

> *It advised older people to avoid social contact and recommended that people work from home, wash their hands regularly and avoid non-essential travel. But borders and schools for under-16s remain open—as do many businesses, including restaurants and bars.* (Paterlini 2020)

How did the Swedish model perform economically? We can calculate year-to-year changes in the two economic indicators from the economic data provided by Statistics Sweden, a governmental agency. The unemployment remained relatively stable and on average ticked up by 1.5% from year to year: 6.8% in 2019 to 8.3% in the 10 months of 2020 (Trading Economics 2020).

For the quarterly GDP growth, the Q1 growth rate was +0.3%, the Q2 growth rate was -8.0%, and the Q3 growth rate was +4.9%. Averaging the three quarters gives -0.9%. This can be compared with the 2019 average quarterly growth rate: +0.2%. So, this brute force analysis gives us 1.1% reduction in the GDP growth from 2019 to 2020 (Trading Economics 2020).

These rough estimates of the comparative economic outcomes from the choices of the three policy options are summarized in the last column of Fig. 2.4. Although these are only crude estimates, their differences are sufficiently large to clearly indicate disparate economic performances of the three policy options. The unemployment rate differs by about 10% between the lockdown-lockdown strategy and the focused protection-safely reopen strategy. Between the two strategies, the GDP growth rate differs by about 30%.

Notwithstanding a clear economic message embedded in Fig. 2.4, it does not provide a definitive answer to the inquiry of which policy option should be chosen by the government because the simple analysis in the figure does not address many other critical policy variables including human fatalities which are of economic value and at the heart of the GBD argument (Viscusi 2014). The health outcomes across the policy options will be analyzed in Chap. 4. It suffices to say at this point that the lockdown-lockdown strategy does not seem to outperform overwhelmingly the no-lockdown strategy in the measure of human fatalities, either (Deccan Herald 2020).

8   Looking Ahead

This chapter provided a review of the economic theories, models, and statistics that are apposite to a systematic exposition of the economics of pandemics as a globally shared experience which is the ultimate goal of this book. It started from the theory of public goods, then moved on to the concept of production technologies, to market failures and governmental interventions, to national health systems, impacts of the pandemic on the economy, and economic policy options.

Although this chapter provides a sound platform for the purpose of this book as far as the intellectual foundation is concerned, it does not unravel a true complexity of pandemics and a full range of economic questions regarding them. Ensuing chapters will lead readers to get to a comprehensive picture of pandemics and pandemic economic considerations through the five pandemic analyses presented in the following five chapters.

Chapter 3, entitled "Pandemic Analysis I," sheds a spotlight on the roles of global governance, especially the World Health Organization, from the angle of pandemic economics (UN 1948; WHO 2015).

Chapter 4, entitled "Pandemic Analysis II," explains a series of policy decisions that have to be made by national governments. Nine key governmental decisions are analyzed, which include a travel suspension, a nationwide lockdown, business closures, a mask mandate, economic relief programs, school closures, potential treatments, and vaccine developments (USDOT 2020; USDHHS 2020; White House 2020).

Chapter 5, entitled "Pandemic Analysis III," describes a host of radical social transformation movements that surfaced in response to the

COVID-19. This includes a Great Reset, a Marxist revolution, and a popular uprising (Schwab and Malleret 2020). An analysis of the disparate impacts of the COVID-19 pandemic on different income or social groups of the society is provided in the chapter.

Chapter 6, entitled "Pandemic Analysis IV," examines the doomsday scenario associated with the pandemics in which the COVID-19 pandemic is just a precursor of an even bigger end-of-the-planet climate catastrophe (Ban and Verkooijen 2020).

Chapter 7, entitled "Pandemic Analysis V," will be devoted to an exposition of vaccine developments. A multi-dimensional look at the vaccines is provided, including history, science, economics, policy decisions, and international cooperation (Plotkin 2009; Azar II 2020).

REFERENCES

Arrow, K.J., M.L. Cropper, G.C. Eads, R.W. Hahn, L.B. Lave, R.G. Noll, P.R. Portney, et al. 1996. Is There a Role for Benefit-Cost Analysis in Environmental, Health, and Safety Regulation? *Science* 272: 221–222.

Azar, Alex M. II. 2020. How Operation Warp Speed Delivered a COVID Vaccine in Record Time. *Fox News*. Published on 12 December 2020. https://www.foxnews.com/opinion/hhs-azar-operation-warp-speed-covid-vaccine-record-time.

Ban, Ki-moon, and Patrick Verkooijen. 2020. Coronavirus Is a Warning To Us All: We Must Heal Nature In Order To Heal Ourselves. *HuffPost*. Published on May 2, 2020. https://www.huffingtonpost.co.uk/entry/coronavirus_uk_5e ac35acc5b65156135c9863.

Barrett, Scott. 2003. *Environment and Statecraft: The Strategy of Environmental Treaty*. Oxford: Oxford University Press.

Baumol, W.J., and O.A. Oates. 1975. *The Theory of Environmental Policy*. Upper Saddle River, NJ: Prentice Hall.

Berry, K., T. Allen, R.D. Horan, J.F. Shogren, D. Finnoff, and P. Daszak. 2018. The Economic Case for a Pandemic Fund. *EcoHealth* 15: 244–258.

Bloom, D.E., and D. Canning. 2017. *Epidemics and Economics. Working Paper #9, Harvard Program on Demography of Ageing*. Harvard University.

Bowen, H.R. 1943. The Interpretation of Voting in the Allocation of Economic Resources. *Quarterly Journal of Economics* 58: 27–48.

Buchanan, James M. 1965. An Economic Theory of Clubs. *Economica* 32: 1–24.

———. 1968. *The Demand and Supply of Public Goods*. Chicago, IL: Rand McNally & Co.

Burns, A., D. Mensbrugghe, and H. Timmer. 2008. *Evaluating the Economic Consequences of Avian Influenza*. Washington, DC: World Bank. http://documents.worldbank.org/curated/en/977141468158986545/pdf/474170WP 0Evalu101PUBLIC10Box334133B.pdf.

Centers for Disease Control and Prevention (CDC). 2012. *Principles of Epidemiology in Public Health Practice (Third Edition): An Introduction to Applied Epidemiology and Biostatistics*. Atlanta, GA: The CDC.

———. 2021a. COVID-19 Pandemic Planning Scenarios. Updated on March 19, 2021. Atlanta, GA: The CDC. https://www.cdc.gov/coronavirus/2019-ncov/hcp/planning-scenarios.html.

———. 2021b. Provisional COVID-19 Death Counts by Sex, Age, and State. Updated on April 15, 2021. Atlanta, GA: The CDC. https://data.cdc.gov/NCHS/Provisional-COVID-19-Death-Counts-by-Sex-Age-and-S/9bhg-hcku.

Ch.Ch. 2020. Health Insurance—Obtaining Basic Insurance, Its Costs and Services. Ch.Ch: A Service of the Confederation, Cantons and Communes. https://www.ch.ch/en/health-insurance/.

Chapman, C.R., and D. Morrison. 1994. Impacts on the Earth by Asteroids and Comets: Assessing the Hazard. *Nature* 367: 33–40.

Coalition for Epidemic Preparedness Innovations (CEPI). 2020. Why We Exist. https://cepi.net/about/whyweexist/.

Coleman, C.M., and M.B. Frieman. 2014. Coronaviruses: Important Emerging Human Pathogens. *Journal of Virology* 8: 5209–5212.

Deccan Herald. 2020. No lockdowns, but Sweden seems to have controlled the Covid-19 pandemic. Published on October 1, 2020. https://www.deccanherald.com/opinion/panorama/no-lockdowns-but-sweden-seems-to-have-controlled-the-covid-19-pandemic-895509.html.

Ellis, J., G. Giudice, M. Mangano, I. Tkachev, and U. Wiedemann. 2008. Review of the Safety of LHC Collisions. *Journal of Physics G: Nuclear and Particle Physics* 35: 115004. https://doi.org/10.1088/0954-3899/35/11/115004.

European Centre for Disease Prevention and Control (ECDPC). 2020. *COVID-19 Coronavirus Dataset*. Solna Municipality, Sweden: The ECDPC. https://data.europa.eu/euodp/en/data/dataset/covid-19-coronavirus-data.

Fan, Victoria Y., Dean T. Jamison, and Lawrence H. Summers. 2018. Pandemic Risk: How Large are the Expected Losses? *The Bulletin of the World Health Organization* 96 (2): 129–134. https://doi.org/10.2471/BLT.17.199588.

Financial Times. 2020. Architect of Sweden's No-Lockdown Strategy Insists It Will Pay Off. Published on May 8, 2020. https://www.ft.com/content/a2b4c18c-a5e8-4edc-8047-ade4a82a548d.

Finkelstein, Amy. 2007. The Aggregate Effects of Health Insurance: Evidence from the Introduction of Medicare. *Quarterly Journal of Economics* 122: 1–37.

Ford, J., and K.M. Katondo. 1977. Maps of Tsetse Fly (Glossina) Distribution in Africa, 1973, According to Subgeneric Groups on a Scale of 1: 5000000. *The Bulletin of Animal Health and Production in Africa* 15: 187–193.

Fox Business. 2020a. Pfizer's Covid-19 Vaccine Proves 90% Effective in Latest Trials. Published on November 9, 2020. https://www.foxbusiness.com/healthcare/pfizers-covid-19-vaccine-proves-90-effective-in-latest-trials.
———. 2020b. Moderna Says Its Vaccine is 94.5% Effective in Preventing COVID-19. Published on November 16, 2020. https://www.foxbusiness.com/healthcare/moderna-coronavirus-vaccine-trial-phase-3.
Fraser, Christophe, C.A. Donnelly, S. Cauchemez, et al. 2009. Pandemic Potential of a Strain of Influenza A (H1N1): Early Findings. *Science* 324: 1557–1561.
Gould, George M., and Walter L. Pyle. 1896. Historic Epidemics. In *Anomalies and Curiosities of Medicine*. New York, NY: The Bell Publishing Company.
Hartwick, J.M., and N.D. Olewiler. 1997. *The Economics of Natural Resource Use*. 2nd ed. New York, NY: Pearson.
Hawking, S., M. Tegmark, S. Russell, and F. Wilczek. 2014. Transcending Complacency on Superintelligent Machines. *Huffington Post*. https://www.huffingtonpost.com/stephen-hawking/artificial-intelligence_b_5174265.html.
Hirshleifer, Jack. 1983. From Weakest-link to Best-shot: The Voluntary Provision of Public Goods. *Public Choice* 41: 371–386.
Hoover Institution. 2020. The Doctor Is In: Scott Atlas and the Efficacy of Lockdowns, Social Distancing, and Closings. Uncommon Knowledge with Peter Robinson. Palo Alto, CA: Hoover Institution, Stanford University. https://www.hoover.org/research/doctor-scott-atlas-and-efficacy-lockdowns-social-distancing-and-closings.
International Energy Agency (IEA). 2020. *Global Energy Review 2020: The Impacts of the Covid-19 Crisis on Global Energy Demand and CO_2 Emissions*. Paris, F.R.: IEA.
Jamison, D.T., and J. Jamison. 2011. Characterizing the Amount and Speed of Discounting Procedures. *Journal of Benefit-Cost Analysis* 2: 1–53. https://doi.org/10.2202/2152-2812.1031.
Johns Hopkins University (JHU). 2020. *COVID-19 Dash Board*. Baltimore, MD: JHU. https://data.humdata.org/dataset/novel-coronavirus-2019-ncov-cases.
Jonas, O.B. 2013. *Pandemic Risk*. Washington, DC: World Bank. https://openknowledge.worldbank.org/bitstream/handle/10986/16343/WDR14_bp_Pandemic_Risk_Jonas.pdf?sequence=1&isAllowed=y.
Kariko, K., H. Muramatsu, J. Ludwig, and D. Weissman. 2011. Generating the Optimal mRNA for Therapy: HPLC Purification Eliminates Immune Activation and Improves Translation for Nucleoside-modified. *Protein-encoding mRNA. Nucleic Acids Research* 39: e142.
Kulldorff, Martin, Sunetra Gupta, and Jay Bhattacharya. 2020. The Great Barrington Declaration. Published on October 4, 2020. https://gbdeclaration.org/.
Kurzweil, R. 2005. *The Singularity is Near*. New York, NY: Penguin.

Le Quere, C., R.B. Jackson, M.W. Jones, et al. 2020. Temporary Reduction in Daily Global CO_2 Emissions during the COVID-19 Forced Confinement. Nature Climate Change 14: 121001. 10.1038\s41558-020-0797-x.

Le Treut, H., R. Somerville, U. Cubasch, Y. Ding, C. Mauritzen, et al. 2007. Historical overview of climate change. In *Climate Change 2007: The Physical Science Basis. The Fourth Assessment Report of the Intergovernmental Panel on Climate Change*, ed. S. Solomon et al. Cambridge: Cambridge University Press.

Liu, J.-T., J.K. Hammitt, J.-D. Wang, and M.-W. Tsou. 2005. Valuation of the Risk of SARS in Taiwan. *Health Economics* 14: 83–91. https://doi.org/10.1002/hec.911.

Lopez, Alan D., Colin D. Mathers, Majid Ezzati, Dean T. Jamison, and Christopher J.L. Murray. 2006. *Global Burden of Disease and Risk Factors*. New York, NY: World Bank and Oxford University Press.

Mahler, D. Gerszon, Christoph Lakner, R.A. Castaneda Aguilar, and Haoyu Wu. 2020. The impact of COVID-19 (Coronavirus) on global poverty: Why Sub-Saharan Africa might be the region hardest hit. *World Bank Blogs*. Updated on June 8, 2020. https://blogs.worldbank.org/opendata/impact-covid-19-coronavirus-global-poverty-why-sub-saharan-africa-might-be-region-hardest.

Martens, P., R. Kovats, S. Nijhof, P. Devries, M. Livermore, D. Bradley, J. Cox, and A. McMichael. 1999. Climate Change and Future Populations at Risk of Malaria. *Global Environmental Change* 9 (Oct.): S89–S107.

Mas-Colell, A., M.D. Whinston, and J.R. Green. 1995. *Microeconomic Theory*. Oxford: Oxford University Press.

Morin, B.R., A.P. Kinzig, S.A. Levin, and C.A. Perrings. 2018. Economic Incentives in the Socially Optimal Management of Infectious Disease: When R0 is Not Enough. *EcoHealth* 15: 274–289.

Musgrave, R.A. 1939. The Voluntary Exchange Theory of Public Economy. *Quarterly Journal of Economics* 53: 213–237.

National Aeronautics and Space Administration (NASA). 2014. NASA's Efforts to Identify Near-Earth Objects and Mitigate Hazards. IG-14-030, NASA Office of Inspector General, Washington, DC.

———. 2017. An Overview: Planetary Defense Coordination Office. NASA, Washington, DC. https://www.nasa.gov/planetarydefense/overview.

National Health Service (NHS). 2020. Guidance: The NHS Constitution for England. NHS, UK. https://www.gov.uk/government/publications/the-nhs-constitution-for-england.

New York Times (NYT). 2020a. Coronavirus Vaccine Tracker. https://www.nytimes.com/interactive/2020/science/coronavirus-vaccine-tracker.html.

———. 2020b. See Coronavirus Restrictions and Mask Mandates for All 50 States. Published on November 25, 2020. https://www.nytimes.com/interactive/2020/us/states-reopen-map-coronavirus.html.

Nordhaus, William D. 1973. The Allocation of Energy Resources. *Brookings Papers on Economic Activity* 1973: 529–576.

———. 1977. Economic Growth and Climate: The Carbon Dioxide Problem. *American Economic Review* 67: 341–346.

———. 1994. *Managing the Global Commons.* Cambridge, MA: MIT Press.

———. 2006. Paul Samuelson and Global Public Goods. In *Samuelsonian Economics and the Twenty-First Century*, ed. M. Szenberg, L. Ramrattan, and A.A. Gottesman. Oxford Scholarship Online.

———. 2008. *A Question of Balance: Weighing the Options on Global Warming Policies.* New Haven, CT: Yale University Press.

———. 2011. The Economics of Tail Events with an Application to Climate Change. *Review of Environmental Economics and Policy* 5: 240–257.

Nordhaus, William D., and Zili Yang. 1996. A Regional Dynamic General-Equilibrium Model of Alternative Climate-Change Strategies. *American Economic Review* 86: 741–765.

Organization for Economic Cooperation and Development (OECD). 2019. *Health at a Glance 2019.* Paris, FR: The OECD.

Pardi, N., M.J. Hogan, F.W. Porter, and D. Weissman. 2018. mRNA Vaccines—A New Era in Vaccinology. *Nature Reviews Drug Discovery* 17: 261–279.

Pareto, Vilfredo. 1896. *Cours d'Economie Politique.* Geneva, CH: Droz.

Paterlini, Marta. 2020. 'Closing Borders is Ridiculous': The Epidemiologist behind Sweden's Controversial Coronavirus Strategy. *Nature* 580 (7805): 574. https://doi.org/10.1038/d41586-020-01098-x.

Patz, J.A., A.K. Githeko, J.P. McCarty, S. Hussein, U. Confalonieri, and N. de Wet. 2003. Climate Change and Infectious Diseases. In *Climate Change and Human Health—Risks and Responses.* Geneva, CH: WHO.

Pfizer. 2020. *All COVID-19 updates.* New York, NY: Pfizer Inc.. https://www.pfizer.com/health/coronavirus/updates.

Pigou, A.C. 1920. *Economics of Welfare.* London: Macmillan.

Plotkin, S.A. 2009. Vaccines: The Fourth Century. *Clinical and Vaccine Immunology* 16: 1709–1719.

Polyakova, Maria, Geoffrey Kocks, Victoria Udalova, and Amy Finkelstein. 2020. Initial Economic Damage from the COVID-19 Pandemic in the United States is More Widespread across Ages and Geographies than Initial Mortality Impacts. *Proceedings of the National Academy of Sciences* 117 (45): 27934–27939.

Polyakova, Maria, Victoria Udalova, Geoffrey Kocks, Katie Genadek, Keith Finlay, and Amy Finkelstein. 2021. Racial Disparities in Excess All-Cause Mortality During the Early Covid-19 Pandemic Varied Substantially Across States. *Health Affairs* 40 (2). https://doi.org/10.1377/hlthaff.2020.02142.

Potter, C.W. 2001. A History of Influenza. *Journal of Applied Microbiology* 91 (4): 572–579.

Reuters. 2020. Your Money: Coronavirus Fears Shake Yale Economist Robert Shiller. Published on 20 March 2020. https://www.reuters.com/article/us-health-coronavirus-shiller-idUSKBN2163LD.

Rice, T., P. Rosenau, L.Y. Unruh, A.J. Barnes, R.B. Saltman, and E. van Ginneken. 2013. United States of America: Health System Review. *Health Systems in Transition* 15 (3): 1–431.

Rogers, David J., and Sarah E. Randolph. 2000. The Global Spread of Malaria in a Future. *Warmer World. Science* 289 (5485): 1763–1766.

Romer, Paul. 2020. Roadmap to Responsibly Reopen America. Accessed from roadmap.paulromer.net. Published on April 23, 2020.

Samuelson, Paul. 1954. The Pure Theory of Public Expenditure. *Review of Economics and Statistics* 36: 387–389.

———. 1955. Diagrammatic Exposition of a Theory of Public Expenditure. *Review of Economics and Statistics* 37: 350–356.

Samuelson, Paul, and William D. Nordhaus. 2009. *Economics.* 19th ed. New York, NY: McGraw-Hill Education.

Schuster, E.F. 1984. Classification of Probability Laws by Tail Behavior. *Journal of the American Statistical Association* 79 (388): 936–939.

Schwab, Klaus, and Thierry Malleret. 2020. *COVID-19: The Great Reset.* Agentur Schweiz.

Seo, S. Niggol. 2016. *Microbehavioral Econometric Methods: Theories, Models, and Applications for the Study of Environmental and Natural Resources.* Amsterdam, NL: Academic Press.

———. 2018. *Natural and Man-made Catastrophes: Theories, Economics, and Policy Designs.* New York, NY: Wiley-Blackwell, John Wiley & Sons.

———. 2019. *The Economics of Global Allocations of the Green Climate Fund: An Assessment from Four Scientific Traditions of Modeling Adaptation Strategies.* Cham, CH: Springer Nature.

———. 2020a. *The Economics of Globally Shared and Public Goods.* Amsterdam, NL: Academic Press.

———. 2020b. A Succinct Mathematical Disproof of the Dismal Theorem of Economics. In *The Economics of Globally Shared and Public Goods*, ed. In: Seo, S. Niggol. Amsterdam, NL: Academic Press.

Shiller, Robert J. 2005. *Irrational Exuberance.* 2nd ed. Princeton, NJ: Princeton University Press.

Sloan, Frank A., and Chee-Ruey Hsieh. 2013. *Health Economics.* 2nd ed. Cambridge, MA: The MIT Press.

Taubenberger, J.K., D.M. Morens, and A.S. Fauci. 2007. The Next Influenza Pandemic: Can It Be Predicted? *The Journal of the American Medical Association* 297: 2025–2027.

Trading Economics. 2020. Sweden GDP Growth Rate & Sweden Unemployment Rate. https://tradingeconomics.com/sweden/unemployment-rate.

United Nations. 1948. *Constitution of the World Health Organization*. New York, NY: The UN.

United States Bureau of Economic Analysis (USBEA). 2020. *Gross Domestic Product, Third Quarter 2020 (Advance Estimate)*. Suitland, MD: USBEA, US Department of Commerce. https://www.bea.gov/sites/default/files/2020-10/gdp3q20_adv.pdf.

United States Bureau of Labor Statistics (USBLS). 2020. *Labor Force Statistics from the Current Population Survey*. Washington, DC: USBLS, US Department of Labor. https://data.bls.gov/timeseries/LNS14000000.

United States Department of Health and Human Services (USDHHS). 2020. Explaining Operation Warp Speed. https://www.hhs.gov/coronavirus/explaining-operation-warp-speed/index.html.

United States Department of the Treasury (USDOT). 2020. *The CARES Act Works for All Americans*. Washington, DC: USDOT. https://home.treasury.gov/policy-issues/cares.

United States Space Force (USSF). 2020. About the United States Space Force. https://www.spaceforce.mil/About-Us/About-Space-Force/.

Viscusi, W. Kip. 2014. The Value of Individual and Societal Risks to Life and Health. In *Handbook of the Economics of Risk and Uncertainty*, ed. M. Machina and W. Kip Viscusi, 385–452. Amsterdam, NL: North-Holland. https://doi.org/10.1016/B978-0-444-53685-3.00007-6.

Weiss, Susan R. 2020. Forty Years with Coronaviruses. *Journal of Experimental Medicine* 217 (5): e20200537. https://doi.org/10.1084/jem.20200537.

Weitzman, Martin L. 2009. On Modeling and Interpreting the Economics of Catastrophic Climate Change. *Review of Economics and Statistics* 91: 1–19.

White House. 2020. *How President Trump Uses the Defense Production Act to Protect America from the China Virus*. Washington, DC: Office of Trade and Manufacturing Policy, White House.

World Health Organization (WHO). 2015. *International Health Regulations (2015)*. Geneva, CH: WHO.

———. 2018. *WHO Releases 2018 Priority Diseases List*. Geneva, CH: WHO. https://ohsonline.com/articles/2018/02/15/who-releases-2018-priority-diseases-list.aspx?admgarea=news&m=1.

———. 2019. *World Malaria Report 2019*. Geneva, CH: WHO.

———. 2020a. *What Is a Pandemic*. Geneva, CH: WHO.

———. 2020b. Timeline of WHO's Response to COVID-19. https://www.who.int/news/item/29-06-2020-covidtimeline.

———. 2020c. *Structure*. Geneva, CH: WHO.

World Meteorological Organization (WMO). 2020. *United in Science 2020*. Paris, FR: WMO.

Zipf, G.K. 1949. *Human Behavior and the Principle of Least Effort*. Cambridge, MA: Addison-Wesley.

CHAPTER 3

Pandemic Analysis I: Global Governance for a Global Pandemic?

1 INTRODUCTION TO THE PANDEMICS AND GLOBAL GOVERNANCE

When it comes to a globally shared good, which is alternatively referred to as global commons or a global public good, a question of governance is a central inquiry to researchers and policy-makers (Seo 2020). Unlike numerous public goods at the national level, for example, national defense, there is no government that is mandated by people to supply a globally shared good for the benefit of all citizens of the planet. As a globally shared good and experience, a global pandemic management must deal with the same governance dilemma.

If you wonder what the governance conundrum would look like in the efforts to provide a globally shared good, then you might just need to reflect on the climate change negotiations during the past 30-year period since the 1992 Earth Summit. After the unprecedented efforts by policy-makers and the dollars invested throughout the three decades, the global community does not yet have a legally binding treaty on climate change (Nordhaus 2010, 2015, Seo 2012, 2017).

In the case of global climate change challenges, a new international organization was created to coordinate global responses, the United Nations Framework Convention on Climate Change (UNFCCC), at the Rio Earth Summit in 1992 (UNFCCC 1992). The counterpart in global health matters is the World Health Organization (WHO).

© The Author(s), under exclusive license to Springer Nature Switzerland AG 2022
S. N. Seo, *The Economics of Pandemics*,
https://doi.org/10.1007/978-3-030-91021-1_3

Table 3.1   WHO in the United Nations system

Types of organizations	UN organizations
UN funds and programs	United Nations Development Programme (UNDP) United Nations Environment Programme (UNEP) UN Population Fund (UNFPA) UN Children's Fund (UNICEF) World Food Programme (WFP) UN Human Settlements Programme (UN-Habitat) United Nations Conference on Trade and Development (UNCTAD) UN High Commissioner for Refugees (UNHCR) United Nations Relief and Works Agency for Palestine Refugees (UNRWA) United Nations Office for Project Services (UNOPS) United Nations Office on Drugs and Crime (UNODC) UN Women
UN specialized agencies	Food and Agriculture Organization (FAO) International Civil Aviation Organization (ICAO) International Fund for Agricultural Development (IFAD) International Labor Organization (ILO) International Monetary Fund (IMF) International Maritime Organization (IMO) International Telecommunication Union (ITU) UN Educational, Scientific and Cultural Organization (UNESCO) United Nations International Development Organization (UNIDO) *World Health Organization (WHO)* United Nations World Tourism Organization (UNWTO) Universal Postal Union (UPU) World Intellectual Property Organization (WIPO) World Meteorological Organization (WMO) World Bank
Other UN entities and bodies	Joint United Nations Programme on HIV/AIDS (UNAIDS) International Trade Centre (ITC) Office of the United Nations High Commissioner for Human Rights (OHCHR) United Nations Framework Convention on Climate Change (UNFCCC) United Nations International Strategy for Disaster Reduction (UNISDR) Organization for the Prohibition of Chemical Weapons (OPCW) Preparatory Commission for the Comprehensive Nuclear-Test-Ban Treaty Organization (CTBTO)
Related international organizations	International Atomic Energy Agency (IAEA) World Trade Organization (WTO) International Organization for Migration (IOM)

The World Health Organization was established in 1948 with a lofty goal of "attainment by all peoples of the highest possible level of health," right after the United Nations Charter was signed in San Francisco (UN 1948). As shown in Table 3.1, the WHO is one of the specialized agencies of the UN system (UNSCEB 2018). Since then, the WHO led the international efforts for achieving the aforementioned health goal and eliminating some of the most feared diseases in human history including smallpox (WHO 2020a).

Likewise, the WHO played a leading role among the international organizations in the battle against the COVID-19 pandemic. However, it has also faced not a few criticisms regarding its handling of the COVID-19 pandemic. To note one, the WHO has not been able to identify the origin of the novel coronavirus and its team of experts had been denied to enter China for investigation until the end of January 2021 (WSJ 2021).

This chapter provides a critical review of the global governance in place for effective responses to global pandemics. Our analysis is centered around the question of whether the WHO is an adequate global governance system for the pandemic responses. The present author will review the critical decisions that the WHO has made during the course of the COVID-19 contagion across the globe, including the declaration of COVID-19 as a pandemic and the naming of the infectious disease as such.

A keen observer must have noticed that the pandemic responses during the COVID-19 were, by and large, nationally coordinated. In any country, a national response center and associated institutions have actively designed necessary measures, enforced regulations, and kept track of all the relevant information. S/he might be puzzled over why the pandemic policy responses are taken up with enthusiasm and urgency by national governments, rather than being led by a global governance system such as the WHO, despite it being a globally shared good or concern.

From another viewpoint, the WHO was not initially conceived as an organization for the global pandemic response, nor does it act as one. It was designed as an all-purpose health organization for all peoples on the planet, meaning that its purview is on all diseases and other health matters. This chapter will shed light on the organization's historical works across the range of different diseases it has tackled.

This point of view, however, begs another question which is addressed in this chapter. That is, does the global community need another organization or treaty devoted exclusively to global pandemics? Unsurprisingly, a call for such a treaty is being made and signed by world leaders including the head of the WHO (2021b).

2   WHO Under the United Nations System

The WHO is one of about 40 organizations belonging to or associated with the United Nations and one of the 15 specialized agencies of the UN. As shown in Table 3.1, there are four types of organizations in the UN System: UN funds and programs, UN specialized agencies, other UN entities, and related UN organizations.

The UN funds and programs are those created by the UN to meet the needs not envisaged at San Francisco in 1945 but later developed. The specialized agencies are legally independent international organizations, brought into by international agreements and treaties. Other UN entities and bodies are the UN organizations that are not members of the Chief Executive Board for Coordination of the UN System. Related organiza tions are not part of the UN System, but similar to the specialized agencies of the UN (UNSCEB 2018).

A specialized agency is, unlike the UN funds and programs, legally independent and established by a separate international agreement. Many influential international organizations belong to this group, including the WHO: to name some, the World Bank, the International Monetary Fund (IMF), the Food and Agriculture Organization (FAO), the World Meteorological Organization (WMO), and the United Nations Educational, Scientific and Cultural Organization (UNESCO).

The long and powerful list of the UN-associated organizations in Table 3.1 represents to many observers the current international order. The order is that of the United Nations created by the treaty in San Francisco in 1945 (UN 1945). The UN was initially conceived as a coun-termeasure against man-made catastrophes such as the two world wars during the first half of the twentieth century. The death toll from World War II alone is estimated to amount to 70–85 million people. The UN's purview has, however, come too far to exceed that of an anti-war regime. As is evident in Table 3.1, this order exerts influences over nearly every aspect of global affairs and more often than not defines the contemporary international affairs.

The Charter of the United Nations (CUN), signed on June 26, 1945, by 51 countries including the 5 permanent members of the Security Council, declares unequivocally in its Article I, where the purview and objectives of the CUN are marked, the foremost purpose of the CUN to be maintaining international peace and security (UN 1945):

[Article I.1] To maintain international peace and security, and to that end: to take effective collective measures for the prevention and removal of threats to the peace, and for the suppression of acts of aggression or other breaches of the peace, and to bring about by peaceful means, and in conformity with the principles of justice and international law, adjustment or settlement of international disputes or situations which might lead to a breach of the peace;

Article I did not end there, though. Portending a truly comprehensive role of the United Nations in determining a myriad of international affairs, the article goes on to declare that solving "economic, social, cultural, and humanitarian (ESCH)" problems of the globe pertains to the purview and objectives envisaged at the establishment of the United Nations (UN 1945):

[Article I.3] To achieve international co-operation in solving international problems of an economic, social, cultural, or humanitarian character, and in promoting and encouraging respect for human rights and for fundamental freedoms for all without distinction as to race, sex, language, or religion;

The signing of the CUN was followed by an establishment of one specialized agency after another: to mention some of them, the Food and Agriculture Organization in 1945, the International Monetary Fund in 1945, the World Bank in 1945, the International Labor Organization in 1946, the International Civil Aviation Organization in 1947, the International Maritime Organization in 1948, the World Health Organization in 1948, and the World Meteorological Organization in 1950.

The Constitution of the World Health Organization was signed on July 22, 1946, by 61 countries, which entered into force on April 7, 1948. As noted in the introduction, the WHO Constitution was written in aspiration of a lofty goal as declared in Article I (UN 1948):

[Article I] The objective of the World Health Organization shall be the attainment by all peoples of the highest possible level of health.

The lofty objective of the Constitution is emphatically expressed also through the declaration of its principles. Within the principles of the WHO, health is not defined just by physical well-being, but shall embrace mental as well as social well-being while the enjoyment of the highest standard of health is one of the fundamental human rights of every human being:

[Principle I] Health is a state of complete physical, mental and social well-being and not merely the absence of disease or infirmity. [Principle II] The enjoyment of the highest attainable standard of health is one of the fundamental rights of every human being without distinction of race, religion, political belief, economic or social condition.

The Constitution defines in Article II the functions of the WHO, one of which is that of the directing and coordinating authority on international health matters:

[Article II] In order to achieve its objective, the functions of the Organization shall be: (a) to act as the directing and co-ordinating authority on international health work; (b) to establish and maintain effective collaboration with the United Nations, specialized agencies, governmental health administrations, professional groups and such other organizations as may be deemed appropriate; (c) to assist Governments, upon request, in strengthening health services.

Since its founding, the WHO has, without any doubt, not accomplished its lofty aspiration. However, its achievements during the past 70 years, summarized in Table 3.2 based on the presentation by the WHO itself in celebration of its 70th anniversary, are remarkable. The milestones include the era of antibiotics, polio vaccines, measles vaccines, International Health Regulations, sexual and reproductive health, tropical diseases, smallpox eradication, polio-free, AIDS discovery, tuberculosis strategy, malaria eliminated in developed countries, tobacco control, H1N1 virus, Ebola virus, and Zika virus (WHO 2020a).

Entering the twenty-first century, the WHO commits to the Millennium Development Goals (MDGs) of the United Nations and adopted the Sustainable Development Goals (SDGs) in 2015. Beginning from 2010, it declares and pushes forward a move toward a universal health coverage, which it believes is a step toward the lofty goal declared in Article I, that is, the best possible health for all peoples.

Today's activities of the WHO can be glimpsed from its annual budget allocations into its basket of priorities (WHO 2020b). For the 2020–2021 biennial period, the total budget was US$5.84 billion. Of the total, US$1.36 billion was allocated to the area of universal health coverage; US$1 billion to the area of country support; US$1 billion to the area of emergency operations and appeals; US$889 million to the area of health emergencies; US$863 million to the area of polio eradication; US$432

Table 3.2 Milestones of the WHO in its 70th anniversary

Date	Heath issues or diseases	Achievements
1948		The WHO's Constitution comes into force and the WHO takes over responsibility for the International Classification of Diseases.
1950	Antibiotics	The era of discovery of present-day antibiotics begins and the WHO starts advising countries on their responsible use.
1952–1957	Polio vaccines	Polio vaccines are discovered, paving the way for WHO-facilitated global campaigns that have led to the near-eradication of poliomyelitis.
1963	Measles vaccine	Vaccine against measles becomes available.
1969	International Health Regulations	The World Health Assembly establishes the first International Health Regulations, an agreement between WHO member states to work together to monitor and control 6 serious infectious diseases: cholera, plague, yellow fever, smallpox, relapsing fever, and typhus.
1972	Sexual, reproductive	The Special Programme of Research, Development and Research Training in Human Reproduction (HRP) is created with a global mandate to carry out research into sexual and reproductive health and rights.
1974	Immunization of children	The WHO founds the Expanded Programme on Immunization to bring life-saving vaccines to children worldwide.
1975	Tropical diseases	WHO founds and begins hosting the Special Programme for Research and Training in Tropical Diseases (TDR). By 2016, 5 of the 8 diseases the program was created to tackle are close to elimination.
1977	Essential medicines list	The first essential medicines list is published. This core list outlines the medicines that a basic health system needs.
1978	Universal health coverage	The International Conference on Primary Health Care, in Alma-Ata, Kazakhstan, sets the historic goal of "Health for All", laying the groundwork for the WHO's current call for universal health coverage.
1979	Smallpox elimination	Following an ambitious 12-year global vaccination campaign led by the WHO, smallpox is eliminated.
1983–1987	HIV/AIDS	Human immunodeficiency virus, which causes AIDS, is discovered.
1995	TB diagnosis	The directly observed treatment (DOTS) strategy for reducing the toll of tuberculosis (TB) is launched. At end of 2013, more than 37 million lives had been saved through TB diagnosis and treatment under this strategy.
2000		World leaders commit to fulfill the Millennium Development Goals (MDGs).

(*continued*)

Table 3.2 (continued)

Date	Heath issues or diseases	Achievements
2002	Polio	The WHO European Region is certified polio-free.
2003	Tobacco Treaty	The WHO Framework Convention on Tobacco Control, the WHO's first global public health treaty, is adopted.
2005		The World Health Assembly revises the International Health Regulations.
2006	Child mortality	The number of children dying before their fifth birthday declines below 10 million.
2008	Noncommu nicable diseases	World Health Statistics note a global shift from infectious diseases to noncommunicable diseases (NCDs).
2009	H1N1	New H1N1 influenza virus emerges. The WHO collaborates with partners in developing influenza vaccines.
2010	Universal health coverage	The WHO issues a menu of options for raising sufficient resources and removing financial barriers so that all people move toward universal health coverage.
2012	Heart disease, diabetes, cancer, and other NCDs	WHO Member States set global targets to prevent and control heart disease, diabetes, cancer, and other NCDs.
2014	Ebola virus	The biggest outbreak of Ebola virus disease in West Africa occurs. The WHO deploys thousands of technical experts, support staff, and medical equipment to stop Ebola.
2015	Malaria free	The WHO European Region is declared malaria free.
2015		The Sustainable Development Goals (SDGs) are adopted.
2016	Zika virus	Infections with Zika virus in South America represent a public health emergency of international concern.
2018		The WHO recommits to the goal of health for all through focused action toward universal health coverage.

million to the area of healthier populations; US$209 million to specialized programs (Fig. 3.1).

Beginning from 2015, the WHO has published its list of priority diseases: the first list in 2015 and the second list in 2018 (WHO 2018). We can tell the priorities of the organization from this list right before the COVID-19 pandemic. The list in 2018 identifies as its priority diseases the following: Crimean-Congo hemorrhagic fever, Ebola virus disease and Marburg virus disease, Lassa fever, Middle East respiratory syndrome coronavirus (MERS-CoV), Severe Acute Respiratory Syndrome (SARS), Nipah and henipaviral diseases, Rift Valley fever, Zika. The Zika virus is the only addition to 2015's first list.

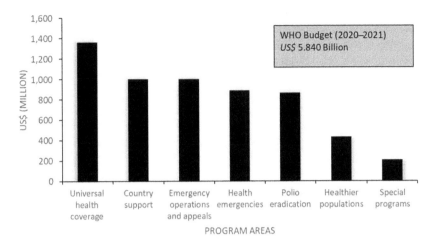

Fig. 3.1 WHO annual budget allocation for 2020–2021

There are two aspects that are notable in the above budget allocations and the priority disease lists. First, the WHO's budget is not structured to deal effectively with a global pandemic. The budget is largely directed to a universal health coverage, healthier populations, and country supports. The share of the annual budget allocated to health emergencies, which may be the pertinent area for pandemic responses by the WHO, is only about 15%. The budget is largely directed to the achievement of the objective of the sustainable development goals and/or the universal health coverage. A heavy shift by the WHO toward the two policy areas or goals may have left the organization ill-prepared for a global pandemic at the scale of the COVID-19.

Second, the list reveals that the coronaviruses have long been a priority of the WHO. The coronaviruses were researched as early as the 1970s while the human coronaviruses, that is, SARS-CoV and the MERS-CoV viruses, have been transmitting human to human since the first outbreak in 2002 (Coleman and Frieman 2014; Weiss 2020). To our dismay, the WHO has not effectively dealt with these viruses, resulting in the novel coronavirus of 2020 which has, as of mid-July 2021, killed over 4 million people globally (JHU 2021).

3   Key Decisions of the WHO During the COVID-19 Pandemic

During the COVID-19 pandemic, citizens of the world witnessed a series of key decisions made by the WHO which appeared to set the course fundamentally for the national-level COVID-19 responses. These decisions are at the core of the "functions" of the WHO responding to the global pandemics. The five decisions that the present author reviews in this section are (1) declaring a human-to-human transmission; (2) declaring a public health emergency of international concern; (3) naming a novel infectious agent and disease followed by declaring a pandemic; (4) declaring the origin of the virus; (5) clinical trials on treatment options (Fig. 3.2).

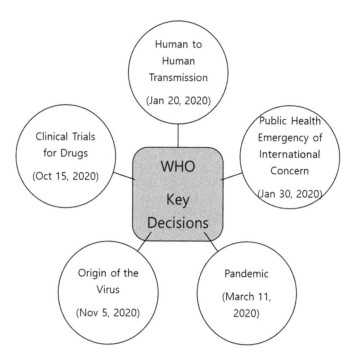

Fig. 3.2   A Diagram of Key Decisions of the WHO

3.1   Declaring a Human-to-Human Transmission

A timeline of the WHO's responses is presented in Table 3.3, as summarized by the WHO itself (WHO 2020c). According to the WHO's timeline of events, it was first informed of the COVID-19 on the last day of 2019, that is, December 31, 2019. It was a website statement from the Wuhan Municipal Health Commission. For over three months since the first information, the infectious disease was called colloquially Wuhan viral pneumonia originated from Wuhan city in the Hubei Province of China.

On January 3, 2020, Chinese officials provided to the WHO information on the cluster of cases of "viral pneumonia of unknown cause" identified in Wuhan. On as early as January 9, 2020, the WHO reported that Chinese authorities have determined that the outbreak is caused by a novel coronavirus. It is notable that Chinese officials were able to switch the identity of the new disease from viral pneumonia to coronavirus in a span of only ten days. On as early as January 11, 2020, Chinese officials provided the genetic sequence of the virus to the WHO (Bloomberg 2021).

The timeline of the outbreak reported by the WHO is at odds with the examination of the blood samples collected by the American Red Cross and other agencies well before the first report by the Chinese officials. The study of the blood samples reveals that the virus was present in the US as early as December 13–16 in 2019 or even as early as September 2019 in Europe (Basavaraju et al. 2020).

More controversially, the WHO stated on January 14, 2020, that preliminary investigations by the Chinese authorities had found "no clear evidence of human-to-human transmission." Even a week later, the WHO tweeted only meekly that there was "at least some human-to-human transmission" (WHO 2020c).

It is rather odd that these statements came even well after Chinese officials confirmed that the disease was caused by a novel coronavirus on January 9, 2020. Even more suspicious to the world citizens is that these statements were made even though the WHO experts were well aware of the coronavirus experiments that had been undertaken at the Wuhan Virology Laboratory, as then CDC Director Robert Redfield confirms (Reuters 2021).

The WHO has been broadly criticized for making these eventually false statements (Fox News 2020a). In looking back at the scale of the damage the virus has inflicted on the people of the planet, many will feel that the WHO did not live up to its mission, which is expected by world citizens,

Table 3.3   The COVID-19 timeline of the WHO

Date	Key decisions	Events
December 31, 2019	First report	The WHO's Country Office in China picked up a media statement by the Wuhan Municipal Health Commission from their website on cases of "viral pneumonia" in Wuhan, China.
January 1, 2020		The WHO requested information on the reported cluster of atypical pneumonia cases in Wuhan. The WHO activated its Incident Management Support Team.
January 2, 2020		The WHO informed Global Outbreak Alert and Response Network (GOARN) partners.
January 3, 2020		Chinese officials provided information to the WHO on the cluster of cases of "viral pneumonia of unknown cause" identified in Wuhan.
January 5, 2020		The WHO shared detailed information about a cluster of cases of pneumonia of unknown cause through the International Health Regulations (IHR) Event Information System, which is accessible to all member states. The WHO also issued its first Disease Outbreak News report.
January 9, 2020	Infectious agent	The WHO reported that Chinese authorities have determined that the outbreak is caused by a novel coronavirus.
January 10–12, 2020		The WHO published a comprehensive package of guidance documents for countries.
January 11, 2020	Genetic sequence	The WHO tweeted that it had received the genetic sequences for the novel coronavirus from China. Chinese media reported the first death.
January 13, 2020		The Ministry of Public Health in Thailand reported the first recorded case outside China.
January 14, 2020	Human-to-human transmission	After a press briefing, the WHO tweeted that preliminary investigations by the Chinese authorities had found "no clear evidence of human-to-human transmission."
January 20–21, 2020		The WHO conducted the first mission to Wuhan. WHO/ WPRO tweeted that it was now very clear from the latest information that there was "at least some human-to-human transmission."
January 21, 2020		The US reported its first confirmed case.
January 22–23, 2020		The WHO Director-General convened an IHR Emergency Committee (EC) regarding the outbreak of a novel coronavirus.
January 27–28, 2020		The Director-General met with President Xi Jinping on January 28.

(*continued*)

Table 3.3 (continued)

Date	Key decisions	Events
January 30, 2020	PHEIC	The Director-General accepted the EC's advice and declared the novel coronavirus outbreak a public health emergency of international concern (PHEIC).
January 31, 2020		The US imposed travel restrictions from China.
February 11, 2020	Name	WHO announced that the disease caused by the novel coronavirus would be named COVID-19.
March 7, 2020		The number of confirmed COVID-19 cases surpasses 100, 000 globally.
March 11, 2020	Pandemic declaration	The WHO declares COVID-19 as a pandemic.
March 18, 2020	Clinical trials	The WHO and partners launched the Solidarity trial, an international clinical trial that aims to generate robust data from around the world to find the most effective treatments for COVID-19.
March 19, 2020		For the first time, China reported zero local infections.
March 24, 2020		The Tokyo Olympics was delayed until 2021.
April 2, 2020		The WHO reported evidence of transmission from symptomatic, pre-symptomatic, and asymptomatic people infected with COVID-19.
April 4, 2020		The WHO reported that over 1 million cases of COVID-19 had been confirmed worldwide.
June 17, 2020		The WHO announced that the hydroxychloroquine arm of the Solidarity Trial to find an effective COVID-19 treatment was being stopped.
October 15, 2020		The WHO announced conclusive evidence on the effectiveness of repurposed drugs for COVID-19. Interim results from the Solidarity Trial indicated that remdesivir, hydroxychloroquine, lopinavir/ritonavir, and interferon regimens appeared to have little or no effect on 28-day mortality or the in-hospital course of COVID-19 among hospitalized patients.
November 5, 2020	Origin	The WHO published terms of reference for the WHO-convened Global Study of the Origins of SARS-CoV-2.
January 14, 2021		The WHO-China joint mission enters China.
February 12, 2021		The WHO-China joint mission held a press conference on the investigation of the origin of the novel coronavirus.

to warn the world of a big health crisis such as the COVID-19 well ahead of time.

It appears that the Chinese government was far better aware of the danger of the virus. It appeared to lock down domestic travels as early as the end of January, according to a traffic data. Notwithstanding, it continued to push its citizens to travel internationally (The Economic Times 2020). In retrospect, the WHO failed to pick up these vital signals swiftly enough for the global citizens.

3.2   Declaring a Public Health Emergency of International Concern

The WHO decision that prompted an immediate response from national governments was the declaration of a public health emergency of international concern (PHEIC). On January 30, 2020, the WHO Director-General declared the COVID-19 as a PHEIC and the US government immediately followed up with an imposition of travel suspension from China on January 31, 2020 (White House 2020a).

Earlier on January 22, 2020, the Director-General, Tedros Adhanom Ghebreyesus, convened an International Health Regulations (IHR) Emergency Committee (EC) whose mission was to advise the Director-General on whether the coronavirus outbreak should be called a PHEIC. The EC was not able to reach a conclusion on that day.

The Director-General met with China's President on January 28, 2020. Soon afterward, the EC advised the coronavirus outbreak met the criteria for a PHEIC. He then declared a PHEIC on January 30, 2020. According to the WHO timeline, there were 98 cases at that time in 18 countries, but no deaths outside China.

The series of events that preceded the declaration reveals the EC's critical role in the pandemic responses of the WHO as well as that of the IHR. The IHR is an important international health treaty which the present author will come back to explain in Sect. 5 of this chapter. That the PHEIC declaration followed the Director-General's meeting with China's President, that is, not preceded it, will remain a source of discomfort for many observers who are concerned about the independence of the WHO.

The IHR Emergency Committee held two meetings on January 22–23 and January 30, 2020. The EC consists of 15 members, each of whom represents each country. The EC's composition appears similar to that of the United Nations Security Council (UNSC), consisting of five permanent members and ten non-permanent members. The EC members include an expert from the US, China, Russia, France, and the UK, as well as from Japan, India, Cameroon, South Africa, Thailand, Saudi Arabia, and Pakistan, respectively.

The IHR EC's composition raises the question of whether the EC is well-deigned to make a rapid decision that is called for at the time of a global pandemic outbreak. In a similar manner to the UN Security Council's decisions in numerous military crises, the EC's decisions will be hampered, to some degree, by competing national interests of the member countries. That is, some countries may want to declare an international public health emergency while other countries may oppose it.

At the time of this writing as of July 2021, we do not know which members of the Emergency Committee supported a PHEIC declaration on the January 22–23 meeting and which members opposed it. We do not know whether all members opposed a declaration on that meeting.

Considering these limitations in the EC decision-making, it can be suggested that each member's decision on the PHEIC declaration be made public, so that the global public is aware of the split decisions. It would give national policy-makers an opportunity to evaluate individual members' decisions and act on them, that is, without waiting for a unanimous decision. Again, this process is similar to that of the UN Security Council.

3.3   Nomenclature and Declaring a Pandemic

The next key decisions of the WHO are a determination of the disease's name and a declaration of a pandemic. As noted above, because the first case was reported from Wuhan, China, and the first community spread occurred there, the disease was called "Wuhan pneumonia" across the world during the first several months of 2020.

On February 11, 2020, the WHO announced that the infectious disease caused by a novel coronavirus be named COVID-19. The COVID-19 is an abbreviation for the Corona Virus Disease of 2019. Before the formal nomenclature, the disease was also informally referred to as "2019 novel coronavirus" or "2019-nCOV."

The WHO did not denominate the disease a Wuhan coronavirus, or a Chinese coronavirus, or a Chinese pandemic. This nomenclature can be contrasted with the 1918 flu pandemic, the deadliest pandemic in history which is estimated to have killed 50 million people globally and infected a third of the global population. The pandemic is named the 1918 H1N1 virus pandemic or the 1918 Influenza pandemic. However, it has been known more commonly to the world as Spanish Flu, despite the place of origin of the pandemic is still hard to determine (Potter 2001).

On March 11, 2020, the WHO determined that the COVID-19 should be characterized as a pandemic. Just several days earlier, on March 7, 2020, the number of cases surpassed 100,000 globally. As explained in Chap. 2, an infectious disease is categorized, based on the spatial scope of contagion and the speed of transmission, into one of the following four: an outbreak, an endemic, an epidemic, and a pandemic (CDC 2012). Of the four, a pandemic is defined to be a worldwide spread of an infectious disease. A pandemic, unlike a globally spreading seasonal flu whose victims are mostly the elderly, tends to result in the deaths of a large number of non-elderly people as well.

The declaration of a pandemic is a threshold event for several reasons. First, it gives the WHO the authority and responsibility in dealing with the infectious disease. Specifically, under the treaty of the International Health Regulations, a pandemic declaration gives the WHO justifications to act "to prevent, protect against, control, and provide a public health response to the international spread of disease" (WHO 2015).

Equally importantly, the pandemic designation means that national governments across the globe will take immediate national policy actions on the basis of the WHO's declaration. Especially, many national policy measures that are unimaginable in normal times of the democratic society would be enforced by national policy-makers on the justification of the WHO's pandemic designation. Such measures, which is the main topic of Chap. 4, include travel restrictions from certain countries, a universal mask mandate, prohibiting a social group gathering, locking down a nation, ordering business closures, forcing school closures, banning an in-person religious gathering.

Immediate consequences of the WHO's key decisions on national policy decisions are illustrated in Fig. 3.3, drawing from the US responses. The declaration of a public health emergency of international concern by the WHO on January 30, 2020, is immediately followed by the US executive order on January 31, 2020, that suspends an entry from China (White House 2020a). The declaration of a pandemic on March 11, 2020, by the WHO is swiftly followed by the US declaration of a national emergency on

March 13, 2020, which is again followed by the recommendation of no social gathering of more than 10 people for 15 days, which is further followed by the invocation of the Defense Production Act (DPA) on March 18, 2020 (White House 2020b, c).

3.4 Etiology: Origin of the SARS-CoV-2

During the first wave in 2020, the disease was widely called a Wuhan pneumonia or a Wuhan virus originating from Wuhan city of Hubei Province in China. However, as of July 2021 more than 18 months after the virus outbreak, the WHO is not able to declare the origin of the virus. As of the middle of July 2021, the WHO's website simply notes that the organization learned the virus for the first time from a Chinese report (WHO 2020d):

> COVID-19 is the disease caused by a new coronavirus called SARS-CoV-2. WHO first learned of this new virus on 31 December 2019, following a report of a cluster of cases of 'viral pneumonia' in Wuhan, People's Republic of China.

The WHO published on November 5, 2020, the terms of references for the WHO-convened global study for the origins of SARS-CoV-2 (WHO 2020f). However, the WHO experts had not been allowed to enter China to investigate the origin of the novel coronavirus through the end of 2020, which prompted a public criticism of China by the WHO on January 6, 2021 (WSJ 2021). The WHO team entered China on January 14, 2021, but it remained unclear whether they would be permitted to travel to Wuhan, what activities they would be conducting, and especially whether they would be able to directly interview initial patients from Wuhan city and Wuhan Virology Laboratory.

In the meantime, the US State Department released a statement on January 16, 2021, that it has the "reason to believe" that the novel coronavirus was originated from the Wuhan Virology Laboratory while two researchers, experimenting on the coronavirus from a bat, fell sick in the fall 2019 with the symptoms consistent with the COVID-19 (Fox News 2020b). The laboratory leak possibility is also supported by, among many scientists, then CDC Director Dr. Redfield who is a virologist (Reuters 2021).

On the other hand, the joint WHO-China mission to investigate the origin of the virus held a press conference in early February 2021, which

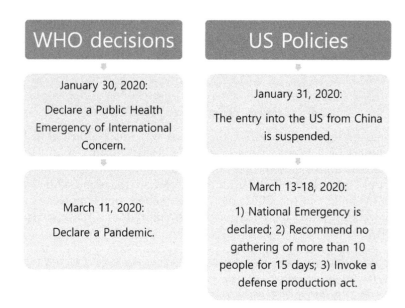

Fig. 3.3 The effects of the WHO key decisions on national policies

dismissed the laboratory leak as "extremely unlikely." It presented four hypotheses (WHO 2021a). The first hypothesis is that the virus jumped directly from an animal species to humans. The animal species under investigation is a horseshoe bat (Wacharapluesadee et al. 2020; Murakami et al. 2020). The second hypothesis is another animal origin hypothesis that the virus jumped to one animal species, then to another intermediary species, and then to humans. The intermediary species, however, has not been found despite an extensive search. The third hypothesis is a food chain origin hypothesis. The fourth is the accidental laboratory leak hypothesis.

As of mid-July of 2021, the WHO is not able to determine the place of origin of the SARS-CoV-2. That some members of the WHO-China joint mission had been participating in the coronavirus research at the Wuhan Virology Institute right before the pandemic outbreak adds a mystery to the etiology of the virus. The present author will revisit the original question in Chap. 9 where some unresolved questions about the pandemic are reviewed.

3.5   Solidarity Trial for Repurposed Drugs

The WHO along with its partners around the world has conducted clinical trials for potential COVID-19 treatments, named the Solidarity Trial. Based on the results, the WHO made recommendations to the member countries on the effectiveness of the treatment options that underwent the WHO trials. Because these recommendations had significantly influenced individual member nations' policy decisions during 2020, the present author reviews the Solidarity Trial as one of the five functions of the WHO.

According to the organization's description, the Solidarity Trial enrolled 12,000 patients in 500 hospital sites in over 30 countries. The four repurposed drugs that were under trials are remdesivir, hydroxychloroquine, lopinavir/ritonavir, and interferon regimens. Although these drugs were originally developed for other diseases, many local doctors who had to treat patients with the COVID-19 reported that they found them to be effective. The WHO trials evaluated these four potential COVID-19 drugs on three measures: mortality, need for assisted ventilation, and duration of hospital stay. For each drug, the trials compared the effects of the drug with the effects of a standard care (WHO 2020g).

On June 17, 2020, the WHO announced that they stopped the further trials on the hydroxychloroquine due to no observed effects of the drug. On October 15, 2020, it further announced the "conclusive evidence" against the effectiveness of all four drugs. To be specific, it reported that the four repurposed drugs "appeared to have little or no effect on 28-day mortality or the in-hospital course of COVID-19 among hospitalized patients" (WHO 2020g).

The clinical trials by the WHO and its partners may have had significant effects on national governments' policy decisions as well as on local hospital decisions concerning COVID-19 patients, although the present author cannot yet provide the empirical evidence of these effects through the national-level or hospital-level data. In fact, before the announcements by the WHO on June 17 and October 15, 2020, many COVID-19 patients had opted to try one of these repurposed drugs, some of whom successfully recovered from the COVID-19 and appeared on the media recommending the drug.

The reason that these four drugs had been considered a potential COVID-19 treatment option was because of the "observed effects" reported by local hospitals and doctors. These positive effects were not supported by the WHO's solidarity trial, argued to be the largest international randomized clinical trial (Ghazy et al. 2020). By the end of May 2021, however, a group of researchers reported that "increased doses of co-administered HCQ (hydroxychloroquine) and AZM (azithromycin) were associated with >100% increase in survival" (Smith et al. 2021).

4   NATIONAL RESPONSES VERSUS THE WHO

Having reviewed the global governance for the pandemics and the key decisions made by the WHO in the preceding chapters, we are now well-positioned to address the core economic questions regarding the global governance system for the pandemic risk management. The first is whether national policy responses or the global governance body's decisions should be the leading force in responding to a worldwide pandemic.

Let me clarify the last sentence. For a pandemic being a global public good, we might be easily led to believe that a global governance body such as the WHO should be the central place where global policy responses to the pandemic are designed and implemented. For comparison, the United Nations Framework Convention on Climate Change (UNFCCC) coordinates and makes a global climate treaty with which each member nation is forced to comply by fulfilling her responsibilities. Consider the Kyoto Protocol or the Paris Agreement (UNFCCC 2015)!

An observer who has closely followed the responses of individual nations during the COVID-19 pandemic might have been quite surprised. Nearly all policy measures and responses to the pandemic were actively designed at the national level by a national control center. Nations did not wait a minute for a global pandemic treaty, nor a globally uniform decision, nor global cooperation. Each nation was on its own in combatting the pandemic.

In the next chapter, a detailed exposition will be given on the governmental and national responses. A series of key decisions were swiftly made by national governments without any intervention from the global body, including travel suspension, a universal mask mandate, an emergency production order, a lockdown order; a business closure, a school closure, economic relief programs, emergency approvals for treatments, and vaccine developments.

All of these decisions were made independently and in urgency by national governments across the planet. To act, there needed no treaty signed by all the governments of the world, nor the rules set by the United Nations or the WHO. As soon as each nation faced a confirmed case of the

COVID-19, it rushed to designate a national response center from which all of the above decisions ensued promptly. The set of response strategies employed by one nation was not the same as that employed by the other nations.

As discussed in the preceding section, the declaration of a public health emergency of international concern as well as the declaration of a pandemic by the WHO resulted in a swift response by the US government. These are the two decisions that distinguished the WHO from governmental decisions.

However, it is an overstatement to say that the WHO's two decisions were decisive for the national actions that followed. Rather, they appeared to assist the national actions in a secondary manner. Each nation has its own science networks as well as data gathering capacities, as such, kept close track of the Wuhan virus outbreak from the first report. A handful of nations may have been in a better position than the WHO in deciding a human-to-human transmission as well as a pandemic designation. The US decisions, for example, on travel suspension, a national emergency declaration, and a 15-day closedown before the end of March 2020 may have had as much influence on the responses of the other national governments as the WHO decisions had.

The central point to which the present author hopes to direct readers' attention is that when it comes to the COVID-19, policy and market responses to the global-scale public good needed neither a global-scale uniform policy response nor a global treaty. Each and every country took on the pandemic challenges to their nations on their own with minimal international coordination or intervention and in the best interests of their countries.

This observation would be sufficient to spark a curiosity of the researchers who are keen on the provisions of global-scale public goods. Is it possible at all to provide a globally shared good efficiently to the global community without any international cooperation? An answer to this question will have profound implications on the economics and policymaking regarding the entire basket of the globally shared goods and resources.

Take for example global climate change negotiations over the past three decades! The policy responses and negotiations on global warming over that time period by the international community have been starkly different from those to the COVID-19 pandemic just described. The former negotiations have concentrated with immense financial resources on ironing out a globally binding legal treaty, which has failed until now, while nations preferred to wait and see what the climate future holds for them (Nordhaus 2010; Seo 2017).

The global pandemic responses, which we all have witnessed up until now, anchored at and initiated with urgency by the national-level responses, are sufficient to shed a refreshing light on the global community's collective efforts on global warming and many other globally shared goods.

5   IS A GLOBAL PANDEMIC TREATY NEEDED?

Why are the efforts to provide a global-scale public good, that is, a pandemic control, not approached via a globally coordinated action or a global treaty? Should a global pandemic treaty be in place in preparation for future pandemics, as world leaders, including the Head of the WHO, recently called for (WHO 2021b)?

To answer this question, let's start with the fact that a global pandemic is a globally shared public good. By definition by the WHO, a pandemic is a worldwide spread of an infectious disease. As such, if a pandemic is declared, then the pandemic pathogen would be present in most places of the planet and be well ready to be transmitted to all people. In reality, not all the pandemics declared by the WHO were of the same magnitude in terms of a spatial scope or health consequences. For the simplicity of arguments, let's assume that the pandemic under examination is affecting all places on the planet and at a scale of the COVID-19 pandemic.

As clarified in Chap. 2, a public good is defined as a collective consumption good (Samuelson 1954). As for a pure public good, it is non-excludable as well as non-rivalrous. In the context of the COVID-19 pandemic, the non-rivalry is easy to understand. Even if a person gets infected by the virus, it does not decrease the possibility that other persons contract the virus. The non-excludability is also apparent. It is very difficult or costly to exclude someone from the pandemic infection.

Having said that, it is also easy to grasp that there is some degree of excludability in more than one aspect of the pandemic experience (Buchanan 1965). To allude to these, a person can live free of pandemic infection through a secluded living environment like a hermit or with an extensive precise testing facility at the gates of her/his residence like a very wealthy family.

In Chap. 2, it is also explained that of the range of public goods, a pandemic, as well as an infectious disease, has a distinct production technology, that is, a weakest-link technology (Nordhaus 2006). Stated simply, this means that the provision of a pandemic's end cannot be accomplished as long as there is a weakest link, that is, the community where the virus is still circulating. It will easily and rapidly spread to other places and regions, making earlier efforts futile.

However, if a highly effective vaccine can be produced for any pandemic, the weakest-link production function loses some of its applicability to pandemics. With the vaccine possibility, the pandemic can effectively be ended within a single nation by the herd immunity obtained from the vaccine shots given to the people in the nation. Therefore, this country can end the pandemic through vaccine shots coupled with selective travel restrictions from the countries where the virus continues to be spreading.

Before addressing the question posed at the top of this section, which is a question of grave concern by the international community, the present author needs to clarify the current treaty in place for global pandemic matters. As surveyed above, the WHO is a United Nations specialized agency, legally independent and established through a separate international treaty (UN 1948). Specifically, the International Health Regulations, a treaty signed in 1969 and last amended in 2005, gives the WHO a legally binding authority over 196 member nations to act as a global governance entity on international spread of diseases. The IHR aims for international collaboration to "prevent, protect against, control, and provide a public health response to the international spread of disease in ways that are commensurate with and restricted to public health risks" considering international traffic and trade. The IHR provides "an overarching legal framework that defines countries' rights and obligations" in health events that may cross national borders such as pandemics (WHO 2015).

After the COVID-19 outbreak, it was the IHR Emergency Committee (EC) that made a decision on a human-to-human transmission of the SARS-CoV-2 virus as well as a declaration of a public health emergency of international concern (PHEIC). The IHR had six meetings since the outbreak of the COVID-19, as of January 20, 2021 (WHO 2020e).

Therefore, the WHO, under the IHR treaty, is set up as a global governance entity in pandemic matters and other cross-border infectious diseases. However, the IHR is not a stringent global treaty, that is, does impose little restrictions on members' activities. Specifically, the IHR regulations are limited to a declaration of a public health emergency of international concern, national IHR focal points, and travelers' rights (WHO 2015).

Back now to the main question, despite possessing the afore-described characteristics of a globally shared (public) good, a global pandemic comes to have several unique features that push individual nations to pursue their own path in dealing with the pandemic, making decentralized provisions more realistic.

The first feature is a backstop solution. An effective vaccine offers the only route to end a global pandemic. Without effective vaccine, herd immunity is nearly impossible to achieve. The science of vaccines, on the other hand, is well established and has long been advanced to the level of high practicality (Plotkin 2009; Pardi et al. 2018). That countries expect that a vaccine will soon provide a backstop to the global pandemic gives individual nations no good reasons to put huge resources and time into ironing out a worldwide coordinated set of actions.

From the opposite point of view, without a high possibility of the vaccine backstop, individual countries should keep track of each other's disease control efforts closely in order to minimize the damage from the pandemic which is certain to last many years, if not a decade. More importantly, individual countries will also be forced to forge an international treaty that specifies, *inter alia*, each member country's responsibilities, penalties when they are violated, and monitoring of each other's efforts.

In the scenario where there is no vaccine feasible in a global pandemic, a provision of the globally shared public good, that is, an end to the global pandemic, should take a globally coordinated policy approach. Each country's efforts should add up while non-participant in the global effort should be sanctioned. Notice the similarity to the climate change policy negotiations: each country's emissions reduction should add up (Nordhaus 2010; Seo 2017).

Consider the 1918 Influenza pandemic, more commonly, Spanish Flu. An effective vaccine against the H1N1 virus was not available at that time. Without a vaccine, a globally coordinated effort, for example, via a treaty, could have made big differences in global health outcomes such as mortality. To make things worse, the world was in the middle of one of the deadliest military conflicts, World War I. For fear of harming the morale of a country at war, individual governments did not report accurately on the pandemic, let alone pushing for global cooperation or a global treaty. A confluence of these factors resulted in the deadliest pandemic in humanity (Potter 2001).

The second feature is excludability, which was alluded in the above. Once the pandemic is in full swing, individual countries have no choice but to close the border entries or, if not, severely tighten border entry requirements. In a normal world without a pandemic, such restrictions would violate international laws (WHO 2015). A pandemic declaration by the WHO would make the border closing a rational decision to any government. As of January 2021, nearly all countries on the planet imposed at least some border restrictions. The most severe one is to prevent all foreigners from entering the country. A less severe one is to require every entrant to the nation to present a negative COVID-19 test result and undergo a two-week self-quarantine.

That an individual country can exclude, that is, block international visitors from the entry into the country without violating international laws forces them to concentrate on a nationally determined set of measures and guidelines instead of pushing for a global policy treaty or cooperation.

For comparison, consider the carbon dioxide problem in global climate challenges. Once a ton of carbon dioxide is released from a power plant in one country, it is not possible to exclude some countries from the effects of the released ton of carbon dioxide. This is because the carbon dioxide molecule is a quickly mixing compound in the atmosphere, leveling the global carbon dioxide concentration immediately (IPCC 1990). Colloquially speaking, no country can stop the carbon dioxide compound from crossing its border in the sky.

Unlike the climate change problem, the pandemic problem permits individual countries a rather high level of excludability. A country can suspend the travels from other countries and require entrants a proof of no virus. This feature is especially pertinent at a final stage of the pandemic. That is, when most countries on the planet are successful in stopping the pandemic virus transmissions, the successful countries may block the travelers from the countries that are still unable to contain the virus.

The third feature is disparate impacts of a global pandemic across the nations. Even a global-scale pandemic is likely to hurt some subgroups of the world population more severely than others. During the COVID-19 pandemic, many European countries and North American countries were the most severely hurt from the pandemic during 2020, that is, before the vaccine creations, in terms of the number of cases, the number of mortalities, and mortality rate (ECDPC 2020). From around March 2021, the most impacted countries appeared to be shifting to India, Brazil, and South Africa owing to differing vaccination rates across the countries (JHU 2021).

The differential impacts from a pandemic virus across the nations can arise because of a number of factors. The first is a physiological factor. For example, some races may turn out to be more vulnerable to a certain pandemic, for example, White people versus Asian people. Second, they could arise from the medical history. For example, some groups may have suffered from a certain disease, for example, pneumonia, for a long time, because of which they have extensive medical facilities and resources to treat the pandemic disease that attacks human lungs. Third is a climate factor. For example, African countries suffered the least from the COVID-19 pandemic. Fourth is a geographical factor. Island nations and the nations farther away from the origin of the pandemic could better cope with the pandemic.

The expected disparity in the pandemic's impact across the nations renders reasons to individual nations to carve out their own strategy in responding to the pandemic. Individual nations are forced to carefully consider the variations in the importance of the physiological, medical, climate, and geographical factors in order to best address the pandemic.

6   Key Conclusions

From the exposition of this chapter, several key conclusions can be drawn out with regard to global governance and, in particular, the WHO in the pandemic responses of the planet. The first is that there is no global governance system set up to address a global pandemic. The IHR renders some degree of authority to the WHO in the global pandemic responses, but the WHO's roles are severely limited to several decisions such as a declaration of a pandemic.

The second conclusion is that the WHO, although it is the primary global governance body during the pandemic, is the institution set up to enhance global health, that is, the best possible level of health for all peoples on the planet, as such, is not a global governance institution established for global pandemics exclusively. As seen in the biennial budget allocations of the WHO, the WHO budget allocated to health emergencies accounts for only 10–20% of its total budget.

Third, because the IHR Emergency Committee is structured as a representation of the world powers, it resembles and acts like the United Nations' Security Council in which opposing geopolitical interests collide and often hinders a rapid decision-making needed during the pandemic outbreaks.

Fourth, it is observed that effective responses to the global pandemic, despite being a globally shared public good, are not coordinated by a global treaty or globally coordinated policy efforts. On the contrary, individual nations are forced to respond urgently and initiate their own unique response strategies. This is the most crucial conclusion of this chapter on global governance. Put differently, a provision of the globally shared good is undertaken predominantly by private actors, that is, individual countries in this context.

Fifth, a rationale for such decentralized decisions and actions can be given by three salient features of the pandemics: a high possibility of a backstop option through an effective vaccine, a high degree of excludability, and disparate impacts of a pandemic across the countries.

The key conclusions thus far summarized can be meaningfully interpreted in comparison with the economics of climate change. Despite being a globally shared good, global climate policy-making has failed to agree on a globally coordinated action plan or a global treaty. In designing responses to climate change, there are many reasons that individual countries should heed the response strategies that are in the nation's best interests that simultaneously provide a part of the global solution (Seo 2017, 2020).

This completes the first of the five pandemic analyses, Pandemic Analysis I, presented in this book.

References

Basavaraju, Sridhar V., Monica E. Patton, Kacie Grimm, et al. 2020. Serologic Testing of US Blood Donations to Identify Severe Acute Respiratory Syndrome Coronavirus 2 (SARS-CoV-2)–Reactive Antibodies: December 2019–January 2020. *Clinical Infectious Diseases* 72: e1004–e1009. https://doi.org/10.1093/cid/ciaa1785.

Bloomberg. 2021. U.S. Confirms Removal of Wuhan Virus Sequences from Database. Published on June 24, 2021. https://www.bloomberg.com/news/articles/2021-06-24/u-s-confirms-removal-of-wuhan-virus-sequences-from-database.

Buchanan, James M. 1965. An Economic Theory of Clubs. *Economica* 32: 1–24.

Centers for Disease Control and Prevention (CDC). 2012. *Principles of Epidemiology in Public Health Practice (Third Edition): An Introduction to Applied Epidemiology and Biostatistics.* Atlanta, GA: The CDC.

Coleman, C.M., and M.B. Frieman. 2014. Coronaviruses: Important Emerging Human Pathogens. *Journal of Virology* 8: 5209–5212.

European Centre for Disease Prevention and Control (ECDPC). 2020. COVID19 Coronavirus Dataset. ECDPC, Solna Municipality, Sweden. https://data. europa.eu/euodp/en/data/dataset/covid-19-coronavirus-data.

Fox News. 2020a. WHO haunted by January tweet saying China found no human transmission of coronavirus. Published on March 18, 2020. https://www. foxnews.com/world/world-health-organization-january-tweet-china-human-transmission-coronavirus.

———. 2020b. State Department drops 'previously undisclosed' info on Wuhan Lab. https://video.foxnews.com/v/6223384424001#sp=show-clips.

Ghazy, R.M., A. Almaghraby, R. Shaaban, et al. 2020. A Systematic Review and Meta-analysis on Chloroquine and Hydroxychloroquine as Monotherapy or Combined with Azithromycin in COVID-19 Treatment. *Scientific Reports* 10: 22139. https://doi.org/10.1038/s41598-020-77748-x.

Intergovernmental Panel on Climate Change (IPCC). 1990. *Climate Change: The IPCC Scientific Assessment*. Cambridge, UK: Cambridge University Press.

Johns Hopkins University (JHU). 2021. *COVID-19 Dash Board*. Baltimore, MD: JHU. https://data.humdata.org/dataset/novel-coronavirus-2019-ncov-cases.

Murakami, Shin, Tomoya Kitamura, Jin Suzuki, et al. 2020. Detection and Characterization of Bat Sarbecovirus Phylogenetically Related to SARS-CoV-2. *Japan. Emerging Infectious Diseases* 26 (12): 3025–3029. https://doi. org/10.3201/eid2612.203386.

Nordhaus, William D. 2006. Paul Samuelson and Global Public Goods. In *Samuelsonian Economics and the Twenty-First Century*, ed. M. Szenberg, L. Ramrattan, and A.A. Gottesman. Oxford Scholarship Online.

———. 2010. Economic Aspects of Global Warming in a Post-Copenhagen Environment. *Proceedings of the National Academy of Sciences USA* 107 (26): 11721–11726.

———. 2015. Climate Clubs: Overcoming Free-riding in International Climate Policy. *American Economic Review* 105: 1339–1370.

Pardi, N., M.J. Hogan, F.W. Porter, and D. Weissman. 2018. mRNA Vaccines—A New Era in Vaccinology. *Nature Reviews Drug Discovery* 17: 261–279.

Plotkin, S.A. 2009. Vaccines: The Fourth Century. *Clinical and Vaccine Immunology* 16: 1709–1719.

Potter, C.W. 2001. A History of Influenza. *Journal of Applied Microbiology* 91 (4): 572–579.

Reuters. 2021. Former CDC Chief Redfield Says He Thinks COVID-19 Originated in a Chinese Lab. Published on March 27, 2021. https://www. reuters.com/article/us-health-coronavirus-origin-redfield-idUSKBN2BI2R6.

Samuelson, Paul. 1954. The Pure Theory of Public Expenditure. *Review of Economics and Statistics* 36: 387–389.

Seo, S. Niggol. 2012. What Eludes Global Agreements on Climate Change? *Economic Affairs* 32: 73–79.

———. 2017. Negotiating a Global Public Good: Lessons from Global Warming Conferences and Future Directions. In *The Behavioral Economics of Climate Change: Adaptation Behaviors, Global Public Goods, Breakthrough Technologies, and Policy-making*, ed. S. Niggol Seo. Amsterdam, NL: Academic Press.

———. 2020. *The Economics of Globally Shared and Public Goods*. Amsterdam, NL: Academic Press.

Smith, Leon G., Nicolas Mendoza, David Dobesh, and Stephen M. Smith. 2021. Observational Study on 255 Mechanically Ventilated COVID Patients at the Beginning of the USA Pandemic. *MedRxiv*. Published on May 31, 2021. https://doi.org/10.1101/2021.05.28.21258012.

The Economic Times. 2020. How China Locked Down Internally for COVID-19, But Pushed Foreign Travel. Published on April 30, 2020. https://economic-times.indiatimes.com/blogs/Whathappensif/how-china-locked-down-internally-for-COVID-19-but-pushed-foreign-travel/.

United Nations (UN). 1945. *Charter of the United Nations and Statue of the International Court of Justice*. San Francisco, CA: UN.

———. 1948. *Constitution of the World Health Organization*. New York, NY: UN.

United Nations Framework Convention on Climate Change (UNFCCC). 1992. *United Nations Framework Convention on Climate Change*. New York, NY: UN.

———. 2015. *The Paris Agreement. Conference of the Parties (COP) 21*. New York, NY: UNFCCC.

United Nations System Chief Executive Board (UNSCEB). 2018. *UN System*. New York, NY: UN. http://www.unsceb.org/directory.

Wacharapluesadee, S., C.W. Tan, P. Maneeorn, et al. 2020. Evidence for SARS-CoV-2 Related Coronaviruses Circulating in Bats and Pangolins in Southeast Asia. *Nature Communications* 12: 972. https://doi.org/10.1038/s41467-021-21240-1.

Wall Street Journal (WSJ). 2021. WHO Criticizes China for Stymying Investigation Into COVID-19 Origins. Published on January 6, 2021. https://www.wsj.com/articles/world-health-organization-criticizes-china-over-delays-in-COVID-19-probe-11609883140.

Weiss, Susan R. 2020. Forty Years with Coronaviruses. *Journal of Experimental Medicine* 217 (5): e20200537. https://doi.org/10.1084/jem.20200537.

White House. 2020a. *Proclamation on Suspension of Entry as Immigrants and Nonimmigrants of Persons who Pose a Risk of Transmitting 2019 Novel Coronavirus*. Washington, DC: White House.

———. 2020b. 30 Days to Slow the Spread. Published on March 16, 2020. https://www.whitehouse.gov/wp-content/uploads/2020/03/03.16.20_coronavirus-guidance_8.5x11_315PM.pdf

———. 2020c. *How President Trump Uses the Defense Production Act to Protect America from the China Virus*. Washington, DC: Office of Trade and Manufacturing Policy.

World Health Organization (WHO). 2015. *International Health Regulations.* Geneva, CH: WHO.

———. 2018. *WHO Releases 2018 Priority Diseases List.* Geneva, CH: WHO. https://ohsonline.com/articles/2018/02/15/who-releases-2018-priority-diseases-list.aspx?admgarea=news&m=1.

———. 2020a. *Milestones for Health over 70 Years.* Geneva, CH: WHO.

———. 2020b. *Structure.* Geneva, CH: WHO.

———. 2020c. *Timeline: WHO's COVID-19 Response.* Geneva, CH: WHO.

———. 2020d. Q&As on COVID-19 and Related Health Topics. https://www.who.int/emergencies/diseases/novel-coronavirus-2019/question-and-answers-hub.

———. 2020e. COVID-19 IHR Emergency Committee. https://www.who.int/groups/COVID-19-ihr-emergency-committee.

———. 2020f. WHO-convened Global Study of the Origins of SARS-CoV-2: Terms of References for the China Part. https://www.who.int/publications/m/item/who-convened-global-study-of-the-origins-of-sars-cov-2.

———. 2020g. Solidarity Clinical Trial for COVID-19 Treatments. https://www.who.int/emergencies/diseases/novel-coronavirus-2019/global-research-on-novel-coronavirus-2019-ncov/solidarity-clinical-trial-for-COVID-19-treatments.

———. 2021a. Global Leaders Unite in Urgent Call for International Pandemic Treaty. https://www.who.int/news/item/30-03-2021-global-leaders-unite-in-urgent-call-for-international-pandemic-treaty.

———. 2021b. Press Conference on February 12th, 2021. The joint World Health Organization-China Mission to Investigate the Origins of COVID-19. https://www.who.int/emergencies/diseases/novel-coronavirus-2019.

CHAPTER 4

Pandemic Analysis II: Governmental Actions During the Pandemic—Lockdown or No Lockdown?

1 Introduction to Governmental Actions During a Pandemic

Considering that a pandemic such as the COVID-19 is a public good on a global scale, it is anticipated that the governments, both federal and states, should play a key role in preventing, containing, and ending the pandemic. This was certainly the case during the spread of the COVID-19 pandemic, but people may have realized all of sudden once again that their governments wield too much control over their lives, especially so when a political power is at risk faced with the grave societal challenge.

To our dismay, nearly all governments around the globe were acting as if unprepared and shocked with a rapid spread of an infectious disease which is "invisible" and highly contagious. The governments anywhere appeared to make a rapid sequence of decisions contrary to the reasons that prevailed at normal times and often for the sake of self-defense of the political power in charge. Governments around the world, with a few notable exceptions, cracked down cold-heartedly on people's gatherings, business activities, religious services, school openings, and even created at the peak a mask police as well as a customer register at all shops. There was little, with a few notable exceptions, counterforce against the governmental orders (WSJ 2020a).

From another point of view, the governments were witnessed to make important contributions to the palette of responses to the coronavirus pandemic. In the US, the Defense Production Act (DPA) was invoked by then President Trump under which essential medical devices needed in urgency were ordered to be produced in a wartime mode. Ventilators, respirators, test kits, field hospitals, and medical treatments were manufactured under this invocation by major US companies that were called upon by the US government (White House 2020a, b). For another example, the Operation Warp Speed (OWS) put together the best pharmaceutical companies in the world and the public sector agencies effectively to successfully develop and distribute multiple highly effective vaccines in record time (USDHHS 2020a).

In retrospect of the first ten months of 2020, the COVID-19 pandemic exposed the governments that were unprepared against a global-scale pandemic as well as their penchant for a heavy-handed policy approach faced with a big risk. At the same time, the pandemic made clear to careful observers a series of key governmental decisions that has to be made in time and acted upon vigorously. This chapter will explain these key decisions and analyze their consequences on both health and economic outcomes relying on the empirical COVID-19 outcome data.

What are the government's key decisions that must be made? When an infectious disease is reported from anywhere on the Planet, the government should keep close eyes on it and determine whether it will become an epidemic and then a worldwide pandemic. At a right time, the government should decide whether to close a national border or not, especially to the travelers from the origin of the pandemic. At roughly the same time, the guidelines on physical distancing, social gathering, personal protective gears such as face masks, and testing should be provided to the public.

When the pandemic eventually hits the country and a fast rise in the number of infection cases is observed, it should determine whether it should order a stay-at-home order, a nationwide business closure, or a national lockdown. With such draconian orders determined to be needed and indeed issued, the government may have an obligation or be forced to financially assist the general public affected by such drastic measures that severely affect the economies of citizens by passing an economic relief bill through the Congress (USDOT 2020). Or alternatively, avoiding such drastic measures, the government may decide to pursue a more focused approach by directing its resources to the protection of the most vulnerable populations, for example, seniors at nursing homes and persons with comorbidity.

During the first wave of the pandemic, the demand for the personal protective equipment (PPE) such as face masks is sure to overwhelm the supply in the market, resulting in shortages of essential PPE goods. The same can happen to essential medical goods such as hospital beds, ventilators, respirators, nurses, doctors, and so on. In the US, the Defense Production Act of 1950, which was intended for a wartime emergency production, was invoked in order to address the supply shortages, calling upon major private sector companies, including General Motors, to produce these goods and devices fast and in large quantities (White House 2020a, b).

Another key decision of the government is to approve for emergency use potential treatment options for the pandemic infected. Since the pandemic is by definition new and not fully known by humanity, it is a painstaking process for medical experts to find an effective cure against the pandemic virus. No treatment is available at the time of a pandemic outbreak. A candidate treatment would be found at the hospitals that treated many pandemic patients and experienced deaths. Even some candidate treatments proposed by local doctors may eventually turn out to be controversial at a larger sample level and/or their effects may turn out to vary across individuals. The candidate treatments such as hydroxychloroquine, remdesivir, and regeneron should go through a governmental approval process, first for an emergency use approval, through a governmental agency such as the Food and Drug Administration (FDA) in the US (USFDA 2020a).

A pandemic may be wished by some people to go away in a natural manner, for example, owing to a high summer temperature, or to disappear naturally through herd immunity gained over time. These wishes will not and did not materialize during the COVID-19. Given this, the government which should be forced from all sides to end the pandemic would therefore pursue with all vigor and resources an effective vaccine. A development of such a vaccine is fundamentally a private sector's task, specifically, the laboratories of premier pharmaceutical companies and research centers in the world.

The government, however, plays an important role in the pursuit of an effective vaccine development. As observed during the COVID-19, the government can get started the vaccine development efforts by the private sector as fast as possible and get an effective vaccine developed as early as possible. The Operation Warp Speed by the US government proved to be a highly effective partnership between the private sector and the public sector (Gupta 2021).

In the ensuing sections, the present author provides a detailed analysis of each of the key decisions made by the US government during the COVID-19 pandemic. A timeline of the US governmental decisions is summarized in Table 4.1. The table focuses on the US federal government responses. State government level responses will also be explained when they need to be explained separately.

2   A BRIEF SUMMARY OF THE KEY DECISIONS BY THE US GOVERNMENT

Let's begin by briefly revisiting the timeline of the sequence of US governmental decisions actually made during the COVID-19 pandemic, summarized in Table 4.1, up to the first vaccine shot. After the first report of the novel coronavirus on December 31, 2019, from Wuhan city in China, the US reported the first confirmed case on January 21, 2020, and the first death on February 29, 2020. On January 30, the World Health Organization declared that the novel coronavirus is a public health emergency of international concern (PHEIC). The first real action by the US government, taken right after the WHO declaration, was to close the US border. To be specific, a travel suspension to and from China was issued on January 31, 2020 (White House 2020c).

On March 13, 2020, President Trump declared a national emergency. This was followed by the Center for Disease Control and Prevention (CDC) recommendations of no gathering of more than 50 people for eight weeks. On March 16, President Trump recommended no gathering in groups of more than 10 people and to avoid discretionary travels for 15 days (White House 2020d). Soon afterward, many states went into a statewide lockdown: California on March 19, New York on March 22, and Georgia on April 3.

On March 18, President Trump invoked the Defense Production Act, calling on major US companies to rapidly produce emergency goods and medical devices (USDHHS 2020b).

On March 27, The US Congress passed and the President signed the Coronavirus Aid, Relief, and Economic Security Act, the CARES Act in short, which provides US$2.2 trillion for economic relief and stimulus of the citizens and businesses (USDOT 2020).

On March 30, as part of the Operation Warp Speed program, US$456 million was provided to Johnson & Johnson for a vaccine development, which was followed by US$486 million funding to Moderna for the same on April 16. The OWS funding was given in the following weeks and months to AstraZeneca, Novavax, and Pfizer pharmaceutical companies for their candidate vaccines (USDHHS 2020a).

On November 9, Pfizer and BioNTech announced their success in the Phase III vaccine trials, which was followed by Moderna announcement a week later on November 16. Both companies reported around 90–95% effectiveness of their vaccines.

Table 4.1 A COVID-19 timeline of US governmental actions until the first vaccine shot

Date	US governmental actions
January 21, 2020	The US reported its first confirmed case of the novel coronavirus.
January 30, 2020	The Director-General accepted the Emergency Committee's (EC's) advice and declared the novel coronavirus outbreak a Public Health Emergency of International Concern (PHEIC).
January 31, 2020	The entry into the US from China is suspended.
February 11, 2020	The WHO announced that the disease caused by the novel coronavirus would be named COVID-19.
February 29, 2020	The US reported a death: a patient near Seattle had died from the coronavirus.
March 13, 2020	President Trump declared a national emergency, and said he was making $50 billion in federal funds available to states and territories to combat the coronavirus
March 15, 2020	The CDC recommended no gatherings of 50 or more people in the US for 8 weeks. The next day, President Trump urged the public to avoid discretionary travel and gathering of more than 10 people for 15 days.
March 18, 2020	Trump invokes the Defense Production Act.
March 19, 2020	California goes into a lockdown, followed by New York on March 22 and Georgia on April 3.
March 27, 2020	Trump signed a stimulus bill, the CARES Act, into law. Trump signed a $2.2 trillion measure.
March 30 and April 16, 2020	Operation Warp Speed: US$456 million in funds for the vaccine development by Johnson & Johnson; US$486 million for the vaccine by Moderna.
July 7, 2020	The Trump administration sent formal notice of US withdrawal from the WHO.
November 9, 2020	Pfizer and BioNTech announced its vaccine is 90% effective.
November 16, 2020	Moderna vaccine is 94.5% effective.
December 11, 2020	FDA approves emergency use authorization of the Pfizer vaccine.
December 14, 2020	A nurse in New York among the first to receive the vaccine shot.

On December 11, 2020, the FDA issued an emergency use authorization for the Pfizer vaccine. On December 14, 2020, a nurse in New York was among the first who received the first shot of the Pfizer vaccine (USFDA 2020c).

Based on the US governmental responses, the set of key decisions that has to be made by the government during the pandemic contagion is diagramed in Fig. 4.1. The first decision is whether the infectious disease reported somewhere in the world is a public health emergency of international concern. The second decision is whether the travels from the origin of the disease should be suspended. The third decision is on social measures such as physical distancing, a gathering of people, and a mask wearing: should these measures be made a mandate? The fourth decision is on the emergency productions of necessary medical devices. The fifth decision is whether the nation should go into a nationwide lockdown to stop a rapid spread of the virus or proceed with the focused protection of the most vulnerable populations. A national lockdown would be implemented in most cases in combination with business closures. The sixth is on economic relief: is it needed? If so, how much money should be allocated to

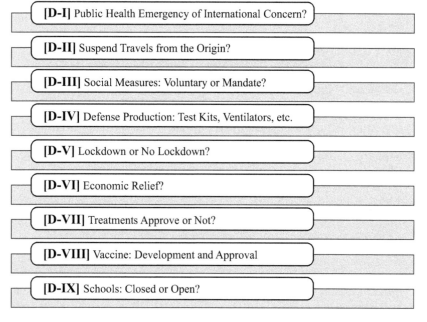

Fig. 4.1 A portfolio of key decisions by the government

whom? The seventh is the decision on the approval of emergency treatments. The eighth is regarding the development and approval of an effective vaccine. The ninth decision is on schools: should primary and secondary schools remain open or closed?

Each of these decisions should be made by the president, federal government, state governments, in concert with the Congress.

3 Decision I: Public Health Emergency of International Concern?

Once the outbreak of an infectious disease is reported from somewhere in the world, the first critical decision that should be made by the government is whether and when it will become a PHEIC. As discussed in detail in Chap. 3 and shown in Table 3.1, the Director-General of the WHO declared the PHEIC on January 30, 2020, following the recommendation by the International Health Regulations' (IHR's) Emergency Committee (EC). This, however, does not mean that individual countries should wait for a WHO declaration.

The WHO declaration came one month after the international organization picked up a website statement on December 31, 2019, on "viral pneumonia" from the Wuhan Municipality Health Commission. The SARS-CoV-2 virus may have already been transmitting human to human in the fall of 2019 (Basavaraju et al. 2020). From the PHEIC declaration, it took another month and a half for the WHO to declare it as a pandemic on March 11, 2020.

The International Health Regulations, a legally binding treaty first adopted in 1969, gives the WHO the authority for a PHEIC declaration. The Article II of the IHR states that (WHO 2015):

> *The purpose and scope of these Regulations are to prevent, protect against, control and provide a public health response to the international spread of disease in ways that are commensurate with and restricted to public health risks, and which avoid unnecessary interference with international traffic and trade.*

To state again, this does not mean that an individual country should not make its own determination on the potential danger of a newly found infectious disease. It may be able to decide earlier than the IHR and corroborate its decision with the IHR decision. An earlier decision may turn out to be a crucial step in controlling the spread of the pandemic.

There is some evidence that supports the importance of an earlier determination and action. In response to the COVID-19 pandemic, the most successful countries are, to our surprise, China's closest neighbors such as Taiwan, Vietnam, and Thailand, that is to say, before the delta (Indian) variant began to sweep the planet at around June 2021. The present author suspects that because of the previous coronavirus outbreaks from China and her neighbors such as SARS and MERS, these geographically neighboring countries might have been able to make a faster decision and act more swiftly than European and North American countries.

As Figs. 4.2 and 4.3 show, as of the middle of November 2020 when the effective vaccines were announced, Taiwan was able to peak the number of cases at 30 per day in the middle of March 2020 and had only a handful of cases since April. Thailand was also able to peak the number of cases at 250 per day in early April 2020 and had only a handful of cases since May. As of December 18, 2020, Taiwan had only in total 7 lives lost from the COVID-19 pandemic and Thailand had in total 60 fatalities. These numbers can be contrasted with the 314,000 fatalities in the US and 144,000 fatalities in India, as of the middle of November 2020 (ECDPC 2020).

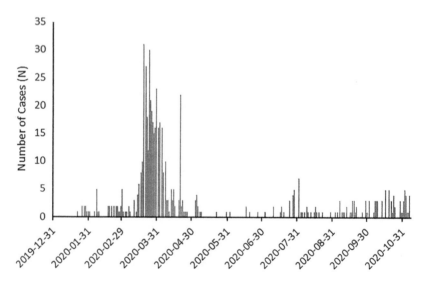

Fig. 4.2 Number of COVID-19 infection cases in Taiwan

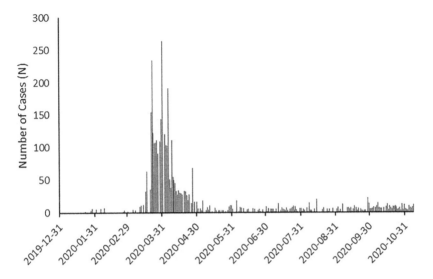

Fig. 4.3 Number of COVID-19 infection cases in Thailand

4 DECISION II: SUSPEND TRAVELS FROM THE ORIGIN?

As Table 4.1 shows, one of the first decisions made by the US government was to suspend the travels from China into the US on January 31, 2020. It came one day after the WHO declared the COVID-19 as a PHEIC. By the time of the executive order on suspension of travels, there were approximately 10,000 cases reported in China, among which roughly 200 people died from the virus. Confirmed cases were reported in 22 other countries.

The executive order made a formal proclamation with the rationale behind it (White House 2020c):

NOW, THEREFORE, I, DONALD J. TRUMP, President of the United States ... hereby find that the unrestricted entry into the United States of persons ... would ... be detrimental to the interests of the United States,... [Section 1] The entry into the United States, as immigrants or nonimmigrants, of all aliens who were physically present within the People's Republic of China ... during the 14-day period preceding their entry or attempted entry into the United States is hereby suspended and limited subject to section 2 of this proclamation.

Why would the decision to suspend the travels from the origin of a pandemic be such a thorny one to make by a policy-maker? According to the above executive order, about 14,000 people traveled from China to the US every day in 2019. Therefore, a travel suspension temporarily from/to the origin of a global pandemic virus should be thought of as the first thing a policy-maker would do and do so without difficulty.

The reality, however, is not that simple. First, as evidenced by the responses of the East and South Asian neighbors to China, owing to China's super dominance in the region, these countries were not able to stop the travelers from/to China, with Singapore being the only exception. In addition, it is not acceptable by international law that a lawful entry by a citizen of a country to another country is banned, that is, in "normal" times.

Without a border closing from the origin country, are there other policy options that a policy-maker can rely on? An alternative is to make a border entrance dependent on the negative result from the COVID-19 test. This, however, is not practical to be effective although it can be politically expedient. This is because during the first wave of a pandemic during which a travel suspension is most effective, test kits are not available in large numbers for foreigners, let alone for domestic citizens. Further, test results may not be precise at an early stage of a pandemic while it takes multiple days to process the results. Furthermore, it is not possible to return the positive-tested travelers to their home countries. Neither is it practical to send the positive-tested travelers to a self-quarantine facility within the border managed by the government.

By the final two months of 2020 when the second wave hit the planet hard, many countries closed their borders entirely to foreign visitors. Many other countries also started to implement a stricter border policy which included a 14-day self-quarantine and a testing at the border.

Is a border closure an effective way for stopping the spread of a pandemic? An answer to this question is often provided by epidemiological models (Chinazzi et al. 2020; Wells et al. 2020). Relying on the Global Epidemic and Mobility Model (GLEAM) and the early COVID-19 data, for example, researchers estimate the impact of a reduction in the number of international travelers on the spread of the pandemic (Chinazzi et al. 2020). Published as early as March 2020, the authors predicted that the travel restrictions can slow the spread of the COVID-19 pandemic by two to three weeks, but the impacts would dissipate thereafter.

As the afore-referenced papers are models based on assumptions, they do not tell actual data regarding the impact of a travel suspension (Nowrasteh 2020). Another way to approach this question is whether border-secure countries performed better in stopping the spread of the pandemic. For this, the present author looked at the COVID-19 contagion in remote small islands in the South Pacific Ocean, specifically in the regions of Melanesia, Micronesia, and Polynesia. The island nations in these ocean regions are remote from the planet's six continents and rarely visited by foreigners.

In Fig. 4.4, the present author compares the responses thereof with the responses in the US, India, and the Maldives. The Maldives is the island in the Arabian Sea south of India, which is a cohort of popular tourist islands. The Maldives can offer an alternative insight since it is a frequently visited island through an open border. The five islands in the aforementioned ocean regions are Fiji, the Solomon Islands, the Marshall Islands, Samoa,

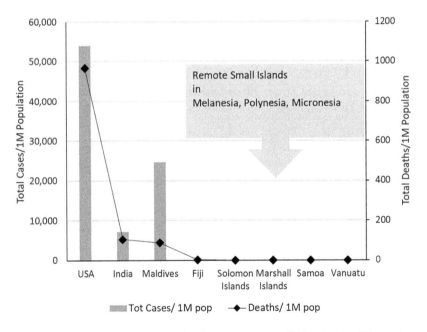

Fig. 4.4 COVID-19 cases and deaths in remote small islands (as of December 19, 2020)

and Vanuatu. These five islands are chosen because of data availability, as of December 19, 2020 (Worldometers 2021).

As for the number of cases per 1 million population, the US has 55,000 cases and India 7000 cases. The remote small islands in the South Pacific had a small number of cases. On the other hand, the tourist islands of the Maldives had a large number of cases: 25,000 cases per 1 million. Fiji had 51 cases and the Solomon Islands had 24 cases per 1 million population.

As for the number of COVID-19 fatalities, the US had 967 deaths per 1 million population, India had 105, the Maldives 88 deaths per 1 million. On the other hand, there were only 2 deaths in the entire five island countries in Melanesia, Micronesia, and Polynesia.

Although the results in Fig. 4.4 are not conclusive at all, it does, however, offer some clue that an early declaration and travel restriction can work to drastically limit the spread of a global pandemic. An important qualification here is "early" because a late travel restriction after a wide virus spread among the population in a nation would not be effective at all at some point. Another qualification is rather obvious: a travel suspension can be more effective when implemented along with the other relevant measures and actions to be described in the following sections.

5   DECISION III: SOCIAL MEASURES BE VOLUNTARY OR MANDATED?

Once a novel infectious disease is declared to be a public health emergency at an international scale and the first case is reported within the national border, the government as well as the private sector should immediately begin designing and implementing a basket of social measures to slow the spread of the epidemic.

The social public health measures should be designed in accordance with the characteristics of the virus, especially its modes of transmission (CDC 2012). Of particular importance is the way the virus is transmitted from person to person. Is it transmitted through physical contacts, fine droplets, foods, or material surfaces? This is a critical question to be answered at the very first stage of mitigation efforts.

A virus, or more broadly, an infectious agent, can be transmitted from human to human through different ways (CDC 2012). There are two types of transmission: direct or indirect. A direct transmission occurs through a direct physical contact with an infected person or a contact with droplets from the person. An indirect transmission occurs through air-borne, vehicle-borne, and vector-borne routes (Fig. 4.5).

Of the direct transmission, the direct contact occurs through skin-to-skin contact, kissing, and sexual intercourse. The droplet spread refers to a transmission through relatively large, short-range aerosols released from sneezing, coughing, or even talking.

Of the indirect transmission, airborne transmission occurs when infectious agents are carried by fine dust or droplet suspended in air. For the vehicle-borne transmission, the vehicles that indirectly transmit an infectious agent include food, water, biological products such as blood, and fomites such as handkerchiefs, bedding, or surgical scalpels. For the vector-borne transmission, the vectors, that is, the carriers, such as mosquitoes, fleas, and ticks, carry an infectious agent.

The transmission mode questions are summarized in Fig. 4.5. In addition to determining the modes of transmission, there are important

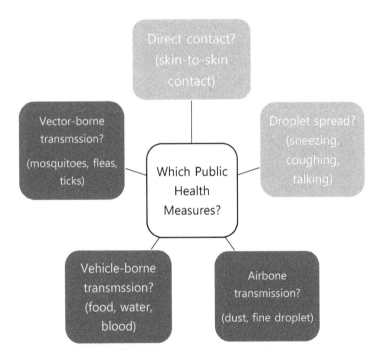

Fig. 4.5 Social public health measures versus modes of transmission

additional questions to be answered. If the virus is determined to be transmitted by droplets from coughing or talking, it should be known how far the droplets could travel in the air and whether the virus can be transmitted in outdoor conditions. For another, if the virus is determined to be capable of staying alive on material surfaces, it should be known how many hours or days it can stay alive on them, the answer to which varies across the materials of concern.

With the transmission modes of the pandemic virus determined, a basket of social public health measures can be designed to help slow the spread of the virus. What are such measures? The measures adopted during the COVID-19 include, *inter alia*, a physical distancing of six feet from other people, avoiding direct physical contacts such as handshakes and hugs, a face mask/shield, washing hands for at least 30 seconds each time, a ban on indoor gathering, a ban on gathering of a large number of people, and seating arrangements.

In the case of the COVID-19 pandemic, the virus was reported by national and international health organizations to be transmitted from person to person by droplets from coughing and talking, in addition to physical contacts. Further, the virus was reported to stay alive in material surfaces for as long as 12 hours and up to 24 hours at maximum. Owing to these transmission routes and patterns, the social measures widely recommended by the health organizations were (1) wearing a mask in enclosed spaces, or when talking to another person, or when visiting a hospital and nursing homes; (2) washing hands frequently using a soap than a foam handwash; (3) avoiding physical human contacts; and (4) avoiding physical contacts against material surfaces (WHO 2020a).

The central policy debate with regard to the recommended social measures is whether they should be advised to the public for voluntary compliance or be universally mandated through a governmental order. If the latter path is chosen by the national policy-maker, then the universal mandate will take the form of a legal order whose violations incur a penalty, financial or physical. For example, a person without wearing a mask may be prevented from taking public transportation. For another, a person without wearing a mask outdoors will face a penalty of US$1000 or be sentenced to jail. By November 25, 2020, 35 US states and Puerto Rico imposed a statewide mask mandate, according to the New York Times tracking (NYT 2020a).

The madness—or, shall I say, pandemonium—of 2020 was characterized by, among other things, the public furor for and against the universal mask mandate. It was frequently witnessed during 2020 that a passenger shouts a curse at another passenger on public transportation or at a person walking on the streets without wearing a mask. A street fight between a mask wearer and a non-wearer broke out frequently.

Does the universal mask mandate outperform the voluntary compliance mask advice in protecting people from getting infected and thereby slowing down the spread of the pandemic virus? The science of a mask mandate appears to point otherwise (Henderson et al. 2009). A Danish study examined the effectiveness of wearing a mask during the COVID-19 pandemic. Researchers compared the rate of infection between the group of mask wearers and the group of non-mask wearers. The study examined 3000 people for each group for about 8 months from March 2020 to October 2020. The researchers reported that there is no significant difference in the infection rate between the two groups (Bundgaard et al. 2020; The Local 2020). The study indicates that the mask wearing is not effective in protecting a mask wearer from being infected. An analysis of the school data from New York, Florida, and Massachusetts arrives at a similar conclusion after comparing the infection rate from the mask mandate states with that from no mandate states (Oster et al. 2021).

An analysis of a randomized cluster trial of Bangladesh's mask promotion program in 600 villages, on the other hand, shows that a tripling—a 200% increase—of mask wearing in the intervention group resulted in the COVID-19-like symptoms in 7.62% of the intervention group compared with 8.62% of the control group. Based on the COVID-19 tests of the symptomatic individuals who consented for the tests, the authors find that the seroprevalence is reduced by 9% in the intervention group (Abaluck et al. 2021). While the reported effect appears to be modest, the decrease may be attributable to an intervention effect, namely a cage effect, via increased physical distancing or government "role modeling," or a self-selection bias, for example, only lower-risk individuals consenting to take a test (Keuhl 1999; Seo 2016).

Another way to tackle the question is to analyze state-level COVID-19 cases and mortality data. In Fig. 4.6, the present author summarizes the COVID-19 health outcomes of the four states. California and New York are the states that enforced the mask mandate while Florida and Georgia did not adopt the mandate (LAT 2020; AARP 2021). The two outcome measures are the number of cases per 1 million population and the number of deaths per 1 million population (Worldometers 2021).

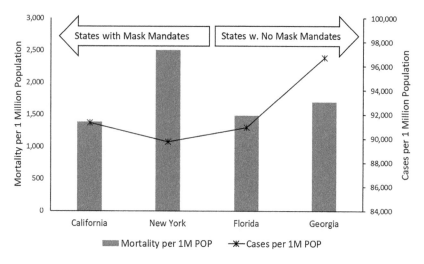

Fig. 4.6   Effectiveness of mask mandates in US state health outcomes (as of March 10, 2021)

In terms of the mortality per 1 million people, Florida, Georgia, and California had similar outcomes while New York performed far worse. In terms of the cases per 1 million population, California, Florida, and New York had similar outcomes, while Georgia performed the worst of them. The figure shows that the mask mandates were not as effective, as far as the COVID-19 health outcomes are concerned, as policy-makers had hoped.

Can scientific rationale explain the ineffectiveness of the universal mask mandate against the voluntary compliance? There are compelling scientific reasons at the core of which lies individuals' behaviors to protect themselves. First of all, when the pandemic turns out to be highly contagious and deadly, individual citizens will take whatever effective measures on their own to protect themselves. On the other hand, a universal mask mandate imposed by the government order will likely prompt individuals to protest against such a heavy-handed policy. These two behavioral incentives created by the government and individuals will make a universal mask mandate to be far less effective than is wished.

Second, a mask wearing mandated at all places all the time will severely hurt the people with pre-existing medical conditions, especially those with lung and bronchitis conditions, and senile citizens.

Third, as the COVID-19 virus turned out to be, an exceptionally efficient virus in transmission can easily outsmart a mask. The virus can stay on the mask for hours through which it can enter the mask wearer's body, in which case a universal mask wearing is rather harmful than helpful. Further, if the virus is transmitted through an airborne mode, say, via fine aerosols, it will penetrate the mask wearer.

Notwithstanding the empirical data and the rationale against it, the universal mask mandate has turned out to be an overwhelmingly favored policy instrument in most countries on the globe in dealing with the COVID-19. There seems to be also a compelling political reason for this. The mask mandate will be a favorite tool for policy-makers and politicians faced with a worldwide pandemic. Under the universal mandate, the burden of controlling the pandemic spread is shifted, to a large extent, from the politicians to the citizens. Under the mask mandate, people who do not wear a mask are viewed as super spreaders. Further, people who die from the pandemic are only themselves to blame because they refused to wear masks against the government policy. Under the voluntary compliance policy, this burden transfer does not occur.

6   Decision IV: Lockdown, No Lockdown, School Closures

When it is observed that the pandemic virus is spreading each day at an "alarming" rate among its population, the government's urgent task becomes a flattening of the curve of the daily numbers of infected people. Alarmed by the rapid spread, the government will most likely perceive that piecemeal policy measures will fail to contain the contagion.

A handy choice for the policy-makers is to lock down the country for a certain period of time. A national lockdown order may be issued for a joint implementation of a business closure order and a stay-at-home order for individual citizens. Some essential businesses, for example, postal service, delivery services, and public transportations, may be allowed to operate.

In most countries, a national policy of pandemic-time restrictions is implemented in stages in tandem with a national emergency level declaration. The latter may be determined in five stages from Stage 1 to Stage 5. The higher the level of the national emergency, the larger the number of business activities ordered to shut down. To give a rough example, at Stage 1, restaurants may be allowed to open with a limited seating arrangement. At Stage 2, restaurants may be allowed to open before, say, 9 p.m. At Stage 3, restaurants may be allowed only for a take-out order. At Stage 4, restaurants may be allowed only for home delivery orders. At Stage 5, restaurants should shut all its activities down.

A draconian nature of a nationwide lockdown is unmistakable, while the restrictions imposed on the civil rights are unprecedented in non-wartimes. A pandemic lockdown policy meant no gathering of people allowed for a political demonstration; no in-person religious services permitted; no schools permitted to open for children and teenagers; no small shops and businesses allowed to open.

A financial, as well as emotional, hardship it causes to every family in the nation is severe. Parents may lose their jobs and monthly incomes; children will lose their educational opportunities through interactions with teachers and classmates; people will not be able to attend a funeral or wedding of family members; people will not be able to go to a hospital for other diseases than the pandemic; people will not be able to attend a religious service; a prolonged lockdown will lead to mental depression, exacerbate drug additions, and increase self-harm as well as household violence (Hoover Institution 2020; Romer 2020b).

A reasoned critique against the national lockdown policy approach was formulated by a group of medical scientists, which was named a focused protection (FP) approach, which was declared as the Great Barrington Declaration (GBD) on October 4, 2020 (Kulldorff et al. 2020). As of December 20, 2020, the number of signatories for the GBD stood as follows: concerned citizens, 702,586; medical and public health scientists, 12,943; medical practitioners, 39,027.

The authors of the GBD argued that the national lockdown will produce "*devastating effects on short and long-term public health*" such as "*lower childhood vaccination rates, worsening cardiovascular disease outcomes, fewer cancer screenings and deteriorating mental health—leading to greater excess mortality in years to come, with the working class and younger members of society carrying the heaviest burden.*" The authors add that "*keeping students out of school is a grave injustice.*"

The focused protection approach proposed by the authors is a policy that "*balances the risks and benefits of reaching herd immunity.*" In the FP approach, people who are at minimal risk of death are allowed to live their normal lives and, at the same time, people at high risk are where governmental resources are directed to protect them.

For clarification, the discussion in this section on the national lockdown policy includes the school closures and opening (D-IX in Fig. 4.1), that is, in addition to a stay-at-home order and a business closure order (D-V in Fig. 4.1). As the GBD emphasized, the impacts of the lockdown policy may have been most severe on school children and their parents. As early as June 2020, the American Academy of Pediatrics (AAP) issued a policy guidance on reopening schools for the fall semester stating that it "*strongly advocates that all policy considerations for the coming school year should start with a goal of having students physically present in school*" (AAP 2020).

However, as Table 1.3 in Chap. 1 reveals, a vast majority of countries decided to fully close the schools during the first half of 2020 (UNESCO 2020). In the US, many states decided to fully close their schools through the end of 2020 and partially open even during the first half of 2021 (Detroit News 2020).

Can we evaluate which of the two policy approaches is superior as a pandemic policy, in particular, for the COVID-19? First, since many states in the US adopted a lockdown policy, we can examine whether an imposition of a statewide lockdown had any effect on the spread of the pandemic. Second, we can compare the outcomes from a lockdown policy in one country with the outcomes from the focused protection policy in another country. For this analysis, Sweden provides an example that approximates the FP policy. Third, we can compare the outcomes from a state with a lockdown policy with those from a state with no lockdowns, as in Fig. 4.6.

Sweden's COVID-19 strategy has received much international attention for being the only outlier (Financial Times 2020; Paterlini 2020). The country devised a strategy which relies on voluntary compliance by the citizens of social measures, deliberately avoiding a lockdown. Under the strategy, primary and secondary schools, restaurants, cafes, shops, and public transportations are allowed to be open as in normal times. Health authorities in Sweden rely on people's voluntary compliance of above-described social measures such as physical distancing, mask wearing, washing hands, avoiding a large gathering, and so on.

Let's begin with the first assessment, which is illustrated in Fig. 4.7. The vertical bar marks the time period when the initial lockdowns of California, New York, and Georgia were issued: March 19, March 22, and April 3 of 2020. We can verify from the figure that the lockdowns in these states were prompted by a public and political fear by a steep rise of the

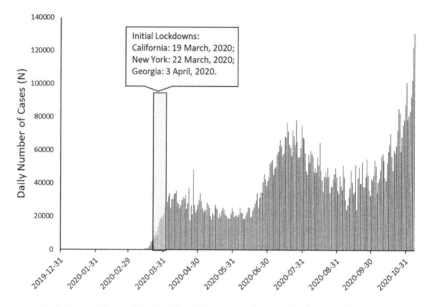

Fig. 4.7   The effects of the US lockdowns on the pandemic spread

number of cases at around this time. Many states followed suit in the coming months after the three states.

The figure indicates that the initial lockdowns do seem to have worked in flattening the curve initially. The increase in the number of cases stopped in early April and the daily number of new cases got flattened thereafter. The number of positive cases started to decline through the middle of June for more than two months. However, the moment of relief was short-lived. The second wave was rushing in by early June and the third wave was hitting the country even harder when October rolled in. Overall, the lockdown policies taken by a majority of the US states have not succeeded in flattening the curve through the middle of November, the time when the effective vaccines were announced by Pfizer-BioNTech and Moderna (Fox Business 2020a, b).

It can be asked whether the failure was attributable to a partial nature of the lockdown. That is, a majority of states implemented a lockdown but some states decided to remain open. However, an analysis at the state level for the lockdown state versus the non-lockdown state, such as the one shown in Fig. 4.6, will reveal more or less the same conclusion.

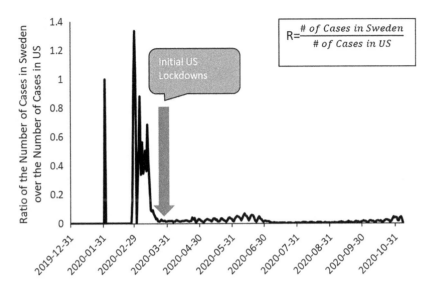

Fig. 4.8 The relative performance of the lockdown versus the no-lockdown

In the second assessment, the present author compares the outcomes from the US lockdown policies with those from Sweden's no-lockdown strategy. In Fig. 4.8, a relative performance of the two policies is illustrated by the ratio of the daily number of cases of Sweden over that of the US. It shows the number of cases in the US started to overwhelm the number of cases in Sweden after the initial US lockdowns, which is marked by a thick gray arrow, began. It is notable that the number of infections in Sweden exceeded temporarily the number of infections in the US before the lockdowns, that is, the ratio>1. After the lockdowns, the fortunes of the two countries diverged to the extremes.

The two figures, Figs. 4.7 and 4.8, lend credence to the critics of the heavy-handed government policies such as a national lockdown. The analysis in this section should be a fodder for serious thoughts by policymakers in future pandemic events.

7   Decision V: Economic Relief

As soon as the government issues a draconian measure such as a national lockdown, a stay-at-home order, or a business closure order, it is practically impossible for it to avoid the burden of providing economic relief to its citizens. The economic toll of a national lockdown on individual households is very severe, but especially so for low-income families. The economic toll is perhaps the highest for small businesses because of monthly rent payments to landowners on top of lost incomes from a closed business (USBEA 2020; USBLS 2020). Political parties, left and right alike, will not be able to withstand without a generous relief package offered by the time a lockdown is issued nationwide.

If, on the other hand, a no-lockdown strategy is adopted by the government, the pressure to provide an economic relief fund to its citizens should not be high because neither businesses nor any other daily activities of individuals will be forced by the government to shut down.

Shortly after the lockdowns are ordered in the aforementioned states in the US, a coronavirus relief package was signed into law with bipartisan supports. The Coronavirus Aid, Relief, and Economic Security (CARES) Act, passed by Congress and signed into law on March 27, 2020, offers a relief package of US$2.2 trillion from which each American citizen was offered a one-time cash payment of US$1200 (USDOT 2020). The American Rescue Plan (ARP) Act, another stimulus and relief act with the size of US$1.9 trillion, was signed into law on March 11, 2021 (WSJ 2020b). Similarly in Europe, the European Commission passed a €750 billion recovery package in July 2020 (EC 2021).

As for the economic relief offered during a pandemic, what should be an appropriate size of the relief package to an individual citizen? There is no rule on this. However, since the economic relief is intended to be a temporary relief during the national lockdown period, it may be determined in consideration of the minimum living expense of an individual citizen as well as the monthly rent payment of small businesses during the period. In addition, the economic relief should not have any wealth redistribution purpose across individual recipients.

On the other hand, a series of unprecedented cash payments to the citizens is expected to increase the prices of goods and services, raising the cost of living for the citizens. The US relief packages—US$2.2 trillion for the CARES, US$1.9 trillion for the ARP, and the US$2.2 trillion for the suggested infrastructure plan—led to an inflation of 4.7% in the US economy from June 2020 to July 2021 (USBLS 2021).

These rationales seem to underlie the universal cash payment of the CARES Act. Every American citizen receives an equal amount of cash of US$1200. It should be reminded that the US approach was not the only economic relief approach taken by the governments around the world.

The other approaches, including the US', are summarized in Fig. 4.9: a universal uniform cash payment, a universal proportional cash payment, a selective low-income cash payment, and a selective ad hoc cash payment.

The A-I in Fig. 4.9 is a universal & uniform cash payment, which is the approach taken by the CARES Act of the US as far as the cash payments to individual citizens are concerned. To clarify, not all of the money approved in the CARES Act was used for cash payments to citizens.

The A-II is a universal proportional cash payment approach. Under the A-II, all individuals are given a cash payment in proportion to, for example, their economic losses during the lockdown period. This approach is attractive to the policy-makers who are concerned about differential impacts of the pandemic across the citizens. Concretely, some businesses would do even better under the pandemic, for example, Big Tech companies such as Amazon, Google, Apple, Facebook, home entertainment device businesses, and home delivery services. It would not be acceptable to many people for the government to give monetary "relief" to these companies and employees who benefited from the pandemic.

The universal proportional cash payment approach, however, suffers from incentive perverseness. Under the A-II, businesses are motivated to

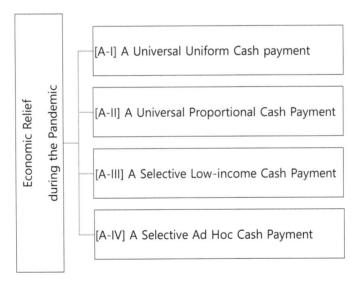

Fig. 4.9 Policy approaches for economic relief

earn as little as possible to receive a larger cash payment or to remain closed as long as possible. Owing to the perverse incentives created by the government, the economy will find it harder to rebound and recover. The larger the proportionality gets, the larger the degree of perverse responses.

The third approach, A-III, is a selective low-income cash payment approach. This approach provides a relief to the selective groups, specifically, of low-income families. Higher-income families are excluded from the economic relief program. The threshold for low-income families should be determined by the policy-maker. This was one of the most popular approaches among the national governments during the COVID-19 pandemic.

The A-III could be justified if the pandemic would cause disproportionately larger harm to the low-income groups than to the higher-income groups. There is some evidence. A group of World Bank researchers argued, for instance, that the COVID-19 pandemic will push 71–100 million people to extreme poverty globally (Mahler et al. 2020). However, the reality is that the pandemic does not stop at the gate of high-income groups. Indeed, rich industrialized nations in Europe and North America suffered the most from the COVID-19 during 2020 (JHU 2020).

A drawback of the selective low-income cash payment approach is that it runs the risk of deteriorating into an income redistribution policy of the economy rather than a pandemic relief policy. If such a selective income redistribution program would remain interminable even after the pandemic is over, it will inflict a lasting impact on the economy.

The fourth approach, a selective *ad hoc* cash payment (A-IV), is a generalized form of the A-III. That is, this approach is the same as the A-III in spirit, but a selection of the groups to which cash payments are disbursed is made by arbitrary criteria picked by the committee in charge, that is, in an *ad hoc* manner. To state it specifically, the committee may decide to provide a large cash payment to the individuals or businesses who are more likely to succeed economically during the pandemic era. These may include artists, solar energy companies, political volunteers, freelance writers, and so on.

Although there is a rationale, *albeit weak*, behind the A-IV, it will be susceptible to favoritism, nepotism, *quid pro quo*, and other bureaucratic malfeasances owing to the nature of case-by-case decisions. If the *ad hoc* program is additionally open-handed in determining the size of each cash payment, the rationale and fairness of the government policy beyond the pandemic relief will be severely damaged.

The analysis thus far points to the conclusion that a pandemic relief can be best done with a universal and uniform cash payment, the A-I. The US and many other countries appeared to go with this model at first, but their relief packages have over time turned out to be a potpourri of many objectives and goals. Many countries proceeded with a blended approach in which more than two policy options from the four shown in Fig. 4.9 were adopted through multiple phases of pandemic relief cash payments during 2020 and 2021.

8 Decision VI: Defense Production Act

The COVID-19 experiences since the first day of 2020 have taught us all citizens that the government should be prepared well and undertake essential tasks during the pandemic in multiple areas. The two areas that particularly stood out are emergency productions of essential medical devices on the one hand and vaccine developments on the other. The two policy areas also revealed that a private-public sector partnership, if well managed, can prove highly effective and beneficial, if not necessary. Let me explain the former in this section and the latter in Sect. 10.

In the US, President Trump invoked the Defense Production Act to produce emergency medical devices and goods needed urgently to deal with the emerging pandemic (White House 2020a, b). The emergency goods to be produced included ventilators, respirators, test kits, emergency medical treatment facilities, masks, needles, and syringes.

Why were these goods not available at the time of the outbreak of the COVID-19 pandemic? Why can't private companies supply these goods during the pandemic, making the government intervention inevitable? These are non-trivial questions connected to fundamental aspects of a global pandemic.

The pandemic in the scale of the COVID-19 would hit the planet only very rarely, say, once in a century. When the pandemic does arrive, the demands for the essential medical devices and services would surge in a short period of time, say, in days after a pandemic declaration. Suppliers in the market do not maintain the stocks of the goods and services that can meet such surges in the demands. Given the life-saving importance of some of these devices, they will have to be produced in an urgent manner.

However, these medical goods, for example, ventilators and field hospitals, cannot be produced in large quantities by the private companies in a short period of time, say, a few weeks. Further, some of the emergency medical devices are technologically complex, for example, ventilators and test kits.

In addition, market responses will be chaotic. There is an incentive for the private companies to limit the supplies in order to prevent price falls owing to oversupplies. There will be panic buyers. Hoarders will attempt to sweep the goods available in the market and then resell them at a later time at higher prices.

The DPA was a civil defense and war mobilization act signed in 1950 during the Korean War. Under the DPA invoked on March 15, 2020, world major companies were called upon by the law to produce the urgently needed goods: to name some, General Motors (GM), Philips, General Electric (GE), and Hamilton.

Table 4.2 summarizes the medical resource types and vendors included in the DPA medical responses, provided by the US Department of Health and Human Services (USDHHS 2020b). Of the requested resources, ventilators dominate the list, for which GM, GE, Philips, Hamilton, and Zoll are requested to produce. A ventilator is an emergency medical device for the patient who is unable to breathe physically which moves the air into and out of the lungs of the patient. Notably, Boris Johnson, the UK prime minister, relied on the ventilator during his COVID-19 hospitalization.

Other notable resources produced under the DPA are medical treatment facilities and alternate medical care facilities. The Department of Defense led the efforts to build these emergency field hospitals.

Despite the grave concern on the lack of hospitals and ventilators during the initial months of the COVID-19 outbreak in the US, a hospital overflowing has not turned out to be a major problem across all states in the US. Nor the lack of ventilators or respirators was a major issue during 2020.

Weighing the empirical data, the DPA proved to be a successful partnership between the public sector and the private sector. This again demonstrates one of the important roles that the government can play during the global-scale pandemic.

Table 4.2 Medical responses under the Defense Production Act (DPA)

Date of approval	Requesting agency	Resource type and quantities	Producers
March 28	FEMA	Upstream machine shop services	Puritan
March 28	FEMA	Blanket request required to invoke DPA	n/a
March 30	HHS	25.5K increase in ventilators	Hamilton
March 30	HHS	18.9K increase in ventilators	Zoll
April 5	FEMA	Memo expediting N95 respirators to NJ	n/a
April 8	HHS	30K increase in ventilators	General Motors
April 8	HHS	43K increase in ventilators	Philips
April 10	FEMA	Applied rating to Zoll ventilator contract	Zoll
April 10	FEMA	Memo compelling sale of filtering face pieces and respirators in shipment	n/a
April 13	FEMA	Authorized construction of alternate care facilities	n/a
April 13	HHS	2.4K increase in ventilators	General Electric
April 13	HHS	3.4K increase in ventilators	Hill-Rom
April 13	HHS	1K increase in ventilators	Medtronic
April 13	HHS	2.5K increase in ventilators	ResMed
April 13	HHS	22K increase in ventilators	Vyaire
April 13	HHS	12K increase in ventilators	Combat Medical
April 16	FEMA	Priority ratings for PPE/equipment for DoD medical treatment facilities	n/a
April 21	HHS	12K increase in powered air purifying respirators	BioMedical Devices
July 8	HHS	50M needles and syringes to support vaccination efforts	Becton, Dickinson

Note: FEMA=Federal Emergency Management Agency; HHS=Department of Health and Human Services; DoD=Department of Defense

9 Decision VII: Emergency Use Authorizations for Treatments

Once the epidemic, soon afterward the pandemic, is declared, the numbers of hospitalizations and human deaths will quickly rise. Besides a rapid contagion of the pandemic virus among the populations, the most troubling aspect of the pandemic is that there is no effective treatment or drug available for a prolonged period of time after the outbreak. The only way to quickly find effective drugs, that is, in a matter of several weeks, is through repeated trial-and-errors at local hospitals with pandemic emergency patients.

Once multiple local hospitals report that a drug developed for the treatment of another disease does seem to work in slowing down or curing the symptoms of pandemic patients, a government's agency, for example, the FDA in the US, has to make a decision on whether or not to authorize the recommended drug for emergency uses. Because there would be no thorough clinical trials completed for the drug at that time, the FDA should make a difficult decision on issuing an emergency use authorization (EUA) for the drug (USFDA 2020a).

The FDA's authority to issue the EUA is given by the Federal Food, Drug, and Cosmetic Act passed by Congress in 1938 by section 564 of the Act which was amended multiple times since then, most recently by the 21st Century Cures Act of 2016. Under the section (USFDA 2020b),

> the FDA Commissioner may allow unapproved medical products or unapproved uses of approved medical products to be used in an emergency to diagnose, treat, or prevent serious or life-threatening diseases or conditions caused by CBRN (Chemical, Biological, Radiological, and Nuclear) threat agents when there are no adequate, approved, and available alternatives.

In Table 4.3, the EUAs issued by the FDA to the drugs for COVID-19 treatments are summarized. There were nine EUAs, including the most touted as well as controversial ones such as Hydroxychloroquine, Remdesivir, COVID-19 convalescent plasma, and a Regeneron antibody cocktail (USFDA 2020b).

Other than the drug products, the FDA issued many EUAs for diagnostic products, different personal protective equipment, ventilators, and other medical devices. Of these, the present author appended to the table two COVID-19 diagnostic tests that garnered much attention during the first wave in 2020 (Romer 2020a). The first is the Abbot Molecular lab's antigen test, also called a rapid test, and the second is the Yale New Haven Hospital's saliva test. The rapid test takes only 15 minutes, while the turnaround time for the saliva test is two to three days, but the latter is more accurate (Yale News 2020). The saliva test is also called a molecular test, an RNA test, or a Polymerase Chain Reaction (PCR) test. The rapid test is also called a swab test.

Table 4.3 FDA's emergency use authorizations for COVID-19 treatments in 2020

Type	Products	Emergency use authorization	Note/source
Drugs (*selected*)	Hydroxychloroquine	March 28	Revoked on June 15, 2020
	Fresenius Medical, multiFiltrate PRO System and multiBic/multiPlus solutions	April 30	
	Remdesivir for certain hospitalized COVID-19 patients	May 1	
	Fresenius Kabi Propoven 2%	May 8	
	REGIOCIT replacement solution that contains citrate for regional citrate anticoagulation (RCA) of the extracorporeal circuit	August 13	
	COVID-19 convalescent plasma	August 23	
	Bamlanivimab	November 9	
	Baricitinib (Olumiant) in combination with remdesivir (Veklury)	November 19	
	Antibody cocktail Casirivimab and Imdevimab	November 21	formerly known as REGN-COV2 or REGEN-COV2
In Vitro diagnostic products (*selected*)	Abbott Molecular: Abbott RealTime SARS-CoV-2 assay	March 18	Antigen test, Rapid test: turnaround time—15 minutes
	Yale New Haven Hospital, Clinical Virology Laboratory: SARS-CoV-2 PCR test	March 31	Saliva test: turnaround time is 2–3 days.

The FDA's EUAs may become controversial. The hydroxychloroquine was the first EUA authorized drug on March 28, 2020, based on local hospital reports, but the effectiveness of the drug got challenged by doctors later on (Ghazy et al. 2020). The drug may have worked on some patients at local hospitals, but was reported to be of no effect to many others in a large sample trial. As noted in Table 4.3, the drug's EUA was revoked on June 15, 2020. By the end of May 2021, however, researchers reported that "increased doses of co-administered HCQ (hydroxychloroquine) and AZM (azithromycin) were associated with >100% increase in survival" (Smith et al. 2021).

10   DECISION VIII: VACCINE DEVELOPMENTS

How does a global pandemic end and how long will it take to get to the end? With human deaths and tragedies that would pile on each day for years during the pandemic, the highest priority of any government should be to finally have an answer to this question.

A scenario for the pandemic's end is that the end will be reached if a vast majority of world citizens would acquire immunity to the virus, which is also known as herd immunity. It may happen naturally if the virus symptoms were mild and a large majority of the population could gain immunity over time without severe health effects. For your reference, an Israeli study in 2021 found that people who were vaccinated by mRNA vaccines in January and February in 2021 were 6–13 times more likely to get infected in June, July, and the first half of August in that year than unvaccinated people who acquired natural immunity from being previously infected with the coronavirus (Gazit et al. 2021). If, on the other hand, the virus was detrimental to individuals' health and a large fraction of the population could not acquire immunity naturally through infections, herd immunity is neither achievable nor desirable.

Another scenario is that the pandemic virus is eliminated by a worldwide immunization of people through an effective vaccine (Schwartz 2001; Plotkin 2011). Notwithstanding the overwhelming rationale for policy-makers to pursue vaccine developments with maximum efforts, it has a major drawback as a pandemic policy. The very nature of a novel pathogen makes it impossible to develop a highly effective vaccine in a short period of time.

The process of vaccine development, which includes identification of vaccine candidates, developments, three phases of clinical trials, and approval by the government agency, is lengthy, complex, and bureaucratic. Many experts during the first wave of 2020 predicted that it would take as many as five years to develop a powerful vaccine against the COVID-19 (NYT 2020b). The drawback of the vaccine pursuit is that by the time that the powerful vaccine becomes available and administered to the public, many millions of people will have fallen victims to the pandemic. As for the novel coronavirus pandemic, the number of the infected reached 80 million and the number of deaths reached 1.8 million by the end of 2020 when Pfizer and Moderna vaccines became distributed to the people (JHU 2020).

As a reference on the time interval needed for the vaccine development (Plotkin 2011), consider a malaria vaccine! Although the malaria parasite has been present for over 10,000 years on the planet, a powerful malaria vaccine is still not widely available. A malaria vaccine named Mosquirix is under clinical trials (WHO 2020b). According to the World Malaria Report 2019, the infectious disease had 228 million new cases and 405,000 new deaths in 2019 globally (WHO 2019).

Despite this risk, the government, especially of the world-leading nations in biomedical research, should take the vaccine pursuit as the first priority in designing a pandemic policy. The reason is that without a powerful vaccine the pandemic virus will continue to spread, infecting people and killing them for many years after the outbreak. As a reference, up to a complete eradication in 1980 of the smallpox viruses, whose emergence can be traced back to as early as the third century BCE, through the vaccine named the Dryvax, the infectious disease had killed an estimated 300–500 million people (CDC 2020).

Another important characteristic to be considered in a vaccine development effort, which is explained in Chap. 2, is that its production function takes on a best-shot technology. That is, only the best effort will eventually matter when it comes to determining whether or not a vaccine is developed. If the best effort would succeed, then a vaccine will be developed. If the best effort would fail, then the second-best effort will by definition fail. This means that only the best pharmaceutical companies or research laboratories in the world will participate in the vaccine development race. As in the COVID-19, only a handful of companies competed, for example, Pfizer-BioNTech, Moderna, Johnson & Johnson, Novavax, and AstraZeneca (refer to Chap. 7 for participants from Russia, China, and India).

In the race for the COVID-19 vaccine, the Trump administration is widely credited to achieving an impossible task, as many experts testified (Gupta 2021). Two vaccines were developed in only nine months: the Pfizer-BioNTech vaccine and the Moderna vaccine (Azar 2020). By the end of 2020, 20 million Americans were expected to receive one of the vaccines free of charge, that is, 1 million people per day, and reportedly about 400 million doses of the vaccines were already secured by then by the US government.

At the heart of the success lay the OWS defined by the federal government as "the national program to accelerate the development, manufacturing, and distribution of COVID-19 vaccines, therapeutics, and diagnostics (medical countermeasures)." The OWS is a partnership among different components of the Department of Health and Human Services (DHHS) and the Department of Defense (DoD). It was initially funded with US$10 billion from the afore-mentioned CARES Act (USDHHS 2020a).

Beyond the DPA invocation, the OWS demonstrated the need and fruitfulness of a successful private-public partnership during the pandemic. The government program placed right incentives for the world's major pharmaceutical companies and research laboratories to start their efforts as early as possible and to develop a vaccine as speedily as possible. First, by selecting the most promising vaccine candidates very early and providing a funding, the OWS was able to achieve a fast start on the vaccine develop-ment efforts. As summarized in Table 4.4, funding recipients for their candidate vaccines are Johnson & Johnson, Moderna, AstraZeneca, Novavax, Pfizer, Sanofi, and GlaxoSmithKline.

Second, by signing a manufacturing and delivery agreement, the devel-opers were guaranteed to have their successful vaccines purchased by the government and have them manufactured even before an FDA approval in order to deliver them to people as early as possible. To give an example, the agreement with Pfizer guarantees a large-scale manufacturing and nationwide distribution of 100 million doses of the company's vaccine. The US government purchased additional 100 million doses from Pfizer in December 2020 after the EUA approval.

Before the FDA approvals for emergency use, the funding to Pfizer amounted to US$1.95 billion, to Moderna roughly US$2 billion, to Johnson & Johnson US$1.5 billion, to Novavax US$1.6 billion, and to AstraZeneca US$1.2 billion, as shown in Table 4.4 (USDHHS 2020a).

The OWS may turn out to be one of the most successful governmental programs at the times of not only pandemics but also all disasters. At the time of this writing only a handful of days left in 2020, the "miracle" vac-cines do seem to offer a glimmer of hope for an end of the novel corona-virus pandemic as the second wave of the COVID-19 is overwhelming the global community. The announcement of a 90–95% effective vaccine by Pfizer-BioNTech was made on November 9, 2020, and a week later Moderna announced its vaccine to be 94.5% effective (Fox Business 2020a, b). The two vaccines were approved for emergency use by the FDA on December 11 and December 18, 2020, respectively (USFDA 2020c).

The vaccines, the Pfizer's and Moderna's given EUAs at the time of this writing, are given to the citizens free of charge by the US government. It decided to have the vaccines administered to the healthcare workers in the

Table 4.4 Operation Warp Speed (OWS) funding

Date	Candidate	Funds	Stage
March 30	Johnson & Johnson	$456 million	Development
April 16	Moderna	$483 million	Development
May 21	AstraZeneca	$1.2 billion	Development
July 7	Regeneron's COVID-19 investigational anti-viral antibody treatment, REGN-COV2	$450 million	Manufacturing
July 7	Novavax	$1.6 billion	Manufacturing
July 22	Pfizer	$1.95 billion	Manufacturing: a large-scale manufacturing and nationwide distribution of 100 million doses of their vaccine candidate
July 31	Sanofi and GlaxoSmithKline (GSK)	$2 billion	Development, trials, manufacturing
August 5	Johnson & Johnson	$1 billion	Manufacturing and delivery
August 11	Moderna	$1.5 billion	Manufacturing and delivery
August 23	Convalescent plasma	Emergency use authorization (EUA), FDA	
October 9	AstraZeneca	Agreement	Late-stage development and large-scale manufacturing
October 28	Eli Lilly and Company	$375 million	The first doses of the company's COVID-19 investigational antibody therapeutic bamlanivimab, also known as LY-CoV555
November 10	Eli Lilly and Company	Emergency use authorization (EUA), FDA	

Intensive Care Unit (ICU) first and then to the most vulnerable populations, especially, people in nursing homes and seniors. The vaccine distribution is another decision that the government should make, especially, the priority groups who will get the shots first. An alternative argument was that black and other minority communities should receive the vaccine shots first. Many countries proceeded with an age cohort approach in the vaccine distribution, from the most senior cohort down.

Globally, countries started to scramble to secure a sufficient number of vaccines for their citizens from the vaccine developers. The vaccine suppliers were not able to manufacture in a short period of time the vaccines in such large quantities to meet the countries' needs. By the end of March 2021, many developing countries were not able to purchase vaccines and vaccination rates were very low, if not near zero. This was in contrast to the rich countries, for example, Israel, UAE, the UK, and others, that were able to make early purchases and achieved a high vaccination rate swiftly (OWID 2021). When the third wave arrived during the first half of 2021, the low vaccination countries, for example, India, suffered unimaginably, with as many as 400,000 infections per day (refer to Fig. 7.6 in Chap. 7).

11   Final Words: Civil Liberty Versus Protecting Lives

This chapter explained the series of governmental decisions made during the COVID-19 pandemic with an emphasis on US decisions. Streamlining a large number of large and small decisions, it presented nine key decisions. The biggest fault line in the governmental actions around the world turned out to be that of civil liberty *versus* containing the virus spread.

The governments around the world, in shock and fear of the virus' unprecedentedly fast spread, did not appear to be concerned about the civil liberty restrictions imposed by their pandemic orders and enforced them with legal and political forces. The only counterforce provided during the entire year of 2020 may have been the US Supreme Court decision to block the New York State's restrictions on in-person church services (WSJ 2020a). Another was Sweden's unique strategy based on voluntary compliance of their citizens (Paterlini 2020).

In retrospect of the entire year 2020, despite the heavy-handed government restrictions and orders that limited citizens' behaviors severely, which "everyone on Earth" has experienced and endured during the year, the governments around the world appear to have made little success in either stopping the spread of the virus or lowering the mortality rate, as elaborated throughout this chapter. By the end of July 2021, the world is again swept by the fourth wave of the pandemic caused primarily by the delta variant. A prudent policy-maker, faced with a shock of the pandemic, would have placed an emphasis on the protection of citizens' decisions and at the same time pursued vigorously a series of sensible actions to expedite an end of the pandemic.

References

Abaluck, J., L.H Kwong, A. Styczynski, et al. 2021. The Impact of Community Masking on COVID-19: A Cluster-Randomized Trial in Bangladesh. The Innovations for Poverty Action (IPA) Working Paper. https://www.poverty-action.org/publication/impact-community-masking-covid-19-cluster-randomized-trial-bangladesh.

American Academy of Pediatrics (AAP). 2020. COVID-19 Planning Considerations: Guidance for School Re-entry. Published on June 23, 2020. Itasca, IL: AAP.

American Association of Retired Persons (AARP). 2021. State-by-State Guide to Face Mask Requirements. Washington, DC: The AARP. Published on March 9, 2021. https://www.aarp.org/health/healthy-living/info-2020/states-mask-mandates-coronavirus.html.

Azar, Alex M. II. 2020. How Operation Warp Speed Delivered a COVID Vaccine in Record Time. *Fox News*. Published on 12 December 2020. https://www.foxnews.com/opinion/hhs-azar-operation-warp-speed-covid-vaccine-record-time.

Basavaraju, Sridhar V., Monica E. Patton, Kacie Grimm, et al. 2020. Serologic Testing of US Blood Donations to Identify Severe Acute Respiratory Syndrome Coronavirus 2 (SARS-CoV-2)–Reactive Antibodies: December 2019–January 2020. *Clinical Infectious Diseases* 72: e1004–e1009. https://doi.org/10.1093/cid/ciaa1785.

Bundgaard, H., J.S. Bundgarrd, D.E.T. Raaschou-Pedersen, et al. 2020. Effectiveness of Adding a Mask Recommendation to Other Public Health Measures to Prevent SARS-CoV-2 Infection in Danish Mask Wearers. A Randomized Controlled Trial. Annals of Internal Medicine. https://doi.org/10.7326/M20-6817.

Centers for Disease Control and Prevention (CDC). 2012. *Principles of Epidemiology in Public Health Practice (Third Edition): An Introduction to Applied Epidemiology and Biostatistics*. Atlanta, GA: The CDC.

———. 2020. *Smallpox*. Atlanta, GA: The CDC.

Chinazzi, Matteo, Jessica T. Davis, Marco Ajelli, et al. 2020. The Effect of Travel Restrictions on the Spread of the 2019 Novel Coronavirus (COVID-19) Outbreak. *Science* 368: 395–400.

Detroit News. 2020. Gov. Whitmer Closing High Schools, Colleges, In-person Dining, Casinos, Movie Theaters. Published on November 15, 2020. https://www.detroitnews.com/story/news/politics/2020/11/15/gov-whitmer-expected-announce-new-covid-19-restrictions-sunday/6304308002/.

European Centre for Disease Prevention and Control (ECDPC). 2020. *COVID-19 Coronavirus Dataset*. Solna Municipality, Sweden: The ECDPC. https://data.europa.eu/euodp/en/data/dataset/covid-19-coronavirus-data.

European Council (EC). 2021. A recovery plan for Europe. EC, Brussels, BE. https://www.consilium.europa.eu/en/policies/eu-recovery-plan/.

Financial Times. 2020 Architect of Sweden's no-lockdown strategy insists it will pay off. Published on May 8, 2020. https://www.ft.com/content/a2b4c18c-a5e8-4edc-8047-ade4a82a548d.

Fox Business. 2020a. Pfizer's Covid-19 Vaccine Proves 90% Effective in Latest Trials. Published on November 9, 2020. https://www.foxbusiness.com/healthcare/pfizers-covid-19-vaccine-proves-90-effective-in-latest-trials.

———. 2020b. Moderna Says Its Vaccine is 94.5% Effective in Preventing COVID-19. Published on November 16, 2020. https://www.foxbusiness.com/healthcare/moderna-coronavirus-vaccine-trial-phase-3.

Gazit, S. R. Shlezinger, G. Perez, R. Lotan, A. Peretz, A. Ben-Tov, D. Cohen, K. Muhsen, G. Chodick, and T. Patalon. 2021. Comparing SARS-CoV-2 Natural Immunity to Vaccine-Induced Immunity: Reinfections Versus Breakthrough Infections. https://doi.org/10.1101/2021.08.24.21262415.

Ghazy, R.M., A. Almaghraby, R. Shaaban, et al. 2020. A Systematic Review and Meta-analysis on Chloroquine and Hydroxychloroquine as Monotherapy or Combined with Azithromycin in COVID-19 Treatment. *Scientific Reports* 10: 22139. https://doi.org/10.1038/s41598-020-77748-x.

Gupta, Swati. 2021. The Application and Future Potential of mRNA Vaccine. COVID-19 & You, Yale School of Public Health, New Haven, CT. Published on May 7, 2021. https://ysph.yale.edu/news-article/the-application-and-future-potential-of-mrna-vaccines/.

Henderson, D.A., Brooke Courtney, Thomas V. Inglesby, Eric Toner, and Jennifer B. Nuzzo. 2009. Public Health and Medical Responses to the 1957–58 Influenza Pandemic. *Biosecurity and Bioterrorism: Biodefense Strategy, Practice, and Science* 7 (3). https://doi.org/10.1089/bsp.2009.0729.

Hoover Institution. 2020. The Doctor Is In: Scott Atlas and the Efficacy of Lockdowns, Social Distancing, and Closings. Uncommon Knowledge with Peter Robinson. Palo Alto, CA: Hoover Institution, Stanford University. https://www.hoover.org/research/doctor-scott-atlas-and-efficacy-lockdowns-social-distancing-and-closings.

Johns Hopkins University (JHU). 2020. *COVID-19 Dash Board.* Baltimore, MD: JHU. https://data.humdata.org/dataset/novel-coronavirus-2019-ncov-cases.

Keuhl, R.O. 1999. *Design of Experiments: Statistical Principles of Research Design and Analysis.* 2nd ed. Pacific Grove, CA: Duxbury Press.

Kulldorff, Martin, Sunetra Gupta, and Jay Bhattacharya. 2020. The Great Barrington Declaration. https://gbdeclaration.org/.

Los Angeles Times. 2020. Californians Must Wear Face Masks in Public under Coronavirus Order Issued by Newsom. Published on June 18, 2020. https://www.latimes.com/california/story/2020-06-18/california-mandatory-face-masks-statewide-order-coronavirus-gavin-newsom.

Mahler, D. Gerszon, Christoph Lakner, R.A. Castaneda Aguilar, and Haoyu Wu. 2020. The Impact of COVID-19 (Coronavirus) on Global Poverty: Why Sub-Saharan Africa Might Be the Region Hardest Hit. *World Bank Blogs*. Updated on June 8, 2020. https://blogs.worldbank.org/opendata/impact-covid-19-coronavirus-global-poverty-why-sub-saharan-africa-might-be-region-hardest.

New York Times (NYT). 2020a. See Coronavirus Restrictions and Mask Mandates for All 50 States. Published on November 25, 2020. https://www.nytimes.com/interactive/2020/us/states-reopen-map-coronavirus.html.

———. 2020b. Coronavirus Vaccine Tracker. https://www.nytimes.com/interactive/2020/science/coronavirus-vaccine-tracker.html.

Nowrasteh, Alex. 2020. *Travel Restrictions and the Spread of COVID-19—What Does the Research Say? Cato at Library*. Washington, DC: The Cato Institute.

Oster, Emily, Rebecca Jack, Clare Halloran, John Schoof, and Diana McLeod. 2021. COVID-19 Mitigation Practices and COVID-19 Rates in Schools: Report on Data from Florida, New York and Massachusetts. medRxiv 2021.05.19.21257467; https://doi.org/10.1101/2021.05.19.21257467.

Our World in Data (OWID). 2021. Coronavirus (COVID-19) Vaccinations. https://github.com/owid/covid-19-data/tree/master/public/data/vaccinations.

Paterlini, Marta. 2020. 'Closing Borders Is Ridiculous': The Epidemiologist behind Sweden's Controversial Coronavirus Strategy. *Nature* 580 (7805): 574. https://doi.org/10.1038/d41586-020-01098-x.

Plotkin, Stanley A., ed. 2011. *History of Vaccine Development*. New York, NY: Springer.

Romer, Paul. 2020a. Even A Bad Test Can Help Guide the Decision to Isolate: Covid Simulations Part 3. Published on March 25, 2020. Accessed from Pualromer.net.

———. 2020b. Roadmap to Responsibly Reopen America. Published on April 23, 2020. Accessed from roadmap.paulromer.net.

Schwartz, M. 2001. The Life and Works of Louis Pasteur. *Journal of Applied Microbiology*. 91 (4): 597–601.

Seo, S.N. 2016. *Microbehavioral Econometric Methods: Theories, Models, and Applications for the Study of Environmental and Natural Resources*. Amsterdam, NL: Academic Press.

Smith, Leon G., Nicolas Mendoza, David Dobesh, and Stephen M. Smith. 2021. Observational Study on 255 Mechanically Ventilated Covid Patients at the Beginning of the USA Pandemic. *MedRxiv*. Published on May 31, 2021. https://doi.org/10.1101/2021.05.28.21258012.

The Local. 2020. Danish Study Finds No Clear Evidence Face Masks Protect Wearer from Covid-19 Infection. Published on November 18, 2020. https://www.thelocal.dk/20201118/danish-study-finds-no-clear-evidence-face-masks-protect-wearer-from-covid-19-infection.

The United Nations Educational, Scientific and Cultural Organization (UNESCO). 2020. Global Monitoring of School Closures Caused by COVID-19. UNESCO Institute of Statistics Data, UNESCO. https://data.humdata.org/dataset/global-school-closures-covid19.

United States Bureau of Economic Analysis (USBEA). 2020. *Gross Domestic Product, Third Quarter 2020 (Advance Estimate)*. Suitland, MD: USBEA, US Department of Commerce. https://www.bea.gov/sites/default/files/2020-10/gdp3q20_adv.pdf.

United States Bureau of Labor Statistics (USBLS). 2020. *Labor Force Statistics from the Current Population Survey*. Washington, DC: USBLS, US Department of Labor. https://data.bls.gov/timeseries/LNS14000000.

———. 2021. Consumer Prices Up 4.7 Percent since February 2020. *The Economics Daily*, USBLS, Department of Labor, USA. https://www.bls.gov/opub/ted/2021/consumer-prices-up-4-7-percent-since-february-2020.htm.

United States Department of Health and Human Services (USDHHS). 2020a. Explaining Operation Warp Speed. https://www.hhs.gov/coronavirus/explaining-operation-warp-speed/index.html.

———. 2020b. Secretary Azar Statement on President Trump's Invoking the Defense Production Act. Published on March 18, 2020. https://www.hhs.gov/about/news/2020/03/18/secretary-azar-statement-president-trumps-invoking-defense-production-act.html.

United States Department of the Treasury (USDOT). 2020. *The CARES Act Works for All Americans*. Washington, DC: USDOT. https://home.treasury.gov/policy-issues/cares.

United States Food & Drug Administration (USFDA). 2020a. *Coronavirus Treatment Acceleration Program (CTAP)*. Washington, DC: USFDA. https://www.fda.gov/drugs/coronavirus-covid-19-drugs/coronavirus-treatment-acceleration-program-ctap.

———. 2020b. *Emergency Use Authorization*. Washington, DC: USFDA. https://www.fda.gov/emergency-preparedness-and-response/mcm-legal-regulatory-and-policy-framework/emergency-use-authorization.

———. 2020c. Pfizer-BioNTech COVID-19 Vaccine EUA Letter of Authorization. https://www.fda.gov/media/144412/.

Wall Street Journal (WSJ). 2020a. Supreme Court Blocks Covid-19 Restrictions on Religious Services in New York. Published on November 26, 2020. https://www.wsj.com/articles/supreme-court-blocks-covid-19-restrictions-on-church-attendance-in-new-york-11606369004.

———. 2020b. House Passes $900 Billion Covid-19 Relief Package. Published on 21 December 2020. https://www.wsj.com/articles/covid-19-aid-package-set-for-final-votes-in-house-senate-11608566895.

Wells, Chad R., Pratha Sah, Seyed M. Moghadas, et al. 2020. Impact of International Travel and Border Control Measures on the Global Spread of the

Novel 2019 Coronavirus Outbreak. *Proceedings of the National Academy of Sciences USA* 117: 7504–7509. https://doi.org/10.1073/pnas.2002616117.

White House. 2020a. Executive Order on Prioritizing and Allocating Health and Medical Resources to Respond to the Spread of COVID-19. White House, Washington, DC. Published on March 18, 2020.

———. 2020b. How President Trump Uses the Defense Production Act to Protect America from the China Virus. Office of Trade and Manufacturing Policy, White House, Washington, DC.

———. 2020c. Proclamation on Suspension of Entry as Immigrants and Nonimmigrants of Persons Who Pose a Risk of Transmitting 2019 Novel Coronavirus. White House, Washington, DC.

———. 2020d. 30 Days to Slow the Spread. White House, Washington, DC. Published on March 16, 2020. https://www.whitehouse.gov/wp-content/uploads/2020/03/03.16.20_coronavirus-guidance_8.5x11_315PM.pdf.

World Health Organization (WHO). 2015. *International Health Regulations (2015)*. Geneva, CH: WHO.

———. 2019. *World Malaria Report 2019*. Geneva, CH: WHO.

———. 2020a. Q&As on COVID-19 and Related Health Topics. https://www.who.int/emergencies/diseases/novel-coronavirus-2019/question-and-answers-hub.

———. 2020b. *Malaria Vaccines*. Geneva, CH: WHO. https://www.who.int/immunization/research/development/malaria/en/.

Worldometers. 2021. Coronavirus COVID-19 Pandemic. Dover, DE. https://www.worldometers.info/coronavirus/.

Yale News. 2020. Quick and Affordable Saliva-Based COVID-19 Test Developed by Yale Scientists Receives FDA Emergency Use Authorization. Yale University, New Haven, CT. Published on August 15, 2020.

Pandemic Analysis III: The Great Reset, People's Uprisings, and Other Radical Change Proposals

1 A GOVERNMENT-AID ECONOMY WITH NO PRIVATE BUSINESSES UNDER THE COVID-19

The experiences during the COVID-19 pandemic are quite odd, unlike any other time since the middle of the twentieth century. On the one hand, it looks as if the world has transitioned itself into another system of global order. International travels are banned; private businesses are ordered to close; people are ordered to stay home while curfews are imposed; indoor religious gatherings are prohibited; people are fined for not wearing a mask and are ordered to wear a full-face mask even in the outdoors; an entry register is required at every building.

On the other hand, it appeared that the government has become sort of invincible. Government policy setters became confident that they should rescue every citizen in the nation from the miseries of the pandemic and keep track of every "bench" in the nation. They even come to believe that the all-powerful government should feed their citizens because private businesses are ordered to remain closed. The government started to send out checks to citizens and businesses, say, every month.

This new government was unimaginable before the COVID-19 pandemic outbreak. The ending of all private businesses for months or even years and the government relief checks sent out in equal amounts to feed the families, among other things, would remind many observers of a communist/Marxist economy similar to the Soviet Union's.

155
S. N. Seo, *The Economics of Pandemics*, https://doi.org/10.1007/978-3-030-91021-1_5

In the academic world, the dire times brought in by the COVID-19 have stirred the debate on transitioning the current economic order to a radically different one. The "Great Reset" is one of such movements put forth during the COVID-19 pandemic by a range of influential figures on the world stage (Schwab and Malleret 2020). A "Marxist Revolution" proposal is another of such movements (IMT 2020; SEP 2020). An "entrepreneurial government" proposal which espouses a largely expanded government is another of such theories (Mazzucato 2020b). The radical social change movements or proposals are depicted in Fig. 5.1 which includes the fourth movement labeled a popular uprising.

A rush of radical social change movements is not unique to the COVID-19 pandemic, nor is it unique to any other pandemic. Rather, it is one prominent feature that characterizes the times of a big social crisis. *Ergo*, the third component of the pandemic analyses of this book was selected by the present author.

These academic and/or political movements appear to have a common theory, *albeit* only implicitly expressed in some: the COVID-19 was

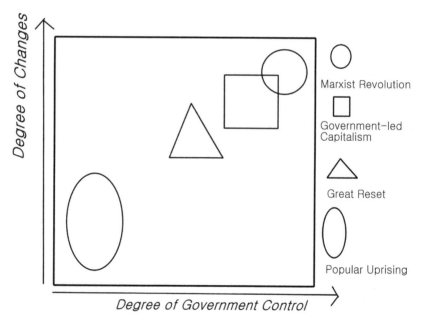

Fig. 5.1   Radical social change movements during the COVID-19

caused by capitalism. The post-COVID-19 world which these movements aspire to build should, therefore, be either a total transition away from a capitalist economy or a set of draconian shifts to correct the capitalist failures. In the extreme of these movements, the post-COVID-19 world should be an opposite side of capitalism, that is, a communist economy where all men and women are more or less equal in wealth and incomes (Marx 1867; Piketty 2014).

Now that the present author has clarified multifarious aspects of the COVID-19 pandemic through Chaps. 1, 2, 3 and 4, it will not be hard for readers to be confident that the COVID-19 pandemic was not caused by capitalism. On the contrary, it was witnessed that the capitalist economy with a better medical system, an advanced virology, cutting-edge pharmaceutical companies, and superior information technologies has equipped humanity with essential tools and expertise needed to fight the novel coronavirus.

In this chapter, the present author will offer a somewhat broad review of the radical social transformation movements spurred by and formulated during the COVID-19 pandemic. The present author will critically evaluate each of the above-mentioned four movements and/or theories, especially with keen eyes on their assertions on the COVID-19 pandemic. An important dimension of the evaluations is the relationships between the COVID-19 pandemic and the poor in the society. The present author will explain some of the emerging studies on the income levels and the COVID-19 examined from the angle of the pandemic's impacts on the low-income groups as well as the angle of the economic recoveries of different income groups of the society (Mahler et al. 2020; ICL 2020; Clark 2020).

2   MOVEMENT I: THE GREAT RESET

The conception of the idea of a "great reset," which was one of the most sought-after ideas in 2020, seems to be originated from the annual World Economic Forum (WEF) held on January 21–24 in Davos, Switzerland. The WEF, in the run-up to the annual meeting, held a virtual series named "The Great Reset Dialogues." The WEF introduced it as a joint initiative of the WEF and the Prince of Wales (WEF 2020a). The agenda of the Great Reset was elaborated later through the publication of "COVID-19: The Great Reset" in July 2020 (Schwab and Malleret 2020). The book's first author is the founder and executive chairman of the WEF.

The essence of the Great Reset movement or proposal is that the COVID-19 pandemic presents to the world community a rare opportunity to reset the existing global economic system. As one of the proponents puts it, "its unprecedented shockwaves may well make people more receptive to big visions of change" (Guardian 2020). A new economic system to which the proponents desire to drive the world varies across the proponents but is centered around the ideas of sustainable development, equity, provisions of public goods.

2.1   A Diagnosis of the Pandemic

The proponents often start with a common theory, which is more accurately a hypothesis, about the cause of the COVID-19 pandemic. They argue that the global pandemic is the result of a breakdown in the relationship between humanity and nature in the capitalist economy. The pandemic, according to them, was caused by the failure in the capitalist market economy (Guardian 2020).

Having explained the literature of the COVID-19 pandemic extensively from Chaps. 1, 2, 3 and 4, the present author does not need to comment at length here on the naiveness of their view on the cause of the pandemic. The coronavirus has been with humanity for a long time and has manifested multiple times to be a global crisis even before the COVID-19 pandemic. The Severe Acute Respiratory Syndrome (SARS) outbreak in 2002 and the Middle East Respiratory Syndrome (MERS) outbreak in 2009 had already killed millions of people worldwide (Coleman and Frieman 2014). The COVID-19 originated from the coronavirus in horseshoe bats, directly or via an intermediate species, or from the Wuhan Virology Institute laboratory's accidental leaks, although the origin is still being investigated (WSJ 2021; WHO 2021). As of August 2021, no person in the world seems to blame capitalism for the pandemic.

A subtler diagnosis about the pandemic by the great reset proponents is that the COVID-19 pandemic exposes "inconsistencies, inadequacies, and contradictions" across the systems in the capitalist market economy (WEF 2020a, b). The COVID-19 pandemic, they argue, is "fundamentally changing" the ways how decisions are made in the economy.

One of the proponents argues that the "neoliberalist ideology has increasingly prevailed" in the world, which can be summarized, according to him, by "the notion that the market knows best and the government should refrain from setting clear rules" in the market. According to

Schwab, these dogmatic beliefs proved wrong by the COVID-19 crisis and other crises (Schwab and Malleret 2020; WEF 2020b).

This diagnosis is, to say modestly, remote and even aloof from the difficult realities that people have had to go through during the COVID-19 pandemic. No ordinary people seemed to care much about the capitalist economy during the year 2020 because they had to fend themselves off from the pandemic virus and cope with the infections and deaths of their family members and friends. Ordinary people were desperate to open their small businesses to feed their families and pay rents, which had been ordered to shut down by the government who was single-mindedly fixated on stopping the spread of the disease.

Did it expose the "inconsistencies, inadequacies, and contradictions" in the systems of the economy? What they mean by this assertion can be known from the agendas put forth to be explained below. It may have or may not, but it is extremely hard to argue that the market economy proved wrong or inferior because of the inconsistencies, among others, revealed by the pandemic. Faced with the pandemic, the national governments had to make a basket of serious decisions which has turned out to be consequential. At those critical moments, the governments around the world were not concerned about the faults of the market economy in place, neither were the citizens.

2.2   The Five-Point Agenda

What is the agenda of the Great Reset movement? Different groups of people presented their unique agendas under the same banner of the Great Reset, but the common areas of their agendas lie in such themes as sustainable development, climate change, equity, and public goods.

One of the Great Reset agendas, so-called the five-point agenda outlined by the Prince of Wales, lays an emphasis on sustainability and climate change policy efforts in an aspirational manner, as readers can verify in the below (Guardian 2020):

> *[Point I] To capture the imagination and will of humanity—change will only happen if people really want it;*
> *[Point II] The economic recovery must put the world on the path to sustainable employment, livelihoods and growth. Longstanding incentive structures that have had perverse effects on our planetary environment and nature herself must be reinvented;*

[Point III] Systems and pathways must be redesigned to advance net zero transitions globally. Carbon pricing can provide a critical pathway to a sustainable market;

[Point IV] Science, technology and innovation need re-invigorating. Humanity is on the verge of catalytic breakthroughs that will alter our view of what is possible and profitable in the framework of a sustainable future;

[Point V] Investment must be rebalanced. Accelerating green investments can offer job opportunities in green energy, the circular and bio-economy, eco-tourism and green public infrastructure.

The five-point agenda is dominantly oriented toward aggressive climate policies to address climate change (Nordhaus 2008). The second point refers to the investments in the planetary environment; the third point refers to net-zero carbon emissions; the fourth point refers to the investments into climate and sustainability technologies; the fifth item refers to green investments.

The readers of this book would wonder quite naturally why the new direction of the world economy should be predominantly directed to a net-zero carbon economy and other climate investments to promote it at the end of a global pandemic which might end up killing tens of millions of people worldwide.

2.3   The Great Reset Agenda

In another rendition of the Great Reset agenda spelled out by Schwab, overarching ideas are equity, sustainability, and public goods. This agenda is expressed in an academic manner and grounded with many suggestions of specific policy changes. According to the WEF version, it has three main components (Schwab and Malleret 2020; WEF 2020b).

The first is a shift toward fairer outcomes and equitable outcomes. The authors argue that such outcomes should be achieved through changes in tax, regulations, and fiscal policy. Specifically, they refer to changes in wealth taxes and the withdrawal of fossil-fuel subsidies, in addition to new rules and regulations on intellectual property, trade, and competition.

The second component is the investments that advance shared goals, for which the authors refer to equality and sustainability. The authors argue that the large economic relief and/or spending programs spurred by the COVID-19 pandemic present a major opportunity for the governments across the world.

In the US, the Coronavirus Aid, Relief, and Economic Security (CARES) Act was passed and signed into law on March 27, 2020, with the size of the relief package amounting to US$2.2 trillion (USDOT 2020). The second relief package, named the American Rescue Plan Act, was signed into law in March 2021, with a total aid of US$1.9 trillion. The European Commission unveiled a €750 billion recovery package in July 2020 (EC 2021).

The authors propose that, instead of using these funds, for example, as cash handouts to relieve the pains of families and small businesses, these funds should be used to create "a new system" that is "more resilient, equitable, and sustainable in the long run." The authors further elaborate that the funds should be directed to building green urban infrastructure and incentivizing industries to improve their record on "environmental, social, and governance metrics."

The third component of the Great Reset agenda is that the innovations of the "Fourth Industrial Revolution" be utilized for the support of the public goods. The authors point to the public goods in health problems and social challenges. The kinds of innovations that are referred to by the authors are collaborations between companies, universities, and others for developing diagnostics, therapeutics, and vaccines; establishing COVID-19 testing centers; tracing infections; delivering telemedicine, that is, remote caring between patients and a provider, during the pandemic.

2.4   A Critique of the Great Reset Agenda

In the above, the present author offered two critiques to the Great Reset movement and its agendas. One was leveled against their diagnosis on the origin of the novel coronavirus. The other was leveled against their push for a draconian climate change policy program as a response to the global pandemic, which the present author argued is only weakly reasoned.

The third critique to be offered presently is concerned with the proposition that the economic relief funds such as those in the CARES Act and others should be directed to a potpourri of social engineering programs that promotes equality and/or sustainability in the society. In Chap. 4, the present author explained that an economic relief package during the pandemic should have a clear goal of providing an economic relief of the distress of the families that result from the government-ordered business closures and lockdowns. That is, it should not be seen by policy setters as an opportunity for income redistributions among the populations.

An income redistribution policy even during a "normal" time is a source of great political turmoil in any democratic country in the world. The political turmoil brought about by such an income redistribution effort by the government during the pandemic time will add to and even accelerate the livelihood disruptions caused by the global pandemic itself. To be elaborate, such a wealth redistribution effort at the time of a pandemic, via changes in wealth tax, selective aid programs, or other regulatory changes, will make the society's effective responses to the pandemic far more difficult. At the same time, it will likely fail in the end to achieve the income redistribution goal.

Why will that be the case? When the government implements a COVID-19 pandemic wealth redistribution program, people will no longer consider the pandemic as a global universal health crisis but will consider it as an economic opportunity. People in the income groups that are aided financially will take more risk and less precaution against the pandemic virus, making the containment efforts far more onerous or be of no consequence in the extreme. Further, the winners from the pandemic created by the government income program will be increasingly separated from the losers, which will increase social tensions among the populations to possibly result in a big social disruption.

There is ample evidence in policy studies that such a large-scale income redistribution policy as a response to another very different policy problem is doomed to fail in achieving the goals in both policy areas (Seo 2020). Take global climate change negotiations for example during the last three decades. Although the Rio Earth Summit in 1992 set the stage nicely for a global big deal for climate change, as soon as the underdeveloped countries demanded a planetwide wealth redistribution as a precondition on account of the historical carbon emissions by rich countries, for example, at Copenhagen Conference in 2009, global talks have failed to progress and but rather deteriorated (UNFCCC 2009; Nordhaus 2010; Seo 2017).

A microbehavioral economic analysis such as the one just described is amply found in many governmental as well as international policy programs. A recent policy focus of the international community lies in the allocations of the Green Climate Fund (GCF) across the countries (GCF 2020). If the Green Climate Fund, an international specialized agency of the United Nations, were to give a monetary aid to the farms in Africa with the most vulnerable agricultural system to climate change, it would give an incentive to the most vulnerable populations in the continent to stick to the same system in anticipation of a continued aid from an international Fund or another (Seo 2019). The consequence is that the funding will hinder the most vulnerable farmers from adapting to climate change efficiently by switching to another more resilient system (Seo 2015, 2016).

The take-home message from this section is this: although we can agree that fairer outcomes, equity, sustainability, and public goods are all an aspiration to be pursued, it is rushed to argue that such efforts should be made at a worldwide scale during a once-in-a-century pandemic. It is even ill-reasoned to propose that such goals should be pursued via a draconian wealth redistribution program such as a certain kind of pandemic relief program.

3   MOVEMENT II: AN ENTREPRENEURIAL GOVERNMENT-LED CAPITALISM

Switching gears from the previous section, let us consider a different proposal which also focuses on the failures of capitalism: a proposal for a transition toward a different kind of capitalism via the experiences of the global pandemic. In the proposed kind of capitalism, the government is the first investor in the economy. The government acts like a private entrepreneur who actively creates markets and invests in the government's priority projects. It can be called an entrepreneurial government capitalism or a government-led capitalism (Mazzucato 2020a).

The diagnosis by the proponent of this theory of the COVID-19 pandemic argues that the government, in this case the UK government, was not prepared to take on the COVID-19 challenge. Faced with many other challenges including "climate breakdown," the government will take actions but not be able to respond effectively. Why so? The author argues as follows (Mazzucato 2020a):

Since the 1980s, governments have been told to take a back seat and let business steer and create wealth, intervening only for the purpose of fixing problems when they arise. The result is that governments are not always properly prepared and equipped to deal with crises such as COVID-19 or the climate emergency.

Notwithstanding that the government will take "desperate" actions to stimulate the economy and contain the spread of the pandemic, even at the scale of a war effort, the above author argues that all actions will add up to be insufficient while already too late. The government has a tendency to wait, according to the proponent, without sufficient preparations until an eventual strike of a big systemic shock.

What does the advocate propose as appropriate government responses to the COVID-19 pandemic? The key argument is that the government should go way beyond just responding to the pandemic. The government should not merely respond to the pandemic nor just fix the market failures that resulted in the pandemic, but actively "shape and create markets that deliver sustainable and inclusive growth" (Mazzucato 2020b). The proposals by the advocate include the following: (1) the government investments and creations of institutions that help to prevent crises, for example, the National Health Service (NHS) in the UK; (2) a better coordination of the Research and Development (R&D) activities in health; (3) the public-private partnerships; and (4) a well-designed bailout plan.

The entrepreneurial government argument is not the idea borne specifically out of the COVID-19 pandemic but seems to be rather concerned with a broader economic system. Having acknowledged that, how could we evaluate their diagnoses and proposals about the pandemic and government responses? First, the governmental capitalism argument has the same diagnosis about the COVID-19 pandemic as the Great Reset proponents in that the pandemic is the result of the failures of capitalism. In addition, it lays an emphasis on the government's failures under the capitalist economy.

The present author can offer several critiques on their diagnoses and suggestions. First, as explained in the previous section, it is difficult to attribute the COVID-19 pandemic origination exclusively to the government failures in the capitalist economy. The origin may be from natural sources or an accident from the laboratory in the communist system, that is, China (WHO 2021).

Second, it is a long stretch to attribute the large number of COVID-19 mortalities exclusively to the government's failures in the capitalist economy. As reviewed extensively in Chap. 4, governmental responses in the US and the UK were anchored by heavy-handed government-imposed restrictions, which would not be usually considered as the responses of the capitalist economy.

With regard to the NHS in the UK, the present author discussed in detail in Chap. 2 that the health systems in other capitalist economies have different types of health systems, for example, the US' private insurance-based system and Germany's national health insurance (NHI) system

(Rice et al. 2013; NHS 2020). As such, the NHS is hard to be seen as a failure in the capitalist economy.

Third, the proposal that the government in the capitalist economy should be the first investor of all investors in the society is most likely not compatible with the capitalist economic system itself. For the capitalist economy to function in the best possible way, it is essential to have a free-market exchange economy, which means that no one should be able to fix market prices. A mammoth government which dominates investment decisions in the society will, by and large, determine prices in the markets, therefore, undermining the success of the capitalist economy (Hayek 1948; Friedman 1962; Mas-Colell et al. 1995).

Fourth, the hands of the government in the capitalist economy are tied rather tightly by regulations, legislations, and the judicial system. Even though an annual government budget is very large in the capitalist country, that is, surpassing any corporation's earnings and any investor's earnings by far, a large fraction of the national budget goes to defense and military while many essential government activities are tightly defined, for example, police works, public works including waste disposals, and provisions of other public goods in the economy (Samuelson and Nordhaus 2009; Seo 2020).

Alternatively stated, the government cannot be a risk-taker as a private investor does. If it does, then it will not able to justify its decisions to the constituents when a big loss event should strike.

Looking into it from a bird's-eye view, the argument for the government capitalism or the entrepreneurial state would be indistinguishable from a socialist economy or a Marxist economy if it should go the distance. It will be hard to draw a line between them. Imagine the national government which taxes 50% of individual incomes and business earnings as well as 70% of individuals' wealth. And imagine further that this government has its hands completely freed, as such, it can invest in any basket of activities it desires for the public goods' provisions including public health. This economy will approximate the communist or Marxist economy.

To sum up, the entrepreneurial government proponents appear to have only weak evidence and rationale to argue that (1) the COVID-19 was originated from the government's failures in capitalism; (2) governmental responses from the capitalist economy were to blame for a large number of mortalities from the pandemic; (3) the government acting as the first investor of the economy will stop future pandemics; and (4) the government-driven capitalism will be a better economic system than a free market-driven capitalism.

4   MOVEMENT III: A MARXIST REVOLUTION

Although the two movements or proposals discussed in the previous two sections seek a new system or another within the capitalist economy by correcting the ills of capitalism, other movements that were triggered by the COVID-19 pandemic expressly call for an end of the capitalist economic system which should be replaced by a revolutionary socialist government. Here the present author briefly reviews the proposals by Marxism-inspired organizations.

The advocates begin with a diagnosis of the COVID-19 pandemic outbreak that global capitalism is the only culprit for it. The International Marxist Tendency (IMT) which is active in over 40 countries states that "the devastation of the coronavirus pandemic is a product of capitalism, a system that puts profit over the lives of people (IMT 2020)." The Socialist Equality Party (SEP), also active in many countries, frames the COVID-19 pandemic as "a trigger event that has both revealed and accelerated the crisis of global capitalism" (SEPA 2020).

The Marxist movement blames the global capitalism as a whole for the COVID-19 pandemic crisis. The proponents do not heed to the facts concerning the origin that the COVID-19 crisis is highly likely to be originated from China; the novel coronavirus may have been transmitted from horseshoe bats, whether or not via another intermediate species, to humans; alternatively, it may have been leaked from the Wuhan Virology Institute's laboratory where coronavirus experiments had been conducted before the COVID-19 outbreak (Fox News 2020; WHO 2021; Reuters 2021).

In addition, the advocates lay the blame on the lack of preparedness and prevention by the governments in power. They level that the governments around the world showed "criminal indifference and negligence" in the preparations against the pandemic as well as the responses to it, resulting in a rapid spread of the pandemic and deaths of millions of people (SEPA 2020).

Based on these interpretations, the advocates argue that the COVID-19 pandemic reveals that a revolutionary socialist program is the only solution to the global capitalism's failures on the pandemic. Further, they assert that the pandemic gives the impetus to the ongoing deeply rooted class struggle between the ruling class and the working class while it necessitates a fundamental social change toward a Marxist government (IMT 2020; SEPA 2020).

Henceforth, based on a rather brief review of this movement, the present author would like to outline several critiques on their proposals. The first is that they look over the fact that the most advanced capitalist economy has succeeded in producing highly effective pandemic virus vaccines in record time, in only nine months, because of the entrepreneurial successes of the leading pharmaceutical companies such as Pfizer, Moderna, Johnson & Johnson, Novavax, and AstraZeneca which are one of the hallmarks of capitalism (USFDA 2020a, b).

In the Marxist economy in which the supplies of medicines and medical services are controlled by the government and the communist party, such successful pharmaceutical companies with cutting-edge technologies would not be possible to build, making it far more difficult to develop rapidly such highly effective vaccines during the pandemic strikes (Azar II 2020).

Second, the vaccine success in 2020 is in turn in large part attributable to the advances in microbiology, medicine, and virology accomplished and dominated by the universities and research centers in the most capitalist economy, say, the US (Kariko et al. 2011; Pardi et al. 2018).

Third, the medical devices that were urgently needed in hospitals around the world during the COVID-19 crisis in 2020 were made available through a successful partnership between the capitalist government and high-tech private businesses. With the invocation of a wartime emergency production system, major private companies were called upon to produce the emergency devices, including General Motors (GM), General Electric (GE), and Phillips. The devices produced included rapid COVID-19 test kits, ventilators, respirators, emergency field hospitals (USDHHS 2020).

These successes demonstrate that the capitalist economy marked by successful high-tech businesses is not a hindrance but an essential weapon in the fight against a highly lethal contagious virus. In addition, the capitalist economic system nestled in a democratic political system proved to be flexible enough to fight the pandemic together when called upon as demonstrated by the partnerships between the government sector and private businesses. For these reasons and others, the capitalist economy is better positioned to fight a pandemic virus than a Marxist economy is.

Fourth, what about the overall government responses? The government's choices in the capitalist economy were clarified in detail in Chap. 4, which showed that the responses were unfortunately focused on restrictions of people's and businesses' activities with heavy-handed measures, like a national lockdown and a universal mask mandate. This does not mean that the government in the capitalist society has to behave in that way. On the contrary, as the present author elaborated in that chapter, a different course of governmental actions was certainly possible and perhaps a more apposite one to the capitalist society, say, based on individual responsibility. The government of Sweden demonstrated it (Deccan Herald 2020; Financial Times 2020).

Fifth, the Marxist advocates may assert that a global pandemic is more likely to occur in a capitalist economy than in a Marxist economy, which is amply implied in the quotations in the beginning of this section. It is an assertion difficult to validate quantitatively, owing in part to only a small number of global pandemics that broke out after, say, the Russian revolution (Marx 1867).

On the one hand, humankind has advanced remarkably in the fields of biology, epidemiology, virology, and medical sciences over the past two millenniums. These advances made it possible for humanity to declare an eradication of many deadly infectious diseases such as smallpox and malaria in developed countries (WHO 2020). These achievements are attributable to a large extent to the success of the market economy in the capitalist society.

On the other hand, humans are not yet able to fully prevent or control infectious diseases, especially highly contagious ones. Every year, an influenza virus kills hundreds of thousands of people globally (Potter 2001; Lopez et al. 2006; Iuliano et al. 2018). Even since the dawn of the twenty-first century, four lethal infectious diseases have hit human society hard, including the SARS, the H1N1 pandemic, the MERS, and the COVID-19 (Coleman and Frieman 2014).

Put the five arguments together, a rush toward a Marxist society, either through a revolution or through an election, on the basis of the miseries brought about by the COVID-19 pandemic would be a grave misstep for humanity, which is possible only in the absence of careful analysis and far-reaching reflection.

5   MOVEMENT IV: A TRIGGER OF THE UPRISINGS AND REVOLUTIONS BY THE MOST HURT

The radical social change movements described thus far are solidly based on an intellectual tradition respectively, that is, are rooted in a respective theoretical model. A populist uprising or revolution that will be explained in this section is distinct from the above because it is an uprising of the people who are hurt during the pandemic, that is, a popular uprising. In addition, as shown in Fig. 5.1, it is shown to be unique among them in that it does not call for an increased and lasting government control over the economy.

According to this line of reasoning, a popular uprising may erupt at the end of the pandemic because the current global pandemic will hurt the people disproportionately, if past revolutions sprung from a widening disparity among the populations are any indication (Davies 1962; Gurr 1968; Tiruneh 2014). If the COVID-19 were to exacerbate the existing gap, for example, between the rich and the poor, the pandemic's tail may arrive with an uprising or revolution led by the poor people who are also hurt the most by the pandemic (Kluth 2020).

According to the advocates, the global pandemic's "trauma and tragedy" endured by people may eventually erupt. People suffered from forced lockdowns, forced business closures, quarantines, deaths, sickness, school closures, restrictions on social gatherings, banning of street protests, and more. All of these repressive policies may trigger an eruption at the tail end of the pandemic (Kluth 2020).

The COVID-19 pandemic has affected all people on the planet in one way or another, more or less, and so have the government's pandemic policies. That being the case, an uprising or revolution, if it were to indeed occur, may take the form of "all the people," that is, not led by a certain group of people, for example, a working class of the society. Such an all-inclusive revolution could be a push back against, *inter alia*, a big brother government during the pandemic which severely restricted people's ways of life.

In sum, a popular uprising can take one of the two forms. The first is an uprising by the people who were hurt the most by the pandemic, for example, the low-income class. The second form is an all-inclusive societal revolution, for example, against a big brother government or for a restoration of pre-pandemic norms.

5.1 The Divergent Economic and Health Impacts of the COVID-19

There are new economic studies, summarized in Table 5.1, that show that the impacts of the pandemic are disproportionate across the income groups and further that the economic recovery may also diverge into two different paths (Mahler et al. 2020; Clark 2020). If these divergencies were to get larger and larger at the tail end of the pandemic, then a popular uprising may be led by a coalition of the most harmed groups of the society against the rest of the society.

Multiple research groups reported that low-income families will be hurt more by the global pandemic than high-income families. First, relying on large-scale household surveys, UK researchers calculated the probability of death during the COVID-19 pandemic across different income rungs (Model I in Table 5.1). The lower-income families have limited health security due to numerous structural factors of which the researchers consider the following three: (1) limited handwashing capacity, (2) occupations that are not amenable to social distancing, and (3) limited access to timely healthcare. Plugging the scores in these three measures into the COVID-19 transmission model, the researchers argued that the lower-income families are 32% more likely to die during the pandemic than the higher-income families (ICL 2020).

In another study led by the World Bank researchers (Model II in Table 5.1), the COVID-19 pandemic will push 71 million to 100 million people worldwide into extreme poverty which was measured by the authors at the international poverty line of US$1.9 per day (Mahler et al. 2020). They argue that the new poor who are born by the COVID-19

Table 5.1 The COVID-19 economic/health impact divergence models

	Indicators	Populations of interest	Predictions
Model I (ICL 2020)	The probability of death	Low-income families	Lower-income families are 32% more likely to die than the higher-income families
Model II Mahler et al. (2020)	Extreme poverty	The global poor earning < US$1.9/ day	71 million to 100 million people worldwide pushed into extreme poverty
Model III (Polyakova et al. 2021)	Excess all-cause mortality (EAM)	Racial groups	The EAM is 6.8 (per 10,000) for Blacks, 4.3 for Hispanics, 2.7 for Asians, and 1.5 for Whites
Model IV (Clark 2020)	K-recovery	Fast recovery industries versus stagnant recovery industries	The winners are high-tech, retail, and software services; the losers may include small businesses, travel, entertainment, hospitality, and food services

pandemic will be different from the existing poor. The new poor will be mostly located in urban areas and employed mostly in informal services, construction, and manufacturing (Sanchez-Paramo 2020).

A third study examines the adjusted excess all-cause mortality (AEACM) relying on the data from January 2011 to April 2020 in the US (Model III in Table 5.1). It finds the AEACM is 6.8 (per 10,000) for Black people, 4.3 for Hispanic people, 2.7 for Asian people, and 1.5 for White people (Polyakova et al. 2021). According to this study, minority groups have suffered far more badly from the pandemic than White people.

A fourth study, Model IV in Table 5.1, reports a divergence in the economic recovery from the pandemic across the range of industries. An economic recovery of the US in 2020 was discussed in detail in Chap. 4, which showed a sharp recovery during the latter two quarters of 2020 after a deep plunge in the first two quarters of 2020 (USBEA 2020; USBLS 2020). The sharp rebound was referred colloquially to a V-shape recovery or a V recovery in short.

On the other hand, the recovery may eventually diverge into two very different paths: on the one side, the path that follows the V recovery and, on the other side, the path where the recovery is not coming and even getting worse. We can call the former the swift recovery group and the latter the stagnant recovery group from the pandemic. This diverging economic recovery model is colloquially referred to as the K recovery model (Clark 2020).

The two recovery groups can be defined by different criteria while the most common criterion was the industrial sectors. The swift recovery group may include the industries such as high-tech businesses (Google, Apple, Twitter, Facebook, Bitcoin, etc.), retail home deliveries (Amazon, etc.), and software services (gaming, home entertainment, etc.). The stagnant recovery group may include the industries such as small businesses, travel services, hotels, and food services (Clark 2020).

Considering the four models in Table 5.1, there are reasons to expect that the COVID-19 pandemic will end up hitting the low-income group more severely than the high-income group. The degree of divergence, on the other hand, will depend on how subgroups in each income group are impacted differently by the pandemic. If the recoveries of the subgroups within the low-income group are uneven, then the degree of divergence would diminish. Similarly, if the recoveries of the subgroups within the high-income group are disparate, then the degree of divergence would diminish as well.

6   WILL THEY HAVE ANY IMPACT ON SOCIETY?

In this chapter, the present author reviewed the four proposals or movements that predict a radical social change inspired by the experiences of the COVID-19 pandemic. I hope they are presented in a brief but comprehensive manner so that readers can appreciate each of these movements and can compare one with another.

The four movements can be distinguished by two dimensions, as done in Fig. 5.1: the degree of social changes called for and the degree of government control advocated. The Marxist revolution, marked by a circle, is placed on the top-right corner of the diagram, which ranks highest in both dimensions. The government-led capitalism, marked by a square, is next to the Marxist revolution. In the middle of both dimensions, the Great Reset movement, marked by a triangle, may be appropriately placed. The popular uprising ranks lowest in the dimension of government control advocated while the degree of social changes called for may have a wide range, which was marked in the figure by an ellipse.

Of the four movements, the present author feels personally that a people's uprising driven by the trauma and tragedy that befell them during the pandemic can be reasonably expected. A revolution of the people, if it were to materialize, would be non-ideology-driven, unlike the Marxist revolution. It may not turn out to be a specific agenda-driven either such as the Great Reset movement which is heavy on sustainability and climate change agenda.

The people's revolution, driven neither by ideology nor by specific agenda, would have a focus on the restoration of normality to the pre-pandemic world. People will likely demand a review of the pandemic-time policies that severely restricted civil liberty with regard to lockdowns, social gatherings, religious services, mask mandates, curfews, business closures, and school closures. Similarly, people will likely demand a review of the abnormal events and policies taken place during the pandemic, especially that led to personal tragedies.

From another viewpoint, did any of these movements have any noticeable effect on the society during the course of the pandemic? Some of them certainly did, although it is difficult to discern and measure at this point. Looking ahead, the Great Reset movement may be best positioned to yield the most influence on the society, among the four proposals, if the Biden infrastructure plan were to eventually pass into a law, as the US$2.2 trillion plan places a high priority on sustainability and climate change agendas (NYT 2021).

Whether or not any of these movements will be realized in the coming years depends on how long the COVID-19 pandemic would last. On the one hand, the US economy rapidly recovered from the crashes in the first and second quarters of 2020. By comparison, during the Great Depression of the 1930s, the US unemployment rate remained above 12% until the end of the entire decade (Shiller 2019; Reuters 2020). On a more pessimistic note, the world has entered into the fifth wave of the pandemic from around June of 2021, even surpassing the peaks in new cases of infection set during the previous four waves, notwithstanding the high vaccination rates in developed countries, for example, over 70% vaccination rate achieved in the EU by the end of July 2021 (JHU 2021).

References

Azar, Alex M. II. 2020. How Operation Warp Speed Delivered a COVID Vaccine in Record Time. Fox News. Published on 12 December 2020. https://www.foxnews.com/opinion/hhs-azar-operation-warp-speed-covid-vaccine-record-time.

Clark, Suzanne. 2020. *What Is the K-Shaped Recovery?* Washington, DC: US Chamber of Commerce. https://www.uschamber.com/series/above-the-fold/what-the-k-shaped-recovery.

Coleman, C.M., and M.B. Frieman. 2014. Coronaviruses: Important Emerging Human Pathogens. *Journal of Virology* 8: 5209–5212.

Davies, J.C. 1962. Toward a Theory of Revolution. *American Sociological Review* 6: 5–19.

Deccan Herald. 2020. No Lockdowns, But Sweden Seems to Have Controlled the Covid-19 pandemic. Published on October 1, 2020. https://www.deccanherald.com/opinion/panorama/no-lockdowns-but-sweden-seems-to-have-controlled-the-covid-19-pandemic-895509.html.

European Council (EC). 2021. *A Recovery Plan for Europe.* Brussels, BE: EC. https://www.consilium.europa.eu/en/policies/eu-recovery-plan/.

Financial Times. 2020. Architect of Sweden's No-Lockdown Strategy Insists It Will Pay Off. Published on May 8, 2020. https://www.ft.com/content/a2b4c18c-a5e8-4edc-8047-ade4a82a548d.

Fox News. 2020. State Department Drops "Previously Undisclosed" Info on Wuhan Lab. https://video.foxnews.com/v/6223384424001#sp=show-clips.

Friedman, Milton. 1962. *Capitalism and Freedom.* Chicago, IL: The University of Chicago Press.

Green Climate Fund (GCF). 2020. *Projects + Programmes.* Songdo City, KR: The GCF. https://www.greenclimate.fund/what-we-do/projects-programmes.

Guardian. 2020. Pandemic is chance to reset global economy, says Prince Charles. Published on June 3, 2020.

Gurr, T.R. 1968. A Causal Model of Civil Strife: A Comparative Analysis of Using New Indices. *American Political Science Review* 62: 1104–1124.

Hayek, Friedrich A. 1948. *Individualism and Economic Order*. Chicago, IL: The University of Chicago Press.

Imperial College London (ICL). 2020. *Equity in Response to the COVID-19 Pandemic: An Assessment of the Direct and Indirect Impacts on Disadvantaged and Vulnerable Populations in Low- and Lower Middle-Income Countries*. London: ICL.

International Marxist Tendency (IMT). 2020. A Socialist Program to Fight COVID-19 and the Economic Crisis. https://socialistrevolution.org/a-socialist-program-to-fight-covid-19-and-the-economic-crisis/.

Iuliano, A.D., K.M. Roguski, H.H. Chang, et al. 2018. Global Seasonal Influenza-Associated Mortality Collaborator Network. Estimates of Global Seasonal Influenza-associated Respiratory Mortality: A Modelling Study. *Lancet* 391 (10127): 1285–1300. https://doi.org/10.1016/S0140-6736(17)33293-2.

Johns Hopkins University (JHU). 2021. *COVID-19 Dash Board*. Baltimore, MD: JHU. https://data.humdata.org/dataset/novelcoronavirus-2019-ncov-cases.

Kariko, K., H. Muramatsu, J. Ludwig, and D. Weissman. 2011. Generating the Optimal mRNA for Therapy: HPLC Purification Eliminates Immune Activation and Improves Translation for Nucleoside-modified, Protein-encoding mRNA. *Nucleic Acids Research* 39: e142.

Kluth, Andreas. 2020. This Pandemic Will Lead to Social Revolutions. Bloomberg. Published on April 11. https://www.bloomberg.com/opinion/articles/2020-04-11/coronavirus-this-pandemic-will-lead-to-social-revolutions.

Lopez, Alan D., Colin D. Mathers, Majid Ezzati, Dean T. Jamison, and Christopher J.L. Murray. 2006. *Global Burden of Disease and Risk Factors*. New York, NY: World Bank and Oxford University Press.

Mahler, D. Gerszon, Christoph Lakner, R.A. Castaneda Aguilar, and Haoyu Wu. 2020. The Impact of COVID-19 (Coronavirus) on Global Poverty: Why Sub-Saharan Africa Might Be the Region Hardest Hit. *World Bank Blogs*. Updated on June 8, 2020. https://blogs.worldbank.org/opendata/impact-covid-19-coronavirus-global-poverty-why-sub-saharan-africa-might-be-region-hardest.

Marx, Karl. 1867. Das Kapital. Kritik der politischen Oekonomie. Verlag von Otto Meisner, Germany.

Mas-Colell, A., M.D. Whinston, and J.R. Green. 1995. *Microeconomic Theory*. Oxford: Oxford University Press.

Mazzucato, M. 2020a. It's 2023. Here's How We Fixed the Global Economy. *Time Magazine*. Published on October 22, 2020.

————. 2020b. The Covid-19 Crisis is a Chance to Do Capitalism Differently. *The Guardian*. Published on March 18, 2020.

National Health Service (NHS). 2020. *Guidance: The NHS Constitution for England*. NHS, UK. https://www.gov.uk/government/publications/the-nhs-constitution-for-england.

New York Times (NYT). 2021. Biden Details $2 Trillion Plan to Rebuild Infrastructure and Reshape the Economy. Published on April 15, 2021. https://www.nytimes.com/2021/03/31/business/economy/biden-infrastructure-plan.html

Nordhaus, William D. 2008. *A Question of Balance: Weighing the Options on Global Warming Policies*. New Haven, CT: Yale University Press.

————. 2010. Economic Aspects of Global Warming in a post-Copenhagen Environment. *Proceedings of the National Academy of Sciences USA* 107: 11721–11726.

Pardi, N., M.J. Hogan, F.W. Porter, and D. Weissman. 2018. mRNA Vaccines—A New Era in Vaccinology. *Nature Reviews Drug Discovery* 17: 261–279.

Piketty, Thomas. 2014. *Capital in the Twenty-First Century*. Cambridge, MA: Belknap Press.

Polyakova, Maria, Victoria Udalova, Geoffrey Kocks, Katie Genadek, Keith Finlay, and Amy Finkelstein. 2021. Racial Disparities in Excess All-Cause Mortality During the Early Covid-19 Pandemic Varied Substantially Across States. *Health Affairs* 40 (2). https://doi.org/10.1377/hlthaff.2020.02142.

Potter, C.W. 2001. A History of Influenza. *Journal of Applied Microbiology* 91: 572–579.

Reuters. 2020. Your Money: Coronavirus Fears Shake Yale Economist Robert Shiller. Published on 20 March 2020. https://www.reuters.com/article/us-health-coronavirus-shiller-idUSKBN2163LD.

————. 2021. Former CDC Chief Redfield Says He Thinks COVID-19 Originated in a Chinese Lab. Published on March 27, 2021. https://www.reuters.com/article/us-health-coronavirus-origin-redfield-idUSKBN2BI2R6.

Rice, T., P. Rosenau, L.Y. Unruh, A.J. Barnes, R.B. Saltman, and E. van Ginneken. 2013. United States of America: Health System Review. *Health Systems in Transition* 15 (3): 1–431.

Samuelson, Paul, and William D. Nordhaus. 2009. *Economics*. 19th ed. New York, NY: McGraw-Hill Education.

Sanchez-Paramo, Carolina. 2020. COVID-19 Will Hit the Poor Hardest. Here's What We Can Do About It. *World Bank Blogs*. https://blogs.worldbank.org/voices/covid-19-will-hit-poor-hardest-heres-what-we-can-do-about-it.

Schwab, Klaus, and Thierry Malleret. 2020. *COVID-19: The Great Reset*. Agentur Schweiz.

Seo, S. Niggol. 2015. Helping Low-latitude, Poor Countries with Climate Change. Regulation, Winter 2015–2016: 6–8.

———. 2016. Modeling Farmer Adaptations to Climate Change in South America: A Microbehavioral Economic Perspective. *Environmental and Ecological Statistics* 23: 1–21.

———. 2017. Negotiating a Global Public Good: Lessons from Global Warming Conferences and Future Directions. In *The Behavioral Economics of Climate Change: Adaptation Behaviors, Global Public Goods, Breakthrough Technologies, and Policy-making*, ed. S. Niggol Seo. Amsterdam, NL: Academic Press.

———. 2019. *The Economics of Global Allocations of the Green Climate Fund: An Assessment from Four Scientific Traditions of Modeling Adaptation Strategies.* Cham, CH: Springer Nature.

———. 2020. *The Economics of Globally Shared and Public Goods.* Amsterdam, NL: Academic Press.

Shiller, Robert J. 2019. *Narrative Economics: How Stories Go Viral and Drive Major Economic Events.* Princeton, NJ: Princeton University Press.

Socialist Equality Party Australia (SEPA). 2020. The Coronavirus Pandemic, the Crisis of Capitalism and the Tasks of the SEP. Published on 26 August 2020. https://www.wsws.org/en/articles/2020/08/26/res1-a26.html.

Tiruneh, Gizachew. 2014. Social Revolutions: Their Causes, Patterns, and Phases. *Sage Open* 4 (3). https://doi.org/10.1177/2158244014548845.

United Nations Framework Convention on Climate Change (UNFCCC), 2009. Copenhagen Accord. UNFCCC, New York.

United States Bureau of Economic Analysis (USBEA). 2020. *Gross Domestic Product, Third Quarter 2020 (Advance Estimate).* Suitland, MD: USBEA, US Department of Commerce. https://www.bea.gov/sites/default/files/2020-10/gdp3q20_adv.pdf.

United States Bureau of Labor Statistics (USBLS). 2020. *Labor Force Statistics from the Current Population Survey.* Washington, DC: USBLS, US Department of Labor. https://data.bls.gov/timeseries/LNS14000000.

United States Department of Health and Human Services (USDHHS) 2020. Secretary Azar Statement on President Trump's Invoking the Defense Production Act. Published on March 18, 2020. https://www.hhs.gov/about/news/2020/03/18/secretary-azar-statement-president-trumps-invoking-defense-production-act.html.

United States Department of the Treasury (USDOT). 2020. *The CARES Act Works for All Americans.* Washington, DC: USDOT. https://home.treasury.gov/policy-issues/cares.

United States Food & Drug Administration (USFDA). 2020a. Pfizer-BioNTech COVID-19 Vaccine EUA Letter of Authorization. https://www.fda.gov/media/144412/.

———. 2020b. Moderna COVID-19 Vaccine EUA Letter of Authorization. https://www.fda.gov/media/144636/download.

Wall Street Journal (WSJ). 2021. WHO Criticizes China for Stymying Investigation Into Covid-19 Origins. Published on January 6, 2021. https://www.wsj.com/

articles/world-health-organization-criticizes-china-over-delays-in-covid-19-probe-11609883140.

World Economic Forum (WEF). 2020a. *The Great Reset*. Davos, CH: WEF. https://www.weforum.org/great-reset/.

———. 2020b. Now is the Time for a 'Great Reset.' WEF, Davos, CH. https://www.weforum.org/agenda/2020/06/now-is-the-time-for-a-great-reset/.

World Health Organization (WHO). 2020. *Milestones for Health over 70 Years*. Geneva, CH: WHO.

———. 2021. WHO-convened Global Study of Origins of SARS-CoV-2: China Part. Published on March 30, 2021. Geneva, CH: WHO.

CHAPTER 6

Pandemic Analysis IV: Is the COVID-19 Pandemic a Doomsday Scenario for Climate Change?

1   A CLIMATE CHANGE DOOMSDAY SCENARIO

For the community of people to be described in this chapter, the COVID-19 pandemic is a miserable event for humanity but perhaps not miserable enough. They say the worst is yet to come. The COVID-19 virus is only a harbinger of the climate catastrophe in the offing that will be truly miserable. The COVID-19 pandemic is only a warning shot by the nature on the coming climate doomsdays, says the former Secretary-General of the United Nations (Ban and Verkooijen 2020a).

Some assert that climate change will be far worse than the COVID-19 pandemic. A climate catastrophe will come as sudden as the COVID-19 pandemic, contrary to the common perception that the climate system is gradually changing, and will turn out to be even more cataclysmic than the pandemic (Giger 2021). The pandemic may kill millions of people on the planet, but climate change can "kill every one" on the planet in the long term, says a prominent climate policy advocate who was also a former mayor of New York City (JustTheNews 2021).

Others would go even further to assert that climate change will cause global pandemics such as the COVID-19. Based on the relationship between climate change and the infectious diseases, they argue that past changes in the climate system is a likely cause of the COVID-19 pandemic and likewise ongoing changes in the climate system will cause pandemics more frequently which are more efficient in transmitting human-to-human and more fatal to humans (Guardian 2020a; Ban and Verkooijen 2020a, b; WHO 2020a).

What these authors are presenting to humanity is a climate change doomsday scenario triggered by the miseries and losses from the COVID-19 pandemic. In this scenario, a tragedy of the global pandemic is only a matter of secondary importance while the matter of the first priority is a climate catastrophe. The climate change doomsday scenario will unequivocally be a strong force for advocating the most stringent climate policy on a global stage. In the previous chapter, the present author reviewed the Great Reset agenda which is at its heart a proposal for a rapid transition of the global economy to sustainability and climate change agendas (Guardian 2020b; Schwab and Malleret 2020).

For a full disclosure, these assertions intrigue the present author very much because I have spent the past 20 years mulling over the planet's climate dialogues (Seo 2006, 2021a). In this chapter, the present author plans to review and clarify the pandemic-based climate change doomsday scenarios, after which two critical analyses on them will be conducted. The first is an analysis of the empirical relationship between the COVID-19 pandemic and the climate change indicators such as carbon dioxide emissions, weekly energy demands, and oil consumption (WMO 2020; IEA 2020).

The second analysis, which constitutes the core of this chapter, is concerned with the causality between climate change and global pandemics (WHO 2020a). In particular, the present author will assess the claim at the core of the doomsday scenarios that the global climate change has caused the COVID-19 pandemic and will cause future pandemics more frequently as well as deadlier pandemics.

These analyses will reveal that the research on the relationships between climate change and infectious diseases, one type of which is a pandemic, has long been a major field of climate research. Up until now, researchers have concentrated on the climate/weather-sensitive diseases, the most prominent of which are malaria in Africa and seasonal influenza (Martens et al. 1999; Rogers and Randolph 2000; Patz et al. 2003). Up until the outbreak of the COVID-19, a pandemic research was rare in the climate community. The COVID-19 pandemic may change that by pushing climate researchers to expand their research horizons to a family of coronaviruses such as Severe Acute Respiratory Syndrome (SARS), Middle East Respiratory Syndrome (MERS), and COVID-19 as well as yet unknown deadly viruses (Coleman and Frieman 2014; Weiss 2020).

2 THE ARGUMENTS FOR THE COVID-19 AS A CLIMATE DOOMSDAY SCENARIO

The COVID-19 has become, at the time of this writing at the end of July 2021, one of the most catastrophic events in human history. It has killed over 4.3 million people worldwide and infected more than 200 million people (JHU 2021). The proposition that the ongoing climate change will cause a global pandemic such as this or even deadlier ones more frequently does indeed pose a serious challenge to the future of mankind, making anyone stop to ponder. It is indeed a doomsday scenario of climate change.

In the economics jargon, the phenomenon that the advocates point to is a fat-tail distribution of climate change (Pareto 1906; Schuster 1984). The fat-tail distribution is characterized by truly catastrophic events whose probabilities of occurrence do not diminish to zero, that is, remain fat even at a far-out tail of the distribution. To state it drastically, if we assume a fat-tail distribution, a truly catastrophic event that culminates in the termination of all human and non-human civilizations in the solar system cannot be treated as a near impossibility, that is, of approximately zero probability. Economists and scientists debated over the past decade, in formal forums and informally, on the appropriateness of a fat-tail distribution as a probability distribution for the impact of climate change (Weitzman 2009; Nordhaus 2011; Wagoner and Weitzman 2015; Seo 2020).

If climate scientists were to be able to prove that the ongoing climate change was indeed the cause of the COVID-19 pandemic and further prove that the ongoing climate change will top the high-end estimate of the IPCC projects, that is, 4.5 °C by the end of the twenty-first century, they could get very close to a proof of the fat-tail distribution of climate change, also referred to as the dismal theorem of climate change (Weitzman 2009; Seo 2020). If the two hypotheses were to be realized throughout the course of this century, the planet community would get overwhelmed even with a consideration of a vaccine solution possibility.

The realization of the two hypotheses simultaneously is, ceteris paribus, a climate change doomsday scenario. Let me review here some of the arguments that pertain to the climate change doomsday scenarios put forth by various authors during the COVID-19 pandemic. An explicit mention of the relationship between the COVID-19 pandemic and climate change appears for the first time in the opinion piece by a former United Nations Secretary-General, published as early as April 9, 2020.

Ban was the UN Secretary-General who was instrumental in the achievement of the Paris Agreement on climate change in December 2015, along with President Obama (UNFCCC 2015; Seo 2017). Ban and Verkooijen wrote as follows (Ban and Verkooijen 2020a):

> *Many experts see a link between the two. Inger Andersen… says Covid-19 is a "clear warning shot" given that 75% of all infectious diseases come from wildlife, and climate change and the destruction of natural habitats are putting humans into ever-closer proximity to animals.*

In the above quote, the two refer to "climate emergency" and the COVID-19 pandemic. In the above, the authors quoted the words from the head of the United Nations Environment Programme (UNEP). But, the quote is at odds with what she was quoted saying to another newspaper, which appeared two weeks earlier (Guardian 2020a):

> *"Never before have so many opportunities existed for pathogens to pass from wild and domestic animals to people," she told the Guardian, explaining that 75% of all emerging infectious diseases come from wildlife.*
> *....*
> *Andersen, executive director of the UN Environment Programme, said the immediate priority was to protect people from the coronavirus and prevent its spread. "But our long-term response must tackle habitat and biodiversity loss," she added.*

The direct quotes of her above statements by the *Guardian* newspaper do not attempt to establish a causal relationship between climate emergency and the pandemic. Rather, she emphasizes the points that the infectious diseases come mostly from wildlife and in the long-term humanity should address habitat and biodiversity loss.

Notwithstanding her stance, the newspaper goes on to declare the following direct causal relationship (Guardian 2020):

> *To prevent further outbreaks, the experts said, both global heating and the destruction of the natural world for farming, mining and housing have to end, as both drive wildlife into contact with people.*

In the above, global heating refers undoubtedly to the phenomenon of global warming. The newspaper article does contain an expert opinion that claims the direct link between the two from the Director of the Center for Climate, Health, and the Global Environment at the Harvard T.H. Chan School of Public Health (Guardian 2020):

> *Aaron Bernstein ... said the destruction of natural places drives wildlife to live close to people and that climate change was also forcing animals to move: "That creates an opportunity for pathogens to get into new hosts."*

Summing up, the direct link between "climate emergency" and pandemics including the COVID-19 is hypothesized by the above authors and newspapers by the two nexus, most clearly by Bernstein and Ban: the first nexus is between climate change and wildlife (especially animals), while the second nexus is between wildlife (especially animals) and pandemics. This is illustrated in Fig. 6.1.

In a follow-up piece, Ban and Verkooijen write that "nature-based climate solutions and climate adaptation" should be placed at the heart of the COVID-19 recovery, with a grim prediction that a climate crisis brought about eventually by failing to do so will come far more devastatingly to humanity than the COVID-19 (Ban and Verkooijen 2020b):

> *So as governments prepare to deal with the economic fallout from Covid-19, we urge them to put nature-based solutions and climate adaptation at the heart of their recovery plans. To do anything less would be to succumb to a crisis that will eventually have far more devastating consequences for humanity than Covid-19.*

The climate change doomsday scenario via pandemics as illustrated in Fig. 6.1 has, as the review here reveals, not a few weak links, which we can say is a relief for humanity. The most fundamental of them is the link between changes in wildlife and changes in the COVID-19 pandemic and other future pandemics. The origin of the COVID-19 is still being

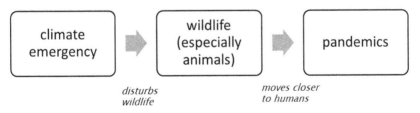

Fig. 6.1 A hypothesis on the connection between climate change and pandemics by advocates

investigated by the WHO team of experts and others (Mallapaty 2020; WHO 2020b). As of this writing, there are four competing theories put forth by the WHO team as possible origins, which are shared widely across scientific communities: (1) a transmission from an animal species to humans; (2) a transmission from an animal species to another animal species and then to humans; (3) a transmission from the food system such as the Wuhan wet market; and (4) accidental leaks from the Wuhan Virology Institute laboratories. On the one hand, it is noticeable that no one from the WHO team of experts is concerned with a climate change origination hypothesis such as the one in Fig. 6.1.

On the other hand, there is ample evidence in the climate science literature that ecosystems, wildlife, and animals are affected by climate change. For one, multiple studies on biodiversity loss and mass extinction due to climate change concluded that climate change will increase a species turnover rate even if the total number of species would remain unchanged in new climate regimes. In other words, there will be a large number of species that will disappear due to climate change but at the same time an even larger number of species that will newly emerge due to climate change (Mayhew et al. 2012; Blowes et al. 2019). This literature, however, tells little, if any, about the impacts of climate change on microbes and pathogens because these studies were concerned with vertebrates, say, far larger animals (Seo 2021b).

In addition, a large number of researchers also report that many animals are able to adapt to changes in climate to survive whether they are domesticated animals, wild animals, birds, or fish (Seo and Mendelsohn 2008; Seo 2021c). For example, an animal species may adapt by increasing heat tolerance, swimming to colder waters, or switching on/off genes (Hahn et al. 2009; Gooding et al. 2009; Lighten et al. 2016). Again, these studies tell little about the effects on microbes and pathogens of pandemics.

Having stated what has been described thus far, a thorny scientific task is to link these macro-scale changes in the biosphere to the pandemic originations which occur at a nano-scale, say, a billionth of a meter scale, the literature of which the present author will clarify in Sect. 6.4 of this chapter. Also, I need to add that, as will be explained in a later section, the World Health Organization (WHO) explicitly refused to accept such the hyped causality between climate change and COVID-19 in its statement entitled "COVID-19 and Climate Change" (WHO 2020a).

3 THE EFFECTS OF COVID-19 ON CLIMATE CHANGE

Changing gears, let us look into the other direction of causality between climate change and COVID-19: the effects of the COVID-19 on climate change indicators. One of the most salient effects of the COVID-19 pandemic that people in East Asia and perhaps the world experienced during 2020 was an exceptionally clear blue sky borne of the shutting-down of factories in Chinese cities which reduced the emissions of fine particulate matter (PM) and other air pollutants drastically. In the normal pre-pandemic years, far East Asian cities suffer greatly every spring from dark gray skies covered by fine PM emitted from, inter alia, Chinese factories. This is one of the changes in the climate/weather system witnessed by world citizens in 2020.

According to the World Meteorological Organization's Air Quality and Climate Bulletin published in September 2021, the PM2.5 concentration in 2020 was about 40% lower than the 2003–2019 average concentration in Southeast Asia, East Asia, Africa, and Latin America where the fine particulate matter pollution is a major health problem. Further, the concentration of NO2 decreased by around 70% globally. The data were from the Copernicus Atmosphere Monitoring Service (CAMS) re-analysis (WMO 2021).

3.1 Global CO₂ Emissions

The first variable of interest is global emissions of carbon dioxide which is the most prevalent greenhouse gas that warms the planet (Le Treut et al. 2007). As explained in Chap. 4, many US states declared a statewide lockdown, which included all business closures except essentials, starting from at the end of March after a global pandemic was declared by the WHO. The same occurred in many countries worldwide, especially China, India, Japan, and European countries. The peak confinement period was April of 2020.

The World Meteorological Organization (WMO) estimates that daily global fossil-fuel CO_2 emissions dropped most in April 2020 by 17% from the daily mean estimate in 2019. The emissions, however, quickly rebounded. By June 2020, the global fossil-fuel CO_2 emissions mostly recovered to within 5% from the same period in 2019 (WMO 2020).

An analysis at the level of fossil-fuel types is available from the International Energy Agency (IEA 2020). In the first quarter (Q1) of 2020, global CO_2 emissions were lower by roughly 5%. The reduction can be attributed to the reduction in emissions from coal by 8%, from oil by 4.5%, and from natural gas by 2.3%.

The reduction in CO_2 emissions in Q1 can be decomposed regionally. The reduction in China amounted to 8%, in the US to 8%, and in the EU to 9%. These three regions are the regions that were hit most severely during the initial phases of the COVID-19, that is, the first wave.

For the entire year of 2020, the IEA predicted that the global CO_2 emissions to decline by 2.6 gigatons of carbon dioxide ($GtCO_2$) for 2020 to reach 30.6 $GtCO_2$, which is about 8% lower than that of 2019. This projection is similar to the Global Carbon Project's analysis whose projection ranges from 4% to 7% reduction (Le Quere et al. 2020). An exceptional nature of the decline is well illustrated in Fig. 6.2 which shows the annual changes in global CO_2 emissions from 1990 to 2020. The reduction in 2020 is nearly seven times larger than the reduction in 2009, the year during which the world was struck hard by the global financial crisis (Shiller 2009).

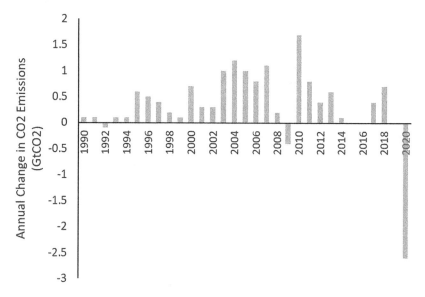

Fig. 6.2   Annual changes in global CO_2 emissions ($GtCO_2$): 1990–2020

The 2.6 $GtCO_2$ reduction is attributed to the reduced uses of fossil fuels: 1.1 $GtCO_2$ reduction attributable to reduced coal burning, 1 $GtCO_2$ reduction attributable to reduced oil burning, and 0.4 $GtCO_2$ attributable to reduced natural gas burning. It is predicted that the US emissions will fall by 0.6 $GtCO_2$, with similar reductions in China and the EU.

3.2 Energy Demands and COVID-19 Policies

The reduction in the global carbon dioxide emissions resulted from the reductions in energy consumptions across the planet owing to the pandemic. The reduction in the energy demands, in turn, depended on the degree of COVID-19 restrictions imposed by the governments. The countries which enforced a full national lockdown had the largest reduction in energy consumption while the countries with limited COVID-19 restrictions had the smallest reduction. This is illustrated in Fig. 6.3 which shows the differences in the change in energy consumption across three COVID-19 policy regimes: full lockdown, partial lockdown, limited restrictions.

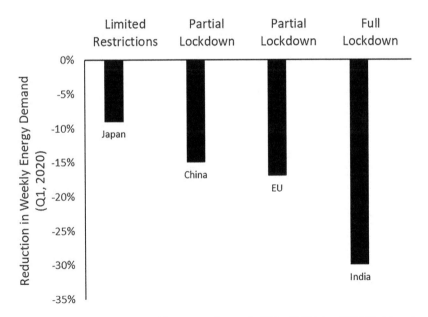

Fig. 6.3 Reduction in weekly energy demands (Q1, 2020) by COVID-19 policy regimes

The reduction in weekly energy demands during the Q1 of 2020 ranged from a 30% reduction in India where a full national lockdown was implemented, roughly 17% reduction in Europe where a partial lockdown was implemented, 15% reduction in China where a partial lockdown was implemented, and 10% reduction in Japan where limited COVID-19 restrictions were imposed (IEA 2020).

The causality between the changes in fossil-fuel use and the changes in global CO_2 emissions can be seen in Figs. 6.4 and 6.5. Monthly changes in the aggregate demand for oil during 2020 relative to 2019 in selected countries are shown in Fig. 6.4. The monthly oil demand started to fall in January, hit the bottom of the trough in April, and largely recovered by October 2020. The reduction is as large as 29 million barrels per day (mb/day) in April and 26 mb/day in May (IEA 2020).

The changes in monthly aggregate oil demands shown in Fig. 6.4 contributed, along with the changes in the demands for the other fossil fuels, to the changes in the carbon dioxide emissions month by month as depicted in Fig. 6.5 in the selected countries including China, India, the US, and the EU. Relative to the monthly amount in pre-pandemic 2019, the largest change occurred in April with 0.65 $GtCO_2$ reduction for the

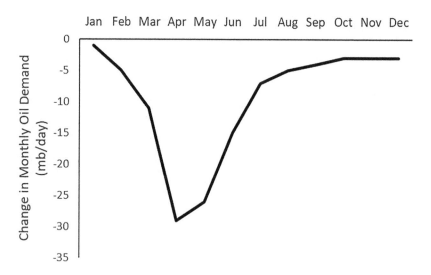

Fig. 6.4 Changes in monthly oil demands in 2020 relative to 2019 (mb/day)

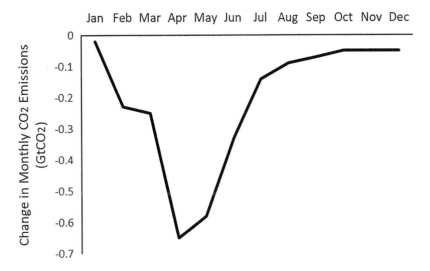

Fig. 6.5 Change in monthly CO_2 emissions in 2020 relative to 2019 $(GtCO_2/month)$

month followed by May with 0.58 $GtCO_2$ reduction for the month. The carbon dioxide emissions mostly recovered by October 2020 to the pre-pandemic level (IEA 2020).

4 Will Climate Change Cause Pandemics More Frequently or Deadlier Pandemics?

Let's change gears one more time and get to the core question of this chapter: will the ongoing climate change cause a global pandemic to occur more frequently or cause more lethal pandemics? The present author alluded to the difficult task of establishing the relationship between climate change and the COVID-19 pandemic in the introduction of this chapter. We can approach this question with reliance upon the literature on climate change and infectious diseases.

The infectious diseases that were concerned most by scientists with regard to climate change are influenza and malaria. The tragedy of the COVID-19 pandemic may force them to refocus their research priority to various types of coronaviruses, that is, SARS-CoV, MERS-CoV, and SARS-CoV-2 (Weiss 2020).

To disentangle the impact of climate change on infectious diseases, three interacting actors should be examined: vectors, pathogens, and hosts (Seo 2021a). A pathogen is an infectious agent, that is, a microbe that causes an infectious disease, such as viruses, bacteria, protozoa, and multicellular parasites. A vector is a carrier of an infectious disease from a host to another, such as mosquitoes, flies, lice, ticks, and dust particles. A host of an infectious agent can be a human or an animal. All three actors are to one degree or another dependent on climate conditions (Patz et al. 2003).

A zoonosis is an infectious disease which is caused by a pathogen which jumped from an animal to a human. The coronaviruses including the COVID-19 are zoonoses. When a pathogen is transmitted from a human to an animal or another human, the infectious disease is called an anthroponosis (Patz et al. 2003).

The deadliest infectious diseases to humanity contemporarily are seasonal influenza and malaria. Malaria is an infectious disease caused by malaria parasites, for example, *P. falciparum*, which are carried by a certain type of mosquitoes to humans. Through the blood vessels, the parasites travel to human liver cells and reproduce.

Malaria has long been declared to be eliminated in developed countries by the WHO, but remains a serious public health problem for Sub-Saharan Africa (WHO 2020c). The number of deaths caused by malaria was estimated to be 1.2 million people worldwide during the 1990–2001 time period, all of which were from developing countries (Lopez et al. 2006). According to the most recent World Malaria Report 2019 published by the WHO, malaria killed 405,000 people globally in 2019 alone (WHO 2019).

Influenza, on the other hand, is the most prevalent infectious disease on the planet (Potter 2001). Of the influenza viruses, the H1N1, an influenza A virus subtype, is the deadliest. It caused two pandemics in history: the 2009 H1N1 pandemic and the Spanish Flu pandemic in 1918. The former is estimated to have killed 284,000 people and the latter up to 50 million people (CDC 2020). It is estimated that 291,000–645,000 seasonal influenza-associated fatalities occur annually across the planet (Iuliano et al. 2018). In the US alone, the influenza deaths ranged from 12,000 to 61,000 annually during the decade of the 2010s (CDC 2020).

The death toll from the two deadliest infectious diseases can be compared with the death toll from the three coronaviruses that humanity experienced since the dawn of the twenty-first century (Fig. 6.6). The figure highlights the heavy disease burdens of malaria and influenza every

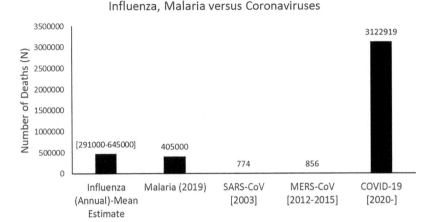

Fig. 6.6 Death tolls from flu and malaria versus coronaviruses (as of the end of April 2021)

year to humanity. It also showcases the deadliness of the COVID-19 pandemic, which should intrigue climate researchers much in the coming years. The number of fatalities from the COVID-19 pandemic stands at 3.2 million people worldwide as of the end of April 2021, which increased to 4.2 million at the end of July 2021.

Can virologists, epidemiologists, or biologists predict a future pandemic that is not known to mankind today but will be caused by the ongoing climate change? It is a monumental task, to state it modestly, because microorganisms that are pathogens such as viruses always evolve to find weaker spots in the immune systems of humans and animals. Besides the pathogens, disease vectors and hosts of infectious diseases also evolve in ways that are difficult to predict. Further, the immune system of an individual human being that depends on many non-physical factors, as such, can be enhanced or deteriorated by mental and social characteristics.

Addressing the question of whether the next pandemic can be predicted, Taubenberger, Morens, and Fauci summarize the remaining challenge and propose the relevant research as follows (Taubenberger et al. 2007):

Despite significant research, fundamental questions about how influenza A viruses switch hosts from wild birds and adapt to domesticated poultry, pigs or horses, and subsequently to humans, remain unanswered, especially those regarding the changes that allow human–to–human transmissibility. Given the potential for high morbidity and mortality, an approximation of the risk that H5N1 viruses will adapt to efficient human–to–human transmission would be extremely helpful for pandemic preparedness planning.

The scientific task may get slightly easier for the known infectious diseases, for example, influenza, malaria, and coronaviruses. Scientists rely on one of the following three methodologies to predict changes in infectious diseases under different climate regimes: a statistical model, a process-based model, and a landscape-based model (Patz et al. 2003). The three methodologies are conceptually analogous to the three methodological traditions applied to the economic studies of changes in agriculture and food productions under different climate regimes (Mendelsohn and Neumann 1999; Seo 2015).

Let me briefly introduce the essence of each of the three methodologies. A statistical model associates characteristics of a concerned infectious disease with a family of explanatory variables that include climate variables. A process-based model links multiple processes that underlie the development of an infectious disease where each process is a sub-module of the model. Some sub-modules would have a climate process. A landscape-based model associates characteristics of a concerned infectious disease with the geographic-geological landscapes across which the disease spreads and becomes prevalent. One of the factors that determine the landscapes is climate (Seo 2019).

A critical conclusion from the epidemiologists' modeling efforts is that the three methodologies yield contrary results regarding the core question of this chapter (Patz et al. 2003). The statistical models predict little changes in the outbreaks of infectious diseases owing to climatic shifts (Rogers and Randolph 2000). The process-based models, on the contrary, predict that a temperature increase by 2–3 °C globally would increase the number of people at risk of malaria by 3–5% globally. To be specific, relying on the Modeling Framework for the Health Impact Assessment of Man-Induced Atmospheric Changes (MIASMA) malaria model, researchers predict that the climate regime in 2080 as predicted by the Hadley Climate Model (HADCM2) model will result in an increase in the number of people at risk of malaria by 260–320 million for *P. falciparum* malaria and by 100–200 million for *P. vivax* malaria (Martens et al. 1999).

To summarize, the review up until now does not give us any confirmation on the dire prediction by many advocates that infectious diseases or pandemics will become more frequent while deadlier pandemics will become more common. The climate change doomsday scenario via pandemics cannot be confirmed by the literature on climate change and infectious diseases.

At this point, we are well-positioned to hear from and evaluate the advice from the World Health Organization on the relationship between climate change and the COVID-19. The following answer is given by the WHO in response to the question of "*Will climate change make COVID-19 worse?*" in the Frequently Asked Questions (FAQs) website of the organization (WHO 2020a):

> *There is no evidence of a direct connection between climate change and the emergence or transmission of COVID-19 disease. ... However, climate change may indirectly affect the COVID-19 response, as it undermines environmental determinants of health, and places additional stress on health systems. More generally, most emerging infectious diseases, and almost all recent pandemics, originate in wildlife, and there is evidence that increasing human pressure on the natural environment may drive disease emergence.*

On the question of "*Do weather and climate determine where COVID-19 occurs?*" the following answer is put forward by the WHO (2020a):

> *No. There is currently no conclusive evidence that either weather (short term variations in meteorological conditions) or climate (long-term averages) have a strong influence on transmission. The SARS-CoV-2 virus which causes COVID-19 disease has been transmitted in all regions of the world, from cold and dry, to hot and humid climates.*

The WHO rightly acknowledges that (1) there is no direct connection between climate change and the emergence of the COVID-19; (2) there is no direct connection between climate change and the COVID-19 transmission; (3) there is no evidence that either weather or climate at the present time determines the transmission of the COVID-19. But, the WHO also acknowledges a portion of the hypothesis shown in Fig. 6.1 while it does not specifically point to climate change but only indirectly to "human pressure on natural environment."

5   FINAL THOUGHTS

Before the COVID-19 pandemic, not a few climate change doomsday scenarios had been promoted, referred to as tipping elements or a runaway climate change in the literature, put forth by a range of climate researchers (Alley et al. 2003; Mann et al. 1999; Lenton et al. 2008, 2019). The climate change doomsday scenario via the connection between climate change and pandemics, however, was rarely discussed, if any. This literature may change significantly in the coming years, motivated by the planetwide experiences of misery and suffering inflicted on humanity by the COVID-19 pandemic. This chapter lays out a gentle warning against a rush toward the pandemic-caused climate change doomsday scenarios, drawing from the pre-pandemic literature on climate change and infectious diseases as well as through an up-close examination of the underlying arguments.

REFERENCES

Alley, R.B., J. Marotzke, W.D. Nordhaus, J.T. Overpeck, D.M. Peteet, R.A. Pielke Jr., R.T. Pierrehumbert, P.B. Rhines, T.F. Stocker, L.D. Talley, and J.M. Wallace. 2003. Abrupt Climate Change. *Science* 299 (5615): 2005–2010.

Ban, Ki-moon, and Patrick Verkooijen. 2020a. Will We Learn Lessons for Tackling Climate Change from Our Current Crisis? CNN. https://edition.cnn.com/2020/04/09/opinions/climate-change-lessons-from-covid-19-ban-verkooijen/index.html. Accessed 9 April 2020.

———. 2020b. *Coronavirus Is a Warning To Us All: We Must Heal Nature In Order To Heal Ourselves.* HuffPost. https://www.huffingtonpost.co.uk/entry/coronavirus_uk_5eac35acc5b65156135c9863. Accessed 2 May 2020.

Blowes, Shane A., Sarah R. Supp, Laura H. Antão, Amanda Bates, Helge Bruelheide, Jonathan M. Chase, Faye Moyes, et al. 2019. The Geography of Biodiversity Change in Marine and Terrestrial Assemblages. *Science* 366 (6463): 339–345.

Centers for Disease Control and Prevention (CDC). 2020. *Influenza.* Atlanta, G.A: The CDC.

Coleman, C.M., and M.B. Frieman. 2014. Coronaviruses: Important Emerging Human Pathogens. *Journal of Virology* 8: 5209–5212.

Giger, Peter. 2021. *Climate Change will Be Sudden and Cataclysmic. We Need to Act Fast.* Davos, CH: World Economic Forum. https://www.weforum.org/agenda/2021/01/climate-change-sudden-cataclysmic-need-act-fast/. Accessed 19 Jan 2021.

Gooding, Rebecca A., Christopher D.G. Harley, and Emily Tang. 2009. Elevated Water Temperature and Carbon Dioxide Concentration Increase the Growth of a Keystone Echinoderm. *Proceedings of the National Academy of the Sciences* 106 (23): 9316–9321.

Guardian. 2020a. *Coronavirus: 'Nature is Sending Us a Message', says UN Environment Chief.* https://www.theguardian.com/world/2020/mar/25/coronavirus-nature-is-sending-us-a-message-says-un-environment-chief. Accessed 25 March 2020.

———. 2020b. *Pandemic is Chance to Reset Global Economy, says Prince Charles.* https://www.theguardian.com/uk-news/2020/jun/03/pandemic-is-chance-to-reset-global-economy-says-prince-charles. Accessed 3 June 2020.

Hahn, G. LeRoy, J.B. Gaughan, T.L. Mader, and R.A. Eigenberg. 2009. Thermal Indices and Their Applications for Livestock Environments. In *Livestock Energetics and Thermal Environmental Management*, ed. J.A. DeShazer, Chapter 5, pp. 113–30. St. Joseph, MI: ASABE. Copyright 2009 American Society of Agricultural and Biological Engineers.

International Energy Agency (IEA). 2020. *Global Energy Review 2020: The Impacts of the Covid-19 Crisis on Global Energy Demand and CO_2 Emissions.* Paris, FR: IEA.

Iuliano, A.D., K.M. Roguski, H.H. Chang, et al. 2018. Global Seasonal Influenza-associated Mortality Collaborator Network. Estimates of Global Seasonal Influenza-associated Respiratory Mortality: A Modelling Study. *Lancet* 391 (10127): 1285–1300. https://doi.org/10.1016/S0140-6736(17)33293-2.

Johns Hopkins University (JHU). 2021. *COVID-19 Dash Board.* Baltimore, MD: JHU. https://data.humdata.org/dataset/novel-coronavirus-2019-ncov-cases.

JustTheNews. 2021. *Bloomberg: 'Climate Change has the Potential to Kill Everybody,' Worse Than Pandemic 'Long-Term.'* https://justthenews.com/government/white-house/bloomberg-climate-change-has-potential-kill-everybody-worse-pandemic-long. Accessed 22 Jan 2021.

Le Quere, C., R.B. Jackson, M.W. Jones, et al. 2020. Temporary Reduction in Daily Global CO2 Emissions during the COVID-19 Forced Confinement. Nature. *Climate Change* 14 (121001). https://doi.org/10.1038/s41558-020-0797-x.

Le Treut, H., R. Somerville, U. Cubasch, Y. Ding, C. Mauritzen, A. Mokssit, T. Peterson, and M. Prather. 2007. Historical Overview of Climate Change. In *Climate Change 2007: The Physical Science Basis. The Fourth Assessment Report of the Intergovernmental Panel on Climate Change.* Cambridge: Cambridge University Press.

Lenton, Timothy M., H. Held, E. Kriegler, J.W. Hall, W. Lucht, S. Rahmstorf, et al. 2008. Tipping Elements in the Earth's Climate System. *Proceedings of the National Academy of Sciences USA* 105: 1786–1793.

Lenton, Timothy M., Johan Rockström, Owen Gaffney, Stefan Rahmstorf, Katherine Richardson, Will Steffen, and Hans Joachim Schellnhuber. 2019. Climate Tipping Points—Too Risky to Bet Against. *Nature* 575: 592–595.

Lighten, Jackie, Danny Incarnato, Ben J. Ward, Cock van Oosterhout, Ian Bradbury, Mark Hanson, and Paul Bentzen. 2016. Adaptive Phenotypic Response to Climate Enabled by Epigenetics in a K-Strategy Species, the Fish Leucoraja Ocellata (Rajidae). *Royal Society Open Science* 3 (10): 160299. https://doi.org/10.1098/rsos.160299.

Lopez, Alan D., Colin D. Mathers, Majid Ezzati, Dean T. Jamison, and Christopher J.L. Murray. 2006. *Global Burden of Disease and Risk Factors*. New York, NY: World Bank and Oxford University Press.

Mallapaty, S. 2020. Where Did COVID Come From? WHO Investigation Begins but Faces Challenges. *Nature* 587: 341–342.

Mann, M.E., R.S. Bradley, and M.K. Hughes. 1999. Northern Hemisphere Temperatures During the Past Millennium: Inferences, Uncertainties, and Limitations. *Geophysical Research Letters* 26: 759–762.

Martens, P., R. Kovats, S. Nijhof, P. Devries, M. Livermore, D. Bradley, J. Cox, and A. McMichael. 1999. Climate Change and Future Populations at Risk of Malaria. *Global Environmental Change* 9 (October): S89–S107.

Mayhew, Peter J., Mark A. Bell, Timothy G. Benton, and Alistair J. McGowan. 2012. Biodiversity Tracks Temperature over Time. *Proceedings of the National Academy of Sciences* 109 (38): 15141–15145. https://doi.org/10.1073/pnas.1200844109.

Mendelsohn, R., and J. Neumann. 1999. *The Impact of Climate Change on the United States Economy*. Cambridge: Cambridge University Press.

Nordhaus, William D. 2011. The Economics of Tail Events with an Application to Climate Change. *Review of Environmental Economics and Policy* 5: 240–257.

Pareto, Vilfredo. 1906. In: ed., A. Montesano, A. Zanni, L. Bruni, J.S. Chipman, and M. McLure. 2014. *Manual for Political Economy*. Oxford: Oxford University Press.

Patz, J.A., A.K. Githeko, J.P. McCarty, S. Hussein, U. Confalonieri, and N. de Wet. 2003. Climate Change and Infectious Diseases. In *Climate Change and Human Health—Risks and Responses*. Geneva, CH: WHO.

Potter, C.W. 2001. A History of Influenza. *Journal of Applied Microbiology* 91 (4): 572–579.

Rogers, David J., and Sarah E. Randolph. 2000. The Global Spread of Malaria in a Future,Warmer World. *Science* 289 (5485): 1763–1766.

Schuster, E.F. 1984. Classification of Probability Laws by Tail Behavior. *Journal of the American Statistical Association* 79 (388): 936–939.

Schwab, Klaus, and Thierry Malleret. 2020. *COVID-19: The Great Reset*. Agentur Schweiz.

Seo, S. Niggol. 2006. *Modeling Farmer Responses to Climate Change: Measuring Climate Change Impacts and Adaptations in Livestock Management in Africa.* Ph.D. dissertation, Yale University, New Haven, CT.

———. 2015. *Micro-Behavioral Economics of Global Warming: Modeling Adaptation Strategies in Agricultural and Natural Resource Enterprises.* Cham, CH: Springer.

———. 2017. Negotiating a Global Public Good: Lessons from Global Warming Conferences and Future Directions. In *The Behavioral Economics of Climate Change: Adaptation Behaviors, Global Public Goods, Breakthrough Technologies, and Policy-making,* ed. S. Niggol Seo. Amsterdam, NL: Academic Press.

———. 2019. *The Economics of Global Allocations of the Green Climate Fund: An Assessment from Four Scientific Traditions of Modeling Adaptation Strategies.* Cham, CH: Springer Nature.

———. 2020. *The Economics of Globally Shared and Public Goods.* Amsterdam, NL: Academic Press.

———. 2021a. A Story of Infectious Diseases and Pandemics: Will Climate Change Increase Deadly Viruses? In *Climate Change and Economics: Engaging with Future Generations with Action Plans.* London: Palgrave MacMillan.

———. 2021b. A Story of Polar Bears and Penguins: A Paradox of Biodiversity and Climate Change. In *Climate Change and Economics: Engaging with Future Generations with Action Plans.* London: Palgrave MacMillan.

———. 2021c. A Story of Coral Reefs, Nemo, and Fisheries: On Biodiversity Loss and Mass Extinction. In *Climate Change and Economics: Engaging with Future Generations with Action Plans.* London: Palgrave MacMillan.

Seo, S. Niggol, and Robert Mendelsohn. 2008. Measuring Impacts and Adaptations to Climate Change: A Structural Ricardian Model of African Livestock Management. *Agricultural Economics* 38: 151–165.

Shiller, Robert J. 2009. *The Subprime Solution: How Today's Global Financial Crisis Happened, and What to Do about it.* Princeton, NJ: Princeton University Press.

Taubenberger, J.K., D.M. Morens, and A.S. Fauci. 2007. The Next Influenza Pandemic: Can It Be Predicted? *The Journal of the American Medical Association* 297: 2025–2027.

United Nations Framework Convention on Climate Change (UNFCCC). 2015. *The Paris Agreement. Conference of the Parties (COP) 21.* New York, NY: UNFCCC.

Wagoner, G., and M. Weitzman. 2015. *Climate Shock: The Economic Consequences of a Hotter Planet.* Princeton, NJ: Princeton University Press.

Weiss, Susan R. 2020. Forty Years with Coronaviruses. *Journal of Experimental Medicine* 217 (5): e20200537. https://doi.org/10.1084/jem.20200537.

Weitzman, Martin L. 2009. On Modeling and Interpreting the Economics of Catastrophic Climate Change. *Review of Economics and Statistics* 91: 1–19.

World Health Organization (WHO). 2019. *World Malaria Report 2019*. Geneva, CH: WHO.

———. 2020a. *Coronavirus Disease (COVID-19): Climate Change*. Geneva, CH: WHO. https://www.who.int/emergencies/diseases/novel-coronavirus-2019/question-and-answers-hub/q-a-detail/coronavirus-disease-covid-19-climate-change.

———. 2020b. *Timeline: WHO's COVID-19 Response*. Geneva, CH: WHO.

———. 2020c. *Milestones for Health over 70 Years*. Geneva, CH: WHO.

World Meteorological Organization (WMO). 2020. *United in Science 2020*. Paris, FR: WMO.

———. 2021. *WMO Air Quality and Climate Bulletin*. Vol. 1. Paris, FR: WMO.

CHAPTER 7

Pandemic Analysis V: The Science and Economics of a Vaccine for Ending the Pandemic

1 THE MIRACLE OF VACCINES

Once an infectious disease that is highly efficient in human-to-human transmission is generated somewhere on the planet, it will quickly spread from one person to another, from one community to another. When the number of the infected in a nation reaches a certain threshold, the rate of contagion in the population will start to accelerate. Sooner or later, it will be declared an epidemic and then a pandemic. If the mortality rate of the disease is high, then the number of fatalities will also keep increasing at an increasing rate. The full basket of mitigation efforts by the government as well as the repurposed drugs explained in detail in Chap. 4 will be able to slow down, *albeit* only to some degree, the rate of transmission and the mortality rate. These efforts will soon turn out to be insufficient to end the spread of the infectious disease.

Consider smallpox! The disease may have been on this planet for over 2000 years. It was extremely fatal for children, killing eight out of ten infected children (refer to Fig. 9.5 in Chap. 9). The disease had been one of the most feared diseases by humanity up until 1980 when it was declared by the World Health Organization (WHO) to be eradicated once and for all. It is estimated that 300–500 million people had died from smallpox until then (CDC 2020a). The point here is that an infectious disease as contagious as smallpox does not simply go away after a few years of devastation. How did smallpox get eradicated after all? It ended thanks to the advancement of vaccine science, specifically, the *Dryvax* vaccine for small-pox (AP 2008).

More generally speaking, how can a global community end a pandemic? A pandemic can end naturally if the disease has such a low mortality rate that people can develop immunity against it naturally over the course of time. When the natural immunity gained by individuals reaches the herd immunity level, the pandemic will be under control. In most pandemics, however, herd immunity would not be attainable naturally because the pathogen will be potent enough to kill an infected individual in most cases before s/he develops natural immunity against it.

Without a possibility of natural herd immunity, the only hope for ter-minating a pandemic may rest on a creation of immunity cells through a vaccine. The immunity cells would have an antibody against the pandemic virus that has the capability of disabling the infectious agent, that is, the novel coronavirus or the SARS-CoV-2 for the COVID-19 pandemic (USFDA 2020d). The science of vaccination, more formally vaccinology, perfected through the early twentieth century, is regarded by many as humanity's greatest achievement in the fights against the infectious dis-eases (Plotkin 2009).

The present author already introduced in Chap. 4 the US government's successful vaccine development program, namely the Operation Warp Speed (OWS), and two highly effective mRNA vaccines resulted from the program (USDHHS 2020). At the time of this writing, two vaccines were issued an emergency use authorization (EUA) by the US federal govern-ment: a Pfizer-BioNTech vaccine and a Moderna vaccine (Fox Business 2020a, 2020b). By the end of 2020, 20 million shots of the two vaccines were reported to have been administered in the US, 1 million shots per day since the authorizations in early December. Whether the two vaccines and the additional vaccines in the third stage clinical trials at the time of this writing will indeed conquer the COVID-19 pandemic is what the world community is anxious to find out in the coming months and years. For an update, a Johnson & Johnson vaccine was approved on the final day of February 2021.

In the economics of pandemics whose description is the primary goal of this book, a high-efficacy vaccine provides an ultimate solution to the problem. Like a miracle, it will bring to an end the misery and suffering of people on the planet. The economics of it is quite incredible: with only a "modest" cost for developing and manufacturing it, the vaccine will yield the benefits immeasurably greater, that is, saving the people on Earth from the pandemic for years. As will be clarified, a key policy variable in the vaccine solution is a time lapse between the pandemic outbreak and the vaccine availability to people which may extend as long as many years.

This chapter proceeds as follows. It starts with an introduction to the science of vaccines and the historical advancement of vaccinations via applications to numerous infectious diseases such as smallpox, malaria, polio, rabies, measles, mumps, and so on. It then goes on to explain the development of COVID-19 vaccines, including the three phases of clinical trials. With these introductions on vaccinology and vaccine applications, the present author will develop the economics of vaccines encompassing the following key economic concepts. First, a time cost of vaccine developments depends on the time lapse it takes to develop a vaccine against the speed of the spread of an infectious disease among the population. Second, a best-shot production technology of a vaccine provision means that only the most advanced pharmaceutical laboratories in the world will participate in the vaccine race. Third, an incredible cost-benefit ratio for the society means that the society with advanced biomedical sciences should be rational to invest in vaccine developments once a pandemic is foreseen or declared. Fourth, there is a key role of the government to play in accelerating the vaccine development at the time of a pandemic including initiating a carefully designed public-private partnership with pharmaceutical laboratories. Fifth, a high-efficacy vaccine provides a backstop solution to a pandemic world. Sixth, a cross-country analysis of the vaccination rates relative to the numbers of new infections in the post-vaccine period will reveal the effectiveness of the vaccine.

2   THE BASICS OF TRADITIONAL VACCINES VERSUS MRNA VACCINES

The scientific name for the novel coronavirus is the SARS-CoV-2. The infectious disease that is caused by the SARS-CoV-2 was formally given by the World Health Organization (WHO) on February 11, 2020, the name of the COVID-19 (WHO 2020a).

Coronaviruses are a family of viruses of which the most well-known to the world are SARS-CoV, MERS-CoV, and SARS-CoV-2 (Coleman and Frieman 2014; Weiss 2020). The infectious disease that each of these coronaviruses causes is called the SARS, MERS, and COVID-19, respectively (Table 7.1). The SARS is short for the Severe Acute Respiratory

Table 7.1   Three types of coronaviruses

Year identified	Virus	Infectious disease	Alternative names
2003	SARS-CoV	Severe Acute Respiratory Syndrome (SARS)	
2012	MERS-CoV	Middle East Respiratory Syndrome (MERS)	
2019	SARS-CoV-2	COVID-19	Novel coronavirus

Syndrome, first identified in 2003. The MERS is short for the Middle East Respiratory Syndrome, first identified in 2012. The coronaviruses survive on a range of hosts, including humans, but most prominently on bats.

Why are they all called a coronavirus? The corona means "crown" in Latin. The coronaviruses have in common the spikes that look like a crown. We saw it in Chap. 1 the shape of the novel coronavirus from which we can understand why it is called a coronavirus (refer to Fig. 1.1, Chap. 1). The coronavirus takes on a shape of a ball whose surface is enclosed by an outer lipid envelope and inside which is a single coiled Ribonucleic Acid (RNA) strand. The ball-shaped coronavirus has many protein spikes on the surface. The spikes look like a crown (USFDA 2020d).

The SARS-CoV-2 is highly efficient in transmitting from human to human. According to the pre-vaccine data, the virus would kill one out of a hundred people infected in the low mortality-rate countries such as Germany and Switzerland to 5 out of 100 people infected in the high mortality-rate countries such as Italy and Spain (refer to Table 2.5, Chap. 2). The virus kills an infected person by killing healthy lung cells in her/him.

The process is explained in Fig. 7.1. The outer lipid envelope in which the virus, that is, the RNA strand in the figure, resides has many protruding spikes. Once the SARS-CoV-2 enters the body of a person, the protein spikes of the virus attach themselves to the healthy lung cell through the receptors of the healthy cell. Being attached, the RNA strand slips into the healthy cell through the cell's receptors. The RNA strand now in the lung cell of a person kills the healthy lung cell, through which spews out multiple new strands of the virus (USFDA 2020d).

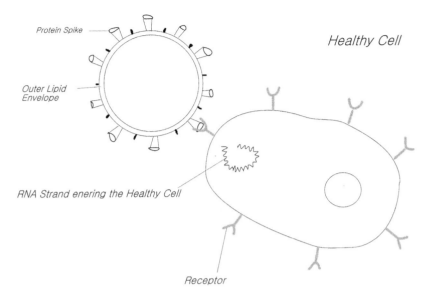

Fig. 7.1 The coronavirus entering and killing the healthy cell

The host, that is, an infected person, has the immune system, which makes her/him survive on this planet, that will react to the entrance of the virus by creating specific antibodies against the virus. The host with a strong immune system will be able to fight the virus to survive, but the host with a weak immune system will not be able to fight and survive the virus. Examples of the latter are persons with pre-existing diseases and the elderly. An effective vaccine is supposed to help both the former and the latter produce specific antibodies against the virus and kill the virus.

A traditional vaccine is a material made of attenuated microorganisms such as bacteria or a virus. Once it is administered to a person, it stimulates the immune system of the person, specifically, the antibody-producing B cells, against a pathogen. The B cells respond when the virus enters the body by producing antibodies (Plotkin 2009).

The concept of a vaccine and vaccination was credited to the laboratory-based microbiology works of Louis Pasteur on chicken cholera, anthrax, and rabies (Schwartz 2001). To give an example, in 1879, an anthrax epidemic killed a large number of sheep in France. Pasteur accomplished the following five steps, which constitute the core of modern vaccinology:

(1) Pasteur isolated the anthrax bacillus from sheep and;
(2) proved that it is responsible for the anthrax epidemic.
(3) He was able to attenuate cultures of anthrax bacillus after weakening the organism's virulence.
(4) In the spring of 1881, he experimented with 70 sheep at the southern outskirts of Paris. Half of the sheep were given a vaccine of low-virulence culture of anthrax bacillus and the other half was a control group.
(5) Two weeks later, the two groups of sheep were inoculated with a virulent strain of anthrax bacillus. All of the vaccinated sheep survived while all the other sheep died.

A vaccine for the COVID-19 is explained in Fig. 7.2. Once an effective vaccine is administered to a person, it will stimulate the B cells which will produce the Y-shaped antibodies against the novel coronavirus. When the SARS-CoV-2 enters the body, the antibodies will bind the protein spikes of the virus and weaken and kill it (USFDA 2020d).

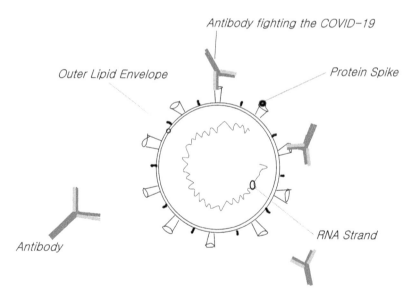

COVID-19 Vaccine

Fig. 7.2 Creating antibody to fight the coronavirus

The COVID-19 virus is an mRNA virus. You can verify it from the RNA strand in Figs. 7.1 and 7.2. Of the COVID-19 vaccines, the Pfizer-BioNTech vaccine and the Moderna vaccine, among all the vaccines being developed, are both an mRNA vaccine (NYT 2020a). These vaccines build on the research on the Messenger Ribonucleic Acid (mRNA) and its applications to pharmaceutical uses (Jacob and Monod 1961; Brenner et al. 1961). The mRNA vaccines are the ones that stood out during the COVID-19 for the reasons to be laid out in this chapter (Kariko et al. 2011; Pardi et al. 2018).

What is the mRNA vaccine? The traditional viral vaccines are founded on the concept and laboratory experiments developed by Pasteur and others, which were explained above (Schwartz 2001; Plotkin 2009). A traditional vaccine carries a weakened or inactivated version of the concerned virus manufactured in a laboratory to a person to stimulate her immune response to the virus. Or, it can be a piece of the virus, that is, a specific protein (Gupta 2021). The former is referred to as a viral vector vaccine and the latter as a protein-based vaccine in this chapter (Table 7.3). The viral vector is an antigen, so is a weakened virus. The term antigen comes from antibody-generating materials.

By contrast, an mRNA vaccine delivers genetic instructions to a person's cells for making a portion of the concerned virus. The body's cells respond by making the protein that is necessary for generating the person's immune response to the virus, that is, anti-COVID-19 B cells and T cells (Thaker 2020). B cells bind with antigens to produce antibodies while T cells directly attack the virus (Pierce 2019). When injected into the body, mRNA vaccines do not integrate into the body cell's Deoxyribonucleic Acid (DNA) and naturally break down in the body, for which reasons scientists generally regard them to be safe (Pardi et al. 2018; Gupta 2021). Emerging studies indicate that the mRNA vaccines provide a high degree of antibody protection against the SARS-CoV-2 at least six months after the second shot (Doria-Rose and Suthar 2021; Pfizer 2021). This means that a fully vaccinated person may need a booster shot, that is, the third shot, after six months.

After an initial success in containing the spread of the virus in high-vaccination countries such as Israel, the UK, and the US from January to June 2021, the Delta variant of Indian origin started to dominate the initial strain, eventually causing the fifth wave of the pandemic. The Delta variant is roughly three times more contagious than the original strain, with $R_0 \approx 7$. A study by the Israel Health Ministry reported only 39%

effectiveness of the Pfizer vaccine against the Delta variant. A British study, on the other hand, reported 88% effectiveness of the Pfizer vaccine against the Delta variant. The Israel study found the Pfizer vaccine is 91% effective in stopping serious cases of the COVID-19 (Jerusalem Post 2021; Bernal et al. 2021). A study of the two mRNA vaccines' effectiveness against the Delta variant by the Mayo Clinic in the US conducted during January–July 2021 finds that the Pfizer vaccine's effectiveness is reduced to 42% and the Moderna vaccine's is reduced to 76% (Puranik et al. 2021).

3   HISTORICAL ACHIEVEMENTS AND FAILURES OF VACCINOLOGY

A vaccine is regarded broadly as the greatest achievement of humanity in the battle against infectious diseases. Since the first publication on vaccine inoculation by Jenner, many infectious diseases surfaced spreading among human and animal populations, against most of which vaccines were developed (Jenner 1801). These vaccines played a pivotal role in containing each respective highly contagious infectious disease.

In Table 7.2, the infectious diseases which were of high international concern and priority historically are summarized, along with the vaccines developed for each of them (WHO 2019a). The list includes smallpox, cholera, measles, polio, swine flu (H1N1), influenza, tuberculosis, Ebola, malaria, and COVID-19. The vaccines in the table are taken from the WHO's list of prequalified vaccines of which the present author chose the earliest vaccine for each disease (WHO 2020b).

Smallpox provides a great success story of vaccination, or equivalently, immunization. As explained in Chap. 4, it was perhaps the most feared disease during the nineteenth and twentieth centuries until the eradication of the disease was declared in 1980. The mortality rate was extremely high, killing eight out of ten infected children (CDC 2020a; refer to Fig. 9.5 in Chap. 9).

The first success in vaccination against smallpox is credited to Edward Jenner who coined the terms "vaccine" and "vaccination." He discovered that the milkmaids who had gotten the cowpox virus did not develop any symptoms of smallpox. Cowpox was another infectious disease similar to smallpox but milder, which causes viral skin infections. It was transmitted from the cows to humans. Jenner published his findings with the title "On the Origin of Vaccine Inoculation" (Jenner 1801). The term "vaccine" comes from the Latin word *Vaccinus*, which means of or from the cow. The oldest smallpox vaccine, the Dryvax, was developed in the nineteenth century by American Home Products (AHP). It was a freeze-dried calf lymph vaccine. Wyeth, a successor to the AHP, was the only

Table 7.2 Vaccines (selected) for major infectious diseases

Infectious disease	Successful vaccines (first, selected)	Eradicated?	Under clinical trials?
Smallpox	Dryvax: American home products, nineteenth century	1980	
Cholera	Shanchol: India, 2011		
Anthrax	Pasteur vaccine: France, 1881		
Rabies	VERORAB: France, 2005		
Measles	Measles vaccine, live, attenuated: India, 1993		
Mumps	Measles, mumps and Rubella vaccine, live, attenuated: India, 2003		
Rubella	Measles, mumps and Rubella vaccine, live, attenuated: India, 2003		
Tuberculosis	Bacille Calmette-Guérin (BCG) Freeze Dried Glutamate vaccine: Japan, 1987		
Diphtheria-tetanus	Diphtheria and tetanus vaccine absorbed (pediatric): India, 1995		
Polio	Polioviral vaccine: India, 2006		
Rotavirus	Rotateq: US, 2008		
Swine flu (H1N1)	Influenza A (H1N1) 2009 monovalent vaccine: US, 2010		
Influenza, seasonal	Fluzone quadrivalent: US, 2015 Fluzone trivalent: US, 2010		
Hepatitis A	Havrix 720 Junior: Belgium, 2013		
Hepatitis B	Engerix: Belgium, 1987		
Yellow fever	STAMARIL: France, 1987		
Dengue	Dengvaxia: France, 2020		
Typhoid	Typhim-Vi: France, 2011		
Japanese encephalitis	IMOJEV MD: Thailand, 2014		
SARS			Yes
MERS			Yes
Ebola Zaire	ERVEBO: US, 2019		Yes
Malaria	RTS, S/AS01 (Mosquirix): Belgium, US		Yes
COVID-19	Pfizer-BioNTech, Moderna: US, 2020		

manufacturer of smallpox vaccines by the 1960s. After smallpox was declared by the WHO to be eradicated in 1980, Wyeth stopped manufacturing the vaccine. The US Centers for the Disease Control and Prevention (CDC) kept the stockpile of Dryvax for emergency use until February 2008 when it disposed of the remaining stock. It is replaced by more modern successors such as ACAM2000 and Imvamune (AP 2008).

After the eradication of smallpox globally, the WHO made the US and Russia the repository for all remaining stocks of smallpox virus, *variola major* and *variola minor*, for research purposes. The US stocks are kept at the Centers for Disease Control and Prevention in Atlanta, Georgia. The Russian stocks are kept at the State Research Centre of Virology and Biotechnology (Weinstein 2011).

Of the vaccines listed in Table 7.2, the most common ones to people are the seasonal influenza vaccines which many people, especially seniors and kids, around the world take annually. For influenza, there are two types of vaccines, Fluzone Quadrivalent and Fluzone Trivalent, depending on the flu virus strains. The efficacy rate of these flu vaccines is in the range of 60 to 70%. Annually, the flu-caused deaths in the US ranged from 12,000 to 61,000 people per year during the decade of the 2010s (CDC 2020b).

Malaria is another deadly infectious disease which kills millions of people around the developing world today, whose detailed description was given in the chapter. The mosquito-borne infectious disease, that is, by carrying malaria parasites, is largely eliminated in developed and high-income countries, but still remains a severe health problem in Sub-Saharan Africa and India (Rogers and Randolph 2000). The number of deaths caused by malaria was 1.2 million people worldwide during the 12-year time period from 1990 to 2001 while the most recent World Malaria Report estimates roughly 400,000 deaths from malaria per year (Lopez et al. 2006; WHO 2019b). The only malaria vaccine available is named RTS, S/AS01, with a trade name Mosquirix. The vaccine is still under clinical trials and of low efficacy, according to the WHO (WHO 2020c). This is astonishing considering that the disease has existed for over 10,000 years.

The infectious diseases listed in the table that are still without an effective vaccine or a candidate vaccine under later phases of clinical trials are two coronaviruses (SARS and MERS), Ebola Zaire, and malaria.

4 THE PROCESS OF VACCINE DEVELOPMENTS FOR COVID-19

What does it take for a pharmaceutical laboratory to develop a vaccine for a rapidly spreading pandemic virus and get it approved by a governmental agency for emergency applications? Let's take a closer look at the vaccine development process relying on the experiences of the COVID-19 vaccines. The process can be divided into four stages: developing a candidate vaccine, three phases of clinical trials, an emergency use authorization, and successful administrations to the people.

4.1 Vaccine Methodologies and Candidate Vaccines

The first stage is developing a candidate vaccine. For this, a pharmaceutical company or a research laboratory should choose a methodology first. Table 7.3 lists the most discussed vaccine candidates during 2020, which shows that multiple methodologies were pursued by then potential developers (NYT 2020a). Participating pharmaceutical companies and

Table 7.3 Vaccine types and candidates

Types	Vaccine candidates	Countries	Trial phases (as of November 9, 2020)
mRNA vaccines	Moderna	US	3
	Pfizer-BioNTech	US, Germany	2–3
Viral vector vaccines	CanSino Biologics	China	3 (approved for limited use in China)
	Sputnik V, Gamaleya Research Institute	Russia	3 (approved for limited use in Russia)
	Johnson & Johnson	US	3
	AstraZeneca	UK, Switzerland	2–3
Protein-based vaccines	Novavax	US	3
	Vector Institute	Russia	3
Inactivated or attenuated coronavirus vaccines	Sinopharm	China	3 (approved for limited use in the UAE)
	Sinovac Biotech	China	(Approved for limited use in the UAE)
	Bharat Biotech	India	

Source: NYT Vaccine Tracker (2020a)

laboratories include Pfizer-BioNTech, Moderna, Johnson & Johnson, and Novavax in the US; CanSino Biologics, Sinopharm, and Sinovac Biotech in China; Gamaleya Research Institute and Vector Institute in Russia; AstraZeneca in Switzerland; and Bharat Biotech in India.

The table shows that four types of vaccines distinguished by their production methodologies were pursued: mRNA vaccines (also known as genetic vaccines), viral vector vaccines, protein-based vaccines, and inactivated or attenuated coronavirus vaccines (NYT 2020a; Gavi 2020). The mRNA vaccines are the ones that stood out during the COVID-19. They were the first to be developed and approved by the FDA. Further, the efficacy rate of the mRNA vaccines was far higher than the other types of vaccines, reaching 95% rate.

First, the mRNA vaccines, as explained in Sect. 2, carry one or more of the novel coronavirus' own genes containing genetic instructions to a person's body cells, from which the person's immune response is provoked, that is, anti-COVID B and T cells. The most successful vaccines relied on this then-novel technology: the Pfizer-BioNTech vaccine and the Moderna vaccine (Kariko et al. 2011; Pardi et al. 2018). The mRNA vaccine technology may have been developed only a few years before the pandemic. The paper entitled "mRNA vaccines—A New Era in Vaccinology" was published in January 2018 (Pardi et al. 2018). Before the pandemic, no DNA or RNA vaccines had been licensed for human use (Gavi 2020).

Second, as for the viral vector vaccines, the vaccine contains a modified virus, that is, the vector, which is engineered to carry coronavirus genes. Once the viral vector vaccine enters human cells, it instructs them to make antigens, thereby triggering an immune response (NYT 2020a). The Johnson & Johnson vaccine and the AstraZeneca vaccine are viral vector vaccines. The Gamaleya Research Institute's vaccine from Russia, called the Sputnik V, is also of this type.

Third, as for the protein-based vaccines, the vaccine contains coronavirus proteins, either the whole proteins or some fragments. However, no genetic material is contained in the protein-based vaccine. The Novavax vaccine from the US and the Vector Institute vaccine from Russia are protein-based vaccines.

Fourth, as for the inactivated or attenuated coronavirus vaccines, the vaccine is created from weakened coronaviruses or killed coronaviruses with chemicals. The Sinopharm vaccine of China and the Bharat Biotech vaccine of India are of this type.

The clinical trial phases of the listed vaccine candidates are shown in the last column of Table 7.3, as of November 9, 2020. This is a notable reference date for the COVID-19 because the first announcement of the successful phase III trials for a vaccine candidate was made by Pfizer-BioNTech with an astonishing 90–95% efficacy (Fox News 2020a).

4.2   Four Phases of Clinical Trials

Once a vaccine candidate is created in a laboratory relying on one of the methodologies just described, the developer should go through a series of clinical trials before it can get reviewed and ultimately approved by, in the case of the US, the Food and Drug Administration (FDA). Four phases of clinical trials should be conducted before any review: pre-clinical testing, Phase I, Phase II, and Phase III clinical trials (NYT 2020a).

For the pre-clinical testing, a candidate vaccine is administered in a laboratory to animals such as monkeys or mice to find out whether the vaccine does stimulate an immune response of the animals. Clinical trials on humans can only begin after a successful pre-clinical testing with an approval from the FDA.

The Phase I clinical trials are, also called safety trials, conducted on humans. The candidate vaccine which passed the pre-clinical testing is administered to a small group of volunteers to test whether it is safe on humans. The phase I trials also test whether or not the expected immune response is actually taking place on human volunteers.

The Phase II clinical trials are expanded trials. The candidate vaccine which passed the Phase I trials is administered to a larger group of people, for example, hundreds of people, who are split into different subgroups such as the elderly, women, children, and so on. In addition to testing the safety and the expected immune responses from the trial participants, the Phase II trials test whether or not the vaccine acts differently on different subgroups of people.

The Phase III clinical trials are, referred to as efficacy trials, conducted on a large population of people in which half of the participants are administered a candidate vaccine and the other half is a control group administered a placebo vaccine. The Phase III trials determine whether the vaccine can protect humans against the infectious agent and especially determine the efficacy rate of the vaccine. In June 2020, the FDA advised the vaccine makers that the vaccine should be at least 50% effective, that is, protect at least 50% of the people who get the vaccine shot for it to be approved for emergency uses.

For the Pfizer-BioNTech vaccine which announced the first successful Phase III trials in the world with the efficacy rate of 90–95%, approximately 43,500 people around the globe participated in the Pfizer vaccine trials, including the enrollees at the Yale New Haven Hospital. Half of the participants were injected with the Pfizer-BioNTech vaccine, while the other half were injected with a placebo. Out of all the enrollees in the global trials, there were 94 confirmed cases of a COVID-19 infection. A majority of the COVID-19 cases, however, occurred in the control group, that is, among the volunteers who received a placebo (Yale Daily News 2020).

4.3   An Emergency Use Authorization

Once the successful Phase III trials are completed and announced by the developer, the results from the clinical trials are reviewed by the governmental agency that is given the authority by law to issue an emergency use authorization (EUA), the FDA in the US for the vaccine. For the COVID-19 vaccine, it took another month for the FDA's approval of the Pfizer-BioNTech vaccine on December 11, 2020, from its announcement of the successful Phase III trials on November 9, 2020.

The FDA's authority to issue the EUA is explained in Chap. 4 of this book, which is given by the Federal Food, Drug, and Cosmetic Act passed by Congress in 1938 and its amendments. Section 564 of the Act gives the FDA Commissioner the authority to "allow unapproved medical products … to be used in an emergency to diagnose, treat, or prevent serious or life-threatening diseases or conditions caused by CBRN (Chemical, Biological, Radiological, and Nuclear) threat agents when there are no adequate, approved, and available alternatives" (USFDA 2020e).

For the FDA approval, the Vaccines and Related Biological Products Advisory Committee reviewed the results from the clinical trials and voted to recommend the EUA of the Pfizer-BioNTech vaccine on December 10, 2020. The EUA letter from the FDA states:

FDA's analysis of the available efficacy data from 36,523 participants 12 years of age and older without evidence of SARS-CoV-2 infection prior to 7 days after dose 2 confirm the vaccine was 95% effective (95% credible interval 90.3, 97.6) in preventing COVID-19 occurring at least 7 days after the second dose (with 8 COVID-19 cases in the vaccine group compared to 162 COVID-19 cases in the placebo group). (USFDA 2020b)

Of the vaccines listed in Table 7.3, five vaccines are from China and Russia. It is notable that some of them were approved without Phase III trials according to the report from the New York Times (NYT 2020a). By January 2021, several reports indicated that despite the Chinese government's efforts to sell Chinese vaccines at cheap prices to other developing countries, many countries were reluctant to buy them over the US vaccines because of safety concerns. On the other hand, the Sputnik V COVID-19 vaccine developed by the Gamaleya Research Institute reported a 91.6% efficacy rate in a peer-reviewed research journal (Logunov et al. 2021).

5 A PARTNERSHIP BETWEEN THE PUBLIC SECTOR AND THE PRIVATE SECTOR: THE OPERATION WARP SPEED

How did the pharmaceutical companies succeed in developing effective vaccines in record time, specifically, in only nine months from the pandemic declaration? Let me start with a timeline of the four most discussed vaccines during 2020 which is presented in Table 7.4. The Pfizer-BioNTech vaccine announced its successful Phase III trials' results on November 9, which was approved for emergency uses on December 11, 2020, by the FDA. The Moderna vaccine announced its Phase III trials' results on November 16, which was approved for emergency uses on December 18, 2020 (USFDA 2020b, 2020c).

The AstraZeneca vaccine announced its success in the Phase III trials on November 25, but their results were questioned soon afterward by the FDA regarding dose changes during the Phase III trials while by March 2021 several European nations suspended the use after serious side effects were observed (NYT 2020b; Reuters 2021). Denmark became the first nation to cease the AstraZeneca vaccine permanently owing to rare blood clots (BBC 2021).

The Janssen COVID-19 vaccine developed by Johnson & Johnson reported that it is 67% effective in preventing the COVID-19 and an EUA was issued by the FDA on February 27, 2021 (USFDA 2021a). By April 14, 2021, the Jansen vaccine was temporarily suspended in the US owing to the reports of rare blood clots in some recipients (USFDA 2021b).

Table 7.4 A timeline of vaccine success announcements, authorizations, and side effects

	Pfizer-BioNTech	Moderna	Oxford-AstraZeneca	Johnson & Johnson
Name of the vaccine	BNT162b2	mRNA-1273	AZD1222	Janssen COVID-19 vaccine
Efficacy rate	90–95%	94.5%	70% on average (62–90%)	67% effective
November 9, 2020	Pfizer's vaccine proves 90% effective (Fox Business 2020a)			
November 16, 2020		Moderna vaccine is 94.5% effective in preventing COVID-19 (Fox Business 2020b)		
November 25, 2020			After admitting mistake, AstraZeneca faces difficult questions about its vaccine (NYT 2020b)	
December 11, 2020	FDA issues an emergency use authorization (USFDA 2020b)			
December 18, 2020		FDA issues an emergency use authorization (USFDA 2020c)		
February 27, 2021				FDA issues an emergency use authorization (USFDA 2021a)
March 12, 2021			The WHO says its advisory committee looking at AstraZeneca vaccine issues (Reuters 2021)	
April 13–14, 2021			Denmark ceases the AstraZeneca vaccine over rare blood clots (BBC 2021)	J&J vaccine paused over rare blood clots (USFDA 2021b)

The remarkable vaccine successes, especially the two mRNA vaccines, at the height of the COVID-19 pandemic in November and December 2020 were widely acclaimed across the planet and largely credited to the US federal government's program named the Operation Warp Speed (OWS). The OWS was a private-public partnership to accelerate the vaccine developments and distributions. Of the private sector, selected pharmaceutical companies were participants. Of the public sector, various components of the Department of Health and Human Services (HHS), including the Centers for Disease Control and Prevention, the National Institutes of Health (NIH), the Biomedical Advanced Research and Development Authority (BARDA), and the Department of Defense (DoD) were participants of the OWS (Azar II 2020).

The OWS' goal was concretely defined to "produce and deliver 300 million doses of safe and effective vaccines with the initial doses available by January 2021." Comprehensively, it was defined as the US government's program under the Trump administration to accelerate the development, manufacturing, and distribution of COVID-19 vaccines, therapeutics, and diagnostics (USDHHS 2020).

The OWS' success can be attributed in large part to (1) selecting early the most promising vaccine candidates and developers; (2) providing a funding to the selected vaccine developers to get the development efforts started as quickly as possible; and (3) investing in a purchase guarantee with the vaccine developers. With the purchase guarantee of several hundred million doses of multiple vaccines, the vaccine developers started manufacturing their vaccine doses after successful Phase II trials. According to this design, the US government would own the purchased vaccines and, with an EUA approval from the FDA, the vaccines would be distributed to people without any delay. In the case of failing to obtain an EUA approval, the vaccines would be discarded.

The vaccine candidates that received the funding from the OWS, as summarized in Table 7.5, are Johnson & Johnson, Moderna, AstraZeneca, Novavax, Pfizer, and Sanofi and GlaxoSmithKline (GSK). The table shows the funding sizes as well as the development stages that are funded. Moderna is given a funding of US$483 million for the development stage on April 16, 2020, and additionally US$1.5 billion for the manufacturing and delivery stages on August 11, 2020. Pfizer is given US$1.95 billion on July 22, 2020, for the manufacturing stage for manufacturing 100 million doses of a successful vaccine. After the emergency use authorization, the US government purchased additional 100 million doses from Pfizer at

Table 7.5   The Operation Warp Speed funding

Date	Candidates	Funding sizes	Stages funded
March 30	Johnson & Johnson	$456 million	Development
April 16	Moderna	$483 million	Development
May 21	AstraZeneca	$1.2 billion	Development
July 7	Regeneron's COVID-19 investigational anti-viral antibody treatment, REGN-COV2	$450 million	Manufacturing
July 7	Novavax	$1.6 billion	Manufacturing
July 22	Pfizer	$1.95 billion	Manufacturing: a large-scale manufacturing and nationwide distribution of 100 million doses of their vaccine candidate
July 31	Sanofi and GlaxoSmithKline (GSK)	$2 billion	Development, trials, manufacturing
August 5	Johnson & Johnson	$1 billion	Manufacturing and delivery
August 11	Moderna	$1.5 billion	Manufacturing and delivery
October 28	Eli Lilly and Company	$375 million	The first doses of the company's COVID-19 investigational antibody therapeutic bamlanivimab, also known as LY-CoV555
December 23, 2020	Pfizer	$1.95 billion	Manufacturing additional 100 million doses

US$1.95 billion on December 23, 2020. The first OWS funding was given to Johnson & Johnson on March 30, 2020 (USDHHS 2020).

As argued in Chap. 4, the Operation Warp Speed demonstrated the value of a well-designed public-private sector partnership during a global scale crisis caused by a highly contagious infectious disease. Built on the strength of the private pharmaceutical laboratories, the partnership has turned out to be much fruitful for the US as well as the global community. The public sector intervention through the OWS, on the other hand, may have accelerated the development of a high-efficacy vaccine by many months or years.

6   The Economics of Vaccines

Having clarified the science of and the government's actions on the COVID-19 vaccines up to this point, we are well-positioned to wait patiently and see whether the vaccine shots, which began to be given in the US on December 14, 2020, will indeed turn out to be so powerful to end the pandemic and the extremely contagious SARS-CoV-2 virus. Before taking up this question in the next section, the present author hopes to delineate hereunder the unique economic aspects of vaccines which lead to some important tradeoffs in policy decisions.

To begin with, the vaccine's economics is incredible. As proven to the world by the smallpox vaccination efforts conducted worldwide which accomplished the eradication of the fatal infectious disease to humankind for many centuries, an effective vaccine gives the global community a solid chance for terminating a pandemic, thereby ending the misery and trauma of people and saving millions of lives at risk. Undoubtedly, monetary benefits of such a vaccine would by far outweigh the monetary cost of developing and manufacturing it. To put it differently, a benefit-cost ratio of a high-efficacy vaccine is truly exceptionally high with reference to a range of governmental intervention programs (Hahn and Dudley 2007).

Second, applying aptly the insights of natural resource economics, an effective vaccine is a backstop technology. Coined in the energy economics and proven to be illuminating in tackling environmental and natural resource economics questions, a backstop was envisioned as an energy source or technology that can supply energy indefinitely to humanity at a constant price (Nordhaus 1973; Hartwick and Olewiler 1997). In everyday language, a backstop is an ultimate solution to the problem under consideration, for example, a nuclear fusion technology to the energy supply problem and a highly effective vaccine to the pandemic disease problem. The *Dryvax* smallpox vaccine proved to be a backstop.

A prominent characteristic of a vaccine backstop is that unlike a backstop energy which would replace all energy sources ultimately, a vaccine is a backstop solution only to the particular infectious agent against which it is specifically developed. For example, mRNA-1273, which is the Moderna vaccine, would be a backstop only against the SARS-CoV-2 virus. The vaccine backstop is only narrowly defined. The mRNA-1273 cannot be a backstop solution against all infectious diseases, nor even against all types of coronaviruses.

On the other hand, a virus, for example, the SARS-CoV-2, can easily evolve into a different strand to become a different variant. The vaccine developed against the first virus strand may or may not be effective against its variants. The Pfizer-BioNTech vaccine, for example, may not be effective for another coronavirus, say, MERS-CoV, SARS-CoV, a British variant of SARS-CoV-2 (Alpha variant), or an Indian variant (Delta variant) (Jerusalem Post 2021).

An important economic implication of a narrow applicability of the backstop vaccine is that a vaccine backstop cannot be prepared ahead of time against a possible future pandemic virus. From another viewpoint, an "all-purpose" vaccine is not available with today's technologies.

Third, the incredible vaccine economics hinges on the time interval from an outbreak of an infectious disease to an emergency use authorization for a vaccine. The shorter the time lapse, the more incredible it becomes. The longer the time lapse, the less incredible it becomes. The time interval is especially a pivotal factor when the infectious agent of concern is highly efficient in transmitting human to human, that is, highly contagious, as well as when it has a high mortality rate. Under each or both circumstances, the number of fatalities from the pandemic will quickly rise worldwide, starting from the outbreak of the disease. Unfortunately, a pandemic, that is, an infectious disease at a worldwide scale, tends to possess both characteristics.

As for the COVID-19 pandemic, it took only nine months from the OWS agreements with the pharmaceutical companies or the pandemic declaration by the WHO to the emergency use authorizations for the Pfizer and Moderna vaccines, which is broadly regarded as a remarkable achievement in the vaccine science. Notwithstanding the great success, the number of deaths worldwide had already passed 1 million people by the time of the EUA approvals while the number of infected people had approached 80 million people by that time. If it had taken two or three years to get an effective vaccine developed and approved, the number of deaths could have reached an unimaginable level by the time of the first vaccine shot. For reference, even with the arduous vaccination efforts worldwide during the first half of 2021, the number of deaths surpassed 4.2 million people by the end of July 2021.

Fourth, given the big responsibility placed on the shoulders of governmental leaders during a pandemic, they have ample reason to get the vaccine developers started working on it as early as possible. As in the

Operation Warp Speed, the government can expedite this process by providing an early funding to selected vaccine candidates. The funding should be directed to the development stage first, but the funding to the manufacturing/delivery stages is equally important in speeding up the vaccine developments.

By selecting the vaccine candidates, the government is limiting the vaccine race in effect to the selected pharmaceutical companies. Is this a big problem because the government is limiting the market competition? This is not because the vaccine supply function has a best-shot technology. That is, it does not have a cumulative technology as some researchers implied (Bloom and Canning 2017). To state simply, the vaccine supply is determined by the success of the most advanced pharmaceutical laboratory. As soon as Pfizer-BioNTech or Moderna got its vaccine approved, the world has the vaccine supplied for people's uses worldwide. As far as the incredible economics is concerned, the second vaccine or the third vaccine does not matter much: one highly effective vaccine would do the job!

In addition, because of the high risk involved in vaccine manufacturing and administrating it to an exceptionally large number of people, only the most advanced companies in the world will attempt to compete in the vaccine race. As the COVID-19 experience reveals, only the world's major pharmaceuticals competed for vaccine developments: Pfizer, Moderna, Johnson & Johnson, Novavax, and AstraZeneca.

Fifth, considering the success of the COVID-19 vaccines, we should wonder why there is still no vaccine for the infectious diseases that have long been with humanity, for example, malaria. Of the priority diseases identified by the WHO (Table 7.6), many have no effective vaccines: MERS-CoV, Ebola, SARS, and Zika (WHO 2018). Is there indeed a market failure in developing the vaccines for these diseases (Bloom and Canning 2017)?

There are two reasons: one is technological, while the other is economic. The technological reason is that it may be difficult to develop a vaccine for a certain infectious disease than the others. The economic reason is that the contagiousness of the infectious disease is limited to a certain group or a certain local area, which makes it difficult for a potential vaccine developer to make a big investment.

Sixth, the inevitable time lapse in vaccine developments means that there is a big void to fill until a high-efficacy vaccine is administered to a

Table 7.6 The lists of WHO priority diseases in 2018 and 2015 (WHO 2018)

Second list in 2018	First list in 2015	Notes
Crimean-Congo hemorrhagic fever	Crimean Congo hemorrhagic fever	
Ebola virus disease and Marburg virus disease	Ebola virus disease and Marburg	
Lassa fever	Lassa fever	
Middle East respiratory syndrome coronavirus (MERS-CoV)	MERS-CoV	
Severe Acute Respiratory Syndrome (SARS)	SARS coronavirus diseases	
Nipah and henipaviral diseases	Nipah	
Rift Valley fever	Rift Valley fever	
Zika		
Disease X		Represents the knowledge that a serious international epidemic could be caused by a pathogen currently unknown to cause human disease

"large" fraction of the population in the country. The mitigation and treatment efforts via either policy measures or behavioral responses should fill that void. The mitigation efforts aim at slowing down the spread of the infectious disease with a variety of actions such as physical distancing, mask-wearing, hand washing, and avoiding social gatherings. This was explained in Chap. 4 of this book.

At the heart of the mitigation efforts lies diagnostics. Early availability of test kits and rapid testing capacities are instrumental in containing the unchecked spread of the virus (Romer 2020; Yale News 2020). For the treatment efforts, hospital capacities, doctors and care workers, medical devices, and therapeutic drugs are essential elements for success.

Note in Table 7.5 that both COVID-19 diagnostics and therapeutics are parts of the Operation Warp Speed funding programs (USDHHS 2020). Of the therapeutics, the REGN-COV2, which is Regeneron's

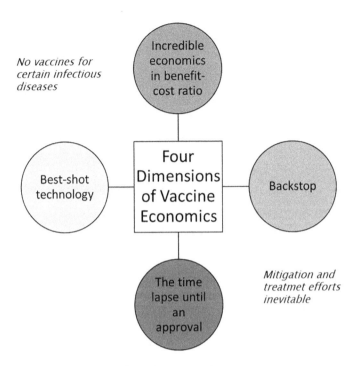

Fig. 7.3 Four dimensions of vaccine economics

COVID-19 anti-viral antibody treatment, is what then President Trump took when he was diagnosed with the virus USFDA 2020a. The other repurposed drugs as well as the WHO-led solidarity tests and recommendations on the drugs were explained in Chap. 4.

The vaccine economics described thus far is summarized as the four dimensions of vaccine economics in Fig. 7.3. The four dimensions are an incredible economics in the benefit-cost ratio, a backstop solution, the best-shot production technology, and the time lapse until the EAU approval. The problem of no vaccines for certain infectious diseases arises from two dimensions: the low benefit-cost ratio and the best shot. The need for mitigation and treatment efforts arises from the other two dimensions: a backstop solution and the long time lapse.

7   WILL THE VACCINES END
THE COVID-19 PANDEMIC?

By the time the Pfizer-BioNTech vaccine and the Moderna vaccine were authorized for emergency uses, the coronavirus pandemic entered into the third wave globally, spurred by the cold weather in November and December of 2020. The daily number of infections as well as the daily number of deaths worldwide did not diminish even after the vaccines arrived and got administered for several months. This final section examines the up-to-date COVID-19 data to evaluate whether the pandemic will indeed be terminated, thanks to the "miracle" vaccines in the not-too-distant future.

To reflect the raw emotions of the world community after the vaccines were approved and administered, this analysis was done in the middle of January of 2021, roughly one month after the two mRNA vaccine approvals. Readers of this book will be able to appreciate the very early signs of the effectiveness of the vaccine shots that began to emerge in the richest countries of the world. By the time that a revision to this analysis was taken place on May 2, 2021, the early signs to be shown below have magnified to enable some countries to open most businesses or have a plan to fully open within a month or so, for example, Israel and the UK (NYT 2021).

The vaccine shots are rolled out to pre-defined priority groups first. The CDC of the US recommended that the initial doses of the vaccines be offered to healthcare personnel and residents of long-term care facilities. Governors and individual jurisdictions, however, will ultimately decide who will get the vaccine shots first.

As of January 10, 2021, 22 million doses are distributed in the US, of which 7.7 million shots are administered across the states. The percentage of shots given is 34.9% of the total number of distributions. The number of shots given is 0.73 million shots in California, 0.7 million in Texas, 0.55 million in Florida, and 0.54 million in New York.

Globally, of the 24 million doses administered, as shown in Table 7.7, 9 million shots were given in China and 7.7 million shots given in the US. The two countries are followed by Israel, the UK, the UAE, and Russia. Per 100 people, Israel gave vaccine shots to nearly 20 people, while the UAE gave shots to nearly 10 people by January 10, 2021 (Bloomberg 2021).

To detect the earliest signs of the effectiveness of the COVID-19 vaccines, the present author examines the trend in the total number of infections before and after the first vaccine shots administered on December 14, 2020. The data are obtained from Johns Hopkins University's global coronavirus dashboard (JHU 2020).

Since the data covers only the 25-day period after the first vaccine shots, you would argue that it is too early to have a definitive conclusion. This is confirmed in our preliminary data analysis summarized in Figs. 7.4 and 7.5. Let's have a look at the US infection data first. At the point of the event on December 14, there is no sign of any change in the trend of the total number of cases (Fig. 7.4). Specifically, there is no discernible kink or change in the slope of the trend that we can detect from the figure during the first 25-day period. This is expected given that the number of doses administered (NDA) is only 2.35 per 100 people in the US by the date.

For a more meaningful analysis, the present author examines in Fig. 7.5 the total case trends in four countries across which the rate of vaccination, that is, the Number of Doses Administered (NDA), is varied. Israel is the high-vaccination country where roughly 20% of the population is already vaccinated, that is, NDA = 19. The UK is the medium-vaccination country where 2.23% of the population is vaccinated. Sweden is the low-vaccination country where 0.39% of the population is vaccinated. Japan is the no-vaccination country at this early date (Table 7.7).

Figure 7.5 reveals a sign of hope, however meager it might be. The trend after the first vaccination is far flatter in Israel, the high-vaccination country, than the trend in Japan, no-vaccination country, as well as the trend in Sweden, the low-vaccination country. This is the only observation from which we can assert a positive effect of the COVID-19 vaccine, without a more sophisticated statistical analysis, as early as January 10, 2021. The uptrends in Japan and Sweden during the third wave are significant in Fig. 7.5.

Unlike Israel's trend, the UK's trend offers a most pessimistic outlook for the vaccination efforts. It appears to show a kink at the time of the first COVID-19 vaccine. The number of cases is increasing at a faster rate after the COVID-19 vaccine administration than before it. This, however, does not negate the effectiveness of the vaccines because the NDA in the UK is only 2.3 per 100 people, but does show that the third wave of the COVID-19 is overwhelming the nation.

Table 7.7   Vaccine shots given per 100 people by country

Country	Number of doses administered (NDA)	NDA per 100 people	Status date (year 2021)
Global	24,746,063	–	January 9
China	9,000,000	0.64	January 8
US	7,725,000	2.35	January 9
Israel	1,692,000	18.69	January 8
UK	1,488,947	2.23	January 7
UAE	1,020,349	9.49	January 9
Russia	800,000	0.55	January 2
Italy	583,050	0.97	January 9
Germany	532,878	0.64	January 9
Canada	294,280	0.78	January 9
Spain	277,976	0.6	January 8
Poland	198,787	0.52	January 9
Saudi Arabia	130,000	0.38	January 7
Denmark	112,427	1.94	January 9
Argentina	107,542	0.24	January 8
Romania	102,301	0.53	January 9
Bahrain	84,157	5.67	January 9
France	80,000	0.12	January 7
Portugal	70,000	0.68	January 8
Mexico	67,468	0.05	January 8
Hungary	42,549	0.44	January 8
Greece	40,163	0.37	January 9
Sweden	40,000	0.39	January 7
Netherlands	30,000	0.17	January 9
Croatia	24,985	0.61	January 8
Lithuania	22,191	0.8	January 9
Czech Republic	19,918	0.19	January 7
Slovakia	19,727	0.36	January 8
Slovenia	19,523	0.94	January 9
Norway	17,337	0.32	January 8
Austria	15,905	0.18	January 7
Ireland	15,314	0.31	January 7
Oman	14,980	0.36	January 9
Bulgaria	13,473	0.19	January 9
Finland	11,135	0.2	January 8
Chile	10,699	0.06	January 9
Estonia	10,197	0.77	January 9
Latvia	4595	0.24	January 7
Kuwait	2500	0.05	December 29
Costa Rica	2455	0.05	January 3

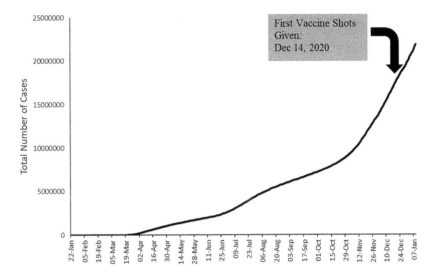

Fig. 7.4 The trend after the vaccine shots in the US (total cumulative cases). (Source: JHU 2020)

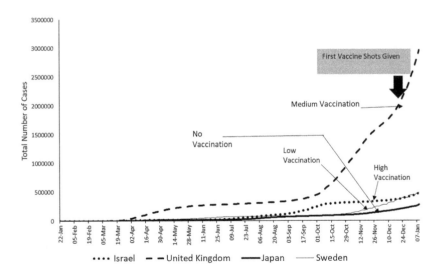

Fig. 7.5 The trends after the vaccine shots across different vaccination rates (total cumulative cases). (Source: JHU 2020)

As noted earlier, by May 1, 2021, the UK becomes one of the few most successful vaccination countries with nearly 65% of the people aged 18 and over vaccinated, opening most businesses (NYT 2021). The dramatic effect of vaccinations can be illustrated by the comparison of the daily confirmed cases in the UK with those in India, as in Fig. 7.6. The shaded area in the figure corresponds to the period after the Pfizer-BioNTech and Moderna EUA approvals up to May 1, 2021. Roughly one month after the first vaccinations, the number of daily cases started to plummet in the UK. On the other hand, the daily number of cases in India began to explode in March 2021. By May 1, 2021, India reported nearly 400,000 confirmed cases per day (JHU 2020).

8   Final Words

Amid the suffering and trauma brought about to the planet by the novel coronavirus of 2020, the vaccine approvals in the last month of the remarkable year shed a ray of hope for a strong recovery in 2021, while

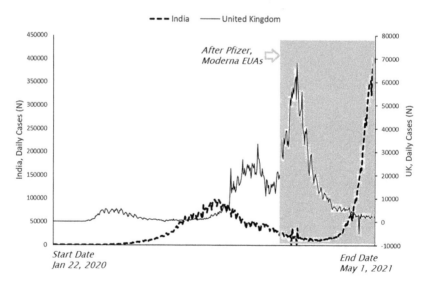

Fig. 7.6 Vaccine effects by May 1, 2021: India versus the UK. (Source: JHU 2020)

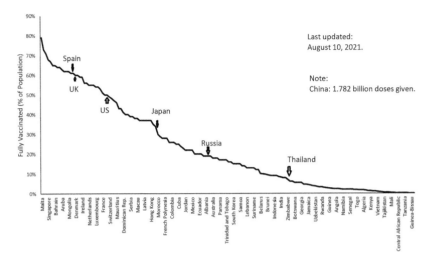

Fig. 7.7 Fully vaccinated (% of population by August 10, 2021)

portending a possibility of a vaccine-assisted miracle, as of January 10, 2021. Regrettably, the advent of the mRNA vaccines coincided with the third COVID-19 wave worldwide. Whether the "miracle" vaccines will be sufficient to end the COVID-19 pandemic by overcoming the new wave of infections remained in doubt, as of May 10, 2021.

By August 10, 2021, the global community is witnessing another big wave of infections across the planet, the fifth wave, driven by the spread of the Delta variant which appears to "breakthrough" a large fraction of vaccinated people (Jerusalem Post 2021; Brown et al. 2021). By then, the full vaccination rate in rich countries has passed 50% of respective populations: over 70% in UAE, over 60% in Spain and the UK, and over 50% in the US (Fig. 7.7). However, the full vaccination rate remains low in many countries that are suffering the most from the Delta variant surge, roughly 10% of the population in India, Indonesia, and Thailand (OWID 2021). Although roughly 60% of the population is vaccinated in the US, the daily number of new cases has surged to pass 100,000 in early August 2021 (JHU 2020). A research just leased by the Mayo Clinic Health System shows that the vaccine effectiveness against the Delta variant is reduced to 42% in the Pfizer vaccine while it is reduced to 76% in the Moderna vaccine (Puranik et al. 2021). Whether the mRNA vaccines will be effective

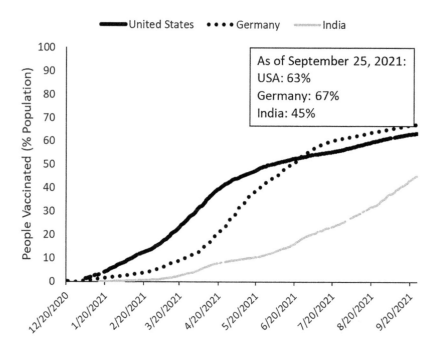

Fig. 7.8 A trajectory of people vaccinated as percentage of population (as of September 25, 2021)

in stopping the Delta variant and the other variants or whether another set of new vaccines must be developed against ever more contagious new variants of the SARS-CoV-2 virus remain unanswered, as of August 10, 2021.

The trajectory of the percentage of people vaccinated in each country, shown in Fig. 7.8, indicates that it will reach a plateau at some date not far away. The figure shows the percentage of people in each country who received at least one dose of the COVID-19 vaccines as of September 25, 2021 (OWID 2021). In Germany, the rate of increase appears to approach zero by early July 2021 while the same appears to be true for the US by early September 2021. It remains to be seen how high the vaccination rate will go and whether it will reach a vaccination plateau soon.

REFERENCES

Associated Press (AP). 2008. CDC to destroy oldest smallpox vaccine. Published on March 3.

Azar II, Alex M. 2020. How Operation Warp Speed delivered a COVID Vaccine in Record Time. *Fox News*. Published on December 12. https://www.foxnews.com/opinion/hhs-azar-operation-warp-speed-covid-vaccine-record-time.

BBC. 2021. AstraZeneca Vaccine: Denmark Stops Rollout Completely. Published on April 14. https://www.bbc.com/news/world-europe-56744474#:~:text=Denmark%20has%20ceased%20giving%20the,vaccination%20programme%20by%20several%20weeks.

Bernal, Jamie Lopez, Nick Andrews, Charlotte Gower, et al. 2021. Effectiveness of Covid-19 Vaccines against the B.1.617.2 (Delta) Variant. *The New England Journal of Medicine*. Published on July 21. https://doi.org/10.1056/NEJMoa2108891.

Bloom, D.E., and D. Canning. 2017. *Epidemics and Economics*. Working Paper #9, Harvard Program on Demography of Ageing, Harvard University.

Bloomberg. 2021. More Than 24 Million Shots Given: Covid-19 Vaccine Tracker. https://www.bloomberg.com/graphics/covid-vaccine-tracker-global-distribution/.

Brenner, S., F. Jacob, and M. Meselson. 1961. An Unstable Intermediate Carrying Information from Genes to Ribosomes for Protein Synthesis. *Nature* 190: 576–581.

Brown, C.M., J. Vostok, H. Johnson, et al. 2021. Outbreak of SARS-CoV-2 Infections, Including COVID-19 Vaccine Breakthrough Infections, Associated with Large Public Gatherings—Barnstable County, Massachusetts, July 2021. Morbidity and Mortality Weekly Report 70:1059–1062. https://doi.org/10.15585/mmwr.mm7031e2externalicon

Centers for Disease Control and Prevention (CDC). 2020a. *Smallpox*. Atlanta, G.A.: The CDC.

———. 2020b. *Influenza*. Atlanta, G.A.: The CDC.

Coleman, C.M., and M.B. Frieman. 2014. Coronaviruses: Important Emerging Human Pathogens. *Journal of Virology* 8: 5209–5212.

Doria-Rose, Nicole, and Mehul S. Suthar. 2021. Antibody Persistence through 6 Months after the Second Dose of mRNA-1273 Vaccine for Covid-19. *New England Journal of Medicine*. https://doi.org/10.1056/NEJMc2103916.

Fox Business. 2020a. Pfizer's Covid-19 Vaccine Proves 90% Effective in Latest Trials. Published on November 9. https://www.foxbusiness.com/healthcare/pfizers-covid-19-vaccine-proves-90-effective-in-latest-trials.

———. 2020b. Moderna Says Its Vaccine is 94.5% Effective in Preventing COVID-19. Published on November 16. https://www.foxbusiness.com/healthcare/moderna-coronavirus-vaccine-trial-phase-3.

Gavi: The Vaccine Alliance. 2020. There are Four Types of COVID-19 Vaccines: Here's How they Work. https://www.gavi.org/vaccineswork/there-are-four-types-covid-19-vaccines-heres-how-they-work.

Gupta, Swati. 2021. The Application and Future Potential of mRNA Vaccine. COVID-19 & You, Yale School of Public Health, New Haven, CT. Published on May 7. https://ysph.yale.edu/news-article/the-application-and-future-potential-of-mrna-vaccines/.

Hahn, R.W., and P.M. Dudley. 2007. How Well Does the U.S. Government Do Benefit-Cost Analysis? *Review of Environmental Economics and Policy* 1: 192–211.

Hartwick, J.M., and N.D. Olewiler. 1997. *The Economics of Natural Resource Use.* 2nd ed. New York, NY: Pearson.

Jacob, F., and J. Monod. 1961. Genetic Regulatory Mechanisms in the Synthesis of Proteins. *Journal of Molecular Biology* 3: 318–356.

Jenner, Edward. 1801. *On the Origin of the Vaccine Inoculation.* London, U.K.: D.N. Shury.

Jerusalem Post. 2021. Is Israel or the UK Right When it Comes to COVID-19 Vaccine Effectiveness? Published on July 24.

Johns Hopkins University (JHU). 2020. COVID-19 Dash Board. JHU, Baltimore, M.D.: JHU. https://data.humdata.org/dataset/novel-coronavirus-2019-ncov-cases.

Kariko, K., H. Muramatsu, J. Ludwig, and D. Weissman. 2011. Generating the Optimal mRNA for Therapy: HPLC Purification Eliminates Immune Activation and Improves Translation for Nucleoside-modified. *Protein-encoding mRNA. Nucleic Acids Research* 39: e142.

Logunov, Denis Y., Inna V. Dolzhikova, Dmitry V. Shcheblyakov, et al. 2021. Safety and Efficacy of an rAd26 and rAd5 Vector-based Heterologous Prime-boost COVID-19 Vaccine: An Interim Analysis of a Randomised Controlled Phase 3 Trial in Russia. *The Lancet* 397 (10275): 671–681.

Lopez, Alan D., Colin D. Mathers, Majid Ezzati, Dean T. Jamison, and Christopher J.L. Murray. 2006. Global Burden of Disease and Risk Factors. New York, NY: World Bank and Oxford University Press.

New York Times (NYT). 2020a. Coronavirus Vaccine Tracker. https://www.nytimes.com/interactive/2020/science/coronavirus-vaccine-tracker.html.

———. 2020b. After Admitting Mistake, AstraZeneca Faces Difficult Questions About Its Vaccine. Published on Nov 25 https://www.nytimes.com/2020/11/25/business/coronavirus-vaccine-astrazeneca-oxford.html.

———. 2021. As Britain Unlocks, Outdoor Pints Are Pure Joy. Published on April 12. https://www.nytimes.com/live/2021/04/12/world/britain-lockdown-reopening-virus.

Nordhaus, William D. 1973. The Allocation of Energy Resources. *Brookings Papers on Economic Activity* 1973: 529–576.

Our World in Data (OWID). 2021. Coronavirus (COVID-19) Vaccinations. https://github.com/owid/covid-19-data/tree/master/public/data/vaccinations.

Pardi, N., M.J. Hogan, F.W. Porter, and D. Weissman. 2018. mRNA vaccines—A New Era in Vaccinology. *Nature Reviews Drug Discovery* 17: 261–279.

Pfizer. 2021. Pfizer and BioNTech Confirm High Efficacy and No Serious Safety Concerns through Up to Six Months following Second Dose in Updated Topline Analysis of Landmark covid-19 Vaccine Study. Pfizer Inc., New York, NY. Published on April 1. https://www.pfizer.com/news/press-release/press-release-detail/pfizer-and-biontech-confirm-high-efficacy-and-no-serious.

Pierce, Benjamin A. 2019. *Genetics: A Conceptual Approach.* 7th ed. New York, NY: W.H. Freeman.

Plotkin, S.A. 2009. Vaccines: The Fourth Century. *Clinical and Vaccine Immunology* 16: 1709–1719.

Puranik, A., P.J. Lenehan, E. Silvert, et al. 2021. Comparison of Two Highly-effective mRNA Vaccines for COVID-19 during Periods of Alpha and Delta Variant Prevalence. *medRxiv* preprint. https://doi.org/10.1101/2021.08.06.21261707.

Reuters. 2021. WHO Says its Advisory Committee Looking at AstraZeneca Vaccine Issues. Published on March 12.

Rogers, David J., and Sarah E. Randolph. 2000. The Global Spread of Malaria in a Future. *Warmer World. Science* 289 (5485): 1763–1766.

Romer, Paul. 2020. Even A Bad Test Can Help Guide the Decision to Isolate: Covid Simulations Part 3. Published on March 25. Pualromer.net.

Schwartz, M. 2001. The Life and Works of Louis Pasteur. *Journal of Applied Microbiology.* 91 (4): 597–601.

Thaker, Raj. 2020. Coronavirus: B Cells and T Cells Explained. *The Conversation.* Published on July 20. https://theconversation.com/coronavirus-b-cells-and-t-cells-explained-141888.

United States Department of Health and Human Services (USDHHS). 2020. Explaining Operation Warp Speed. https://www.hhs.gov/coronavirus/explaining-operation-warp-speed/index.html.

United States Food & Drug Administration (USFDA). 2020a. Coronavirus Treatment Acceleration Program (CTAP). Washington, DC: USFDA. https://www.fda.gov/drugs/coronavirus-covid-19-drugs/coronavirus-treatment-acceleration-program-ctap.

———. 2020b. Pfizer-BioNTech COVID-19 Vaccine EUA Letter of Authorization. https://www.fda.gov/media/144412/.

———. 2020c. Moderna COVID-19 Vaccine EUA Letter of Authorization. https://www.fda.gov/media/144636/download.

———. 2020d. Vaccine Development—101. https://www.fda.gov/vaccines-blood-biologics/development-approval-process-cber/vaccine-development-101.

————. 2020e. Emergency Use Authorization. Washington, DC: USFDA. https://www.fda.gov/emergency-preparedness-and-response/mcm-legal-regulatory-and-policy-framework/emergency-use-authorization.

————. 2021a. Janssen COVID-19 Vaccine EUA Letter of Authorization 2021-02-27. Washington, DC: USFDA.

————. 2021b. Joint CDC and FDA Statement on Johnson & Johnson COVID-19 Vaccine. Washington, DC: USFDA.

Weinstein, R.S. 2011. Should Remaining Stockpiles of Smallpox Virus (Variola) Be Destroyed? *Emerging Infectious Diseases* 17 (4): 681–683.

Weiss, Susan R. 2020. Forty Years with Coronaviruses. *Journal of Experimental Medicine* 217 (5): e20200537. https://doi.org/10.1084/jem.20200537.

World Health Organization (WHO). 2018. WHO Releases 2018 Priority Diseases List. Geneva, CH: WHO. https://ohsonline.com/articles/2018/02/15/who-releases-2018-priority-diseases-list.aspx?admgarea=news&m=1.

————. 2019a. International Travel and Health. Ch 6. Vaccine-Preventable Diseases and Vaccines. Geneva, CH: WHO.

————. 2019b. World Malaria Report 2019. Geneva, CH: WHO.

————. 2020a. Timeline of WHO's Response to COVID-19. Geneva, CH: WHO. https://www.who.int/news/item/29-06-2020-covidtimeline.

————. 2020b. WHO Prequalified Vaccines. Geneva, CH: WHO. https://extranet.who.int/pqvdata/Default.aspx?nav=1.

————. 2020c. Malaria Vaccines. Geneva, CH: WHO. https://www.who.int/immunization/research/development/malaria/en/.

Yale Daily News. 2020. Pfizer Vaccine, Which Early Data Found to be 90 Percent Effective, Enrolled Patients in Yale Trials. Yale University, New Haven, CT. Published on Nov 13.

Yale News. 2020. Quick and Affordable Saliva-based COVID-19 teSt developed by Yale Scientists Receives FDA Emergency Use Authorization. Yale University, New Haven, CT. Published on August 15.

The Economics of Pandemics as a Globally Shared Experience: A Theory

1 INTRODUCTION

The preceding seven chapters have set the stage nicely for an exposition of this chapter, which is the core chapter of this book, whose ultimate goal is to establish the economics of pandemics as a globally shared experience. Chapters 1 and 2 provided an introduction to the book focusing on the COVID-19 pandemic in the former and to the economics literature on the pandemic in the latter. The succeeding five chapters provided the ensemble of five analyses: global governance in Chap. 3, governmental decisions in Chap. 4, radical social transformation movements in Chap. 5, a climate change doomsday scenario in Chap. 6, and vaccine developments in Chap. 7.

The economics of pandemics as a globally shared good has never been written before in a comprehensive manner. A primary reason for this salient void is the fact that a pandemic at the scale of the COVID-19 does not occur often at all. It occurred once in the twentieth century and once in the twenty-first century: Spanish Flu in 1918 and the COVID-19 in 2020. A global pandemic at the scale of the COVID-19 occurred only once in a century. It is natural that such a hard-to-predict rare event would escape the close attention of economists who should heed to day-to-day fluctuations in prices and month-to-month changes in economic indicators (Taubenberger et al. 2007; Jonas 2013).

For the same reason, the descriptions of pandemics by economists were framed in the context of a broader category of infectious diseases in which a worldwide pandemic was a small portion (Burns et al. 2008; Bloom and

© The Author(s), under exclusive license to Springer Nature
Switzerland AG 2022
S. N. Seo, *The Economics of Pandemics*,
https://doi.org/10.1007/978-3-030-91021-1_8

Canning 2017; Morin et al. 2018). Recent studies, which were undertaken after the H1N1 Flu pandemic in 2009, had a narrow focus, for example, on the question of how much money or fund the global community should set aside optimally for the risk of pandemics and/or infectious diseases (Fan et al. 2018; Berry et al. 2018) or on the question of market incentives (Morin et al. 2018). Infectious diseases have long been recognized in the economic literature of public goods, but only in the context of a limited geographical scale, for example, West African malaria or regionally communicable diseases (Kaul et al. 2003; Barrett 2003; Nordhaus 2006).

The economics of pandemics described in this chapter departs from the currently available economic literature of pandemics in multiple major ways. It begins by defining a worldwide pandemic as a globally shared good or experience, for which the present author will rely on the COVID-19 pandemic contagion data. It highlights the COVID-19 pandemic as a globally shared public good in contrast to other infectious disease problems which are nationally or regionally germane economic issues (Seo 2020). The COVID-19 spread rapidly from a city in China to the entire planet and the COVID-19 cases were occurring across the planet simultaneously.

Next, departing from the literature focusing on a single decision of importance to policy-makers, this chapter elaborates a full basket of economic decisions pertinent to a socially optimal management of the risk of pandemics. The first set of decisions belongs to the global governance organizations. The second set belongs to national governments. The third set belongs to the private sector and businesses. The fourth set belongs to individual citizens.

Another novel feature in the pandemic economics described in this chapter is the presentation of four fault lines. The four fault lines that were observed to emerge during the COVID-19 pandemic played a pivotal role in shaping the pandemic policy responses. They offer an important insight into the exposition of the economics of pandemics in this chapter. The first is that of the private sector *versus* the public sector. The second is that of governmental mandates *versus* civil liberty. The third is that of the global governance *versus* the national actions. The fourth is that of vaccine efforts *versus* containment efforts.

With these foundational concepts clarified in the early sections of this chapter, the present author elucidates the three components of the economics of pandemics as a globally shared good: microbehavioral efficient decisions, foresighted decisions, and technological backstop decisions (Seo 2020). A microbehavioral risk management framework for the pandemics is presented in Sect. 5. The foresighted or forward-looking decisions for the pandemic risk management are presented in Sect. 6. The decisions to advance the breakthrough technologies, including the vaccine backstops, crucial for pandemic risk management, are explained in Sect. 7. An integrated pathway comprising the three decision components is presented in Sect. 8.

2   THE PANDEMICS AS A GLOBALLY SHARED GOOD

Since the first report of the Wuhan viral pneumonia on the last day of 2019, the COVID-19 pandemic has spread in an astonishingly rapid way to the neighboring countries and then to the globe. As depicted in Figs. 1.5 and 1.6 in Chap. 1, all the countries on the planet were impacted heavily, to varying degrees, by the pandemic, which renders credence to the argument that the COVID-19 pandemic was indeed a globally shared experience, put differently, a globally shared bad.

That the COVID-19 pandemic that has become a global-scale public good in a hurry can be illustrated by the cumulative distribution function drawn in Fig. 8.1. It is the number of countries with newly reported infections at each week of the year since the first week of 2020. The data come from the European Center for Disease Prevention and Control (ECDPC) 2020). By the first week of 2020 denoted by 2020-01 in the figure, there was only one country with reported cases, that is, China. By 2020-08 and 2020-09 which are roughly the last week of February and the first week of March, the COVID-19 started to spread rapidly across the planet: from about 20 countries in the former to about 60 countries the latter. By 2020-13 and 2020-14 which are roughly the early weeks of April, nearly all countries on Earth had the cases reported, that is, over 200 countries. By 2021-05 and 2021-06 which are early February of 2021, roughly over 200 countries reported new cases of COVID-19.

We can verify this also through the single cross-section on February 20, 2021. As of that date, the Worldometers statistics on the COVID-19 tells that 221 "countries" had the COVID-19 cases (Worldometers 2021). Given that there are 195 independent countries in the world, this means that the pandemic has affected all countries on Earth without exception.

To be more detailed, the largest number of cases were reported from the US, followed by India, Brazil, Russia, the UK, France, Spain, Italy,

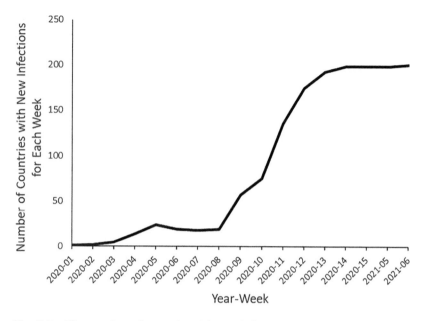

Fig. 8.1 The number of countries with new infections at each week

Turkey, and Germany. The US had 28 million cases, India 11 million, and Brazil 10 million cases by the aforementioned date. The smallest number of cases were reported from South Pacific Islands: the Marshall Islands with 4 cases, Samoa with 3 cases, Micronesia 1 case, Vanuatu 1 case. Even these remote islands in the middle of the Pacific Ocean were not spared by the COVID-19 pandemic.

The three different analyses of the COVID-19 spread data presented above also reveal that the COVID-19 pandemic, more generally, global pandemics, is distinct from the other infectious diseases that are extensively studied by researchers, for example, malaria or influenza, but affect only a sub-population of the global community. Malaria, for example, is eradicated from the developed countries and new malaria cases occur only in some developing regions such as Sub Sahara and India, according to the World Malaria Report (Lopez et al. 2006; WHO 2019).

The three analyses also confirm that the COVID-19 pandemic is substantially different from the other pandemic of the twenty-first century declared by the WHO, that is, the H1N1 influenza pandemic of 2009.

During the latter, countries in Africa, the Middle East, Central Asia, and Russia were largely spared from the severe impacts of the 2009 pandemic (refer to Table 1.1 in Chap. 1).

The scale of contagion is also far greater in the COVID-19 than in the 2009 H1N1 pandemic. For example, the number of infections during the COVID-19 for the US is around 44 million, as of the end of September 2021, compared with that during the 2009 H1N1 pandemic which was about 0.1–0.2 million (Bloom and Canning 2017; CDC 2020b). For Mexico, the number of cases for the 2009 H1N1 influenza was fewer than 0.1 million while that for the COVID-19 pandemic is over 2.4 million by the aforementioned date (JHU 2020).

This discussion reveals that the concept of a globally shared good (or bad), which is an economic term, is not equivalent to the concept of a pandemic, which is a scientific term. The pandemic is defined as a worldwide spread of an infectious disease by the WHO, but a declaration of a pandemic by the WHO is made when an infectious disease is considered by the WHO Committee to have spread to a "sufficiently" large number of countries on the planet. For this reason, the present author in this book often refers to a worldwide pandemic, instead of a pandemic, as a globally shared good.

3 The Decision Array by Economic Actors During the Pandemics

For an exposition of the economics of pandemics as a globally shared good, the present author starts with an enumeration of the array of economic decisions that have to be made during and before the pandemics. The array encompasses the decisions made not just by national governments, but also the decisions by other economic actors such as international organizations, small businesses and big enterprises, and individual citizens. The four economic actors are depicted in Fig. 8.2.

The decision array of the four economic actors is a novel approach introduced in this book in an effort to build the economics of pandemics beyond a set of governmental policy decisions. The economics to be elaborated in this chapter shortly is built upon a comprehensive array of decisions by the four economic actors pertinent to a pandemic risk management.

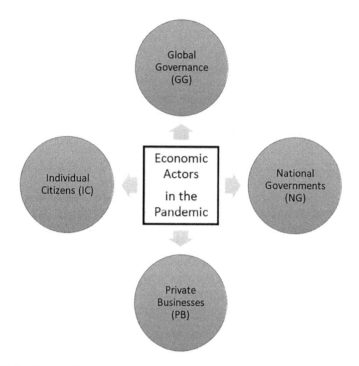

Fig. 8.2   Economic actors in the pandemic

Table 8.1 presents the decision array during the pandemics. There are four actors under each of which major decisions by the actor are listed: global governance (GG), national governments (NG), private businesses (PB), and individual citizens (IC). The decisions in the array include both the short-term responses to a pandemic outbreak and the decisions pertaining to the long-term preparedness and prevention. The lists of the decisions in the table are not exhaustive but highlight those that stood out most prominently during the experiences of the COVID-19.

As per the global governance, or more specifically, the WHO, three major decisions vis-à-vis the pandemic are a declaration of the public health emergency of international concern (PHEIC), a declaration of a pandemic, and an investigation of the origin of the pandemic. These decisions were the focus of Chap. 3 of this book.

As per the national governments, 13 major decisions are listed: declaring a national emergency; a border policy; setting up a control center and testing; a mask mandate, social distancing, and other social measures; a

Table 8.1 The decision array by economic actors during the pandemic

ID	WHO: global governance (GG)	National governments (NG)	Private businesses (PB)	Individual citizens (IC)
1	A PHEIC declaration	Declaring a national emergency	A business mode of operation	Physical distancing
2	A pandemic declaration	Border policy	Relying on non-personal AI services	Mask wearing
3	Investigating origin	Setting up a control center and testing.	Switching to home deliveries	Washing hands
4		Mask mandate, social distancing?	Giving days off to employees when asked	Going to work or staying home
5		A lockdown or stay-at-home order?	Providing medical services	Riding public transportations
6		Business closure?	Developing test kits	Taking a test
7		Closing schools?	Developing potential treatments	Taking vaccine shots
8		Contact tracing?	High-tech companies developing emergency medical devices	Dining outside
9		Emergency production	Pharmaceutical firms developing vaccines	Attending church services
10		Treatments		Avoiding a group gathering
11		Vaccines		
12		Economic relief programs		
13		National health insurance		

lockdown or stay-at-home order; business closure; school closure or opening; contact tracing; emergency production; developing and/or approving effective treatments; developing and/or approving vaccines for emergency use; economic relief programs; a choice of a national health insurance system. These decisions were in the focus of Chap. 4 of this book.

As per the private businesses, nine major decisions are listed: deciding on a mode of business operation; relying on the Artificial Intelligence (AI)-based non-contact services instead of person-to-person services; switching to home deliveries; giving days off to employers when asked; providing medical services; developing test kits; developing potential treatments; high-tech companies developing emergency medical devices; pharmaceutical firms developing vaccines. The business mode of operation includes the decision of whether the business will be fully operational, 50% operational, 25% operational, or be closed during the pandemic. It is also pertinent to the business' decision to allow work from home. Many of these decisions were explained in detail in Chap. 7 and other chapters of this book.

As per the individual citizens, ten major decisions are listed in the table: physical distancing (2 meters or 6 feet); mask wearing; washing hands; going to work or staying home; riding public transportations such as a bus and a subway; taking a test; taking vaccine shots; dining outside or at home; attending church services; avoiding a group gathering. These choices were elaborated throughout this book, especially in Chap. 4. These choices are widely advised measures to the public by the WHO and the CDC of the US (WHO 2021).

A reader who has read through this book up to Chap. 7 will be able to appreciate each of the decisions in the decision array in Table 8.1. Further, s/he has become sophisticated enough to grasp effortlessly that each decision in Table 8.1 may be multi-layered. To elaborate one example, the economic relief program choice in the NG column should decide a size of monetary relief at the first stage, but also determine the principle of economic relief at the second stage, for example, a universal aid or a selective aid.

4   The Four Fault Lines in the Pandemic Risk Management

A careful observer of the COVID-19 pandemic would be quick to discern major fault lines in the choices made during the pandemic from the decision array in Table 8.1. At each fault line, the two distinct faults, that is, interests and/or principles, collided, resulting in a major division and conflict of views in the society. At the very beginning of this book, the present author hinted at these fault lines as one of the key pillars of the pandemic experiences by the global community.

Let me introduce anew the following four fault lines (Fig. 8.3). The first fault line is that of the global governance *versus* the national actions. The second fault line is that of the private sector *versus* the public sector. The third fault line is that of the big government with numerous orders

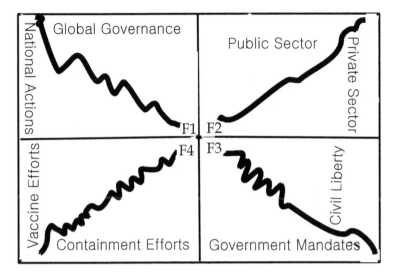

Fig. 8.3   The four fault lines in the pandemic decisions

and mandates *versus* civil liberty. The fourth fault line is that of the containment efforts *versus* the vaccine development efforts.

The first fault line lies between global governance and national actions. National actions may or may not agree with the recommendations of the WHO, the *de facto* global governance in pandemic events by the International Health Regulations (WHO 2015). A nation may also agree or disagree with the reports on the scientific aspects of the pandemic disease from the WHO. In Chap. 4, this book spotlighted that the responses to the COVID-19 pandemic were by and large designed and implemented by national agencies or actions despite it being a global-scale problem, that is, a globally shared good.

The second fault line lies between the public sector and the private sector. In designing response strategies, one of the key questions is whether they should be anchored at the private sector or at the public sector, that is, at a long series of governmental interventions. The government may collide with private businesses by ordering business closures or other restrictions. A successful public-private partnership occurred through the Operation Warp Speed (OWS) in developing vaccines as well as the Defense Production Act (DPA) in producing emergency medical devices and tests, both of which were highlighted in Chap. 7 (USDHHS 2020a, 2020b).

What form would a private sector anchored policy approach take in pandemic responses and preparedness? Having gone through the COVID-19, readers may react with skepticism: is such an outlandish policy framework possible at all in a pandemic at a COVID-19 scale? To the skeptics and especially policy analysts, the no-lockdown policy model adopted in Sweden should be a fresh wake-up call, just to mention one alternative perspective. The Sweden model avoided a national lockdown and other heavy-handed governmental restrictions. Instead, the country resorted to voluntary compliance of individual citizens and private businesses. As analyzed in Chap. 4, Sweden's strategy may have outperformed the countries that resorted to repeated lockdowns and forced closures, up to the point of the world's first vaccine shots (Deccan Herald 2020; Detroit News 2020).

In the private sector anchored approach, private businesses would decide on numerous decisions such as whether they would close the business, operate in a limited capacity, give employers days off, perform COVID-19 tests at the entrance, provide face coverings to the employers, modify offices for sufficient physical distancing, and so on. A private business may decide to accept certain customers, for example, a public bus or subway accepting passengers with a mask. Under this approach, the public sector would still play a critical role as a provider of information and guidelines, developing test kits, developing/approving vaccines. An individual citizen would comply voluntarily with the government guidelines while s/he makes independent decisions on critical matters such as going to work, going to school, social gatherings, and wearing a mask.

The third fault line lies between governmental mandates and civil liberty. The governmental power-based response strategies will infringe upon civil liberty severely. A mask-mandate, a forced business closure, a stay-at-home order, a prohibition of a group gathering, a prohibition of an in-person church service, a travel ban, forced school closures, and a register of civilians' phone numbers for contact tracing are such policy measures that rely on governmental power.

Some of these policies were ruled unconstitutional, for example, by the Supreme Court of the United States (SCOTUS) on a ban on in-person church services in New York and California (WSJ 2020). For another, despite a lockdown order, the riots and protests that raged during May and June of 2020, which occurred in over 500 cities per day during the peak, were left to unfold by respective cities (US Crisis Monitor 2020).

Such an intervention by the SCOTUS, however, was an exception which was nearly absent across the societies in the world during the COVID-19 pandemic. The protests and riots that raged in the US cities were also exceptional in their scale, as explained in Chap. 1. In other words, national governments across the world faced little resistance from the citizens against such severe civil liberty restricting policies.

In this regard, a study of the effectiveness of mask mandates during the COVID-19 pandemic is an emerging research area (Bundgaard et al. 2020; Abaluck et al. 2021). Similarly, a study of the effectiveness of a travel ban or a border control is relevant to an analysis of the third fault line (Chinazzi et al. 2020; Wells et al. 2020).

The fourth fault line lies between virus spread containment efforts and vaccine development efforts. As clarified in Chap. 7, an effective vaccine may offer the only hope for ending such a worldwide pandemic as the COVID-19, as was the case for smallpox during the twentieth century (Weinstein 2011; WHO 2020). Notwithstanding, it may take more than 5 years, or even as long as 20 years, until a high-efficacy vaccine is developed and approved for use (Gupta 2021). During the intervening period, however, the pandemic may end up unleashing unbearable suffering and tragedies on the world communities. As per the COVID-19 pandemic, the number of fatalities and infections are on track to surpass 5 million people and 200 million people, respectively, worldwide by the end of 2021 which marks the two years since the COVID-19 outbreak. That being the case, the containment efforts for stopping the spread of the virus should be an essential policy component that cannot be set aside especially during the first several years without a vaccine since the pandemic outbreak.

The vaccine efforts are, however, a key policy variable in the countries with the high-technological capacities and capabilities that are needed to have a shot at a successful vaccine development (USDHHS 2020a; Azar II 2020). As reviewed in Chap. 7, serious vaccine development efforts were concentrated in a handful of countries: the US, Germany, Russia, China, UK/Switzerland, and India (NYT 2020).

For other than the vaccine developer countries, the containment efforts should be an overwhelming policy priority until a vaccine is approved and made available for purchase. As soon as an effective vaccine is developed and in the wait for an approval, the non-developer countries' policy priority should switch from the containment efforts to the vaccine efforts, which involves vaccine purchases, vaccination efforts, and domestic vaccine production agreements with the vaccine developers.

5   THE ECONOMICS I: A MICROBEHAVIORAL DECISION FRAMEWORK FOR THE PANDEMIC MANAGEMENT

The objective of the economics of pandemics can be defined as an exposition of a socially welfare optimizing management of pandemics at a global scale (Samuelson 1954; Nordhaus 1994). The social optimum can be defined as Pareto optimality or efficiency. The Pareto efficiency is achieved at a state of the world in which the society cannot improve an individual's welfare without decreasing another individual's welfare in the society (Pareto 1906; Mas-Colell et al. 1995). At other allocations than the Pareto optimum, the society will face welfare loss. The objective of achieving Pareto efficiency given economic constraints is the benchmark for a wide range of economic analyses that involves societal decisions, for example, economic growth, pollution control, climate change, sustainability (Koopmans 1965; Baumol and Oates 1988; Nordhaus 1992; Solow 1993; Muller and Mendelsohn 2009).

In elucidating the economics of pandemics as a globally shared good, we need to start with an analysis of microbehavioral decisions of individual citizens and private businesses. Without a careful analysis of the incentives that individuals are faced with in making a large basket of decisions, a societally efficient management of the pandemics cannot be reachable or designable, as has been demonstrated in the other fields of the economics of public goods (Coase 1960; Friedman 1962; Buchanan 1968; Seo 2015a, 2019, 2020).

For an individual citizen, she has to make a series of choices in order to deal with the pandemic in an efficient way. Let's define her objective to be a minimization of the aggregate cost under the pandemic. The cost can occur from numerous sources: lost earnings due to business closures (c_1), the cost of a quarantine due to an infection (c_2), the cost of purchasing personal protective equipment and taking a test for infection (c_3), the cost of hospital treatments (c_4). The ultimate cost would be the loss of her life as well as the loss of her loved ones (c_5). Let the other remaining cost be ω. With the total cost denoted as Φ:

$$\Phi = \sum_{k=1}^{5} c_k + \omega. \tag{8.1}$$

The ten key decisions of an individual are enumerated in Table 8.1. These include social distancing, mask wearing, washing hands, going to work or staying home, riding public transportations, taking a test, taking a vaccine, dining outside or at home, attending church services, and avoiding a group gathering.

Let the total cost of the pandemic for an individual (i) be Φ_i and the options that the individual can choose from are $j = 1, 2, ..., J$. Then, the decision to be made is written as follows:

$$\arg\min_j \Phi_{ij}, \text{where } j = 1, 2, ..., J. \tag{8.2}$$

Let the choice that satisfies Eq. (8.2) be alternative j^*, which is the optimal choice for the decision-maker. Since there are ten decisions for the individuals, the total number of alternatives is $J = 2^{10}$ if all decisions were binary. What would an optimal choice, j^*, be like? It is important to note that an optimal choice can vary from an individual to another, depending upon the different circumstances that individuals are faced with. An example of an optimal choice by individual i can be as follows:

$$j^* = \begin{cases} \text{physical distancing} \\ \text{mask wearing in public gatherings only} \\ \text{washing hands} \\ \text{taking weeks off from work when feel needed} \\ \text{using public transportations with mask wearing} \\ \text{taking a test} \\ \text{dining at home but dining outside sometimes} \\ \text{attending church services} \\ \text{avoiding a group gathering} \\ \text{taking a vaccine when available} \end{cases} \tag{8.3}$$

The decision framework explained in Eqs. (8.1), (8.2), and (8.3) is applicable to private businesses (PB), especially small/family businesses.

The bundle of options faced by private businesses shall be different from that shown in Eq. (8.3). Let $j^{*,PB}$ be an optimal choice for a small business, which again will be varied from a business to another. Let's suppose, for the sake of continued discussion, that the optimal choice by the small business is the following combination of decisions:

$$j^{*,PB} = \begin{cases} \text{operating at 25\% of the capacity} \\ \text{switching to AI services} \\ \text{increasing home deliveries} \\ \text{giving days off to employees when asked} \\ \text{providing personal protective equipment at work} \\ \text{designing physically distanced office space} \end{cases} \quad (8.4)$$

The set of Eqs. (8.1), (8.2), (8.3), and (8.4), along with Eq. (8.5), lies at the core of the microbehavioral framework for the pandemic risk management. The micro decision-maker would choose one alternative over the others because it enables her to achieve the minimum damage during the pandemic, that is,

$$\Phi_{j^*} < \Phi_k, \forall k \neq j^*. \quad (8.5)$$

For an analysis of the pandemic policies, a policy designer would be interested in predicting the probability of an alternative, which is policy relevant, being adopted by an individual citizen (Seo 2016a). A probabilistic model can enable researchers to identify the factors that affect the choice decision of an individual citizen. Further, it will show that the choices of individuals across the society are varied from one individual to another.

The probability of choosing alternative j^* by an individual decision-maker can be succinctly expressed with several assumptions (McFadden 1999a, 1999b). If, first, the total cost of the pandemic is assumed to be dependent on a family of explanatory variables (X) linearly and an error term (ε) and, second, the error terms were to follow a Gumbel distribution, the probability can be written simply as a logit, with spatial spillover effects incorporated in the model (McFadden 1974; McFadden and Train 2000; Seo 2016a).

With the cumulative distribution function (CDF) of the Gumbel in Eq. (8.6), the probability is written as a logit in Eq. (8.7) as follows:

$$\varepsilon_j \sim G(\varepsilon_j) = \exp(-e^{-\varepsilon_j}), \forall j. \qquad (8.6)$$

$$P_{j^*} = \frac{\exp(X\beta_{j^*})}{\sum_{j=1}^{J} \exp(X\beta_j)}. \qquad (8.7)$$

The β_j (with $j = 1, 2, \ldots, J$) is the parameters in the model to be estimated according to a statistical principle, which is done most often with a Maximum Likelihood Estimation (MLE) method (McFadden 1999a). The probability model for the microbehavioral decision framework can be built in several different ways, depending upon the interest of policy analysts. To give just one example, if the policy analyst is interested in only one of the key decisions outlined in Eqs. (8.3) and (8.4), say, an option of using public transportations with a mask on, s/he can build a choice model of a sequence of ten decisions by the individual. Applying a multivariate probit model, s/he can estimate the set of the ten probabilities by individual i (Bliss 1934; Chib and Greenberg 1998; Train 2003):

$$P_i = \begin{cases} P_i(\text{physical distancing}) \\ P_i(\text{mask wearing in public gatherings only}) \\ P_i(\text{washing hands}) \\ P_i(\text{taking weeks off from work when feel needed}) \\ P_i(\text{using public transportations with mask wearing}) \\ P_i(\text{taking a test}) \\ P_i(\text{dining at home but dining outside sometimes}) \\ P_i(\text{attending church services}) \\ P_i(\text{avoiding a group gathering}) \\ P_i(\text{taking a vaccine when available}) \end{cases} \qquad (8.8)$$

The policy analyst can unravel even deeper policy implications of individuals' best choices by specifically modeling the objective of the decision-maker as a function of relevant explanatory variables (Seo 2016a, 2016b):

$$\Phi_{j^*} = X\beta_{j^*} + M_j(P_1, \ldots P_J) + \eta_{j^*}. \qquad (8.9)$$

In the above equation, the second term on the right side is a selection bias correction term while the third term is a white noise error term (Heckman 1979; Dubin and McFadden 1984). From Eq. (8.9), the researcher can reveal many important additional insights on individuals' best choices, that is, after the equation has been estimated. Note that the selection bias term is expressed as a function of the choice probabilities of all the alternatives considered by the decision-maker (Seo 2016a). Put differently, the choice made in the first stage by the decision-maker will affect the economic outcome in the second stage.

A specific form of the selection bias correction takes on the following form, with σ, ω being parameters to be estimated (Dubin and McFadden 1984; Seo 2016a);

$$M_j = \sigma_j \sum_{k \neq j}^{J} \omega_k \times \left\{ \frac{P_k \times lnP_k}{P_k} + lnP_j \right\}. \qquad (8.10)$$

The rationale behind the microbehavioral decision framework outlined thus far is that it is only the individual who can make the best decision, that is, the total cost-minimizing decision for her. The government can never make such a decision for every individual in the society or even a single individual. As such, individuals' best decisions will add up, as far as the rationale is concerned, to the society level to approximate the society's best decision.

Let me state just a few examples to clarify this point that a nationwide blanket policy will turn out non-optimal for the society. A national/statewide lockdown may have inflicted significant harm on the persons with mental distress and disorder, on the persons with physical disabilities, or on young children (Boserup et al. 2020; Japan Times 2020). A forced business closure by the government may have hurt certain businesses and income groups the most, for example, small businesses and low-income groups (Sanchez-Paramo 2020; Polyakova et al. 2021). A universal mask mandate, that is, *versus* a voluntary mask policy, may have harmed the health of the general public, especially those with existing respiratory problems, by forcing them to wear masks even outdoors and isolated places.

Having said that, there is an unresolved question that the microbehavioral framework cannot stand without addressing it, which is also a central question to the pandemic economics described in this book. That is whether the best choices of individual economic actors in the society during the pandemic times will be indeed welfare optimizing at the level of the wider society, say, the global community or the nation as a whole.

A satisfactory answer to this question depends on two important economic parameters: foresighted decisions on the one hand and technological advancements on the other (Seo 2020). First, a Pareto efficient pandemic risk management has to consider pandemic events in a century-long time frame. A pandemic such as the COVID-19 or the 1919 Influenza pandemic may occur only once in a century. However, no individual citizen is as forward looking as 100 years ahead of time in consideration of future pandemics. The short-sightedness of individuals will result in inadequate preparedness and prevention measures against the pandemics in the society (Fisher 1930; Arrow et al. 1996; Weitzman 1998). For example, without foresighted decisions or forward looking, it would be impossible for the society to establish a national health insurance system, which an important element in pandemic preparedness and responses (Sloan and Hsieh 2013; Rice et al. 2013; NHS 2020). The economics of foresight in pandemics is the topic of the next section.

Second, as evidenced during the COVID-19, advanced technological capacities and capabilities offer the society a chance for developing a backstop solution, that is, a highly effective vaccine, in a short period of time. The society as a whole would, therefore, be benefited and therefore willing to invest in the medical and pharmaceutical sciences as a way to defend against future pandemics. Will the private pharmaceutical companies and academic laboratories invest efficiently into the pertinent sciences for this purpose?

The answer may be yes if we root for the theories of economic growth powered by efficient economic decisions (Ramsey 1928; Solow 1956; Koopmans 1965). As one of the endeavors for achieving economic growth, private laboratories will invest in research and development (R&D) activities while the government will strive to protect intellectual property rights (Griliches 1979, 1998). The growth in medical sciences and the pharmaceutical sector are driven by the money, that is, capital invested in by the people for their health and life. Under the economic growth theory, these investments into novel medical and pharmaceutical technologies are efficient (Romer 1990, 1994). If, on the other hand, the benefits of a technological innovation in the medical/pharmaceutical sector are a public consumption good, as long as the benefits cannot be divided and made exclusive by the developers, these investments will turn out to be suboptimal, calling for a corrective policy (Nordhaus 1994, 2006). The economics of efficient technological developments is the topic in Sect. 7 of this chapter.

6   THE ECONOMICS II: FORESIGHTED DECISIONS ON PANDEMICS

The microbehavioral decisions by individual economic agents described in the preceding section are near-sighted decisions. To be specific, they are by and large short-term responses by individuals and private businesses to the spread of a worldwide pandemic. If individuals' decisions were mostly near-sighted, then the microbehavioral decision framework cannot describe the society's efficient response to the pandemics.

Can an individual actor take a far-sighted decision in preparation or anticipation of a pandemic outbreak which is highly uncertain in terms of both the time of the outbreak and the seriousness of the outbreak (Arrow 1963; Cutler and Zeckhauser 2000)? Are there systems in the society and/or incentives in the market system that make individuals take such a precautionary action against a highly uncertain pandemic event?

Far-sighted decisions by an individual agent for the sake of pandemic preparations are not easy to imagine. The reason for this is clear: a pandemic at a scale of the COVID-19 does not occur often at all, perhaps occur only one time in a century (Potter 2001; Taubenberger et al. 2007). Given the rarity of the pandemics, it would be difficult for one to imagine an individual agent who takes a costly action today in preparation of a future pandemic (Jonas 2013). After all, it may not occur in her/his lifetime at all.

This does not mean, however, that a full basket of economic decisions that an individual makes today does not have any bearing on the pandemic preparedness of the individual. Some of the individual's decisions, to be explained presently, are forward looking in the sense that they should place the individual in a better position to deal with an unexpected outbreak of the pandemic (Seo 2020). Further, these forward-looking decisions in most cases are not made specifically as a strategy (or investment) against a pandemic but rather as a strategy (or investment) against the generic health and life risk.

That an individual agent places a high, if not the highest, value on her health and life-years means that such forward-looking behaviors of individuals are found to be particularly stronger in health and life matters than other matters in the person's life (Nordhaus 2000; Viscusi and Aldy 2003; Mendelsohn and Olmstead 2009; Muller et al. 2011; Deaton 2013). In this section, the present author elaborates three such decisions: an increase in health spending, AI non-contact technologies, and a national health insurance system.

6.1 An Increase in Health Spending

A foresighted generic investment in personal health and life-years is seen in the annual health/medical spending of individuals. A large fraction of an individual's income is spent on medical/health products and services. The medical/health expenses are most often dual-purposed: to cure a specific illness of an individual on the one hand and to improve the general health of the individual on the other.

Individuals spend an increasingly larger amount of money on medical/health products and services in pace with a growth in personal income, or equivalently, national income per capita (Deaton 2013; Case and Deaton 2015). The increased spending would then go to numerous medical services: *inter alia*, a national health insurance premium, a private health insurance premium, hospital visits, regular check-ups, adequate immunizations against infectious diseases, medicine purchases, nutritional products, nursing homes, home cares, physical exercises, psychiatric treatments, drug and addiction treatment (rehabilitation) centers, and meditations (Bhattacharya et al. 2013).

The total health expenditures per capita per annum of the Organisation for Economic Co-operation and Development (OECD) member countries are shown in Fig. 8.4, which is drawn from the OECD.Stat's health statistics for 2019 (OECD.Stat 2021). The top spender is the US with US$11,000 per capita per year spent on health. The next top spenders are Switzerland with US$7700 per year, Germany with US$6600 per year, Sweden with US$5700 per year, the UK with US$4600 per year, Italy with US$3600 per year. The bottom spenders are Poland, Slovak, and Greece with roughly US$2500 per capita per annum.

An increase in health spending over time since the beginning of the twentieth century has helped increase the life expectancy of people in many countries remarkably during that time period. In the US, the life expectancy at birth in 1900 was around 47–48 years for men and women, which increased to 75–80 years for men and women in 2100. For China, the life expectancy in 1960 was around 43 years, which has increased in

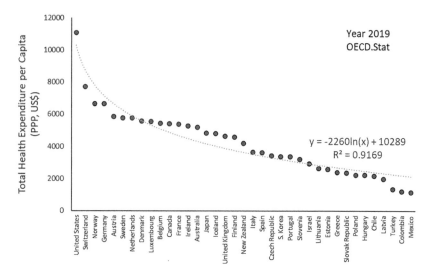

Fig. 8.4 Annual total health expenditure per capita across the countries

pace with the increase in personal income to around 75 years in 2100 (Deaton 2013).

An increased health spending certainly gets individuals better prepared against the pandemic. During the COVID-19 pandemic, the most vulnerable, that is, the highest mortality groups, were senior citizens over 65 years and the people with comorbidity (NCHS 2021a, 2021b). The persons with existing diseases as well as the persons with poor health owing to old age suffered the most by the COVID-19. Conversely, the increased health spending during multiple decades before the COVID-19 may have helped people to maintain good health and thereby better cope with the pandemic, including the ability to acquire natural immunity from the COVID-19 infection (Gazit et al. 2021). In this sense, the increase in health/medical spending of an individual is a foresighted, or equivalently, a forward-looking decision in preparation of the pandemic risk.

In Fig. 8.5, the total number of US COVID-19 deaths during the period from January 1, 2020, to February 20, 2021, is broken down by age cohorts. Of the total number of mortalities amounting to 478,912, senior citizens over 65 years accounted for 81% while the age cohort of 50–64 years accounted for another 15% (NCHS 2021a). The two age cohorts accounted for 96% of the total fatalities. A similar mortality

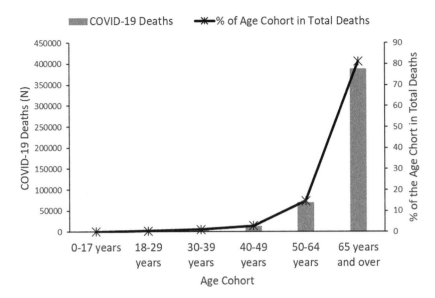

Fig. 8.5 COVID-19 mortalities by age cohorts (January 1, 2020–February 20, 2021)

distribution across age cohorts is also found in the UK fatality data (Smith et al. 2021).

Figure 8.6 breaks down the total number of COVID-19 deaths in the US during the same time period by comorbidities. It is astonishing that roughly 45% of the total number of mortalities occurred in the people with the preexisting conditions of influenza and pneumonia. Another 37% of the deaths occurred in the people with the comorbidity of respiratory failure while another 20% of the deaths occurred in the people with the comorbidity of hypertension, that is, high blood pressure. Note in the figure that a deceased one may have had more than one preexisting conditions (NCHS 2021b).

6.2 AI-Based Non-contact Technologies

An aspect of the business and office environment that is apt to the discussion of forward-looking decisions against future pandemics is non-contact technologies. The non-contact technologies refer to a multitude of

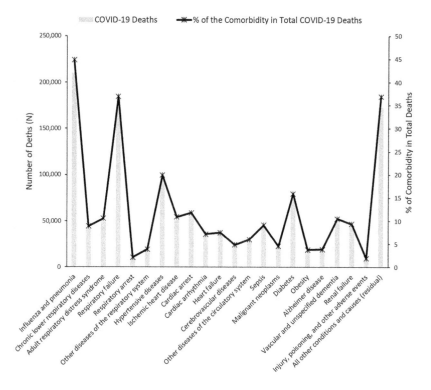

Fig. 8.6 COVID-19 mortalities by comorbidities (January 1, 2020–February 20, 2021)

AI-based robot technologies that enable remote working or replace person-to-person contact-based services.

That AI robots have replaced many types of human labor in businesses during the past two decades is undoubted. The AI robots are rather ubiquitous today: to name just some, AI waitresses in restaurants, AI workers at gas stations, AI tellers at banks, AI toll collectors, and AI medical checkups. Further, remote working is enabled for most of the businesses in developed countries. Remote online-based education has been increasing for the past two decades before the COVID-19 pandemic, offering numerous degrees and course certificates. During the COVID-19 pandemic, schools and universities in developed countries are actively tapping into the existing remote education capacity to switch from an in-person class-room to a virtual classroom.

At the level of individual businesses, the AI capacity of a private business proved to be one of the deciding factors for the business' success during the COVID-19. The winners of the COVID-19 pandemic from the profit viewpoint are the businesses that are, broadly speaking, AI business leaders such as Google, Apple, Facebook, Amazon, Twitter, and Microsoft (GAFATM). Home delivery businesses which rely heavily on mobile phones and Global Positioning System (GPS) technologies are also winners. Small businesses are also able to reduce the risk of contagion among their employers and guests by adopting, for example, an AI-based ordering system.

From the society's viewpoint, the AI capacity proved to be a critical tool in the response to the COVID-19 pandemic. Besides the aforementioned switches to remote education and remote working, the AI capacity was utilized for numerous essential tasks, including the real-time COVID-19 updates provided through individuals' mobile phones and tailored to the recipient's neighborhood.

In hindsight, the advances in the AI technologies were indeed a forward-looking decision against pandemic risk, especially the AI non-contact technologies. An adoption of these technologies is expected to increase after the COVID-19 pandemic by businesses, schools, governments, and individuals, which would be their forward-looking decisions against future pandemics. Of course, not all of these economic agents will expand the AI capacities.

The AI capacity of a private business is endogenous for some companies while exogenous for others. The endogeneity is pertinent to the AI leaders, that is, the GAFATM above. They intentionally developed the AI technologies for their businesses' success. Therefore, the AI capacity of a GAFATM firm is determined by its investment decision. The exogeneity is pertinent to the businesses that only utilize the AI technologies. For them, the AI capacity is determined by the growth of the overall economy, that is, AI technologies become available to them as the overall economy develops, for example, an automated ordering system at restaurants. The firms purchase them like another production input.

In other words, the exogeneity of the AI capacity to most private businesses is in fact endogenous from the macro economy's standpoint (Romer 1994; Nordhaus 2007). That is, the technological development in the macro economy, more specifically, the AI technology's growth, is accomplished as a means for the macro economy's productivity growth. Put differently, as individual businesses pursue higher profits, the AI technologies are developed and advanced, which then improves the macro economy's productivity.

When a private enterprise decides to adopt a bundle of selected AI technologies, the decision is made primarily to increase the firm's profit by making a costly investment in new technologies. Therefore, it is not a decision made in consideration primarily of a potential pandemic outbreak at future dates. Notwithstanding, such a costly investment would turn out to help defend the firm's profit if a pandemic should break out, as amply evidenced during the COVID-19 pandemic. Although there is no published empirical estimate on this yet, businesses that had a built-in AI capacity or were able to switch swiftly to AI-based services may have outperformed the businesses that hadn't or weren't.

An AI technology investment by a firm is therefore a foresighted decision against the pandemics, as is an increased health spending by an individual consumer, explained in the previous subsection. The rationale for is strong vis-à-vis virology and epidemiology: the pandemic virus thrives by contagion through contacts while the AI technology thrives by the need for non-personal contacts.

6.3   A National Health Insurance System: Private Versus Public

The array of decisions presented up to this point in this chapter, whether microbehavioral or forward-looking, are anchored at the private sector. In particular, the two forward-looking decisions are by and large individuals' and private business' decisions. On the other hand, it is often asserted that the public sector is better placed for making a long-term investment decision that may last many decades or even centuries. One of the most prominent examples in today's society is a national pension fund, also called a national retirement insurance or a 401(k)-retirement plan in the US (Diamond and Orszag 2005; Barr and Diamond 2006).

As per the pandemic risk, a forward-looking decision by the public sector is a choice of a system of health insurance for the nation (SHIN). The choice is made for the sake of the health of its citizens, which is expected to have long-term effects on the nation's health outcomes (Sloan and Hsieh 2013). However, the ways how the choice of a SHIN affects the pandemic preparedness and health outcomes of the nation have received little attention up until the COVID-19 outbreak.

In Chap. 2, the present author introduced the three systems of national health insurance that are adopted by the nations across the globe and provided a comparative analysis descriptively. The first is a free national health service (NHS). The second is a nationally managed health insurance (NHI). The third is a privately oriented health insurance system (PHI).

The first system, that is, the NHS, is adopted by the UK, Spain, Italy, and others. The NHS system provides health services to its citizens free of charge. The funds for the NHS are derived from the general taxation of the nation (NHS 2020). As such, there is no national health insurance corporation.

The second system, that is, the NHI, is adopted most frequently across the globe, including Switzerland, Germany, France, Japan, and South Korea. The NHI system is a nationally managed health insurance system in which the citizens of the nation are obligated by law to join the NHI scheme and pay insurance premiums monthly to a national health insurance corporation (NHIC) (Ch.Ch. 2020). The premiums are then invested in financial and tangible assets by the NHIC for profits. Relying on the revenue thus generated from the investments, the NHIC pays a partial cost of the treatment by the citizens while the rest is paid by them. The fraction of the total cost paid by the citizens varies from 20% to 60% of the total cost of the treatment, which depends on the types of the disease treated and the types of the hospital where the treatment is conducted.

The third system, that is, the PHI, is uniquely adopted by the US. The US system is a system of private health insurances (Cutler and Zeckhauser 2000; Finkelstein 2007; Dafny 2010). In the PHI of the US, there is no nationally managed universal insurance, although the system of private insurances is augmented by various public sector programs such as Medicare, Medicaid, and the Affordable Care Act (Rice et al. 2013; Sloan and Hsieh 2013).

The value of a health insurance can be explained mathematically for the simplest situation in which sickness requires a fixed cost of treatment and the insurance is priced to be actuarially fair (Cutler and Zeckhauser 2000). Let's assume that there is one disease and a person can be sick with probability p. Let d be an indicator of whether the person is sick ($d = 1$) or healthy ($d = 0$). The medical spending needed for the treatment of the disease is z. The health of the person after the medical spending is $\theta = \Theta[d, z]$. In the simple case where the medical treatment restores the person to perfect health, $\Theta[1, z] = \Theta[0, 0]$.

The utility of the person depends on the consumption (x) and health, that is, $u = U(x, \theta)$. Let the person have an initial income endowment of y. Let insurance premium be π. For the uninsured, her consumption is $x = y$ when in good health and $x = y - z$ when sick, assuming no savings by the consumer. For the insured, her consumption is $x = y - \pi$ in both states, that is, either healthy or sick, assuming a 100% payment by the NHIC.

How should the insurance premium be determined? An insurance premium is a monthly fixed amount of money an insurance company charges an insurance holder in return for an insurance payout when the insured person gets sick with the disease at an indeterminate time. In the actuarially fair insurance, for the sake of simplicity of this explanation, the insurance premium is determined at the price at which the insurer breaks even (Sharpe 1964; Cutler and Zeckhauser 2000), which occurs when

$$\pi = pz. \tag{8.11}$$

Should the individual purchase this insurance? The person's expected utility without this health insurance, denoted by V_N, is Eq. (8.12), while the individual's expected utility with this insurance, denoted by V_I, is Eq. (8.13):

$$V_N = (1-p)U(y) + pU(y-z). \tag{8.12}$$

$$V_I = U(y-\pi). \tag{8.13}$$

The value of the health insurance for the person is the difference between the utility with the insurance and the utility without it (Cutler and Zeckhauser 2000):

$$\frac{V_I - V_N}{U'} = (1/2)\frac{-U''}{U'}\big(\pi(z-\pi)\big). \tag{8.14}$$

The left-hand side is the difference in the person's utilities between the insured state and the uninsured state, scaled by the marginal utility. The second term on the right-hand side, $-U''/U'$, is the coefficient of absolute risk aversion, which is positive. The third term is also positive because $z > \pi$. Therefore, owning the actuarially fair health insurance improves the welfare of the person, that is, $(V_I - V_N)/U > 0$. In other words, the insurance makes a Pareto welfare improvement to the society (Pareto 1906). The coefficient of absolute risk aversion (CARA) is the degree to which uncertainty about marginal utility makes the person worse off (Arrow 1971):

$$CARA = \frac{-U''}{U'}. \tag{8.15}$$

The value of the insurance depends, as clarified in Eq. (8.14), on the person's attitude toward the risk of contracting the disease. The larger the coefficient of absolute risk aversion of the individual, the larger the value of the insurance to her. In other words, the larger the coefficient of absolute risk aversion of the individuals in the society, the larger the size of the Pareto welfare improvement to the society. This conclusion holds for a wide range of methods for determining insurance premium beyond Eq. (8.11).

The differential performances of the three SHINs were analyzed in Chap. 2. Key comparative statistics of the three SHINs, drawn from the OECD health report in 2019, are shown in Fig. 8.7. When it comes to the

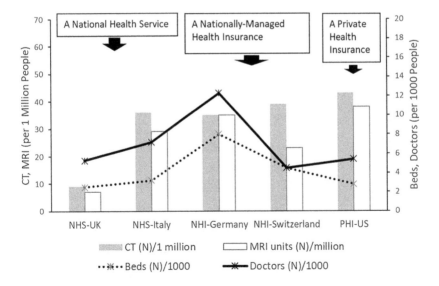

Fig. 8.7 Key comparative statistics of the national health systems

number of Computed Tomography (CT) scanners and that of Magnetic Resonance Imaging (MRI) units (per 1 million people), the PHI in the US is outperforming the other systems. The US has 43 CT scanners and 38 MRI units per 1 million citizens. As for the number of hospital beds and doctors, the nationally managed health insurance system in Germany is outperforming the other systems. Germany has 8 hospital beds and 4.3 doctors per 1000 citizens (OECD 2019). Germany has more than twice as many hospital beds and doctors per 1000 citizens as the UK has.

Which of the three SHINs performed best during the COVID-19 pandemic? In Fig. 8.8, the present author compares the COVID-19 health outcomes across the three systems (JHU 2021). The case-fatality ratio and the number of cases (per 100,000 people) are drawn from the Johns Hopkins University database last updated on February 26, 2021. The reference date is chosen because the comparisons are most meaningful for the pre-vaccine period.

The figure presents compelling evidence that the privately oriented health system (PHI) outperformed the other systems as far as mortality is

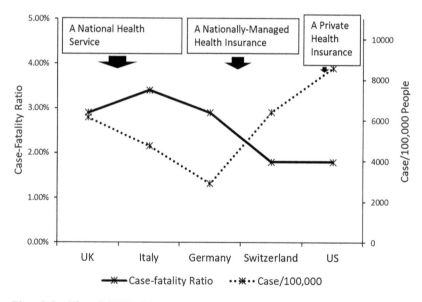

Fig. 8.8 The COVID-19 outcomes versus national health systems (as of February 26, 2021)

concerned. The US mortality rate is 1.8%, which can be compared with a 2.9% mortality rate of the UK, 3.4% mortality rate of Italy, and 2.9% mortality rate of Germany. The mortality rate is the case-fatality ratio in the figure.

When it comes to the number of infections, the US performed the worst of the countries represented in the figure. The US has 8500 persons infected, the UK has 6100 persons infected, and Germany has 2800 persons infected per 100,000 people. The high number of US infections may be due, among other things, to the riots and protests that raged during May and June of 2020 (US Crisis Monitor 2020). At the peak, nearly 100 riots occurred daily and roughly 600 protests per day across the US cities, which coincided with a pivotal spread period of the COVID-19 pandemic in the US before the third wave that started at around mid-October 2020.

The examination of Figs. 8.7 and 8.8 indicates, with a caveat of small samples, that the foresighted decision embedded in the establishment of the health insurance system of a nation has borne fruits most successfully in the privately oriented health system in terms of case-fatality ratio and in the nationally managed health insurance system in terms of the number of cases. This may be attributable to the financial incentives created more amply for the medical/pharmaceutical sectors under the privately based insurance system, which forces these sectors to innovate technologically voluntarily, including installations of MRI units and CT scanners (refer to Fig. 8.7).

Why would then a free national health service be less effective during the times of a pandemic, as per the case-fatality ratio? The NHS system seems to be better positioned to offer basic care to its citizens during "normal" times, but poorly positioned to offer advanced care which is needed during the times of a pandemic.

Since the data presented in Figs. 8.7 and 8.8 are selective while the measures presented in the figures are not comprehensive, it is too early to draw a general conclusion on this question from the figures. A rigorous study is guaranteed. A key takeaway message from this section is that a system of health insurance in the nation can be either privately based or publicly managed, which is a forward-looking decision, to some degree or another, against the pandemic risk.

7   THE ECONOMICS III: TECHNOLOGICAL
DEVELOPMENTS FOR A BACKSTOP

The concept of a backstop technology arose from the literature of energy economics during the 1970s. The emergence of the concept was perhaps inevitable because the total amount of fossil fuels on Earth from which most of the energy that humanity consumes is generated is limited. Hubbert predicted in the 1950s that the US oil production would peak in 1970 (Hubbert 1956). Economists started to ask what alternative energy sources could be appropriated when all fossil fuels on the planet would be exhausted in a not-distant future. The pursuit led them to the concept of an ultimate energy source or technology. The ultimate energy generation technology was referred to as a backstop technology, which was a newly coined terminology. The backstop energy technology is an energy generation technology that can supply energy to humanity indefinitely at a constant price (Nordhaus 1973). When the idea was first formulated during the early 1970s, a nuclear fusion technology appeared to hold such a promise as a backstop (Hartwick and Olewiler 1997).

If a backstop energy source or technology were to be found or developed, it would offer an ultimate solution to the problem of humanity's energy supply and consumption indefinitely. Recently, the concept of a backstop technology was applied as a key element to the economics of global climate challenges and globally shared goods (Seo 2020). If a solar radiation reflector or a carbon dioxide removal and sequestration technology can be perfected in the near future for a geographically large-scale application, either of these would turn out to be more or less an ultimate solution to the climate challenges facing the planet (NRC 2015a, 2015b).

Figure 8.9 illustrates the concept of a backstop technology. The society relies on Technology 1 in the initial phase whose price is increasing over time owing to the scarcity of the resources needed for the technology. When time T1 arrives, Technology 1 is replaced by Technology 2 as the former becomes more expensive than the latter at T1. The transition from Technology 1 to Technology 2 occurs at T1. As the price of Technology 2 increases over time again, a transition from Technology 2 to Technology 3 occurs at T2 at which point the price of Technology 3 becomes cheaper than that of Technology 2. Similarly, a transition from Technology 3 to the Backstop occurs at T3 at which point the price of Technology 3 becomes more expensive than that of the backstop technology. Unlike the other preceding technologies, the price of the Backstop remains constant

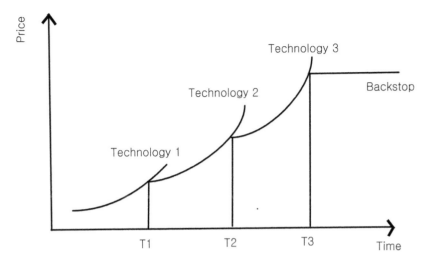

Fig. 8.9 An illustration of a backstop technology

over time, making sure that it is the ultimate technology for consumers throughout an indefinite future.

Applied to the real world of energy economics, Technology 1 can be interpreted as bio energy sources such as timber, horsepower, castor oil, whale oil; Technology 2 as fossil fuel energy sources such as coal, oil, and natural gas; Technology 3 as renewable energy technologies such as solar energy (NREL 2020). Technology 4, which is the backstop, may correspond to a nuclear fusion technology which the world does not yet have perfected (ITER 2015).

Applied to the climate change economics literature, Technology 1 may correspond to forest and grassland carbon sinks; Technology 2 may correspond to a transition from oil- and coal-fired power plants to natural gas-fired power plants; Technology 3 may correspond to still expensive mitigation technologies such as a carbon capture technology from fossil fuel-fired power plants, a solar energy, or an electric vehicle (EV) transition; the backstop technology, Technology 4, may correspond to a solar radiation reflector or a direct air carbon dioxide removal technology (Seo 2020). It goes without saying that climate change solutions are by far more complex than the transitions described in this paragraph, which is only for the purpose of a clear illustration of the transition to the backstop.

The economic problem of pandemics can be analyzed in parallel with the economics of energy supply as well as the economics of global climate change challenges. In particular, when it comes to a backstop technology, the three problems share a solid common ground: respective backstop technologies turn out to be a crucial element in solving each of these big challenges.

Having said that, the backstop for the pandemics is a by far more proven technology than those discussed for the energy supply problem as well as those discussed for the global climate change problem. The backstop energy technologies, for example, nuclear fusion or solar energy, are still yet to be proven to be a real backstop energy for the planet. The backstop climate technologies, for example, a solar radiation reflector or a direct carbon capture, are yet to be proven at a practical level. By contrast, the backstop technology for the pandemic problem, which is a high-efficacy vaccine, is already well established in science and has already been proven successful multiple times (Schwartz 2001; Plotkin 2009).

The smallpox disease had been one of the deadliest infectious diseases during the nineteenth and twentieth centuries. The fatality rate was especially high among children: eight out of ten children infected by the *Variola* virus died and three out of ten people infected died (CDC 2020a; refer to Fig. 9.5 in Chap. 9). It was declared by the World Health Organization (WHO) in 1980 to be eradicated from the planet owing to the development of an effective vaccine and a worldwide immunization effort (Weinstein 2011). The oldest smallpox vaccine, the Dryvax, was developed by American Home Products and, after the eradication of the smallpox virus, all of the stockpiles of the Dryvax were destroyed in 2008 (AP 2008). For the vaccines for a large list of infectious diseases, readers may refer to Table 7.2 in Chap. 7. For the World Health Organization (WHO) declaration, readers may refer to Table 3.2 in Chap. 3.

The declaration by the WHO of the smallpox virus eradication in 1980 is a landmark event in the economics of pandemics (WHO 2020). The reason for the assertion is that it vindicates the theory of a backstop for the pandemic economics, which is featured in this chapter as one of the three components thereof. To be more concrete, the event validated that the smallpox vaccine did indeed provide a backstop to the grave challenges posed by the smallpox disease: it ended the smallpox contagion. From an opposite viewpoint, the declaration proved that the smallpox disease might have continued to rage on in humanity until today, had the Dryvax vaccine not been developed.

The silver lining of the COVID-19 pandemic, if I am permitted to say this, is that the pandemic "offered" to the world an opportunity to show-case remarkable advances in the science of vaccine, vaccinology, and virol-ogy, during the past decades. As elaborated with great effort in the previous chapter of this book, two vaccines were developed, manufactured, and approved for emergency use within just nine months after the start of the development efforts. The Pfizer-BioNTech vaccine and the Moderna vac-cine were approved during the first two weeks of December 2020 (USFDA 2020a, 2020b). At the end of February 2021, the Janssen COVID-19 vaccine developed by Johnson & Johnson was also authorized for emer-gency use (USFDA 2021). As explained in Chap. 7, there are other vac-cines developed or approved elsewhere from Switzerland/UK, Russia, and China.

Do the COVID-19 vaccines hold the promise to end the COVID-19 pandemic? At the time of this writing on March 1, 2021, they do seem to hold a high promise to end the pandemic, that is, be proven to be a back-stop technology for the pandemic. Pfizer-BioNTech and Moderna reported in November 2020 after their respective Phase-III clinical trials that their vaccines are effective in preventing the COVID-19 infections with about 95% efficacy rate (USFDA 2020a, 2020b).

The experiments after the mass vaccination efforts yielded an even stronger hope. The Pfizer-BioNTech vaccine was given shots starting from December 14, 2020. Israel was a leading nation in the mass vaccination efforts. By the middle of February 2021, nearly 42% of the entire popula-tion of the country were given the first shot of the Pfizer-BioNTech vac-cine while 28% fully vaccinated. A study by Clalit, Israel's largest healthcare provider, showed that the fully vaccinated group was 94% less likely to develop a symptomatic COVID-19 disease compared to the unvaccinated group (Dagan et al. 2021). Readers may refer to the analyses in Figs. 7.5 and 7.6 in Chap. 7 to see a dramatic effect of vaccination in the UK by May 1, 2021. For the discussion of the vaccines' effectiveness against the Delta variant that caused the fifth wave globally, also refer to the studies explained Chap. 7 including the Mayo Clinic study (Puranik et al. 2021).

What explains the historical advancement in the biomedical sciences and the pharmaceutical industry that have paved the way for the develop-ment of the mRNA vaccines in such record time? The vaccine success is attributed, to some degree, by many to the successful private-public part-nership through the Operation Warp Speed by the Trump administration (USDHHS 2020a). But the OWS cannot explain the strength of the aforementioned biomedical fields that existed before the pandemic as well as before the OWS program.

The capacity and capabilities of the biomedical fields that laid the groundwork for the rapid development of the COVID-19 vaccines can be in large part attributed to the growth in the economy, more specifically, the accumulation of technological knowledge or the investments in technological innovations that have driven the past economic growth (Nelson 1959; Griliches 1979). The technological progresses under the spotlight in this section are the advances in biomedical sciences, virology, and pharmaceutical applications (BMVP), including the DNA and mRNA discoveries (Avery et al. 1944; Watson and Crick 1953; Brenner et al. 1961; Jacob and Monod 1961). The growth in the economy is achieved by, *inter alia*, technological innovations which in turn are induced by the economic agents who make profit-maximizing investment decisions (Lucas 1986; Romer 1994; Nordhaus 2002, 2014). A technological change is simply and succinctly defined as an improvement in the instruction for mixing raw materials together for producing a good.

Let me explain in a formal way how technological changes drive the economic growth, put alternatively, how technological advances are made by the economic agents each of whom pursues a higher profit from her/his investments. The goal here is obviously to explain the growth in the BMVP sector driven by such economic agents. Let Y be the final output of the macro economy, that is, the whole economy we are concerned with. Let Y be expressed as a function of the three inputs of production: the amount of physical labor (L), the amount of human capital devoted to the production of the final goods (H_Y), the amount of physical capital expressed as an infinite number of durables $x = \{x_i\}_{i=1}^{\infty}$ (Romer 1990). The human capital, H_Y, is the key variable of this growth model literature (Solow 1956). Let's imagine an economy with three sectors: a research sector, an intermediate-goods sector, and a final-goods sector.

The variable of primary interest in this modeling is the human capital, an increase of which can be interpreted to be a rate of technological change. It is a factor of production distinct from physical labor as well as the amount of durable goods. In the context of pandemics, the human capital can capture the accumulation of the biomedical and virological science knowledge as well as the technical capabilities of the pharmaceutical companies. Let the human capital pertinent to the pandemics be denoted by H_{BMVP}.

Let $A_{BMVP,\,t}$ be the level of accumulated technological knowledge in the BMVP sector at time t. Then, the rate of technological change, the left-hand side of Eq. (8.16), is written as follows:

$$\frac{\dot{A}_{BMVP,t}}{A_{BMVP,t}} = \phi\left(R_{BMVP,t}, \tilde{H}_t\right). \tag{8.16}$$

The right-hand side is the "innovation-possibility frontier" which is expressed as a function of the stock of knowledge available at time t across the society ($\tilde{H}_t$) and the research and development efforts in the BMVP sector at time t, that is, $R_{BMVP,\,t}$ (Nordhaus 2002).

An optimization decision of the macro economy can be written as follows, using the Cobb-Douglas (CD) production function, to determine the levels of the durable goods, taking the levels of physical labor and the levels of human capital as given, to be produced in the economy (Romer 1990):

$$\max_{i\,L,H_Y} \int_0^\infty \left[H_Y^\alpha L^\beta x_i^{1-\alpha-\beta} - p_i x_i \right] di. \tag{8.17}$$

In the above model, the decision is made at one point in time. α and β are technological parameters of the CD production function. Differentiating the terms under the integral sign of Eq. (8.17) leads to the demand function, more precisely, the inverse demand function for durable goods i:

$$p_i = \left(1 - \alpha - \beta\right) H_Y^\alpha L^\beta x_i^{-\alpha-\beta}. \tag{8.18}$$

A profit-maximizing firm, m, which is a producer of the single final good x will take the prices in Eq. (8.18) as given and, having incurred the fixed cost of investment, that is, the sunk cost, will choose the level of output to maximize its net revenue, that is, profit:

$$\pi_m = \max_x p_x x - \gamma \varphi x. \tag{8.19}$$

In the above, γ is the interest cost, that is, the rental cost, on φx units of output needed to produce the durable goods x. The firm's decision can be more explicitly written as follows by inserting Eq. (8.18) into Eq. (8.19):

$$\pi_m = \max_x \left(1 - \alpha - \beta\right) H_\gamma^\alpha L^\beta x^{1-\alpha-\beta} - \gamma\varphi x. \tag{8.20}$$

To proceed further, let's assume that the society's preference can be written as the utility function with a constant rate of relative risk aversion (σ), often referred to as the Ramsey model (Ramsey 1928; Weitzman 2009). With C being the consumption,

$$U\left(C\right) = \frac{C^{1-\sigma} - 1}{1 - \sigma}. \tag{8.21}$$

Then, the intertemporal optimization condition in the competitive market for a consumer faced with a fixed interest rate (γ) is the following, with the discount rate ρ (Weitzman 2009):

$$\frac{\dot{C}}{C} = \frac{\gamma - \rho}{\sigma}. \tag{8.22}$$

Referring back to Eq. (8.16) which specifies two types of knowledge, the total human capital has two components: a rival component of knowledge (Γ) and a nonrival component of knowledge (Ω) (Griliches 1979, 1998). The rival knowledge is an exclusive knowledge to the firm such as years of formal education and on-the-job training for the employers at a specific firm. Take, for example, a worker's ability to add, read, or use a specific machine. The nonrival knowledge is a shared knowledge in the society, for example, a new design for a good. Once the new design is created, it can be used or copied by other producers and in other activities as desired. Specifically, the Ω can be measured by a count of new designs (Romer 1990; Nordhaus 2002). H_Ω can be interpreted as the human capital employed in research, as per Eq. (8.16).

Assuming that any person can allocate his/her human capital to either a final-goods production sector or a research sector, a human capital constraint in the model is, at the aggregate, that the two types of the human capital add up to the total human capital (H) (Romer 1990):

$$H_Y + H_\Omega = H. \tag{8.23}$$

The optimization decisions by individual economic agents, Eq. (8.19), in the three sectors determine the level of human capital devoted to the production of the final output. The price of a new knowledge or a new design is determined by the net present value of the net revenues earned from the design:

$$P_\Omega = \frac{\pi(t)}{\gamma(t)}. \tag{8.24}$$

The wage for human capital, which should be equalized across the sectors, is determined by the marginal product of the knowledge:

$$\omega_H = P_\Omega \delta \Omega. \tag{8.25}$$

δ is a productivity parameter of a researcher from nonrival knowledge (Ω). From Eqs. (8.24) and (8.25), in the balanced growth model in which the capital grows at a constant exponential rate, the following can be derived (Romer 1990):

$$H_Y = \frac{1}{\delta} \frac{\alpha}{(1-\alpha-\beta)(\alpha+\beta)} \gamma. \tag{8.26}$$

As explained before, ρ in the above is a constant discount rate; σ is a constant rate of relative risk aversion; α and β are technological parameters in the Cobb-Douglas production function.

The rate of economic growth (ξ) in the balanced growth model satisfies the following equalities:

$$\xi = \frac{\dot{C}}{C} = \delta H_\Omega = \frac{\delta H - \Psi \rho}{\sigma \Psi + 1}. \tag{8.27}$$

Human capital components are H, a rival component of human capital; H_Ω a nonrival component of human capital; δ, the productivity parameter for the nonrival component of human capital (Ω). The Ψ is a function of the technological parameters α and β, specifically, the middle term of the product on the right-hand side of Eq. (8.26). The other important parameters of the balanced growth model are discount rate (ρ) and risk aversion (σ) of the society. What Eq. (8.27) says is that the economic growth is determined by the human capital which drives technological changes (Romer 1990).

As for the pandemic economics, what are some examples of a rival component of knowledge (Γ) and a non-rival component of knowledge (Ω)? During the COVID-19 pandemic, mRNA research and mRNA vaccines are examples of the rival knowledge, that is, Γ_{BMVP} (Kariko et al. 2011; Pardi et al. 2018). The accumulated knowledge on biology, medicine, infectious diseases, and vaccines shared broadly across the society are examples of the nonrival knowledge, that is, Ω_{BMVP} (Plotkin 2009; CDC 2012).

In the economic system in which technological advances are achieved via economic agents who make every effort to gain higher profits from their investments, the human capital in the BMVP areas will increase via private investments of, *inter alia*, pharmaceutical companies, universities, and consumers of medical products (Eq. (8.19)). The growth of the macro economy will hinge on the total human capital, both in the form of the rival component of scientific knowledge and in the form of the nonrival component, which drives technological changes, that is, new designs.

From the vantage point of the technology-driven economic growth theory, an advancement in the aforementioned rival component of knowledge in the BMVP areas during the pre-pandemic period made possible the US development of the COVID-19 vaccines in record time (Gupta 2021). To put it differently, the COVID-19 vaccines demonstrate a power of the economy that is driven primarily by profit-maximizing motives of individuals in the competitive market economy.

This theory does not assert that there is no role for the government in economic growth or pandemic responses. As highlighted in Chap. 7, the successful private and public partnership, that is, the Operation Warp Speed, not only laid out a clear rule of engagements by the public sector in the vaccine development efforts but also created appropriate incentives for candidate vaccine developers to start as early as possible and as swiftly as they can (Azar II 2020; USDHHS 2020a; Gupta 2021).

By selecting the vaccine candidates early and providing funds to them, the OWS made the developers to start at the earliest possible dates. In addition, by "betting big" by agreeing to purchase billions of doses of vaccines and start manufacturing them even before an emergency use approval issued by the Food and Drug Administration (FDA), the OWS was able to create incentives for the pharmaceutical companies to develop vaccines as swiftly as they possibly can. The OWS is one of the rare examples of a successful government intervention during the COVID-19 pandemic.

8   A Society's Optimal Pathway for the Pandemic Risk Management

Having clarified the three focal points of the pandemic economics, that is, the microbehavioral decisions, foresighted decisions, and the economics of a backstop technology, the present author is in a good position to present an integrated pathway for the society's optimal management of the pandemic risk. In the optimal trajectory to be described presently, all three decision focal points are at work at one point in time, which are utilized by the society as a powerful force when a pandemic befalls.

The present author first proposed the framework of the three focal point decisions in the book entitled *The Economics of Globally Shared and Public Goods* (Seo 2020). The three focal points can be interpreted as the three reference points for observing Earth from the atmosphere. Depending on your reference point which is fixated at the centroid of the Atlantic Ocean (say, the Greenwich reference point), or at the centroid of the Pacific Ocean (say, the Mauna Loa observatory), or at the centroid of the Indian Ocean (say, the archipelago of the Maldives), the planet will look very different to you. The truth is you are looking at the same planet from three different reference points. Similarly, the three focal points in the economics of pandemics are the three reference points in time in the pandemic risk management.

The focal point of microbehavioral decisions explicates individual economic agents, that is, individuals and private businesses, who make efficient choices for them when faced with a large basket of decisions to be made. The basket of decisions for private individuals includes choices vis-à-vis physical distancing, mask wearing, washing hands, taking days off from work, avoiding public transportations, avoiding dining out, skipping in-person church services, taking an infection test, getting vaccine shots. The basket for private businesses includes choices vis-à-vis choosing a mode of operation, giving employers paid days off, providing personal protective equipment at work, providing a rapid test, a physically distanced office spacing, switching to AI-based services, switching to home deliveries or take-out services.

The essence of the microbehavioral decision focal point is that the set of choices by one economic agent in response or anticipation of a pandemic will be different from the set of choices made by another economic agent, owing to many factors including, among other things, a personal economic status, a health status, geographic conditions, and virus characteristics. The mosaic of individually varying choices at the society level would yield a more efficient outcome, be it health or economic, than the blanket of individually unvarying choices, for example, the mandate set by the government applied homogenously across all citizens.

The focal point of foresighted decisions explicates the decisions of the economic agents in both the private sector and the public sector which pertain to a long-term risk management strategy for each of them. Three foresighted decisions are explained in this chapter. The first is an increased health expenditure by an individual in pace with an increase in personal income as a long-term health risk management strategy by the individual. The second is an increase in the adoption of AI-based non-contact technologies by private businesses. The third is a choice of a system of health insurance for a nation that can respond to future pandemic outbreaks most efficiently.

That the choices actually made by the economic agents many years before an outbreak of a pandemic faced with these decisions will make a big difference in both health and economic outcomes of unexpected pandemics was amply justified and demonstrated in this chapter with references to the actual health and economic outcomes from the COVID-19 pandemic. An increased health spending by an individual will reduce her/his comorbidity which was perhaps the single most important condition that leads to the COVID-19 mortality. An adoption of non-contact services relying on AI technologies makes private businesses more resilient against pandemic contagion, which would help their business operations as well. A system of private health insurances or national health insurances for the nation may make the nation better equipped and positioned to deal with worldwide pandemics.

The third focal point is the economics of a backstop technology. A highly effective vaccine is practically the only option for ending the pandemic at a scale of the COVID-19. In other words, the vaccine is a backstop technology in the pandemic risk management. The COVID-19 pandemic showcased the science of vaccines as a backstop technology for pandemics. The mRNA vaccines were developed and approved miraculously in less than a year with a remarkable 95% efficacy, shining a glimmer of hope in humanity's fight against the COVID-19.

The COVID-19 vaccine miracle can be ascribed to the economic growth which is powered by technological developments. Technological innovations achieved through private businesses' pursuits for higher profits lay the foundation for developing a vaccine backstop in the times of pandemics. Pharmaceutical companies and private research laboratories accumulate knowledge and technologies through their efficient operations in the market economy in response to the demands for medical services, which are appropriated by themselves and the society when future pandemics strike.

9 WHAT LIES AHEAD IN PANDEMIC ECONOMICS

The economics of pandemics is elucidated in this chapter as a society's optimal transition pathway in which the three focal points unravel a society's efficient management of the pandemic risk. The economics of pandemics thus explained is the economics of a globally shared good, in other words, a global-scale public good. That is, the full array of choices described in this chapter are pertinent at the global scale in which local, national, and global actors play important roles in the planet's pandemic risk management.

The economics of globally shared goods with three focal points was introduced for the first time for the exposition of the economics of global climate challenges, another globally shared good that has received the most attention by policy-makers and the public for the past three decades (Seo 2015b, 2020).

The pandemic economics, however, is a novel emerging field that can stand alone and high in a not-distant future. The present author can predict this for two reasons. One is increasingly greater interests and investments by the public on their health and life years (Deaton 2013; OECD. Stat 2021). The other is the notable advances in medicine, genetics, and virology (Kariko et al. 2011; Pardi et al. 2018; NHGRI 2021).

REFERENCES

Abaluck, J., L.H Kwong, A. Styczynski, et al. 2021. The Impact of Community Masking on COVID-19: A Cluster-Randomized Trial in Bangladesh. The Innovations for Poverty Action (IPA) Working Paper. https://www.poverty-action.org/publication/impact-community-masking-covid-19-cluster-randomized-trial-bangladesh.

Arrow, Kenneth J. 1963. Uncertainty and the Welfare Economics of Medical Care. *American Economic Review* 53 (5): 941–973.

———. 1971. *Essays in the Theory of Risk Bearing.* Chicago, IL: Markham Publishing Co.

Arrow, K.J., W. Cline, K.G. Maler, M. Munasinghe, R. Squitieri, and J. Stiglitz. 1996. Intertemporal Equity, Discounting, and Economic Efficiency. In *Climate Change 1995: Economic and Social Dimensions of Climate Change,* ed. J.P. Bruce, H. Lee, and E.F. Haites. Cambridge, UK: Cambridge University Press.

Associated Press (AP). 2008. CDC to Destroy Oldest Smallpox Vaccine. Published on March 3.

Avery, Oswald T., Colin M. MacLeod, and Maclyn McCarty. 1944. Studies on the Chemical Nature of the Substance Inducing Transformation of Pneumococcal Types: Induction of Transformation by a Deoxyribonucleic Acid Fraction Isolated from Pneumococcus Type III. *Journal of Experimental Medicine* 79: 137–158.

Azar II, Alex M. 2020. How Operation Warp Speed Delivered a COVID Vaccine in Record Time. *Fox News.* Published on December 12. https://www.foxnews.com/opinion/hhs-azar-operation-warp-speed-covid-vaccine-record-time.

Barr, Nicholas, and Peter Diamond. 2006. The Economics of Pensions. *Oxford Review of Economic Policy* 22: 15–39.

Barrett, Scott. 2003. *Environment and Statecraft: The Strategy of Environmental Treaty.* Oxford, UK: Oxford University Press.

Baumol, W.J., and O.A. Oates. 1988. *The Theory of Environmental Policy.* 2nd ed. Cambridge, UK: Cambridge University Press.

Berry, K., T. Allen, R.D. Horan, J.F. Shogren, D. Finnoff, and P. Daszak. 2018. The Economic Case for a Pandemic Fund. *EcoHealth* 15: 244–258.

Bhattacharya, Jay, Timothy Hyde, and Tu. Peter. 2013. *Health Economics.* New York, NY: Macmillan International Higher Education.

Bliss, C.I. 1934. The Method of Probits. *Science* 79: 38–39.

Bloom, D.E., and D. Canning. 2017. *Epidemics and Economics.* Working Paper #9, Harvard Program on Demography of Ageing, Harvard University.

Boserup, Brad, Mark McKenney, and Adel Elkbuli. 2020. Alarming Trends in US Domestic Violence during the COVID-19 Pandemic. *The American Journal of Emergency Medicine.* https://doi.org/10.1016/j.ajem.2020.04.077.

Brenner, S., F. Jacob, and M. Meselson. 1961. An Unstable Intermediate Carrying Information from Genes to Ribosomes for Protein Synthesis. *Nature* 190: 576–581.

Buchanan, J.M. 1968. *The Demand and Supply of Public Goods*. Chicago, IL: Rand McNally & Co.

Bundgaard, H., J.S. Bundgarrd, D.E.T. Raaschou-Pedersen, et al. 2020. Effectiveness of Adding a Mask Recommendation to Other Public Health Measures to Prevent SARS-CoV-2 Infection in Danish Mask Wearers. A Randomized Controlled Trial. *Annals of Internal Medicine*. https://doi.org/10.7326/M20-6817

Burns, A., D. Mensbrugghe, and H. Timmer. 2008. Evaluating the Economic Consequences of Avian Influenza. Washington, DC: World Bank. Accessed from: http://documents.worldbank.org/curated/en/977141468158986545/pdf/474170WP0Evalu101PUBLIC10Box334133B.pdf.

Case, Anne, and Angus Deaton. 2015. Rising Morbidity and Mortality in Midlife among White Non-Hispanic Americans in the 21st Century. *Proceedings of the National Academy of Sciences (PNAS)* 112: 15078–15083.

Centers for Disease Control and Prevention (CDC). 2012. Principles of Epidemiology in Public Health Practice (Third Edition): An Introduction to Applied Epidemiology and Biostatistics. Atlanta, GA: The CDC.

———. 2020a. *Smallpox*. Atlanta, G.A.: The CDC.

———. 2020b. *Past Pandemics*. Atlanta, G.A.: The CDC.

Ch.Ch. 2020. Health Insurance—Obtaining Basic Insurance, Its Costs and Services. Ch.Ch: A Service of the Confederation, Cantons and Communes. https://www.ch.ch/en/health-insurance/.

Chib, S., and E. Greenberg. 1998. Analysis of Multivariate Probit Models. *Biometrika* 85: 347–361.

Chinazzi, Matteo, Jessica T. Davis, Marco Ajelli, et al. 2020. The Effect of Travel Restrictions on the Spread of the 2019 Novel Coronavirus (COVID-19) Outbreak. *Science* 368: 395–400.

Coase, Ronald. 1960. The Problem of Social Costs. *Journal of Law and Economics* 3: 1–44.

Cutler, David, and Richard Zeckhauser. 2000. The Anatomy of Insurance. In *Handbook of Health Economics*, ed. Anthony Culyer and Joseph Newhouse, vol. 1A. Amsterdam, N.L.: Elsevier.

Dafny, Leemore S. 2010. Are Health Insurance Markets Competitive? *American Economic Review* 100: 1399–1431.

Dagan, Noa, Noam Barda, Eldad Kepten, Oren Miron, Shay Perchik, Mark A. Katz, Miguel A. Hernán, Marc Lipsitch, Ben Reis, and Ran D. Balicer. 2021. BNT162b2 mRNA Covid-19 Vaccine in a Nationwide Mass Vaccination Setting. *New England Journal of Medicine*. https://doi.org/10.1056/NEJMoa2101765.

Deaton, Angus. 2013. *The Great Escape: Health, Wealth, and the Origins of Inequality*. Princeton, NJ: Princeton University Press.

Deccan Herald. 2020. No Lockdowns, but Sweden Seems to Have Controlled the Covid-19 Pandemic. Published on October 1. https://www.deccanherald.com/opinion/panorama/no-lockdowns-but-sweden-seems-to-have-controlled-the-covid-19-pandemic-895509.html.

Detroit News. 2020. Gov. Whitmer Closing High Schools, Colleges, In-person Dining, Casinos, Movie Theaters. Published on November 15. https://www.detroitnews.com/story/news/politics/2020/11/15/gov-whitmer-expected-announce-new-covid-19-restrictions-sunday/6304308002/.

Diamond, Peter A., and Peter R. Orszag. 2005. Saving Social Security. *Journal of Economic Perspectives* 19 (2): 11–32.

Dubin, J.A., and D.L. McFadden. 1984. An Econometric Analysis of Residential Electric Appliance Holdings and Consumption. *Econometrica* 52: 345–362.

European Centre for Disease Prevention and Control (ECDPC). 2020. COVID19 Coronavirus Dataset. Solna Municipality, Sweden: The ECDPC. https://data.europa.eu/euodp/en/data/dataset/covid-19-coronavirus-data.

Fan, Victoria Y., Dean T. Jamison, and Lawrence H. Summers. 2018. Pandemic Risk: How Large are the Expected Losses? *The Bulletin of the World Health Organization* 96 (2): 129–134.

Finkelstein, Amy. 2007. The Aggregate Effects of Health Insurance: Evidence from the Introduction of Medicare. *Quarterly Journal of Economics* 122: 1–37.

Fisher, I. 1930. *The Theory of Interest*. New York: Macmillan.

Friedman, Milton. 1962. *Capitalism and Freedom*. Chicago, IL: The University of Chicago Press.

Gazit, S. R. Shlezinger, G. Perez, R. Lotan, A. Peretz, A. Ben-Tov, D. Cohen, K. Muhsen, G. Chodick, and T. Patalon. 2021. Comparing SARS-CoV-2 Natural Immunity to Vaccine-induced Immunity: Reinfections versus Breakthrough Infections. https://doi.org/10.1101/2021.08.24.21262415

Griliches, Zvi. 1979. Issues in Assessing the Contribution of Research and Development to Productivity Growth. *Bell Journal of Economics* 10: 92–116.

———. 1998. *Patents and Technology*. Cambridge, MA: Harvard University Press.

Gupta, Swati. 2021. The Application and Future Potential of mRNA Vaccine. COVID-19 & You, Yale School of Public Health, New Haven, CT. Published on May 7. https://ysph.yale.edu/news-article/the-application-and-future-potential-of-mrna-vaccines/.

Hartwick, J.M., and N.D. Olewiler. 1997. *The Economics of Natural Resource Use*. 2nd ed. New York, NY: Pearson.

Heckman, J. 1979. Sample Selection Bias as a Specification Error. *Econometrica* 47: 153–162.

Hubbert, M.K. 1956. *Nuclear Energy and the Fossil Fuels*. Presented before the Spring Meeting of the Southern District, American Petroleum Institute, Plaza Hotel, San Antonio, Texas, March 7–8–9.

International Thermonuclear Experimental Reactor (ITER). 2015. ITER: The World's Largest Tokamak. https://www.iter.org/mach.

Jacob, F., and J. Monod. 1961. Genetic Regulatory Mechanisms in the Synthesis of Proteins. *Journal of Molecular Biology* 3: 318–356.

Japan Times. 2020. Japan Suicides Rise as Economic Impact of Coronavirus Hits Home. Published on November 11. https://www.japantimes.co.jp/news/2020/11/11/national/japan-suicide-rise-coronavirus/.

Johns Hopkins University (JHU). 2020. COVID-19 Dash Board. JHU, Baltimore, MD. https://data.humdata.org/dataset/novel-coronavirus-2019-ncov-cases.

———. 2021. Mortality Analyses (Last Updated on February 26). Coronavirus Resource Center, JHU, Baltimore, MD. https://coronavirus.jhu.edu/data/mortality.

Jonas, O.B. 2013. Pandemic Risk. Washington, DC: World Bank. https://openknowledge.worldbank.org/bitstream/handle/10986/16343/WDR14_bp_Pandemic_Risk_Jonas.pdf?sequence=1&isAllowed=y.

Kariko, K., H. Muramatsu, J. Ludwig, and D. Weissman. 2011. Generating the Optimal mRNA for Therapy: HPLC Purification Eliminates Immune Activation and Improves Translation for Nucleoside-modified. *Protein-encoding mRNA. Nucleic Acids Research* 39: e142.

Kaul, I., P. Conceicao, K.L. Goulven, and R.U. Mendoza, eds. 2003. *Providing Global Public Goods: Managing Globalization.* Oxford, UK: Oxford University Press.

Koopmans, T.C., 1965. On the concept of optimal economic growth. Acad. Sci. Scr. Varia 28 (1): 1–75.

Lopez, Alan D., Colin D. Mathers, Majid Ezzati, Dean T. Jamison, and Christopher J.L. Murray. 2006. *Global Burden of Disease and Risk Factors.* New York, N.Y.: World Bank and Oxford University Press.

Lucas, R.E. 1986. On the Mechanics of Economic Development. *Journal of Monetary Economics* 22: 3–42.

Mas-Colell, A., M.D. Whinston, and J.R. Green. 1995. *Microeconomic Theory.* Oxford, UK: Oxford University Press.

McFadden, Daniel L. 1974. Conditional Logit Analysis of Qualitative Choice Behavior. In *Frontiers in Econometrics,* ed. P. Zarembka. New York, NY: Academic Press.

———. 1999a. Chapter 1. Discrete Response Models. Lecture Note. University of California at Berkeley, CA.

———.. 1999b. Chapter 2. Sampling and Selection. Lecture Note. University of California at Berkeley, CA.

McFadden, D., and K. Train. 2000. Mixed MNL Models for Discrete Response. *Journal of Applied Econometrics* 15: 447–470.

Mendelsohn, R., and S. Olmstead. 2009. The Economic Valuation of Environmental Amenities and Disamenities: Methods and Applications. *Annual Review of Resources* 34: 325–347.

Morin, B.R., A.P. Kinzig, S.A. Levin, and C.A. Perrings. 2018. Economic Incentives in the Socially Optimal Management of Infectious Disease: When R0 is Not Enough. *EcoHealth* 15: 274–289.

Muller, N.Z., and R. Mendelsohn. 2009. Efficient Pollution Regulation: Getting the Prices Right. *American Economic Review* 99: 1714–1739.

Muller, N.Z., R. Mendelsohn, and W. Nordhaus. 2011. Environmental accounting for pollution in the United States economy. *American Economic Review* 101: 1649–1675.

National Center for Health Statistics (NCHS). 2021a. Provisional COVID-19 Death Counts by Sex, Age, and State. Washington, DC: NCHS, CDC. https://www.cdc.gov/nchs/nvss/vsrr/covid_weekly/index.htm.

———. 2021b. Conditions Contributing to Deaths involving Coronavirus Disease 2019 (COVID-19), by Age Group and State, United States. Washington, DC: NCHS, CDC. https://www.cdc.gov/nchs/nvss/vsrr/covid_weekly/index.htm.

National Health Service (NHS). 2020. Guidance: The NHS Constitution for England. NHS, UK. https://www.gov.uk/government/publications/the-nhs-constitution-for-england.

National Human Genome Research Institute (NHGRI). 2021. The Human Genome Project. The NHGRI, National Institutes of Health, Bethesda, MD. https://www.genome.gov/human-genome-project.

National Renewable Energy Laboratory (NREL). 2020. Perovskite Solar Cells. Washington, DC: The NREL, Department of Energy. https://www.nrel.gov/pv/perovskite-solar-cells.html.

National Research Council (NRC). 2015a. *Climate Intervention: Reflecting Sunlight to Cool Earth. Committee on Geoengineering Climate: Technical Evaluation and Discussion of Impacts.* Washington, DC: The National Academies Press.

———. 2015b. *Climate Intervention Carbon Dioxide Removal and Reliable Sequestration.* Washington, DC: The National Academies Press.

Nelson, R.R. 1959. The Simple Economics of Basic Scientific Research. *Journal of Political Economy* 67: 297–306.

New York Times (NYT). 2020. Coronavirus Vaccine Tracker. https://www.nytimes.com/interactive/2020/science/coronavirus-vaccine-tracker.html.

Nordhaus, William D. 1973. The Allocation of Energy Resources. *Brookings Papers on Economic Activity* 1973: 529–576.

———. 1992. The Ecology of Markets. *Proceedings of the National Academy of Sciences of the United States of America* 89: 843–850.

———. 1994. *Managing the Global Commons.* Cambridge, MA: MIT Press.

———. 2000. New Directions in National Economic Accounting. *American Economic Review Papers and Proceedings* 90: 259–263.

———. 2002. Modeling Induced Innovation in Climate Change Policy. In *Technological Change and the Environment*, ed. A. Grubler, N. Nakićenović, and W.D. Nordhaus. New York, NY: Routledge.

———. 2006. Paul Samuelson and Global Public Goods. In *Samuelsonian Economics and the Twenty-First Century*, ed. M. Szenberg, L. Ramrattan, and A.A. Gottesman. Oxford Scholarship Online.

———. 2007. Two Centuries of Productivity Growth in Computing. *The Journal of Economic History* 67: 128–159.

———. 2014. The Perils of the Learning Model for Modeling Endogenous Technological Change. *The Energy Journal* 35: 1–13.

OECD.Stat. 2021. Health Expenditure and Financing. OECD, Paris, Fr. https://stats.oecd.org/Index.aspx?DataSetCode=SHA

Organization for Economic Cooperation and Development (OECD). 2019. *Health at a Glance 2019*. Paris: OECD.

Pardi, N., M.J. Hogan, F.W. Porter, and D. Weissman. 2018. mRNA vaccines—A New Era in Vaccinology. *Nature Reviews Drug Discovery* 17: 261–279.

Pareto, Vilfredo. 1906. A Critical and Variorum Edition. In *Manual for Political Economy*, ed. A. Montesano, A. Zanni, L. Bruni, J.S. Chipman, and M. McLure. Oxford, UK: Oxford University Press.

Plotkin, S.A. 2009. Vaccines: The Fourth Century. *Clinical and Vaccine Immunology* 16: 1709–1719.

Polyakova, Maria, Victoria Udalova, Geoffrey Kocks, Katie Genadek, Keith Finlay, and Amy Finkelstein. 2021. Racial Disparities in Excess All-Cause Mortality During the Early COVID-19 Pandemic Varied Substantially Across States. *Health Affairs* 40 (2). https://doi.org/10.1377/hlthaff.2020.02142

Potter, C.W. 2001. A History of Influenza. *Journal of Applied Microbiology* 91 (4): 572–579.

Puranik, A., P.J. Lenehan, E. Silvert, et al. 2021. Comparison of Two highly-effective mRNA Vaccines for COVID-19 During Periods of Alpha and Delta Variant Prevalence. medRxiv preprint. https://doi.org/10.1101/2021.08.06.21261707.

Ramsey, Frank P. 1928. A Mathematical Theory of Savings. *Economic Journal* 38: 543–559.

Rice, T., P. Rosenau, L.Y. Unruh, A.J. Barnes, R.B. Saltman, and E. van Ginneken. 2013. United States of America: Health System Review. *Health Systems in Transition* 15 (3): 1–431.

Romer, Paul M. 1990. Endogenous Technical Change. *Journal of Political Economy* 98: S71–S102.

———. 1994. The Origins of Endogenous Growth. *The Journal of Economic Perspectives.* 8: 3–22.

Samuelson, Paul. 1954. The Pure Theory of Public Expenditure. *Review of Economics and Statistics* 36: 387–389.

Sanchez-Paramo, Carolina. 2020. COVID-19 Will Hit the Poor Hardest. Here's What We Can Do About It. *World Bank Blogs*. https://blogs.worldbank.org/voices/covid-19-will-hit-poor-hardest-heres-what-we-can-do-about-it.

Schwartz, M. 2001. The Life and Works of Louis Pasteur. *Journal of Applied Microbiology*. 91 (4): 597–601.

Seo, S. Niggol. 2015a. Helping Low-latitude, Poor Countries with Climate Change. *Regulation*. *Winter* 2015–2016: 6–8.

———. 2015b. Adaptation to Global Warming as an Optimal Transition Process to a Greenhouse World. *Economic Affairs* 35: 272–284.

———. 2016a. *Microbehavioral Econometric Methods: Theories, Models, and Applications for the Study of Environmental and Natural Resources*. Amsterdam, NL: Academic Press.

———. 2016b. The Micro-behavioral Framework for Estimating Total Damage of Global Warming on Natural Resource Enterprises with Full Adaptations. *Journal of Agricultural, Biological, and Environmental Statistics* 21: 328–347.

———. 2019. *The Economics of Global Allocations of the Green Climate Fund: An Assessment From Four Scientific Traditions of Modeling Adaptation Strategies*. Cham, CH: Springer Nature.

———. 2020. *The Economics of Globally Shared and Public Goods*. Amsterdam, NL: Academic Press.

Sharpe, William F. 1964. Capital Asset Prices: A Theory of Market Equilibrium under Conditions of Risk. *Journal of Finance* 19: 425–442.

Sloan, Frank A., and Chee-Ruey Hsieh. 2013. *Health Economics*. 2nd ed. Boston, MA: The MIT Press.

Smith, C., D. Odd, R. Harwood, J. Ward, M. Linney, M. Clark, D. Hargreaves, S. Ladhani, E. Draper, P. Davis, S. Kenny, E. Whittaker, K. Luyt, R. Viner, and L. Fraser. 2021. Deaths in Children and Young People in England following SARS-CoV-2 infection During the first Pandemic Year: A National Study Using Linked Mandatory Child Death Reporting Data. https://doi.org/10.21203/rs.3.rs-689684/v1

Solow, Robert M. 1956. A Contribution to the Theory of Economic Growth. *Quarterly Journal of Economics* 70: 65–94.

———. 1993. An Almost Ideal Step toward Sustainability. *Resources Policy* 19: 162–172.

Taubenberger, J.K., D.M. Morens, and A.S. Fauci. 2007. The Next Influenza Pandemic: Can It Be Predicted? *The Journal of the American Medical Association* 297: 2025–2027.

Train, Kenneth. 2003. *Discrete Choice Methods with Simulation*. Cambridge, UK: Cambridge University Press.

United States Department of Health and Human Services (USDHHS). 2020a. Explaining Operation Warp Speed. https://www.hhs.gov/coronavirus/explaining-operation-warp-speed/index.html.

———. 2020b. Secretary Azar Statement on President Trump's Invoking the Defense Production Act. Published on March 18. https://www.hhs.gov/about/news/2020/03/18/secretary-azar-statement-president-trumps-invoking-defense-production-act.html.

United States Food & Drug Administration (USFDA). 2020a. Pfizer-BioNTech COVID-19 Vaccine EUA Letter of Authorization. https://www.fda.gov/media/144412/.

———. 2020b. Moderna COVID-19 Vaccine EUA Letter of Authorization. https://www.fda.gov/media/144636/download.

———. 2021. Janssen COVID-19 Vaccine EUA Letter of Authorization 2021-02-27. FDA, Washington, DC.

US Crisis Monitor. 2020. Data. The Armed Conflict Location & Event Data Project (ACLED) and the Bridging Divide Initiatives (BDI) at Princeton University. https://acleddata.com/special-projects/us-crisis-monitor/.

Viscusi, W.K., and J.E. Aldy. 2003. The Value of a Statistical Life: A Critical Review of Market Estimates throughout the World. *Journal of Risk and Uncertainty* 5: 5–76.

Wall Street Journal (WSJ). 2020. Supreme Court Blocks Covid-19 Restrictions on Religious Services in New York. Published on November 26. https://www.wsj.com/articles/supreme-court-blocks-covid-19-restrictions-on-church-attendance-in-new-york-11606369004.

Watson, J.D., and F.H. Crick. 1953. Molecular Structure of Nucleic Acids; a Structure for Deoxyribose Nucleic Acid. *Nature* 171: 737–738.

Weinstein, R.S. 2011. Should Remaining Stockpiles of Smallpox Virus (Variola) Be Destroyed? *Emerging Infectious Diseases* 17: 681–683.

Weitzman, Martin L. 1998. Why the Far-distant Future Should be Discounted at Its Lowest Possible Rate. *Journal of Environmental Economics and Management* 36: 201–208.

———. 2009. On Modeling and Interpreting the Economics of Catastrophic Climate Change. *Review of Economics and Statistics* 91: 1–19.

Wells, Chad R., Pratha Sah, Seyed M. Moghadas, et al. 2020. Impact of International Travel and Border Control Measures on the Global Spread of the Novel 2019 Coronavirus Outbreak. *Proceedings of the National Academy of Sciences USA* 117: 7504–7509. https://doi.org/10.1073/pnas.2002616117.

World Health Organization (WHO). 2015. *International Health Regulations (2015)*. Geneva, CH: WHO.

———. 2019. *World Malaria Report 2019*. Geneva, CH: WHO.

———. 2020. *Milestones for Health over 70 Years*. Geneva, CH: WHO.

———. 2021. *Coronavirus Disease (COVID-19) Advice for the Public*. Geneva, CH: WHO.

Worldometers. 2021. Coronavirus. Dover, DE. https://www.worldometers.info/coronavirus/?utm_campaign=homeAdvegas1.

CHAPTER 9

Some Yet Unresolved Questions and Mysteries About the COVID-19 Pandemic

1 Introduction

This final chapter examines some of the as of yet unresolved questions with regard to the COVID-19 pandemic that remain critical to a comprehensive exposition of the pandemic, both epidemiologically and economically. The questions to be explained in this chapter are at the core of the empirical questions regarding the pandemic; therefore, we should hope that they will be paid attention to and answered by researchers sooner than later.

The first question is the origin of the novel coronavirus. The SARS-Cov-2 virus was first reported on December 31, 2019, as a cluster of cases of viral pneumonia from the city of Wuhan in Hubei Province in China. In the first three months, it was widely referred to in Asia as Wuhan pneumonia while Chinese authorities determined that the disease was caused by a novel coronavirus on January 9, 2020 (WHO 2020a). Since then, a number of theories on the origin of the virus were put forward. The joint WHO-China mission to Wuhan, China, to investigate the origin of the virus during January and February of 2021 did not reach a conclusion on the question of whether the virus was indeed originated from Wuhan, China. Instead, it proposed four hypotheses (WHO 2021).

The second question we examine is the question of why the richest nations in the West, including the US and the EU member nations, have suffered the most from the virus. Of the 2.6 million deaths from the

© The Author(s), under exclusive license to Springer Nature
Switzerland AG 2022
S. N. Seo, *The Economics of Pandemics*,
https://doi.org/10.1007/978-3-030-91021-1_9

COVID-19 as of early March 2021, roughly 540,000 deaths occurred in the US alone and roughly 670,000 deaths occurred in EU/EEA including the UK. The death tolls in these rich western regions far outnumbered those from the other world regions. Most notably, the number of deaths in China is roughly 4600, which is less than 1% of that of the US or the EU/EEA (JHU 2021).

The third question to be considered is the question of why the Southeast Asian nations were affected little by the COVID-19 pandemic despite the proximity to China and sometimes shared borders with China. Taiwan, Vietnam, Cambodia, Thailand, and other Southeast Asian nations were exempted from the fury of the COVID-19, especially during the pre-vaccine time period. As of the aforementioned date, the cumulative death toll in Thailand stands at 85, Vietnam at 35, Taiwan at 9, and Cambodia at 0 (JHU 2021).

A hypothesis put forth by some was that these countries' citizens by and large have already antibodies against the novel coronavirus; specifically, 7 out of 10 citizens have them. The hypothesis is that the citizens in these countries had been exposed before the COVID-19 to the coronavirus multiple times in the past two decades through the Severe Acute Respiratory Syndrome (SARS) outbreak in 2002 and the Middle East Respiratory Syndrome (MERS) outbreak in 2012. Both of these were caused by a coronavirus, that is, the SARS-CoV for the former and the MERS-CoV for the latter (Weiss 2020).

It remains unanswered whether the abovementioned ratio of antibody possessors was accurate as well as whether the ratio of antibody possessors was significantly lower in the US population or the EU population. For an interesting reference, a US study finds that 10 out of 10 people who were admitted to intensive care unit because of the COVID-19 had T cells which generate an immune response. Interestingly, 2 out of 10 people who did not contract the COVID-19 had also T cells (Pierce 2019; Weiskopf et al. 2020).

The fourth rather mysterious question is why the SARS-CoV-2 virus had little effect on the cohort of infants, kids, and school-age children (NCHS 2021a). This cohort is commonly one of the most vulnerable groups to any infectious diseases, including smallpox, polio, influenza, malaria, and so on (O'Neal 2020). By contrast, the COVID-19 pandemic has turned out to be deadly to the cohort of senior citizens as well as the cohort of people with comorbidities.

The fifth intriguing question is how accurate the COVID-19 tests have been in the US and also other countries. In the first two months since the COVID-19 first report, COVID-19 test kits were not available in the US (Romer 2020). The Abbott Laboratory's RealTime SARS-CoV-2 Assay was approved in the middle of March and Yale University's saliva test, called the PCR (Polymerase Chain Reaction) test or an RNA (Ribonucleic Acid) test, was approved in the middle of August 2020 (Yale News 2020). The accuracy of these test kits was often challenged during 2020. On the other hand, the daily number of COVID-19 positive cases, which critically depends on the accuracy of these tests, proved to be perhaps the single most important indicator that informed numerous policy decisions in the US.

The number of COVID-19 cases in the US stands at nearly 30 million by early March 2021. Intriguingly, it is nearly 35 times larger than the number of positive cases of China and roughly 3 times larger than that of India or Brazil (JHU 2021). For comparison, 30 million is roughly one-tenth of the entire population of the US. More notably, the population of China is roughly four times larger than that of the US. By September 1, 2021, the total number of cases surpassed 40 million in the US.

These questions, although critical for a full exposition of the COVID-19 pandemic, remain as yet unresolved by the research community, for which reason this final chapter felt inevitable to the present author. In the next five sections, the present author will go through each of these five questions, describe a range of hypotheses put forth on each until this date, and provide an initial assessment of them.

2 UNRESOLVED QUESTION I: THE ORIGIN OF THE NOVEL CORONAVIRUS

As of early September 2021, the global community is not yet able to pinpoint where and how the SARS-CoV-2 virus was originated. This has been from the very beginning of the pandemic a serious setback for a clear analysis of the COVID-19 pandemic as well as for designing appropriate policy measures against the pandemic. This book could have been presented in a different way if the exact origin of the virus had become established by the scientific community at the time of writing.

The facts established early by the World Health Organization (WHO) on the SARS-CoV-2 virus origin are as follows (WHO 2020a): (1) the

WHO first learned on December 31, 2019, of the virus through a report of a cluster of cases of viral pneumonia in Wuhan, Hubei Province, China; and (2) on January 9, 2020, Chinese authorities determined that the outbreak was caused by a novel coronavirus.

However, the Chinese government rejects the hypothesis that the novel coronavirus was originated from China. It promotes the hypothesis that the novel coronavirus, or its most recent ancestor, came from an animal outside China to humans and it was already circulating in humans outside China. Once it had been circulating in people, it could have spread on frozen wildlife and other cold packaged products, for example, traded in the Wuhan wet market (Mallapaty et al. 2021).

On the other hand, the US State Department proposed a Wuhan Virology Laboratory leak hypothesis. In its formal statement on mid-January 2021, it offered that it has the "reason to believe" that the virus was accidentally leaked from the abovementioned laboratory. As the evidence to support it, it offered that several researchers experimenting on the bat coronavirus in the laboratory fell sick in the fall of 2019 with the symptoms consistent with the COVID-19 (USDS 2021). The experiment is called a "gain-of-function" research which examines whether the coronavirus existent in bats can be artificially enhanced to gain additional functions to make it transmissible among humans. The US intelligence further reported on May 23, 2021, that three researchers at the Wuhan Institute fell sick with the symptoms consistent with the COVID-19 and sought hospital care (WSJ 2021).

Whether you support the US State Department's laboratory leak hypothesis or the Chinese government's animal origin hypothesis, the SARS-CoV-2 virus may have had been circulating well before the first report of Wuhan pneumonia on December 31, 2019. A study by Red Cross America, which provides one of the evidences, of the blood samples collected during the latter half of 2019, showed that the novel coronavirus was present in the blood samples collected in early December of 2019 (Basavaraju et al. 2020).

The WHO team of experts has been investigating the origin. It published the terms of references for the WHO-convened global study for the origins of the virus in July 2020 (WHO 2020b). After an entry into China in January 2021 and a month-long investigation, the team held a press conference in early February 2021. It did not reach a conclusion, but offered four hypotheses, as shown in Fig. 9.1 (WHO 2021).

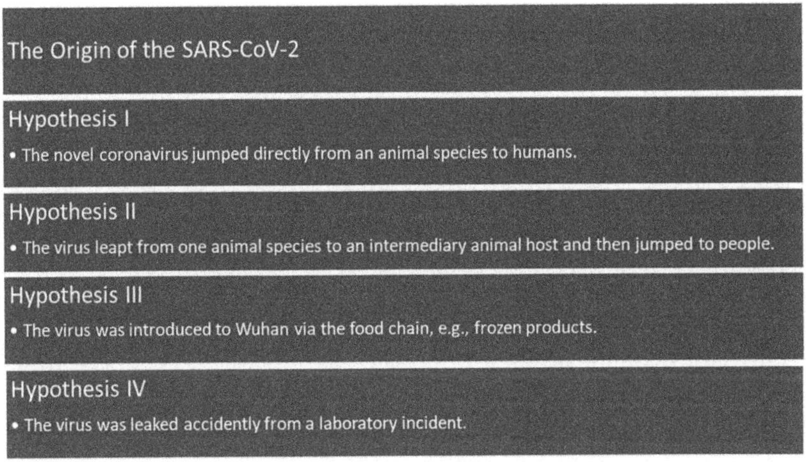

The Origin of the SARS-CoV-2

Hypothesis I
• The novel coronavirus jumped directly from an animal species to humans.

Hypothesis II
• The virus leapt from one animal species to an intermediary animal host and then jumped to people.

Hypothesis III
• The virus was introduced to Wuhan via the food chain, e.g., frozen products.

Hypothesis IV
• The virus was leaked accidently from a laboratory incident.

Fig. 9.1 The four hypotheses on the origin of the SARS-Cov-2

The four hypotheses are as follows: (1) the virus jumped directly from an animal species to humans; (2) the virus jumped from an animal species to an intermediary animal and then to humans; (3) the virus was introduced to Wuhan via the food chain, for example, frozen products; and (4) the virus was leaked from a laboratory accident.

The joint WHO-China mission after its investigation stated that all four hypotheses remain a possibility. However, the mission's press conference emphasized that the unintentional Wuhan lab-leak hypothesis is "extremely unlikely" (Calisher et al. 2020; WHO 2021; Mallapaty et al. 2021).

The animal origin hypotheses, Hypotheses 1 and 2, are supported by multiple research groups, although indirectly, especially by the Lancet letter in March 2020 (Calisher et al. 2020). Researchers find that the coronavirus closely related, although not exactly the same, to SARS-CoV-2, which is found in bats in Japan, Cambodia, Thailand, and China. The bats captured in a cave in Thailand in June 2020, concretely acuminate horseshoe bats, are found to contain a new coronavirus named RacCS203 which shares 91.5% of the genome with SARS-CoV-2 (Wacharapluesadee et al. 2021). This is the only example that a virus similar to the novel coronavirus is found in the animals currently circulating.

Other studies support the horseshoe bat origination of the COVID-19 virus, although based on the captured bats 'long time' ago. The virus named RC-o319 found in a little Japanese horseshoe bat captured in 2013 shared 81% of its genome with the SARS-CoV-2 (Murakami et al. 2020). The virus named RaTG13 was found in intermediate horseshoe bats captured in Yunnan Province of China in 2013, which shares 96% of its genome with the SARS-CoV-2 (Zhou et al. 2020).

The SARS-CoV-2 was found in the Shamel's horseshoe (*Rhinolophus*) bats captured in the north of Cambodia in 2010. This is the only example where the novel coronavirus is found in animals. However, the genetic sequence has not been fully completed. The genome should be at least 99% similar to the SARS-CoV-2 for it to be an immediate predecessor (Mallapaty 2020, 2021).

In sum, the animal origin hypothesis has not yet been proven to be true. Further, the above studies up to this point seem to indicate that the task would be a very difficult one. More seriously, scientists have not been able to find an intermediary species in the SARS-CoV-2 virus despite the extensive search for nearly 20 months, as of this writing, while the intermediary species for the SARS coronavirus, that is, Asian palm civets, was found within 6 months of the outbreak (Guan et al. 2003).

After the WHO-China joint mission's press conference, the Wuhan laboratory leak hypothesis seems to be gaining increasing supports. The US State Department's press conference in January 2021 which gave weight to the lab-leak hypothesis was already mentioned above (Fox News 2021). On March 27, 2021, the former CDC Director, Robert Redfield, gave an interview that he believes that the SARS-CoV-2 was originated accidentally from the Wuhan laboratory (Reuters 2021). As a virologist himself, he asserted that an animal transmission hypothesis lacks credibility because of the extremely high contagiousness of the SARS-CoV-2. Although widely ridiculed in the media, his assertion garnered increasing supports from scientists, doctors, science journalists, and the general public (Wade 2021; Fox News 2021).

On May 23, 2021, it was reported that three researchers at the Wuhan Institute fell sick enough to seek hospital care in November 2019 (WSJ 2021). Immediately afterward, on May 25, 2021, Anthony Fauci, the National Institute of Allergy and Infectious Diseases (NIAID) Director, admitted to the US House Appropriations Committee that the National Institutes of Health gave US$600,000 to the Wuhan Institute of Virology, through the EcoHealth Alliance, to study whether bat coronavirus could be transmitted to humans (CNN 2021). According to the more than 900 pages of documents on the works of the EcoHealth Alliance obtained through the Freedom of Information Act (FOIA) lawsuit:

> *The bat coronavirus grant provided EcoHealth Alliance with a total of $3.1 million, including $599,000 that the Wuhan Institute of Virology used in part to identify and alter bat coronaviruses likely to infect humans.* (Lerner and Hvistendahl 2021)

Scientists and the general public are increasingly giving weight to the Wuhan laboratory leak hypothesis in large part because the Joint WHO-China Mission in January–February 2021 was not able to examine thousands of blood samples of the persons in Wuhan that were collected by China in November 2019. These samples were destroyed by China before the Joint Mission investigation (WHO 2021).

3   UNRESOLVED QUESTION II: WHY HAVE THE RICHEST NATIONS IN THE WEST SUFFERED THE MOST?

To everybody's surprise, the richest nations on the planet have suffered the most from the COVID-19 pandemic during 2020. After the initial spike in the cases in China, the world was shocked to witness the novel coronavirus overwhelming the rich European nations such as Italy, France, Span, and the UK. The shockwave soon reached the US.

Table 9.1 shows the comparative COVID-19 statistics across selected nations. In order to analyze the impact of the virus itself, the present author focuses on the time period before vaccination effects take control of the COVID-19 data. Concretely, the data in Table 9.1 cover the time period up to March 7, 2021 (Worldometers 2021).

The table shows that the rich nations in the West, that is, the G-7 nations, suffered the most from the pandemic in terms of human fatalities as well as infections: the US, the UK, Italy, France, and Germany. Of the five nations, Germany suffered the least. Among the rich nations, Japan suffered the least. Specifically, the mortality per 1 million population was 1618 for the US and similar magnitudes for the UK, Italy, and France. It was 864 for Germany and only 65 for Japan.

These fatality statistics can be compared with those from China, India, Thailand, and Vietnam. The mortality per 1 million population was only 3 for China, 1 for Thailand, and 0.4 for Vietnam. It was 114 for India. Even for Brazil which was hit the hardest among developing nations, the

Table 9.1 Comparative COVID-19 statistics across nations (as of March 7, 2021)

	Mortality	Cases	Mortality per 1 M pop	Cases per 1 M pop	Mortality per cases
Total, planet	2,605,094	117,437,928	334	15,066	0.0222
The West					
US	537,838	29,696,250	1618	89,359	0.0181
UK	124,501	4,218,520	1827	61,919	0.0295
Italy	99,785	3,067,486	1652	50,785	0.0325
France	88,574	3,904,233	1355	59,723	0.0227
Germany	72,532	2,508,655	864	29,877	0.0289
Brazil	265,500	11,019,344	1243	51,591	0.0241
The East					
Japan	8227	438,956	65	3478	0.0187
China	4636	89,994	3	63	0.0515
India	157,890	11,229,271	114	8083	0.0141
Thailand	85	26,370	1	377	0.0032
Vietnam	35	2512	0.4	26	0.0139
Taiwan	10	976	0.4	41	0.0102

mortality per 1 million population was lower than France and higher than Germany. Be reminded again that the India and Brazil data in the table cover the period before the worldwide fourth wave began.

Why have the rich nations in the West suffered from the pandemic 100 times to 1000 times more than the developing nations such as China, India, Thailand, and Vietnam? An answer to this question has not yet been given by the scientific community, as of this writing, although the present author came across several reasons or clues offered by various people who appeared in the world media. Empirical researches on this question are still hard to find.

The factors that may have contributed to this surprising outcome are summarized by the present author in Fig. 9.2. There are five factors: behavioral, policy, epidemiological, genetic, and geo-climate factors (CDC 2012; Bloom and Canning 2017).

Of the five, one that struck the present author was the argument that the least impacted countries were "compliant" societies to the government rules and regulations. The riots and protests that raged during April, May, and June of 2020 in the midst of the first wave of the COVID-19 pandemic, which was explained in detail in Chap. 1, certainly made a

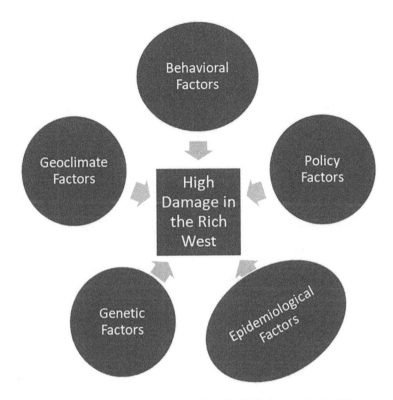

Fig. 9.2 The five factors that could explain the high damage in the West

strong impression to the present author that the US is a different kind of a nation, that is, a non-compliant one appearing nearly unruly (US Crisis Monitor 2020). This aspect of the responses can be categorized as a behavioral factor in Fig. 9.2.

However, the attitude of non-compliance may explain only a small fraction of the totality of the severe harm inflicted upon the rich western countries because some of the European nations deemed more orderly and compliant suffered an even larger number of fatalities than that of the US.

Like the behavioral factor, the policy factor does seem to offer only a small degree of explanatory power at first thought. The US and the European nations implemented the strictest policy measures such as repeated national lockdowns, mask mandates, ordered business closures, school closures, and so on, which were certainly more stringent than the COVID-19 policies implemented in Vietnam, Thailand, and China. Notwithstanding, the western nations suffered far more from the COVID-19. On second thought, the strict policy measures in the form of a universal mandate may have contributed significantly to the far worse health outcomes in the western countries.

Is there an epidemiological factor in play? It appears so. Specifically, the citizens from Southeast Asia and East Asia suffer more from lung diseases than the citizens in the western nations (WHO 2019). Table 9.2 compares death rates from lung diseases in Asian countries with those from the

Table 9.2   Death rate from lung diseases in Asia versus the West (WHO 2019)

Global rank	Countries	Regional categories	Death rate per 100,000 people
1	North Korea	Asia	112.26
2	India	Asia	89.36
3	Nepal	Asia	77.08
5	Myanmar	Asia	64.49
6	Bhutan	Asia	63.66
7	Bangladesh	Asia	61.82
10	Pakistan	Asia	54.47
12	China	Asia	53.43
16	Philippines	Asia	45.61
23	Laos	Asia	41.85
25	Afghanistan	Asia	41.05
31	Indonesia	Asia	37.89
56	US	The West	30.74
57	Denmark	The West	29.41
58	Cambodia	Asia	28.81
64	Thailand	Asia	28.06
87	UK	The West	23.07
90	Sri Lanka	Asia	22.82
91	Belgium	The West	22.7
93	Vietnam	Asia	22.65
98	Netherlands	The West	22.24
112	Germany	The West	20.04
125	Spain	The West	18.03
131	Australia	The West	17.29
136	Canada	The West	16.99
167	South Korea	Asia	11.73
169	Japan	Asia	11.61
173	France	The West	10.28
182	Singapore	Asia	6.98

western countries (WHO 2019). Asian countries top the WHO's list of death rates from lung diseases. It is 112 for North Korea, 89 for India, 53 for China, 11 for Japan. By contrast, it is 30 for the US, 23 for the UK, 20 for Germany, and 10 for France.

Did a high death rate from lung diseases make Asian countries more resilient to the COVID-19 virus than the western countries? There are two sides to consider for an answer. On the one hand, the availability of the hospitals and medical care staff that are specialized in lung diseases may have made the Asian countries to be more responsive to the COVID-19 outbreak. On the other hand, existing lung conditions, which are a comorbidity, may have made the Asian countries more vulnerable to the COVID-19 pandemic (NCHS 2021b).

The fourth is a genetic factor. As surveyed in the previous section, multiple groups of scientists report that close relatives to the SARS-CoV-2 virus are found in the bats circulating or captured in Southeast Asian countries such as Thailand, Cambodia, and China (Mallapaty 2020, 2021; Zhou et al. 2020; Wacharapluesadee et al. 2021). This may mean that a large fraction of people in Southeast Asia may have obtained antibodies to the coronaviruses, making them more resilient to the SARS-CoV-2. This hypothesis has not yet been proven by any scientific group.

The fifth factor is a variation in geo-climate conditions. To be specific, colder climate regimes in Europe and North America, compared with those in South Asia, may have increased the contagiousness or virulence of the novel coronavirus, especially during the winter months of 2020 and 2021. As far as the high rates of infections in April and May of 2021 in India and Brazil are concerned, the geo-climate factors seem to be dominated by the other aforementioned factors in determining the transmission rates in these countries.

4   Unresolved Question III: Did Southeast Asians Have Antibodies Before the COVID-19 Pandemic?

Southeast Asian nations, including Vietnam, Thailand, and Taiwan listed in Table 9.1, reported some of the best health outcomes in the world against the COVID-19 pandemic during 2020. In these countries, the mortality per 1 million population was only 1/1000th to 1/4000th of that of the US and the EU/EEA. The outcome of China is not far apart from that of the Southeast Asian countries. Figure 9.3 compares the

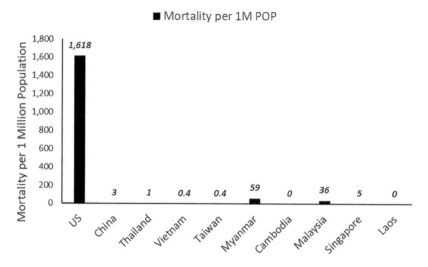

Fig. 9.3   Remarkable outcomes in Southeast Asia (as of March 7, 2021)

number of fatalities per 1 million population in the Southeast Asian nations against that of the US, with additional data on Cambodia, Myanmar, Singapore, Laos, and Malaysia (Worldometers 2021). The fatality per 1 million amounts to 1618 for the US, which is shockingly high compared with 3 for China, 1 for Thailand, and 0.4 for Vietnam.

How did the Southeast Asian nations achieve such a remarkable success against the COVID-19 pandemic relative to the richest nations in the West? Of the five factors in Fig. 9.2, two factors may offer a most plausible explanation for their success: epidemiological and genetic. As explained before, behavioral as well as policy responses appear to be more stringent in the western nations than in Southeast Asia. Note also that Bangkok city in Thailand is the most visited city in the world in terms of the number of visitors per year. As per the geo-climatic factor, a warmer climate condition appears to have contributed to their success to some degree, especially during the first half of 2020.

By the genetic factor, the present author refers to the evidence of the existence of multiple SARS-CoV-2 related viruses found in the horseshoe bats in China, Thailand, and Cambodia during the decade just before the COVID-19 outbreak (Zhou et al. 2020; Wacharapluesadee et al. 2021). Through contacts unknowingly with the close relatives to the novel coronavirus, people may have obtained an immune system mechanism to resist the COVID-19 virus better. This has not been proven by the scientific community, as far as the present author is aware of.

The epidemiological factor refers specifically to the past outbreaks of the coronaviruses in this region: the SARS outbreak in 2004 and the MERS outbreak in 2012, which were diseases caused by different types of coronaviruses, i.e., SARS-CoV and MERS-CoV (Weiss 2020). Through contacts with these past coronaviruses, people in Southeast Asia may have obtained the antibodies or immune system responses against the SARS-CoV-2.

Again, to emphasize, the present author cannot offer any definitive explanation for the success of the Southeast Asian nations, nor can any scientist at this point. Hence, it is included in this chapter as one of the unresolved questions. Having said that, new research seems to be emerging to shine a light on this issue. An Israeli study, for example, conducted from June 1, 2021, to August 14, 2021, at the height of the delta variant spread found that people who were vaccinated in January and February in 2021 were 6–13 times more likely to get infected in June, July, and the first half of August in that year than unvaccinated people who were previously infected with the coronavirus (Gazit et al. 2021; Wadman 2021). The researchers relied on the database of the Maccabi Healthcare Services in Israel.

In South Asia, probably the worst health outcomes during the entire pandemic were observed in India during the fourth wave of the COVID-19 pandemic driven by the delta variant between April and May 2021. Readers may go back to check Fig. 7.6 in Chap. 7. At the peak, the country recorded over 400,000 new infections per day and 5000 new deaths per day. As for the Indian outcomes, behavioral as well as policy factors seem to be dominating factors during the fourth wave, for example, a high population density and a poor sanitation system.

5   Unresolved Question IV: Why Little Effect on Kids and School Children?

A stunning characteristic of the COVID-19 pandemic was that it had little effect on infants, kids, and school children. Also, the pandemic virus had only very limited effects on young people in their 20s, 30s, and even 40s.

Lethal impacts of the COVID-19 were concentrated in the two cohorts: the elderly over 65 years and the people with comorbidities.

The differential impacts can be seen in the number of fatalities by age cohorts, as in Fig. 9.4. According to the most recent data from the National Center for Health Statistics (NCHS), the number of deaths caused by the COVID-19 pandemic from January 1, 2020, to April 14, 2021, for the [65–74] age cohort amounts to roughly 130,000, for the [75–84] age cohort to roughly 150,000, and for the [85–] age cohort to roughly 160,000 (NCHS 2021a).

By contrast, the number of fatalities for the [<1 year], [1–4], [5–14], and [15–24] age cohort, respectively, amounts to only a really tiny fraction of the number of fatalities for the old-age cohorts mentioned earlier, which is evident in Fig. 9.4 (NCHS 2021a).

An analysis of the UK's National Child Mortality Database (NCMD) for the one-year period from March 2020 to February 2021 corroborates the findings of the Centers for Disease Control and Prevention (CDC) data from the US summarized in Fig. 9.4. The mortality rate of children under age 18 was only 2 in 1 million children (Smith et al. 2021).

This is surprising because infants, kids, and school children are one of the most vulnerable cohorts to a host of infectious diseases. Take smallpox for example. The mortality rate of the disease was as high as 80% in the

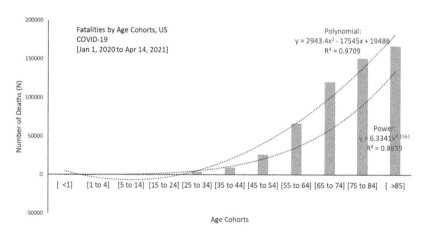

Fig. 9.4   The number of COVID-19 mortalities, US

children (Potter 2001; CDC 2020). For another example, consider seasonal influenza. One of the most vulnerable age groups to the flu is again kids and children. Infants and kids are among the most vulnerable cohorts to seasonal influenza because their immune systems are not yet fully developed. In addition, they are in a highly active stage of life, therefore, are more exposed to contagions of flu viruses than other age cohorts. For still another example, the Zika virus epidemic in Brazil in 2015–2016 caused birth defects of infants including microcephaly (WHO 2018).

In Fig. 9.5, the present author puts together age-cohort mortality rates of the COVID-19 pandemic against those of the smallpox disease during the 1870s. The age cohorts are defined to be only roughly the same for the two diseases owing to data availability. For smallpox, the health outcome measure is the mortality rate while it is the number of deaths for the COVID-19, again owing to data availability. The infant mortality rate of smallpox was 30% in Leipzig and the [1–5] age cohort's mortality rate was

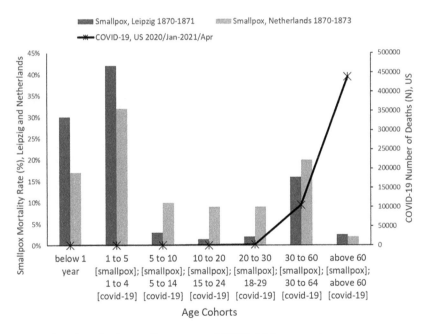

Fig. 9.5 Mortality by smallpox versus COVID-19 by age cohorts

42% in the city (O'Neal 2020). By contrast, the mortality rate of the [60–] cohort was only 2%.

6   Unresolved Question V: How Accurate Was the COVID-19 Test?

People's perception of the COVID-19 pandemic was heavily influenced by the daily number of reported new infections, especially during the first and second waves of the pandemic. Governmental responses too depended critically on daily new cases, whose goal is often expressed as "flatting the curve."

During the first three months after the novel coronavirus outbreak, reliable infection tests were not available in the US. The Abbott RealTime SARS-CoV-2 Assay was approved on March 18, 2020. The turnaround time for the Abbott test was reported to be 15 minutes, so it was called a rapid test. The Yale New Haven Hospital's SARS-CoV-2 PCR test, colloquially called a saliva test, was approved on March 31, 2020, whose turnaround time was reported to be two to three days (USFDA 2020).

The Polymerase Chain Reaction (PCR) test is referred to as by scientists the gold standard of the novel coronavirus testing because it actually detects the Ribonucleic Acid (RNA) that is specific to the virus (refer to Fig. 1.3 in Chap. 1). Further, the PCR test can detect the SARS-CoV-2 virus in a person within days from the moment of infection, that is to say, even for the non-symptomatic COVID-19 infected individuals.

How accurate were these tests? A study by the CDC compared the test results from the Antigen rapid tests with the results from the PCR tests in two university campuses in Wisconsin (Pray et al. 2021). The finding is striking. The rapid test is accurate only 80% of the time for the symptomatic persons. For the non-symptomatic persons, the accuracy drops to only 41.2%.

The results indicate that the COVID-19 case statistics relied upon heavily by the governments around the world in designing their policy responses may not have been close to being accurate. In reporting the number of new cases, the rapid test may have played a far larger role than the PCR test because the former is a lower-cost option with a rapid turnaround time. If the rapid tests conducted during the year 2020 in the US had been accurate only half of the time, the COVID-19 case statistics could have been significantly skewed. That is, unless a follow-up PCR test was undertaken after a positive result from the rapid test.

There is no data available, as far as the present author is aware of, on what fraction of the reported COVID-19 positive results was from the rapid tests and what fraction was from the PCR tests. Also, the Pray et al. study is limited by its narrow geographical scope in the two Wisconsin campuses while a more comprehensive study is not available. At this point, it is hard to assess how accurate the COVID-19 case statistics during 2020 were in the US.

The description in this section should shed a light on the importance of the infection tests' accuracies during the pandemic, that is, in addition to the importance of a shorter turnaround time of the test results as well as an earlier availability of the test kits (Romer 2020). It is also acknowledged that there are alternative ways to report daily cases of infection, for example, a ratio of the number of new infections over a fixed population size.

7   Final Words in Concluding the Book

A worldwide pandemic at the scale of the COVID-19 in 2019 and the Spanish Flu in 1919 is a once-in-a-century rare event. Once it strikes, it would likely end up killing more people than any other event in history up to that point, be it a war, an infectious disease, or a natural disaster.

A worldwide pandemic would certainly turn out to be a globally shared experience. That is, people that have undergone a pandemic would have a large basket of shared memories. This book is made possible by and has given spotlights on these shared experiences and memories of the global citizens who lived through the COVID-19 pandemic.

Elucidating the economics of pandemics as a globally shared experience has been the core mission of this book. This mission is comparable to the scientific tasks of epidemiology, virology, and vaccinology, that is, the study of infectious agents, viruses, and vaccine development methodologies, respectively. The economics of pandemics lays out the least cost option, alternatively speaking, a socially optimal option, to deal with the pandemics in consideration of the full array of behavioral, policy, and technological response options in the society. The economics of pandemics is the economics of globally shared goods or resources wherein global cooperation *versus* individual actions is a key policy decision variable.

The brightest point in the global community's experiences in the COVID-19 pandemic is viewed by many to be the developments of highly effective vaccines in record time, not one but multiple vaccines within a year of the pandemic outbreak as well as with a novel mRNA technology. On the other hand, the present author gave ample explanations to the critical decisions—be they behavioral, policy, or technological—that were made in an urgent manner during the COVID-19 pandemic, which readers of this book can fully appreciate at this point and reevaluate in the coming years retrospectively.

In retrospect of the economics literature, the biggest hurdle in the economists' endeavors has been the rareness of global pandemic events. When a once-in-a-century pandemic strikes, many resourceful economists would experience it deeply. It will, however, soon go out of their memories as well as people's memories, making it hard to trace the entire intricate universe of the pandemic experience painstakingly elaborated in this book. For your reference, Irving Fisher's *The Theory of Interest* was published in 1930, John Maynard Keynes' *The General Theory of Employment, Interest and Money* in 1936, and Paul Samuelson's doctoral dissertation entitled "Foundations of Economic Analysis" was submitted to Harvard University only in 1941, all long after the 1919 H1N1 influenza pandemic (Fisher 1930; Keynes 1936; Samuelson 1947). Surely, the economics profession today is far better positioned and equipped for a lucid and enlightening analysis of the economic aspects of the COVID-19 pandemic of 2020.

The present author has taken on this important task, having clearly experienced all the happenings of the COVID-19 pandemic with all other global citizens, considering the rareness of such a pandemic unfolding at the present author's active academic years.

References

Basavaraju, Sridhar V., Monica E. Patton, Kacie Grimm, et al. 2020. Serologic Testing of US Blood Donations to Identify Severe Acute Respiratory Syndrome Coronavirus 2 (SARS-CoV-2)–Reactive Antibodies: December 2019–January 2020. *Clinical Infectious Diseases* 72: e1004–e1009. https://doi.org/10.1093/cid/ciaa1785.

Bloom, D.E., and D. Canning. 2017. *Epidemics and Economics*. Working Paper #9, Harvard Program on Demography of Ageing, Harvard University.

Calisher, Charles, Dennis Carroll, Rita Colwell, Ronald B. Corley, Peter Daszak, Christian Drosten, Luis Enjuanes, Jeremy Farrar, Hume Field, Josie Golding, Alexander Gorbalenya, Bart Haagmans, James M. Hughes, William B. Karesh,

Gerald T. Keusch, Sai Kit Lam, Juan Lubroth, John S. Mackenzie, Larry Madoff, Jonna Mazet, Peter Palese, Stanley Perlman, Leo Poon, Bernard Roizman, Linda Saif, Kanta Subbarao, and Mike Turner. 2020. Statement in support of the scientists, public health professionals, and medical professionals of China combatting COVID-19. *Lancet* 395: E42–E43.

Centers for Disease Control and Prevention (CDC). 2012. *Principles of Epidemiology in Public Health Practice (Third Edition): An Introduction to Applied Epidemiology and Biostatistics.* Atlanta, GA: The CDC.

———. 2020. *Smallpox.* Atlanta, G.A.: The CDC.

CNN. 2021. Fauci Defends 'modest' Collaboration with Wuhan Scientists, Says NIH didn't Fund 'gain of function' Research. Published on May 25. https://www.foxnews.com/politics/fauci-gain-of-function-wuhan-collaboration-spillover.

Fisher, Irving. 1930. *The Theory of Interest.* New York, NY: Macmillan.

Fox News. 2021. Fox News Poll: Majority believes COVID-19 Leaked from Lab in China. Published June 23. https://www.foxnews.com/politics/china-coronavirus-lab-link-covid-19-poll.

Gazit, S. R. Shlezinger, G. Perez, R. Lotan, A. Peretz, A. Ben-Tov, D. Cohen, K. Muhsen, G. Chodick, T. Patalon. 2021. Comparing SARS-CoV-2 Natural Immunity to Vaccine-Induced Immunity: Reinfections versus Breakthrough Infections. https://doi.org/10.1101/2021.08.24.21262415

Guan, Y., B.J. Zheng, Y.Q. He, X.L. Liu, Z.X. Zhuang, C.L. Cheung, et al. 2003. Isolation and Characterization of Viruses Related to the SARS Coronavirus from Animals in Southern China. *Science* 302: 276–278. https://doi.org/10.1126/science.1087139.

Johns Hopkins University (JHU). 2021. *COVID-19 Dash Board.* JHU, Baltimore, M.D.: JHU. https://data.humdata.org/dataset/novel-coronavirus-2019-ncov-cases.

Keynes, J.M. 1936. *The General Theory on Employment, Interest and Money.* London, UK: Palgrave Macmillan.

Lerner, S., and Hvistendahl, M. 2021. New Details Emerge About Coronavirus Research at Chinese Lab. *The Intercept.* Published on September 7.

Mallapaty, S. 2020. Coronaviruses Closely Related to the Pandemic Virus Discovered in Japan and Cambodia. *Nature* 588: 15–16.

———. 2021. Closest Known Relatives of Virus Behind COVID-19 Found in Laos. *Nature.* https://doi.org/10.1038/d41586-021-02596-2

Mallapaty, S., A. Maxmen, and E. Callaway. 2021. 'Major Stones Unturned': COVID Origin Search Must Continue after WHO Report, Say Scientists. *Nature* 590: 371–372.

Murakami, S., T. Kitamura, J. Suzuki, R. Sato, T. Aoi, M. Fujii, H. Matsugo, H. Kamiki, H. Ishida, A. Takenaka-Uema, M. Shimojima, and T. Horimoto. 2020. Detection and Characterization of Bat Sarbecovirus Phylogenetically

Related to SARS-CoV-2. *Japan. Emerging Infectious Diseases* 26 (12): 3025–3029.

National Center for Health Statistics (NCHS). 2021a. Provisional COVID-19 Death Counts by Sex, Age, and State. Washington, DC: NCHS, CDC. https://www.cdc.gov/nchs/nvss/vsrr/covid_weekly/index.htm.

———. 2021b. Conditions Contributing to Deaths involving Coronavirus Disease 2019 (COVID-19), by Age Group and State, United States. Washington, DC: NCHS, CDC. https://www.cdc.gov/nchs/nvss/vsrr/covid_weekly/index.htm.

O'Neal, Aaron. 2020. Share of Total Deaths Due to Smallpox by Age during the Great Pandemic of 1870–1875. *Statista*. Published on April 23. https://www.statista.com/statistics/1107867/smallpox-share-smallpox-total-deaths-by-age-great-pandemic-historical/.

Pierce, Benjamin A. 2019. *Genetics: A Conceptual Approach*. 7th ed. New York, NY: W.H. Freeman.

Potter, C.W. 2001. A History of Influenza. *Journal of Applied Microbiology* 91(4): 572–579.

Pray, I.W., L. Ford, D. Cole, et al. 2021. Performance of an Antigen-Based Test for Asymptomatic and Symptomatic SARS-CoV-2 Testing at Two University Campuses—Wisconsin, September–October 2020. *Morbidity and Mortality Weekly Report* 69: 1642–1647. https://doi.org/10.15585/mmwr.mm695152a3.

Reuters. 2021. Former CDC Chief Redfield Says He Thinks COVID-19 Originated in a Chinese Lab. Published on March 27. https://www.reuters.com/article/us-health-coronavirus-origin-redfield-idUSKBN2BI2R6.

Romer, Paul. 2020. Even A Bad Test Can Help Guide the Decision to Isolate: Covid Simulations Part 3. Published on March 25. Pualromer.net.

Samuelson, Paul A. 1947. *Foundations of Economic Analysis*. Cambridge, MA: Harvard University Press.

Smith, C., D. Odd, R. Harwood, J. Ward, M. Linney, M. Clark, D. Hargreaves, S. Ladhani, E. Draper, P. Davis, S. Kenny, E. Whittaker, K. Luyt, R. Viner, L. Fraser. 2021. Deaths in Children and Young People in England Following SARS-CoV-2 Infection During the First Pandemic Year: a National Study using Linked Mandatory Child Death Reporting Data. https://doi.org/10.21203/rs.3.rs-689684/v1

United States Department of State (USDS). 2021. Fact Sheet: Activity at the Wuhan Institute of Virology. USDS, Washington, DC. Published on January 15. https://2017-2021.state.gov/fact-sheet-activity-at-the-wuhan-institute-of-virology/index.html.

United States Food & Drug Administration (USFDA). 2020. Emergency Use Authorization. FDA, Washington, DC. https://www.fda.gov/emergency-preparedness-and-response/mcm-legal-regulatory-and-policy-framework/emergency-use-authorization.

US Crisis Monitor. 2020. Data. The Armed Conflict Location & Event Data Project (ACLED) and the Bridging Divide Initiatives (BDI) at Princeton University. https://acleddata.com/special-projects/us-crisis-monitor/.

Wacharapluesadee, S., C.W. Tan, P. Maneeorn, et al. 2021. Evidence for SARS-CoV-2 Related Coronaviruses Circulating in Bats and Pangolins in Southeast Asia. Nature. *Communications* 12 (972). https://doi.org/10.1038/s41467-021-21240-1.

Wade, Nicholas. 2021. The Origin of COVID: Did People or Nature Open Pandora's Box at Wuhan? Bulletin of the Atomic Scientists. Published on May 5. https://thebulletin.org/2021/05/the-origin-of-covid-did-people-or-nature-open-pandoras-box-at-wuhan/.

Wadman, M. 2021. Having SARS-CoV-2 Once Confers Much Greater Immunity Than a Vaccine—but No Infection Parties, Please. *Science*. Published on August 26. https://www.sciencemag.org/news/2021/08/having-sars-cov-2-once-confers-much-greater-immunity-vaccine-no-infection-parties.

Wall Street Journal (WSJ). 2021. Intelligence on Sick Staff at Wuhan Lab Fuels Debate on Covid-19 Origin. Published on May 23. https://www.wsj.com/articles/intelligence-on-sick-staff-at-wuhan-lab-fuels-debate-on-covid-19-origin-11621796228?mod=hp_lead_pos3.

Weiskopf, D., K.S. Schmitz, M.P. Raadsen, et al. 2020. Phenotype and Kinetics of SARS-CoV-2–specific T Cells in COVID-19 Patients with Acute Respiratory Distress Syndrome. *Science Immunology* 5 (48): eabd2071. https://doi.org/10.1126/sciimmunol.abd2071.

Weiss, Susan R. 2020. Forty Years with Coronaviruses. *Journal of Experimental Medicine* 217 (5): e20200537. https://doi.org/10.1084/jem.20200537.

World Health Organization (WHO). 2018. Zika Virus. Geneva, CH: WHO. https://www.who.int/news-room/fact-sheets/detail/zika-virus#.

———. 2019. *Global Health Estimates: Leading Causes of Death.* Geneva, CH: WHO.

———. 2020a. *Timeline: WHO's COVID-19 Response.* Geneva, CH: WHO.

———. 2020b. *WHO-convened Global Study of the Origins of SARS-CoV-2.* Geneva, CH: WHO.

———. 2021. *Press Conference on February 12. The joint World Health Organization-China Mission to Investigate the Origins of COVID-19.* Geneva, CH: WHO. https://www.who.int/emergencies/diseases/novel-coronavirus-2019.

Worldometers. 2021. Coronavirus COVID-19 Pandemic. Dover, DE. https://www.worldometers.info/coronavirus/.

Yale News. 2020. Quick and Affordable Saliva-based COVID-19 Test Developed by Yale Scientists Receives FDA Emergency Use Authorization. Yale University, New Haven, CT. Published on August 15.

Zhou, P., X.L. Yang, X.G. Wang, et al. 2020. A Pneumonia Outbreak Associated with a New Coronavirus of Probable Bat Origin. *Nature* 579: 270–273.

INDEX

CPSIA information can be obtained
at www.ICGtesting.com
Printed in the USA
LVHW081115210222
711615LV00006B/280

9 783030 910204